Educational Psychology in
a Changing World

Educational Psychology in a Changing World

GERDA SIANN

Department of Psychology, Moray House College of Education

DENIS C. E. UGWUEGBU

Department of Psychology, University of Ibadan

London
GEORGE ALLEN & UNWIN
Boston   Sydney

First published in 1980

GEORGE ALLEN & UNWIN LTD
40 Museum Street, London WC1A 1LU

© George Allen & Unwin (Publishers) Ltd, 1980

British Library Cataloguing in Publication Data

Siann, Gerda
   Educational psychology in a changing world.
   1. Educational psychology
   2. Underdeveloped areas – Education
   I. Title   II. Ugwuegbu, Denis C E
   370.15   LB1051   80–40892

   ISBN 0–04–370099–3
   ISBN 0–04–370100–0 Pbk

Set in 10 on 11 point Times by Computacomp (UK) Ltd.,
Fort William, Scotland
and printed in Great Britain by Lowe & Brydone Limited,
Thetford, Norfolk

Contents

Preface   *page* ix

Acknowledgements   xi

PART ONE: THE WORLD OF CHILDHOOD

1   The Needs of Children   3
2   The Early Years at Home   15
3   Language Development and the
    Functions of Play   28
4   Cognitive Development   41

PART TWO: THE PRIMARY SCHOOL YEARS

5   Social and Emotional Adjustment
    in the Primary School Years   71
6   Learning and Instruction   88

PART THREE: ADOLESCENCE AND YOUTH

7   Developmental Changes in
    Adolescence   127
8   The Adolescent in Society   152

PART FOUR: SCHOOL AND SOCIETY

9   The School as a Social System   183
10   The School and Its Social Setting   199
11   The Nature and Assessment of
     Intelligence and the Assessment
     of Academic Achievement   220

Bibliography   241
Index   249

Preface

Most textbooks of developmental psychology, written in English, are published either in the United Kingdom or in the United States of America. Because of this, certain assumptions are nearly always present. For example, it is taken for granted that the readers come from a background where the nuclear family is the norm, where parents, though they may differ in their degree of education, are in the great majority literate and where children grow up surrounded, in even the poorest homes, by many examples of modern technology.

But many teachers and educationalists in other parts of the world deal with children who do not come from the sort of background just described. Although they themselves may live in families which are very similar in structure to those found in Europe or America, their pupils may live in families which are not nuclear but are instead rich in the emotional warmth and security of an extended family system. In many cases such as West Africa and areas which are largely Muslim the children may live in homes where there is more than one wife. Further, parents, though they may be extremely interested in what education can offer their children, may themselves be illiterate. It may not be possible for these teachers and educationalists to assume that children are familiar with the everyday examples of modern technology that much of the world takes for granted. For example, water may be drawn rather than come from a tap and there may be no electricity in children's homes. In fact, perhaps the only exposure children may have to modern technology may be through the mass media – transistor radios, visiting film shows and, in some countries, television.

In this book we try to discuss children and their development with this kind of environment very much in mind. We are particularly interested in the bearing such home backgrounds may have on the child's ability to integrate into a formal educational system which, with certain notable exceptions, still owes much to its origins outside the indigenous country.

It has been customary to call societies such as these 'developing'. This term is not at all appropriate in our opinion. Though such environments may not be highly developed industrially or technologically, they are anything but 'underdeveloped' or 'developing' in terms of social structure. Indeed the traditional concern such societies have shown for the old, the young and the poor provide an example that more technologically developed societies would do well to follow. Nevertheless, it is clear that we will need a shorthand term to cover societies where many of the young live in rural backgrounds within an extended family system and within an emotional and social environment which is still largely dominated by customary values. We will refer to societies where such homes are in the majority as Third World countries.

We are, of course, aware how coarse such distinctions are and we hope the reader as he or she moves through the book will appreciate that we are fully aware that no matter whether his home is in a tiny village in a tropical rain forest or in a modern flat in a busy city, what is most important to the child is the way those who care for him meet his emotional and social needs. His welfare is dependent on the people around him rather than on the physical environment.

Much of the psychological research done in Third World countries has been done within a cross-cultural framework. The researchers, whether expatriate or indigenous, tended to ask questions that sprung from the preoccupations of American and European educational systems. A prime example of this has been the emphasis often found on testing, problem-solving and intellectual development. In common with many other contemporary psychologists we feel that this has often led to the baby being thrown out with the bathwater. An incident from our own experience may help.

Some years back one of the authors was conducting an experiment in Zambia into children's perception of visual illusions. During this experiment children were brought to the University of Zambia in university transport and asked to judge whether or not a line was in a vertical position. It was made very clear to the children (or so we thought) that we were only concerned with how they perceived the line in question. Yet after the experiment a number of children approached the research assistant and asked privately, 'Why is she [the chief experimenter] trying to trick us? We know she's really measuring our intelligence.' The children knew that lots of tests were given at the university, they also knew that some of these were attempts to produce a test of intelligence, and like most of us they were determined not to be put off by any persuasive and possibly deceptive chat when something that might affect their future was at stake. In this case they were wrong – 'intelligence' was not under consideration – but we are sure you will see how the children's perception of the true aim of the experiment may have distorted their responses.

In this book we try to put ourselves in the place of those Zambian children who refused to be tricked. We try to respect the healthy tendency, found in the young all over the world, to try to make sense of the demands of their societies and we try to describe some of the ways children adapt to and modify these demands. We try also to outline those psychological needs, common to children all over the world, that we as adults who care for them must meet.

Acknowledgements

A number of people have been of great assistance in the preparation of this book, and we would like to thank all of them very much while, naturally, absolving them from blame for any deficiencies in the text.

The following read and commented on parts or the whole of the manuscript, and we are most grateful to them for this help: Harry Donaldson, Barbara Lloyd, Paquita McMichael, Judith Watson, Frances Ugwuegbu.

The ideas for the illustrations are the work of Les Brown and B. Allen-Taylor and we would like to thank them very much for their patience and sensitivity in interpreting our drafts.

The section on the organisation of play areas owes a great deal to the experience of Sheena Johnstone and we are most grateful for this assistance. We are similarly grateful to Judy Gay for her assistance in those sections of the book that deal with initiation rites. John Young helped us with the presentation of the case history in Chapter 6 and we would like to acknowledge our thanks to him for this and to the Lothian Region Child Guidance Service for permission to use the case history.

In addition we would like to acknowledge our gratitude to the authors and publishers for permission to reproduce the following:

Table 3.1   Scott, Foresman and Co., and Professor D. I. Slobin
Figure 4.10   *Journal of Social Psychology* and Dr. William Hudson
Figure 6.5   Dr Jim Calder
Figure 6.6   American Orthopsychiatric Association and Dr L. Bender.

Finally, we would like to record our very great debt to Isaac Adefisoye, Annie Davis, Ellen Dissanayike and Violet Moncrieff for typing and helping us to organise the manuscript.

GERDA SIANN
DENIS C. E. UGWUEGBU

PART ONE
THE WORLD OF CHILDHOOD

In the first part of this book we look at those background factors that affect the child as he moves through the educational system.

In Chapter 1 we examine the nature of children's psychological needs.

In Chapter 2 we look at the influence of home background on the way in which children adapt to the social and cognitive (thinking) demands of school.

In Chapter 3 we look at the course of language development and also at the functions of play.

In Chapter 4 we look at the course of cognitive development (development of thought) and the influence of culture on cognitive development.

THE NEEDS OF CHILDREN

1

Introduction

In common with most adults you probably find it quite difficult to remember just what it felt like to start school. While you may perhaps be able to recall some details of that important time – what you wore, who accompanied you to school, what the teacher and the classroom looked like – the *feel* may be more elusive. Yet, as someone involved in the educational process, you probably agree with us that the successful practitioner in this field is someone who is in sympathy with children, who understands their needs and is able, in imagination, to put him- or herself in their place. Some of us find that such understanding is aided by having children or younger relatives of our own. Others are not so fortunate. But perhaps all of us can gain some insight into children's perceptions and feelings, their thoughts and emotions, by trying to analyse for ourselves what the psychological needs of children are.

Now a list of human needs is something each and every one of us can draw up. Your needs as a student or educationalist may differ from your best friend's. And you may feel that you do not require any academic psychological research to arrive at these needs. Similarly, many psychologists have proposed human need models. In general these have dealt with the psychological needs of adults. We are going to suggest that you consider a need model that was formulated with children in mind. While this model is based on empirical research, it is of course only one of a number of alternative formulations. Nevertheless, we feel that it has the advantage of being simple without being simple-minded, and we have also found it most helpful in our own dealing with children.

This chapter, then, is concerned with children's needs. But before discussing them we would like to present the four fundamental assumptions on which the whole of this book is based.

The Child at School – Four Basic Assumptions

The last fifteen years have been a revolutionary time in educational psychology. Attention has shifted back to the *subject* after half a century of concentrating on the psychologist and his methodology. Whereas during this half-century the psychologist concerned himself with situations where he did something (conducted an experiment, gave a test, measured an attitude) to the subject and then attempted to summarise and quantify the resulting behaviour on the part of the subject, we are now equally concerned with the subject's perception and evaluation of the psychologist and his actions. We are beginning to realise that these are of prime importance.

Thus the four basic assumptions we are going to describe are related to an interactive and transactional view of the child at school. That is, we, the educators, do not simply do things to children – teach them, socialise them, possibly punish them. They in turn, by their evaluation of us and their responses to us, affect our behaviour. And their evaluation and responses to us have, in turn, been mediated by their past experience of life and their previous interactions with other people. We are attempting in this book to cast some light on an area that is constantly in flux; any school is not the same from day to day and year to year and each of the members of that school, whether teacher, headteacher, ancillary staff or child, is not the same from day to day or encounter to encounter. No situation in a school is exactly the same as any other, just as no individual who has ever lived is exactly the same as any other, for we all bear with us not only our own genetic constitution but also our own individual and special life histories and our own interpretation of these life histories.

own particular family, his physical and social environment as well as his own temperament.

(3) This is not to say we must take a deterministic* approach. In *Early Experience: Myth and Evidence* (1976) Clarke and Clarke conclude, after surveying the literature on early experience, that children are far more resilient than has been supposed and that it *is*

O	FOUR BASIC ASSUMPTIONS
1	The child is an active agent in his own development
2	The child cannot be separated from his total environment
3	Intervention is always possible, if the early environment is unfavourable
4	The teacher has an important role in shaping the child's perception of himself, his environment, and his mastery of that environment

Figure 1.1

We can summarise this point of view as follows (see Figure 1.1):

(1) The child is an *active* agent in his own development. When considering his behaviour or his attitudes or his beliefs, we must always remember that as we observe and make judgements about him, so does he continually strive to make sense of his own environment and relate it to his growing perception of himself.

(2) The child cannot be separated from his total environment. His behaviour and his understanding of himself are influenced by his

possible to compensate for early deprivation. *Directly* we can try to modify poor conditions in the emotional, social and physical environment. *Indirectly* we can help the child to view himself as an effective agent in shaping his own future.

(4) The teacher thus has an important role in shaping the child's perception of himself; his environment and his mastery of that environment in such a way that he faces the future confidently and hopefully.

* By a 'deterministic' approach we mean an approach that suggests that early experience inevitably dictates a particular result.

Children's Needs

Our need model is based on that presented by Mia Kelmer Pringle in her book *The Needs of Children* (1974). Although this book is based primarily on British data, we feel that her treatment of children's needs has universal application. Throughout the world, children are born with the same basic emotional and intellectual needs (Figure 1.2), although each culture will answer these needs in ways that are appropriate to differing social, economic and political conditions. Furthermore, societies themselves generate different secondary psychological needs and we will touch briefly on this aspect at the end of the chapter.

For infants the two most important channels of communication are sight and sound, and their responses to both of these are discriminative. Hutt *et al.* (1968) show that children are most likely to pay attention to speech-like sounds. Similarly, Condon (1975), who attached sensitive instruments to the bodies of infants, shows that they swayed their bodies in response to the conversational inflections in their mothers' speech.

Studies of visual responses show the same pattern. The work of Fantz (1967) has been pre-eminent in this field. He hung displays above the cribs of young infants and noted which configurations on these displays stimulated the

THE NEEDS OF CHILDREN	
1	The need for love and security
2	The need for new experiences
3	The need for praise and recognition
4	The need for responsibility

Figure 1.2

The first need – the need for love and security
In the last ten years psychologists have been conducting intensive observational studies of the early social and emotional relationships of young children. All these studies suggest that children, wherever they are born, come into the world 'pre-programmed' for social relationships. We know that from the first few weeks of their lives children respond selectively to the world around them.

most attention and the most smiling. His results and those of others show clearly that configurations most similar to human features produce the most attention.

In evolutionary terms we should not find this at all surprising. The young human infant will need attention and care for at least the first three or four years of his life and thus needs to bind his caretakers to him in a sensitive and responsive relationship. Careful and detailed studies in the United Kingdom (Schaffer, 1977) and in Nigeria (Trevarthen, 1979) show quite clearly how important the infant's part is in the loving relationship that a child makes in his early years.

These detailed studies of the interactions between young infants and their caretakers all point to the conclusion that the human infant enters the world well equipped to behave selectively – he pays attention to those features of his environment that are the most likely to lead to social relationships. And these social relationships as they develop are clearly two-way. Not only does the mother stimulate responses from the child, the child also plays his own part in stimulating social behaviour in the mother and others who care for him. Schaffer terms this process reciprocity and it is this reciprocity that gives rise to the child's sociability or his ability to make and maintain social and emotional relations with adults. But is this two-way process dependent on the presence of the natural mother alone?

The work of Bowlby (1969) suggests that this is indeed so. He argues that in order to develop a secure emotional base infants need to have a prolonged period of uninterrupted contact with at best their mother, and if not, with one mother-substitute or 'surrogate'. He argues further that this relationship is different in *quality* and intensity from the relationship that the infant makes with others and he calls this phenomenon monotropy.

Bowlby's work has been severely criticised (Rutter, 1972). The general consensus now among psychologists would appear to be that young babies need to form one or more (but not too many) close relationships with people of either sex. Schaffer and Emerson (1964), for example, show that in some cases equally close relationships as that with the mother were formed with the father, grandparents and siblings (brothers and sisters).

If Bowlby had been correct in his claim that mothers should not leave their young children for protracted periods in the day, then many adults in a number of traditional communities would have been irretrievably harmed in infancy. Particularly in many parts of Africa it has been the practice for some mothers to leave the young child in the day while she works in the fields. Thus many young Tanzanian infants are cared for by 'nursemaids'. In Nigeria, too, Ware (1975) writes that children 'naturally learn to relate to a number of mother substitutes' (p. 5).

Indeed with regard to the more general African context, Ware writes that 'in an African context all children are in a sense everybody's children, or at least the concern of a great number and range of relatives, and there is much less stress upon the individual mother's role in the socialization of the child' (p. 4).

Durojaiye too emphasises the important role the extended family plays in the upbringing of African children (1976, p. 23):

> ' The traditional system of child-rearing and family life promotes strong bonds of loyalty between family members and the child grows into adulthood with a strong feeling of security. Co-operation and mutual help are inculcated from infancy and extended family members are confident that help, support and protection will always be forthcoming from other members of the family whenever needed. The child thus develops an apparently healthy and secure personality which is protected against the rough and tumble of deprivation and want. He is well adjusted, both to his environment and within himself. '

But it is not only in Africa that the extended family share the care of young infants. Philips (1972) writes that in the North American Indian community she studied the care of young children was a shared responsibility. And writing about child-rearing patterns in India, Kuppuswamy (1974) notes: 'It is well-known that in the Indian context of child upbringing many infants and children have, to start with, deeper attachment to the grandmother or widowed paternal aunt than to the mother herself ...' (p. 148).

In the USSR too, according to Bronfenbrenner (1974), young infants are often left in collective day care centres, as mothers tend to resume work soon after birth. This is also the pattern in other East European countries like the German Democratic Republic where young mothers form a stable part of the work force.

Thus there is ample evidence to suggest that while a young infant does need tender loving care throughout the first few years of his life, it is not necessary for him to have a *sole* caretaker such as the natural mother or mother-substitute. However, it is equally clear that he does require *individual* attention on a one-to-one basis from interested and sensitive caretakers and that these should neither change too frequently nor be too many in number. Many studies of institutions show the very bad effect of establishments where infants, although perhaps well cared for physically, are denied the opportunity to make attachment bonds with other people. See, for example, the work of Dennis (1976) in Lebanon and Goldfarb (1945) in the USA, both of which are described in the Clarke and Clarke book on early experiences (1976) and the study done by Oyemade (1974) in Nigeria.

These loving relationships that a child makes in his early years will give him confidence and an inner sense of security that will help him in his later social encounters. If a child does not have love specifically directed towards him in the first years of life he may need very special and compensating attention later on. However, such compensation is always possible as has been shown by Kadushin (1976) and also by Barbara Tizard (1977).

Tizard made a detailed study of young children who were adopted from an institutional setting. Though the institutions were well run and the children's welfare was carefully considered, there were frequent changes of staff. (Sometimes as many as twenty-four people tended one child in the first two years of his life.) Tizard visited and interviewed twenty of these children who had been adopted between the ages of 2 and 4 years. In sixteen out of the twenty cases, at age 8, the children had formed loving and stable relationships within their new families. However, they still tended to have difficulty in their social relationships at school.

In addition to love and affection a young child requires security. By this we mean that children should not be subjected to too much change in their day-to-day circumstances. In order to be able to build up a realistic picture of the world, a child needs to be able to predict what is going to happen in the *immediate* future with a fair degree of certainty. Thus it helps for a 3-year-old to be able to anticipate the daily pattern of events. All young children need a familiar background with a stable routine.

The reason for this is not difficult to understand in the light of current thinking about the nature of human cognitive (intellectual) processes. Cognitive theorists consider that in many ways the human organism functions as an information-processing machine. New information coming into it from the environment is coded, and if it is meaningful it is absorbed into the cognitive network. (We will return to this aspect of human functioning in Chapter 4.) But a young child has had comparatively little experience and many things that we are familiar with, or at least have heard

about, may seem very threatening to him on his first encounter. For example, a young child from a small village with no piped water may find the first sight of water rushing out of a tap very disturbing. Nothing in his previous experience has prepared him for this and he has nothing to relate the sight and sound to.

Similarly, a child taken to a crèche or day care centre for the first time may find the numbers of people and objects very bewildering. It is not surprising then that he will cry and cling to his mother. Even when he is settled in he may still prefer to keep with him a favourite blanket or a cuddly toy.

In the West many observers have reported that young children often cling to a piece of blanket or soft-textured material which they have become attached to. Winnicott (1964) has termed these comforters 'transitional objects' and they are perhaps best viewed as helping the child to make the transition from a familiar environment, with its attendant security, to a new situation. While we have not encountered any reports of such behaviour in more traditional societies, during observation in an Ibadan day care centre we did see a number of children fingering and sometimes sucking their handkerchiefs, or sucking their thumbs.

Related to this need for predictability, many mothers and infant teachers will be aware of the love young children have for rituals. By this we mean that they like to do the same thing in precisely the same way at similar times of the day. Thus a well-loved story must be told in exactly the same words each time or when they go to sleep they like to see their toys arranged in much the same way round their beds each night.

Related to the need for security is the significance to the young child of consistency. As we shall discuss in greater detail in Chapters 7 and 11, the evidence on parental modes of discipline suggests that the most important component is the consistency with which the parent rewards some, and disapproves of other, behaviour. As Pringle writes (1974, p. 38): 'Knowing what is expected of him and, as soon as he can understand, the reasons why, makes growing up a less difficult business.'

I am sure you can imagine for yourselves how confusing it must be for a young child to find that a certain piece of behaviour is treated one day with indifference, perhaps because the mother is thinking of something else, and yet to discover on another day that the self-same piece of behaviour is greeted with an angry slap.

While it is clearly not possible for teachers to love their pupils in the same way that we would expect parents to, many studies of teachers' behaviour indicate that teachers who demonstrate warmth in their interactions with pupils tend to be more effective than teachers who do not (Washburne and Heil, 1960; Rosenshine, 1971). Further, the consistency of school values within a particular school helps the pupils to know and understand what sort of behaviour is expected from them. In a recent large-scale study of twelve schools in London, Rutter and his colleagues showed that the most effective teaching was done in those schools where there is 'some kind of consensus on how school life should be organised' (Rutter *et al.*, 1979, p. 194). Thus it would seem that schools as well as homes can contribute to fulfilling children's needs for affection and security.

There is no doubt that this need for love and security is basic. Observation of any society anywhere in the world will yield the information that where children are emotionally secure they are best able to cope with any demands that may be put on them. Similarly, academic studies of child development have yielded the same conclusion. Even the child's basic physical needs such as those for food and shelter cannot be separated from his requirement for love and security, as many studies document that children deprived of this do not thrive, no matter how good their physical environment (Pringle, 1974).

The second need – the need for new experience
In the previous section we mentioned that in some ways we can compare the human organism to an information-processing machine such as an electronic computer. In order to function effectively such a mechanism needs new information to encode and process, and in the case of the human mind such information is actively sought. We all know how bored we get when we are required to do nothing at all for long periods. Bexton, Heron and Scott (1954) demonstrated this most effectively when they asked some Canadian undergraduates to do precisely that for quite a large sum of money. College students were paid substantial sums of money to do nothing all day but lie in bed with their eyes covered in such a way that no effective vision was possible and their ears covered with earphones which only emitted a constant buzzing. In addition their hands were enclosed in tubes. Thus their lives were reduced to a monotonous existence in which they could do nothing except eat or go to the toilet. Despite the payment they were offered, few lasted more than two or three days and the longest time was six days.

Thus it will be seen that human beings do need to be exposed for much of the time to new and interesting stimuli which will increase their level of what is called 'arousal'. But how does this tie up with our claim in the preceding section that children should not be exposed to too much change in routine? Hebb (1972) has suggested that there is

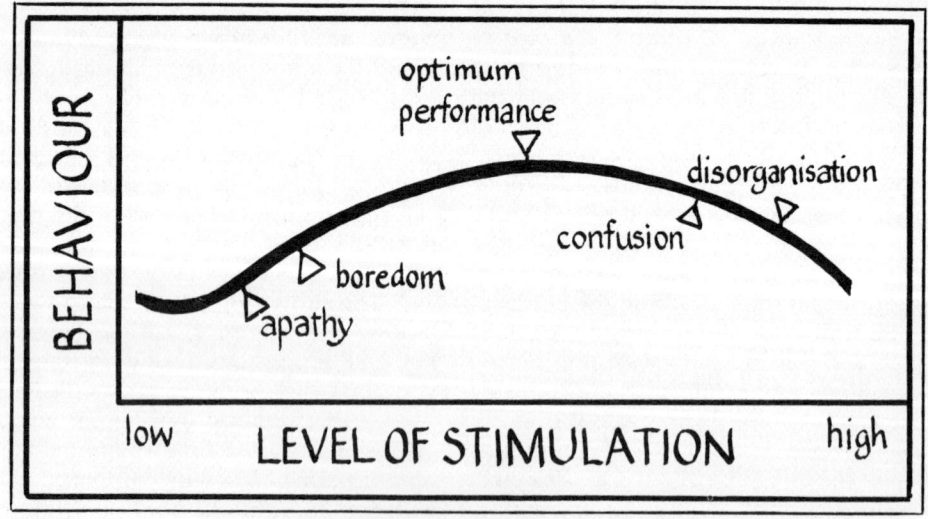

Figure 1.3
Relation of level of stimulus to behaviour

in fact a curvilinear relationship between arousal and optimum functioning. If you look at Figure 1.3 this claim may perhaps become clearer. You will notice that the highest level of satisfaction is experienced at medium levels of stimulation. Too little stimulation makes us bored and apathetic, while too much stimulation may make us feel threatened and confused.

These observations should relate to your own experience. In addition, you will probably agree that this optimum level of functioning differs from individual to individual. Thus some people prefer a quiet life while others are continually seeking out more and more exciting and challenging experiences. Similarly, sometimes you yourself may prefer more excitement and novelty in your environment than at other times.

How do we extend this concept to dealing with children? It would seem that some new experiences are for them a prerequisite of mental development. Without new experience to assimilate into his growing picture of the world, the child's senses and mind cannot reach their full development.

Children can only learn through actively interacting with their environment. Thus children will never learn to speak unless they are spoken to. We can see this, for example, in some of the case studies described by Clarke and Clarke in their book on early experience (1976). Isabelle, for example, is a particularly interesting case.

Isabelle was an illegitimate child who had been brought up by a deaf-mute mother in a dark room shut off from other contact. When she was discovered by outside professionals at the age of 6½ years, Isabelle had no speech – she communicated with her mother by means of gestures. Davis writes: 'Her behaviour towards strangers, especially men, was almost that of a wild animal, manifesting much fear and hostility. In lieu of speech she made only a strange croaking sound' (Davis, 1976, p. 41). Clearly, as a result of the limited interaction, Isabelle, though actually aged 6½ years, behaved like a very young child without speech. This story, however, has a happy ending because after two years of intensive care Isabelle attained normal development. Nevertheless it illustrates the point we are making: without adequate stimulation and interaction, speech cannot develop.

As with learning language, so it is with learning about the physical environment. If children are discouraged from actively exploring the world around them, they not only become irritated and apathetic but also may fall behind their peers in cognitive development. As Pringle writes (1974, p. 42):

> ❛ new experiences enable the child to learn one of the most important, because basic, lessons of early life: learning how to learn; and learning that mastery brings joy and a sense of achievement. This is demonstrated by the exultant cry of "I can do it for myself", which illustrates the link between emotion and learning, between cognitive [thinking] and affective [feeling] experiences. Competence brings its own reward while the mother's or other adults' pleasure in the child's newly acquired skill further reinforces his willingness to seek new fields to conquer. ❜

The two most important avenues of mental development related to this need, then, are play and language, and we shall return to these important topics in Chapter 3.

In most Western countries, children are encouraged to ask questions and explore the environment. Both these practices undoubtedly help the child to assimilate new experiences and absorb them into his ever-expanding cognitive grid. However, Vernon (1969) has suggested that in many traditional societies children are discouraged from asking adults too many questions and are not encouraged to experiment too actively in activities that are not regarded as the province of children. Thus Hake summarises child-rearing practices in northern Nigeria as follows (1972, p. 29):

> ❛ In the northern Nigerian family, restrictions are also placed upon children's conversations with their parents. When the respondents were asked whether they were allowed to join their parents' conversations nearly 60 per cent of the sample answered negatively ... These restrictions suggest the attitude of Nigerian parents toward the correct method of raising children. In the traditional family, children are taught to respect and sometimes fear adults, especially those in authority. Learning respect for elders must take place primarily in the home. So the development of humility is an important developmental task for the northern Nigerian child. Because of this widespread belief, it is only natural that Nigerian parents feel that "children should be seen, but not heard". ❜

Uka (1966, p. 60) makes much the same point about Nigeria when he writes of the strict patterns in the Nigerian family where 'often the child is to be seen and not to be heard. Loquacity [talking too much] particularly in girls, is regarded as a lack of decorum.' Indeed, many studies of child-rearing in Africa stress the importance placed on obedience to elders. For example, Munroe and Munroe (1972) point out how much more obedient Kenyan children between 5 and 7 years of age are in comparison with American children of the same age.

Studies of child-rearing in traditional societies in other parts of the world also indicate that children are expected to be submissive to their elders. Writing about the Punjab, in India, Ghuman (1975, p. 63) says:

> Children are expected to conform and be utterly obedient from the age of about five onwards ... Any form of individuality is actively discouraged ... The children must not argue with adults – even when they could be right. Children in India respect the whole village; all children are known to all adults and they can be corrected or reprimanded by anyone.

This observation ties in with the experience of one of the authors who has for some years conducted child development tutorials with headteachers and inspectors from Third World countries ranging from the Solomon Islands to the West Indies. All agree that in the rural areas such attitudes are commonly found.

What, then, are the implications for the mental development of children brought up in these ways? In line with the conclusions of Clarke and Clarke (1976) we may assume that although children who are discouraged from too much intellectual and physical exploration of the environment may perhaps lag behind Western developmental standards, with exposure to schooling and skilled and sympathetic teaching they will soon catch up. We shall return to this topic in the later chapters, but in general it may be concluded that it is possible that children from such backgrounds 'enter school (even when they are fortunate enough to do so) inadequately prepared to benefit from the experiences that school can potentially give' (Wober, 1975, p. 51).

However, two important points should always be borne in mind. The first is that the work of Kagan (1976) in Guatemala has shown that even if children remain in a more traditional environment, their intellectual and cognitive skills will continue to develop on lines that are attuned to the needs of their own society. Similarly, Cole and Scribner (1974) also conclude that while living in a traditional society may lower performance on Western-type tests, this does not imply that intellectual skills more appropriate to village life do not continue to flourish. And indeed the complex and subtle board games played throughout Africa show this. For example, the game played in Nigeria called Ayo, Dara or Okwe requires a high level of cognitive skills.

But perhaps a more fundamental second point needs to be made as well. While a traditional upbringing, such as that described by Hake, for instance, may perhaps place a premium on quiet and undemanding behaviour in young children, and consequently put these children at a disadvantage on Western-type tasks, other considerations must also obtain even if at a more subjective level. It is by no means a matter of general agreement that the attainment of a highly technologically and economically developed society caters in the end more effectively for human psychological needs than a society that places more stress on human interaction.

The third need – the need for praise and recognition
In Chapter 5 we shall be talking about the child's self-concept. This is a kind of shorthand term we use to describe an individual's private picture of himself. In common with many other psychologists we believe that it is only a child with a positive view of himself and his abilities who can maximally benefit from, and contribute to, the school experience. If a child has a healthy self-image, that is, if he sees himself as a valued and recognised member of society, he will be able to cope with the pressure of school life.

One of the chief ways a child learns to feel positive about himself is through the way other people treat him. If they praise and recognise his efforts to cope with the demands of life, he will begin to gain the confidence and security he needs for optimum development.

However, empty and unrealistic praise does not fool children. It is the considered appraisal of his efforts that makes the child feel that the other is responding to him as an individual. Thus a mother who fobs her child off with repeated and casual remarks of 'Very good, darling' will not foster as much self-confidence in her child as the mother who looks carefully at what her child has been doing and comments accordingly.

You can perhaps relate to this by imagining the following situation. As a student you are required to submit a lengthy essay. You lavish much time, research and thought on this. You hand it in and after a long wait it is returned to you, with, say, a B + inscribed on the bottom. Although this is quite a respectable grade you may perhaps be left with a slight feeling of anti-climax. How much more satisfactory would it have been for you had the tutor bothered to comment individually on any of your points, directed you to another reference, or indeed made any suggestion that indicated that he had thought at any length at all about your particular essay.

A colleague who was attached to a teacher training college in Tanzania told us the following anecdote which we think serves to illustrate further the point we are making. In one rural classroom, the children had only slates to work on. The teacher, at the start of a particular lesson, proceeded as follows:

'Good morning, children. Please take out your slates. Now, please draw me a picture of your mother.'

With much enthusiasm the children set to work. The teacher remained in position at his table. After all the children appeared to be finished he said, 'Good. Now write "Mother" underneath it.' As he said this he demonstrated the writing of the word on the blackboard. He continued to remain in place while the children carefully and painstakingly copied the word down. Then he said, 'Right. Now wipe your slates clean and we will do some arithmetic.'

Perhaps you can imagine that the children felt slightly let down at this lack of acknowledgement of their hard work – the teacher had merely given empty and meaningless praise in an automatic manner as he had never actually indicated an interest in the children's individual efforts.

In the recent study of twelve secondary schools in London to which we have previously referred, Michael Rutter and his co-workers (1979) also observed that immediate and direct feedback in terms of praise or approval was strongly associated with constructive pupil behaviour.

We think you will agree, then, that both the home and the school are important places for the child to start building up a realistic and constructive view of himself as a valued member of the community who has something to contribute at both the individual and social level.

It is in this area that the needs of children with special handicaps must be carefully considered. In many traditional societies such children were, to quote Uka, 'regarded as an abomination' (1966, p. 38). And even in present times such attitudes die hard. For example, in a recent survey of handicapped children in Tanzania, Chowo (1978) found that many villagers regarded such children as a sign that the parents had been guilty of some indiscretion or misdeed.

Children who are handicapped or deformed are at a psychological disadvantage in less traditional societies as well. It is very difficult for them to feel positively about themselves when the mass media (television, newspapers, cinema) show examples of people not only without physical handicaps, but of particularly attractive and prepossessing appearance. We shall return to this in the chapter on adolescence.

It will be seen, then, that the child starts building up a picture of himself not only directly from the attitudes and behaviours of others to him but also by comparing himself both with others and with the accepted images of his society.

Clearly we could not control all the child's interactions so that they always are rewarding even if we wanted to do so. However, we can help the child always to feel accepted. In this way we can fulfil what has been called the need for 'unconditional positive regard'. By this we mean that while perhaps attempting to change a child's behaviour or explain to him where he has erred, we must always be careful to reject the behaviour and not the child himself. We must clearly distinguish our rejection of the deed from our rejection of the individual. In other words, our attitude should be, 'I don't approve of what you are doing now and I'd like to change your behaviour, but that doesn't mean that I reject you as a human being nor does it extend to other, constructive, aspects of your behaviour'.

Such an attitude of *recognition* of the basic worth of all human beings fosters within the child the confidence to confide in the adult when he thinks he cannot cope or when he thinks he has behaved badly. Furthermore, to the extent that the adult attempts to understand why the child has indulged in a particular bit of undesirable behaviour and discusses this with the child, to that extent the child will cease to be paralysed by feelings of guilt and lack of worth which themselves may interfere with the acquisition of more acceptable behaviour.

More behaviourally inclined psychologists stress the need for 'reinforcement'. By this they mean, and we shall return to the topic in Chapter 6, that the basic tool of socialisation lies in the rewarding of behaviour that we wish to encourage. Although the basic orientation of such psychologists differs from the theoretical position we are taking, both viewpoints stress the positive value of praise and recognition of children's constructive behaviour: the behaviourally inclined psychologist because he considers that reinforced behaviour tends to be repeated, the humanistic psychologist because he considers that it is the child's *attitude to himself* that mediates his behaviour and that this attitude derives largely from the way others treat him. The more they recognise and encourage his efforts both at home and school, the more confidence in himself the child will gain.

The fourth need – the need for responsibility
Much evidence ranging from work done in prisons to research in hospitals and industry indicates that involving people in their own development makes for their optimum progress. Institutions that are run from above with strict and inflexible hierarchies may look efficient, but very often the people who work, live or learn in them will be very unhappy and their loyalties to the institution itself will be shallow and ambivalent. Children too, whether in the home or in school, need to be involved in some decision-making. (Clearly, of course, the younger the child the less prominently does this need figure.)

In the first assumption we outlined on page 4 we stressed that children are active agents in their own development and, within limits that are clearly set out for them, should be helped to be responsible for their own actions. Homes have a vital contribution to make here. In more traditional societies this need was clearly met. Many anthropological descriptions stress how girls and boys are slowly brought into the life of the village. Girls may begin to care for their younger siblings at a very early age whereas boys will often accompany the men of the village on hunting trips or into the fields. In such societies where there was no formal schooling as such, this slow socialisation, together perhaps with prescribed initiation ceremonies, helped to bring the younger members of society gradually into their adult roles. Thus responsibility came comparatively young and helped young people to feel effective.

The stress is often very different in more technological and urbanised societies. Children become aware from an early age that they are excluded from the more responsible and important areas of living. While this has clear advantages in allowing time for both informal play and formal learning at school, it leads in some cases to an infantilisation of even quite old children. Children should be prepared well before adolescence for the contribution they can make to the general well-being. At home a democratic form of decision-making clearly aids easier social relationships within the family, as studies on adolescence have shown (see Chapter 8). Further, treating children as rational and useful human beings both helps to foster their self-image and teaches them to examine constructively parental values.

Schools, too, can make an important contribution in this respect. As Pringle writes (1974, p. 57),

‘ In the conventional classroom setting, where both work and discipline are laid down by the teacher, there is relatively little room for allowing each child a measure of responsibility for his own actions and learnings. A more pupil-centred regime gives each child a sense of involvement and participation in planning their own activities according to their different interest and ability levels; while rules evolved jointly with the teacher help to make the reasons for necessary constraints understood and hence more readily accepted by the pupils. ’

In Mays's book, *The Social Treatment of Young Offenders* (1975), the effectiveness of granting responsibility in an attempt to help deviant young people is shown in the studies described by both Bloom and Mays himself.

One of the major contributions to constructive outcomes for pupils that emerged from the Rutter survey of twelve secondary schools was whether or not pupils were encouraged to take positions of responsibility. Giving children positions of responsibility aided individual children in that it conveyed 'trust in pupils' abilities' and because it set 'standards of mature behaviour' (1979, p. 197). But in addition, encouraging pupils to identify with the running of the school encourages commitment to education. A Cypriot headmaster reports that since he has set up pupil councils in each class to aid in the day-to-day running of the classroom there has been a marked improvement in the morale of the school (Ioannou, 1979).

It will be seen that if the child's need for responsibility is met, he will be more likely to view himself as an effective and valuable member of society. And, as we have stressed before, it is through our own perception of the world and our place in it that we are able to play a constructive part in social life.

How Different Societies affect Children's Needs

Before presenting Pringle's model of the needs of children we stressed that while a survey of cross-cultural literature on child development would indicate that these needs are universal, such a model can by no means be regarded as proven. Instead we encouraged you to regard this description of children's psychological needs as a useful tool – a device for examining a particular child's environment. We have argued that to the extent that the needs we have described are met, to that extent will the child be able to cope constructively with life at home and at school.

We also mentioned that any such listing of needs is bound to be at least partially subjective. Nevertheless, we feel that the model outlined has the advantage of being simple and is based, as we have attempted to show, on a number of empirical studies.

We also noted that each culture will meet these needs in differing ways. Thus in some societies, the need for love and security is met within a nuclear family of mother, father and children while in other societies it is met within an extended family system.

But in addition to these primary psychological needs, other needs may be generated within any particular society. To a large extent these needs become particularly important when a child feels in some way different from his peers.

Let us take an example from Britain. Institutions for child care in Britain have undergone a radical change in the last twenty years. Whereas before then many children were cared for in large impersonal orphanages, in recent years children in care have tended to be cared for in small family-sized units with a very high standard of physical amenities and a serious attempt to respond to each child on an individual basis. Children in these institutions are usually there not because they are orphans but because they have been removed from the care of their parents who neglected and in many cases maltreated them. Yet although realistically such children know that they are far better off in care than they were in their homes, a wistful desire for a more 'normal' way of life often shows in their thoughts.

Thus in the National Children's Bureau publication *Who Cares?* we meet children who were removed from parents who both neglected and abused them. For example, one child came into care because 'I was born in Trafalgar Square. My mum she nearly fell under a bus and they couldn't get her into an ambulance, so I was born there. They took me into hospital and put me into an incubator. My mum and dad didn't get on well and used to have fights. My younger brother was born, and my dad tried to cut off his ears and we was all under the table screaming and the rest of the family were trying to help my younger brother. Then my dad threw me mum out of the window. I was put into a children's home' (Page and Clark, 1977, p. 12).

Other children have similar tragic stories to tell. The institutions they are moved to are often well equipped with dedicated and kind staff who endeavour to give as much support and nurture as possible. The children often realise this, as for example the child who noted: 'The place I'm at now is a very good place and I wouldn't like to be anywhere else. I don't think I'd even like to go home because I've found a place where somebody trusts me and I can be left alone and I can be understood (ibid., p. 19).

Nevertheless the stigma (shame or disgrace) of coming from an institution is deeply felt by the majority of children who live in them. Even though they may prefer the institution to their homes, they remain aware that the majority of British children do live in their own homes and that they are different. So a typical comment with respect to being in care is: 'Being in care you feel you've got a cross on your back. You feel marked' (ibid., p. 17); and 'I met a very nice girl and I wouldn't tell her that I came from a children's home but she found out. I was so embarrassed at the fact. I was ashamed' (loc. cit.).

The children thus demonstrate another psychological need – the need to conform to the norms that they think society has laid down that each child should be cared for in the nuclear home by at least one, and preferably both, of their natural parents.

Let us consider another case of a culturally generated need. It is known that all societies throughout history have produced a varying proportion of individuals who prefer to work mainly with their left rather than right hand. Yet a child who is born left-handed in some traditional societies may be placed under enormous pressure to conform to what is regarded as the right-handed norm. As Uka writes in eastern Nigeria, 'Informants said that left-handed persons are regarded as queer. They are called names, slighted or mocked at' (1966, p. 55).

In other parts of Nigeria and in other African countries like Tanzania this prejudice against left-handed dominance is also felt. For example, LeVine (1962, pp. 13–14) writes of the memory a Nigerian student had of the way he was punished for eating with his left hand instead of his right when he was 8 years of age.

‘ My father was so annoyed that he started to beat me mercilessly. My mother then removed the food and said that if I could not eat with my right hand she would no more give me food and that I would no more eat with them. To add to my punishment, my father got a big stone and tied it to my left hand and in addition, he tied a living frog which I detested to it. He then commanded me to be eating in his presence with my right hand. Little by little I suffered for three days because of this offence. I shall never forget the day when a big stone and a living frog were tied to my left hand to prevent my eating with it. ’

It can be seen, then, that secondary psychological needs are often generated in individual societies if a child feels different from his peers. However, to the measure that his caretakers meet his needs for love and security, novelty, praise and recognition and responsibility, to that measure will he feel sufficiently confident of himself to deal with the fact of his difference or differences.

Chapter 1: Selected Bibliography

Abiola, E. T., 'Understanding the African school child', *West African Journal of Education*, vol. XV, no. 1 (1971), pp. 63–7.

Clarke, A. M., and Clarke, A. D. B., *Early Experience: Myth and Evidence* (London: Open Books, 1976).

Durojaiye, M. O. A., *A New Introduction to Educational Psychology* (London: Evans, 1976).

Pringle, M. K., *The Needs of Children* (London: Hutchinson, 1974).

Schaffer, R., *Mothering* (London: Fontana/Open Books, 1977).

THE EARLY YEARS AT HOME

2

Introduction

In this chapter we shall be looking at some of the home factors that may affect the child's behaviour and achievement at school. It is often tempting for the teacher to assume that all the silent attentive little faces gazing up at him or her on the first day of school belong to very similar little people. In fact, as we shall see, children may bring with them very different attitudes and expectations when they enter school. In addition, even though they may be of similar chronological ages, they may have developed thus far at different rates and so may be able to cope with the intellectual and social tasks of the school to varying extents.

However, it is always very important indeed to bear in mind that such differences in ability level are neither fixed nor unchanging. The child who finds learning to read more difficult than his peers is not necessarily always going to perform at a lower level than others. Many people who have later achieved at high intellectual levels did not show much promise in their early years at school. In fact, the greatest physicist of this century, Albert Einstein, who laid the theoretical foundations that enabled us to split the atom, was a poor student in his early schooldays.

So you must bear in mind, when we describe some of the factors that may affect the child's achievement level at school, that early achievement levels do not necessarily determine later achievement and that where a child is apparently falling behind the others of his age remediation is always possible, except in the case of that very small proportion of the population who are sometimes designated as 'mentally retarded'. These children perform markedly worse than other children of their age and in some cases such children show evidence of some precipitating physiological factors such as damage incurred during the birth process. We shall return to the topic of the special learning needs of such children in Chapter 6.

In this chapter, then, we shall consider the factors in the home that influence the child's behaviour at school under the following headings: pre-natal influences; emotional and social factors; motor, perceptual and cognitive factors; temperamental factors; and developmental rate (see Figure 2 .1).

Pre-natal Influences

Even while the mother is pregnant, various factors can affect the child's potential. Experiments with rats have led us to believe that malnutrition in pregnancy can affect the growth of brain cells. Clearly no one would wish to perform similar experiments with human beings. However, throughout the world, there are areas of extreme poverty where pregnant mothers have only inadequate and unsatisfactory diets both while pregnant and while lactating (nursing their infants). It is quite clear that children born to such mothers will be less robust than children born to adequately fed mothers, and that the first group of children will continue to thrive less well (see the survey we discuss later on by Ashem and Janes). This can lead to a progressive and cumulative disadvantage. As Abiola (1971, p. 64) writes: 'Apathy and irritability accompany many children's illnesses, the frequency or severity of which may build up a behaviour pattern that limits the child's exploration

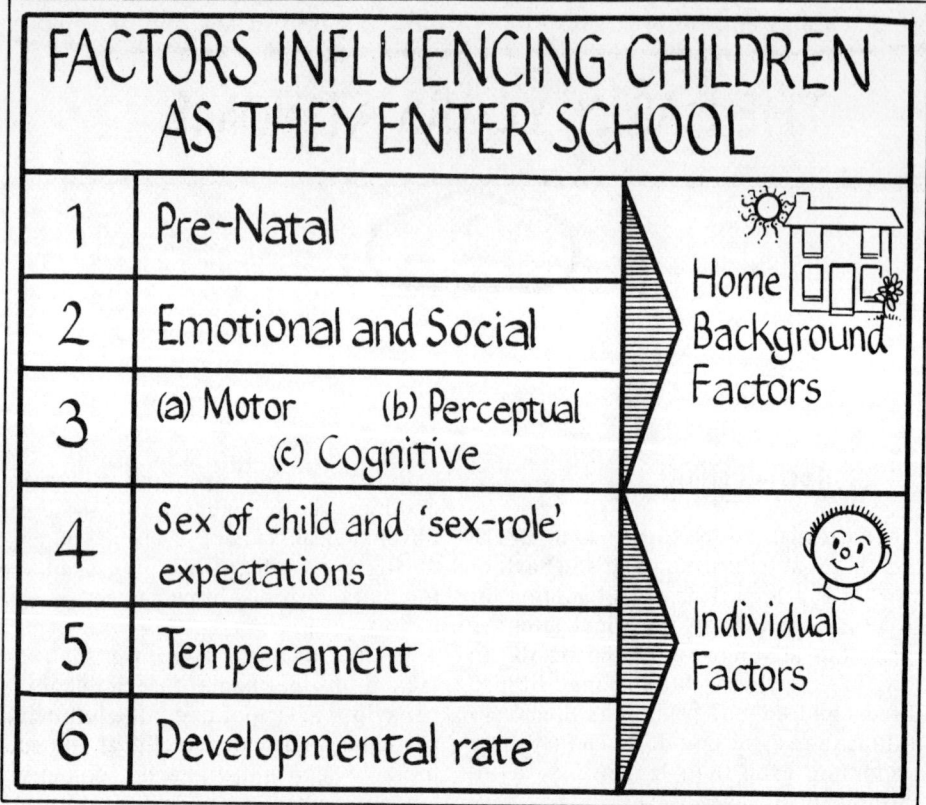

FACTORS INFLUENCING CHILDREN AS THEY ENTER SCHOOL

1	Pre-Natal	
2	Emotional and Social	Home Background Factors
3	(a) Motor (b) Perceptual (c) Cognitive	
4	Sex of child and 'sex-role' expectations	
5	Temperament	Individual Factors
6	Developmental rate	

Figure 2.1 Structure of Chapter 2

and experimentation that ... are involved in the development of intellectual functions.' It is of course well known that mothers who smoke tend to have smaller babies, probably because of a less-than-satisfactory oxygen supply to the baby.

Certain drugs, if taken during the first twelve or so weeks of pregnancy, can have very bad effects on the growing foetus. For example, the thalidomide pills taken during the early 1960s by mothers in Western Europe produced gross malformations in the children concerned. Addictive drugs, such as heroin, can affect the baby if taken frequently at any stage in the pregnancy. And some people like Stott (1977) claim to have shown that even the mother's emotional state during pregnancy can affect the baby's development physically in the first few years of life by making such children more likely to be physically ill during these years.

Certain physical illnesses in the mother, particularly German measles (rubella) during the first twelve weeks of pregnancy, may also produce both sensory defects (e.g. deafness and blindness) and mental defects. Finally, the birth process, if the baby's oxygen supply is very badly restricted, can affect the baby's central nervous system.

Clearly if any of these ill-effects has occurred, there is little that educational institutions can do to reverse it. However, a knowledge of the optimum conditions during pregnancy should be part of the education of all children, whether male or female. So all young people should be aware of the importance of a balanced diet during pregnancy and of the ill-effects of smoking during that period. They should also know that drugs (whether medicinal or not) should not be taken during pregnancy without medical advice, most particularly during the first twelve or thirteen weeks. Finally, they should be aware that the child whose mother is in a relatively happy and balanced emotional state during pregnancy is likely to have a better chance of satisfactory early development than a child whose mother's pregnancy is marred by continual and severe emotional upsets.

Emotional and Social Influences

In the first chapter we tried to show that if a child's emotional needs are met, and in particular his need for love and security, praise and recognition, he will be well prepared for later life. In addition, we tried to indicate that a child needs to know the limits within which his behaviour will be acceptable. Such children who feel secure and valued will approach the new social relationships of the school, whether with the teacher or with the other children, with trust and confidence.

As we pointed out in Chapter 1, it is important then for the child to have had during his early years warm and affectionate relationships with at least one, and preferably more, sensitive caretakers. In addition, it has been shown that emotional and social problems later in life are seldom encountered in children whose homes have been *in general* warm and relatively free from quarrelling and emotional upsets (Rutter and Madge, 1976).

A child from such a home will be prepared to trust his teachers, and if a teacher should perhaps unjustifiably punish the child he will be able to accept this without feeling devalued and worthless. On the other hand, a child who has received little confirmation of his own self-worth and who has been exposed to a lack of harmony in his own home will need very special attention and responsiveness from his teacher. In this way he can perhaps be helped to build up a faith both in himself and in other people.

Many contemporary writers on child development such as Michael Rutter and Rudolf Schaffer stress that it is the *quality*, not the quantity, of interaction that matters in the child's early relationships. It is of course easy to understand that a child fares better with, say, two hours a day intensive interaction with a relaxed and stimulating caretaker than he would with eight hours a day interaction with a bored and unresponsive one.

Thus it is not surprising that Israeli children brought up in a communal way on what are called *kibbutzim* form close and rewarding relationships with their parents even though they may see them for a total of three or four hours a day at most. This hypothesis, that it is the *kind* of interaction that counts rather than the time spent, may also be used to account for the fact that surveys of the children of working mothers have not found them to be disadvantaged in any way when compared with their peers. The general conclusion to be reached from surveys of the effect of working mothers is that their children do not suffer in any way provided that the mother feels happy about working, enjoys her work and provides adequate substitute care (Pugh, 1976).

Unfortunately not all working mothers in developed countries are able to provide satisfactory alternative care. Particularly in Britain, until recently, numbers of unskilled baby-minders looked after young infants in the centre of big cities and some, though not all, surveys of these baby-minders found them to be supplying an unsatisfactory and unstimulating environment for their charges. Further, although in some countries, notably in Scandinavia, crèches are well run and young infants attending them receive individual attention from trained and responsive caretakers, this is by no means the case in all developed countries. In Third World countries too, as can be seen from the study by Ayonrinde, Ashem and Ugwuegbu (forthcoming), many institutions providing daily care for the children of working mothers are woefully inadequate.

There is, however, another side to the coin. Surveys of young mothers who do not work and live in isolation in big cities show that these mothers tend to become depressed and may be prescribed tranquillisers or anti-depressants and thus are ill-equipped to provide sensitive attention to their young infants. Thus Brown and his co-workers in a survey in London (1975) found that 42 per cent of the working-class mothers with children under 6 years that they interviewed could be regarded as suffering from a definite psychiatric disorder. Two of the four major factors identified as producing this disturbance were the emotional isolation of the mothers and lack of interest or employment outside the home.

In more traditional settings the mothers of young children are far more fortunate. The existence of the extended family allows the mother to work if she wishes, in the knowledge that satisfactory substitute care can be provided by a number of relatives, for example, aunts, cousins, older siblings and grandmothers, and sometimes co-wives.

The support the extended family offers to young mothers may help to account for the fact that cases of child abuse (baby-battering and child neglect) would appear to be less common in Third World countries than in developed ones. It seems that one of the precursors of child abuse is the lack of support experienced by young mothers who live in isolated circumstances. They may live in busy and overcrowded towns but they have no one close to turn to when they need help and support in child-rearing. (Of course, another reason may be that the collection of statistics on such cases is more efficient in developed countries.)

In this subsection we have tried to suggest that if the child's home is a happy one, and if his parents or caretakers are responsive and loving, the child will be optimally prepared for the social and emotional aspects of school life. We have further gone on to propose that at the heart of a loving relationship lies the *quality*, not the *quantity*, of interaction, and that the amount of time the child's parents spend with him is less important than the use they make of that time.

Unfortunately, not all children are fortunate enough to have loving and responsive parents or caretakers who can help to build up the child's self-image and so help the child to learn to approach social relationships in a trusting manner. Some children may be brought up under conditions of domestic strife, or in homes where, harassed by financial problems, busy parents simply do not have the time or energy to devote to the child's emotional needs.

What can the teacher do in such circumstances? In principle, it seems clear from adoption studies that removing children from unsatisfactory to happy and caring homes can radically change their prospects. We have already referred to the study by Tizard of adopted children (see page 7). Kadushin (1976) reports on a number of other studies that reached conclusions similar to Barbara Tizard's. In particular he describes a study made by the Division of Children and Youth in Wisconsin over a ten-year period. Ninety-one families who adopted children over the age of 5 years were studied. Two measures of success of outcome were developed, both related to the parents' satisfaction with the adoption. On the one measure 82 per cent of the cases were regarded as successful and on the other measure 87 per cent.

But adoption is not a solution that can be contemplated by the teacher. It remains for him or her to try and help the child to build up a more satisfactory picture of himself than he is likely to get from the non-supportive conditions of his home. He or she can do this by perhaps occasionally seeing the child alone, by discriminating praise, by offering the child special

responsibilities and by keeping an eye on the child's relationships with his classmates, for it seems that unsupportive home conditions can lead to children having difficulty with social relationships (McMichael, 1977). In addition, the teacher can try to build up social contacts with the parents without in any way antagonising them.

The concept of community schools where parents help to run and sometimes to finance the schools can contribute to breaking down the barriers between parents and teachers. Such schools are now found in settings as varied as Tanzania, Scandinavia and Scotland.

Motor, Perceptual and Cognitive Factors

Motor factors

While motor skills are largely determined by developmental rate and therefore affected by the child's physical constitution, they are still liable to improve with practice. There is no doubt that children who are allowed the freedom to move around and explore their immediate environment learn a great deal about spatial relationships and about how to use their own bodies. Both a knowledge of spatial relationships and the feedback gained from using one's body and limbs contribute to higher levels of motor performance so that, even within the limits of a particular individual's physical constitution, improvement in motor skills may be brought about with practice. Thus free play is most important for these skills.

An interesting finding that has been reported from areas as diverse as Latin America, Asia and Africa is that Third World infants have been found to be more developmentally advanced in their motor skills than infants from more developed countries. In addition, there is the suggestion that the less traditional the Third World home is, the less this advantage is likely to hold. This subject is discussed in great detail in Mallory Wober's book (1975). While there has been some conflicting evidence (for example, Warren, 1972), in general it is true to say that most studies in this area, particularly in Africa, find that right from birth, Third World infants are more advanced on measures of motor development like the ability to hold up their heads (Hausa infants in northern Nigeria), the ability to co-ordinate hand and eye movements (Zambia), locomotion and posture (Senegal) and sitting and walking (Kenya). This comparative advantage in motor skills is usually referred to in the cross-cultural literature as the 'precocity' finding.

Many theories have been advanced to account for precocity, amongst them differences in feeding methods, physical care, and handling and maternal attitudes. Perhaps the most interesting of these theories are concerned with the last two factors just mentioned.

With respect to physical care it seems a matter of general observation that in many of the cultures showing precocity the infants are carried on the backs of their caretakers and this undoubtedly contributes to postural control. In addition, in many areas in Central Africa, young infants are placed in padded holes in the ground while their mothers work (Chowo, 1978, in Tanzania). Both these practices undoubtedly give the baby more opportunity for practising different motor skills than is obtained by babies who lie in cribs, cots and prams.

Strong evidence for environmental effect on motor development comes from Charles Super's work in Kenya (1976). He found that the motor skills of walking and sitting, on which Kenyan babies showed precocity, were specifically *taught* by caretakers and could be practised in the course of the daily routines. This applied to children who were reared in a traditional way. But Kenyan children who were of the same ethnic background but were brought up in the cities in a more Western way did not show the same degree of precocity. His work seems to supply strong evidence for the point we made earlier that the environment contributes to how fast motor skills develop.

The hypothesis that precocity is influenced by the mothers' attitudes to their young infants is advanced by Geber and Dean (1957). They point out that 'the state of the newborn African child may be related to the attitude of the mother to her pregnancy'. It does seem that having babies in more traditional societies is a very highly valued activity and a barren woman may indeed find her position very difficult. Thus Hake (1972), in a study of cultural variation in child-rearing, reports that in traditional societies mothers are far more likely to view child-bearing with unqualified happy anticipation than are mothers in the USA. In support of this we can note that Uka says of his northern Nigerian sample of mothers that 'All mothers interviewed said they were usually delighted to be pregnant and that pregnancy is regarded by all and sundry as a joyous event in the family, and a happy omen for the couple' (1966,

p. 29), whereas Sears and his co-workers in the USA found that only 62 per cent of their sample of expectant mothers were 'delighted' that they were having their first child (Hake, 1972, p. 7).

We can therefore perhaps conclude that early motor development is related to the physical environment afforded to the child to move around in as well as his physical condition and that in addition it is possible that close and positive aspects of maternal care may also contribute to greater motor ability.

Perceptual factors
When a young child comes to school the teacher often expects him to be able to make various perceptual discriminations. For example, the teacher may require all the children to be able to discriminate and name colours, to be able to differentiate geometric shapes such as, say, a triangle from a circle, and to be able to reproduce a particular note in singing. There is no doubt that such perceptual discriminations are aided by practice.

An example of perceptual learning that you can demonstrate for yourself is given by Hebb (1972, pp. 29–30). This is the ability to distinguish two points on the skin. A subject is blindfolded and the skin on, say, his upper arm, is touched sometimes with one, sometimes with two, points of a set of dividers (the kind you get in sets of mathematical instruments). Each time the subject is asked to report whether he feels one or two points on testing. Prolonged testing in the area will decrease the distance at which the distinctiveness of the two points can be felt. By definition this is perceptual learning.

You will appreciate, then, that some children come to school with more finely trained perceptual skills than others. Thus a child from a home where, let us say, both parents are teachers may be better able to cope with some of the classroom tasks than a child from a home where both parents are perhaps illiterate and too busy in addition to talk to him very much. The former may be able to discriminate and name colours easily; he may, from playing with educational toys, be able to identify geometric shapes; and he may, because he has spent some time singing and listening to music with his parents, be more able than the other child to hear the difference between, say, the consonants 'b' and 'p' when he is first learning to read in English.

Thus it should be clear that for some children the

routine tasks of the classroom may be easier than they are for others.

Cognitive factors

What do we mean by cognitive skills? We will define cognition as 'a general term covering all aspects of thinking – perception, memory, concept formation and reasoning'. So you can see these are the skills associated with thinking and reasoning. In Chapter 4 we shall examine in some detail the course of cognitive development. In this chapter we are concerned only with the extent to which home background factors may influence the child's cognitive ability as he enters school.

Perhaps the most important aspect of cognition is the ability to manipulate symbols. And the most elaborate use of symbols, of course, lies in language. As you will learn in Chapter 3, language develops primarily as a means by which the child can communicate about his thoughts, needs and feelings with others. Another important function of language lies in our use of language to clothe our concepts – the very young child may feel love for his mother but is only able to express this in words long after he has first experienced the feelings of happiness and contentment he has when she is with him. So you will note that another fundamental aspect of language is its mediating function. You have perhaps noticed this yourself if you have heard young children speak to themselves when they are doing something: 'Now, I'll put this in the box … that's it', as he puts his car away.

A great deal of research both with children who live with their parents and with children who grow up in institutions has shown that language development is accelerated when children are spoken to a great deal by their caretakers. Indeed, you will remember the extreme case described in Chapter 1 where the young girl, Isabelle, failed to learn to speak because no one had ever spoken to her. So it is reasonable to suppose that as homes vary in the amount of time that parents and other people devote to talking to the child, so will children vary in their facility with language. And in general it can be stated that the more developed the child's linguistic (language) skills are, the better he will be able to cope with the cognitive tasks of the classroom.

Language has two important functions in the classroom. The first function concerns its use in instruction. In many classrooms language is the only explicit medium of instruction and such classrooms are often said to be havens for 'chalk and talk'. It is important to point out that other classrooms make more use of other media such as copying physical movements, hand-eye co-ordination exercises and body-thought, and we shall return to ways of teaching such skills in Chapter 4. Nevertheless, in most classrooms the teacher tends to teach mainly through language.

One of the most important things a child has to learn in the first years of school is, of course, how to read. Once again the child with comparatively advanced linguistic skills is at an advantage here. As you will see in Chapter 6, contemporary reading experts see reading as a psycho-*linguistic* skill and argue that it is the child's linguistic ability to predict what will come next in a reading passage that is the most important determinant of his ease in learning to read.

Clearly language plays a major part in the cognitive tasks of the early school years. But this is not its only important function in the classroom. Another area in which it plays a very important role is in the 'socialising of the child into the norms' of the school and the classroom. By 'socialising' we mean helping the child to adjust to and fit into the society in which he moves. By 'norms' we mean the accepted values and attitudes held by any group. Thus the teacher will tell the children about the kind of behaviour he or she expects of them and will use language to shape and control the child's behaviour.

So language can be seen to have two most vital aspects in the classroom. It is often the chief means of socialisation and it is always the major medium through which the cognitive tasks are taught. Thus a teacher must always be on her guard to help remedy deficiencies both in the children's ability to use language themselves (performance) and in their ability to understand language (competence).

We have tried to show, then, that with regard to linguistic development the child's home background plays a most important part. And we have also argued that it is a vital aspect of the teacher's role to help remedy deficiencies in this area.

Another important contributor to cognitive development lies in the acquisition of *analytic skills*. By this we mean the ability to codify and sort out information and then to draw conclusions from this organisation. In Vernon's work on aptitude testing in various cultures (1969) he argues that such analytical skills are first shaped in the home. If the parents encourage children to ask questions about why things happen or how things work, children will be helped to think in a way that is compatible with the tasks of a technological nature.

A certain amount of work in Third World countries has suggested that more traditional homes do not encourage such attitudes in children (you will recall that we discussed this in Chapter 1). Such conclusions were reached by, for example, Okonji in Nigeria (1971) and Otaala (1971) in Uganda. On the other hand, Cole and others' work in Liberia disputes this (1974). But it does seem that certain cognitive tasks such as sorting and classifying and making inferences may be dependent, in the beginning in any event, on the child's early environment.

In this chapter, in the next section and in Chapter 4 we shall look at some studies which suggest that certain factors influence the acquisition of cognitive skills. In the next section we shall look at the effect of the *social class* of the parent and in Chapter 4 we shall look at the degree of *urbanisation*. (By degree of urbanisation we mean the extent to which the home is similar to those in the most developed city in the country under consideration.) Here we simply wish to make the point that such factors can be influenced by teaching. If a child is behind the rest of his peers in analytical skills the concerned teacher can help him to catch up by encouraging him to develop effective and appropriate cognitive strategies (see Chapter 4).

However, it is important to stress here that teaching alone may not be enough. If a child comes from a more disadvantaged home than his classmates, or if he comes from the village and is now in a city school, then he may feel inferior academically to his classmates. Thus, in addition to offering extra academic help, the teacher will also have to make sure that the child does not suffer from feelings of inadequacy which may prevent him from taking advantage of the extra help.

In summary, then, we have argued that in the last three areas we have discussed – motor, perceptual and analytical skills – early home environment is very important. We now pause to consider what are the factors in the early environment that underlie these differences (see Figure 2.1).

What differentiates early home environments?
Perhaps the simplest area to look at is the *physical environment*. In this we include the facilities available. Clearly some children grow up in far from adequate physical environments. Not only may they be overcrowded, small and lacking in toys (whether of a traditional nature or bought toys), they may also be so poverty-stricken that the children are malnourished or at worst suffer from the diseases of malnutrition.

As we showed on page 15, the effects of malnutrition in the early years of life may have far-reaching effects. For example, Stoch and Smythe (1967) studied children in South Africa who had suffered severe malnutrition in the first two years of life and compared them to a group of adequately fed children from similar homes. The first group scored significantly lower on tests of intelligence and were also shown to have EEG (electroencephalograph or 'brain wave') patterns similar to the patterns of people with brain damage. Similarly in Nigeria Ashem and Janes (1978) conducted a study of the effects of chronic under-nutrition on the cognitive abilities of children. The subjects were 118 children between the ages of $2\frac{1}{2}$ and 6 years who came from three groups: 'well-to-do' urban, poor urban and poor rural environments. They concluded that an impoverished environment was responsible for the relatively worse performance of the poor children in comparison to their better-off peers. But in addition to the bad effect of poor home conditions in restricting play and exploratory experiences, there was also evidence that the children who were most malnourished (as judged by their physical growth) performed worst. This means that over and above the effect of a poor environment, these children were handicapped by their poor nourishment in their performance on a wide variety of cognitive tasks.

However, a note of caution must be introduced. As we have said before, most poor environmental effects are reversible and it is clear from other evidence (Waterlow, 1975; Winick *et al.*, 1975) that if children who are malnourished for a comparatively short time are removed from their poor environments, they can catch up with other children. As Waterlow writes, 'what matters in practice is the total environment of the child throughout the period of growth and development. It is not an *episode* of malnutrition in early life that leads to handicap' (our italics).

Overall, however, evidence suggests that malnutrition in infancy and later on in childhood relates to poor performance on cognitive tasks in later life. It clearly also contributes to poorer physical development and consequently poorer motor and perceptual development.

But there are other more subtle ways in which

homes can affect school performance. For example, the *attitude* of the parents toward the utility of what is learned at school must colour the way children approach school. In Tanzania, Joy Mbilinyi (1970) has shown that, particularly with respect to the education of girls, parental attitudes vary widely in this respect and, not surprisingly, attendance at school is poor when parental attitudes to school are not favourable.

Another vital area is *child care practices*. Lloyd (1966) describes in Nigeria how 'elite' parents place a major emphasis on their interaction with their children in the areas that bear on school performance. Thus (p. 169),

> Familiar with Nigerian education institutions, elite mothers see their tasks as taking an interest in their children's schooling, giving help when necessary, and continuously offering support and encouragement. To improve their children's creative and intellectual capacities, parents are prepared to spend as much time as their financial means permit in order to provide teachers, books, toys and recreation. *Mothers take special care to answer their children's questions, since the belief is widespread that ignoring questions from children stifles their curiosity.* (our italics)

Another rather more abstruse area to try and describe is what Margaret Donaldson (1978) calls the capacity for 'disembedded thought'. She argues that the more elaborate and vital cognitive tasks of school require the capacity to isolate oneself from the everyday world and subject oneself to a particular abstract and logical system of organising one's cognitive processes. Bruner (1973) comes to the same conclusion in his book *Beyond the Information Given*, chapter 21, where he claims that children from certain homes in Third World areas do not realise that the majority of concepts (ideas) they meet in school are abstract ones because in their own homes concepts are more likely to have clear concrete referents.

Although this particular aspect is perhaps rather hard to grasp, the reader will agree, we think, that much school work – in particular, mathematics and science – does require an approach that is rigorous, objective and logical, and that the more the parents themselves have access to this 'disembedded' mode of thinking, the better the match between their children's preparation for school and the cognitive tasks of school.

In the Western world the four areas we have just been exploring (see Figure 2.2) – the physical environment in the home, parental attitudes to school, child care practices and preparation for

HOME BACKGROUND VARIABLES	
1	Physical environment in the home
2	Parental attitudes to school
3	Child care practices
4	Preparation for the kind of thought helpful in the school situation ('disembedded' thought)

Figure 2.2

disembedded thought – are often interpreted in terms of socio-economic class (SEC). Research in Scandinavia, the USA and Great Britain has shown that middle-class homes tend to prepare children better for school because of the closer match they show to the attitudinal and conceptual qualities of school, compared with working-class homes. Even at the university level in Western Europe and in particular in Great Britain, a far higher proportion of students are likely to have come from middle-class homes than the proportion of middle-class homes in the country would warrant.

In the USA the same trend has always been shown for white students and very recently the same effects have been shown for black students as well. Sociologists (like Christopher Jencks) argue that as class differences become entrenched, so will the comparative advantage of middle-class children within the educational system become pronounced.

It is clearly of interest to readers of this book to ask whether such social class effects hold in Third World countries as well. We believe that there is some evidence that they do. That is, children from homes that are termed 'elite' not only enter schools at an advantage, but are likely to retain that advantage right through their academic careers.

Before citing evidence to support this claim, we should point out that it is more difficult to measure social class accurately in Third World countries than it is in the West. Ogunlade (1973) writes that this is mainly because of the operation of the extended family system. The demands of the members of a large extended family may make such financial claims on a wage-earner's salary that, according to Ogunlade, even a highly paid person may not be able to 'afford to live like a middle-class family' (p. 429). Because of this we shall continue to refer to more privileged families as 'elite', rather than use the Western term 'middle class'.

'Elite' families are well placed to provide the four advantages we mentioned earlier: a good and stimulating physical environment, constructive parental attitudes to school, more child-centred child-rearing practices and preparation for the kind of abstract thought demanded by schools.

Physical care. We have already mentioned that some homes offer the very minimum of physical facilities to children. But even homes that offer adequate food and shelter may, in comparison with elite homes, lack other facilities. For example, in a survey done in Kenya, Prewitt (1974) reports that 90 per cent of 'mid-elite' families bought their children educational toys. This may be relevant because when Dastoor and Emovan (1972) tested Nigerian children on tests of visual perception and logical reasoning they concluded that the children who did well were those whose parents bought them constructional toys. Further, they thought that some children scored poorly because they had to help their families by hawking (selling goods in the street) and thus had less time to devote to reading.

Parental attitudes. Parental attitudes to school clearly influence school performance. For instance, if parents think that school performance is very important, they may, as parents do in the larger cities of Nigeria and Kenya, arrange for their children to have extra coaching for important examinations. Further, according to Prewitt, they may make sure that their children go to the best schools available in their area.

We have already quoted Barbara Lloyd's description of the *child care practices* of elite parents (see page 22). Beatrice Ashem who worked in Nigeria also reported that when mothers of young children were asked to help them with problem-solving tasks, middle-class (her term) mothers gave more praise, more verbal instructions and more positive feed-back (1974) than the mothers who were not middle class did. Lloyd's work (1966, 1977) clearly shows that the children of her 'elite' sample outstripped the children of her traditional ('oje') sample in school performance.

Finally, having literate parents is clearly an advantage. This is reported by Ogunlade, who showed that children of illiterate parents did worse than children of literate parents attending the same schools. Prewitt also showed that the educational level of parents is important. These two studies provide support for our claim that children are better prepared for school if they come from homes where parents have experience of school and what we called 'disembedded' ways of thinking. That is the ability to think logically about the problem in hand and not bring unrelated factors into play.

Perhaps by now you are persuaded that elite homes do prepare children more adequately for school. But you may wonder, does this advantage last? It seems that for at least three countries it does. In Kenya, Ghana and Nigeria it appears that students at university and at the top end of secondary schools are more likely to come from urban and well-educated homes (Weiss, 1979).

What are the implications for the teacher? Does it mean that she must always expect that children from non-elite homes will perform comparatively poorly at school? The answer to this question must surely be that in many cases this will be true: children from more advantaged homes will be better prepared for school than those from less advantaged ones. However, it is important to remember that the relationship between income and occupation is not *always* so straightforward. For example, Lake (1979) discovered that in Zimbabwe, in the urban area she investigated, the poorest children were not the most backward on scales of cognitive (intellectual) ability.

She used tests of perception, language ability and number ability and using the McCarthy scales she divided her children up into three socio-economic classes. She found that, in her study, children from middle-income homes did worse on these tests than children from richer homes. This was not very surprising. But she also found that they did worse than children from poorer homes. How can we account for this? Lake speculates that when people move from a more informal education system into a more formal one, the poorest economically may not always be the most deprived educationally. The richest group of children in her investigation may have been well prepared because of parental attitudes and parental education. And the poorest children may have also been comparatively well prepared because they had had the advantages of the traditional child-rearing system, whereas the group who were in the middle income band may have had neither set of advantages.

Similarly, working in Guatemalan villages, Kagan found that children from comparatively wealthy homes did worse than children from poorer homes on difficult memory tests (Kagan, 1979; Kagan *et al*., 1979). Kagan interprets that as being due to the fact that, in these villages, the richer homes had child-rearing practices that were 'highly restrictive of the child' (1979, p. 230). He thinks that these practices may have made the children from the richer homes less confident at the tasks, less keen to do well, and more suspicious of the examiner than children from the poorer homes.

So it would seem that teachers must not automatically assume that income and degree of preparation for school are always linked in such a way that a child whose father earns more is necessarily better prepared than one whose father earns less. Furthermore, she must always remember that even if a child is not well prepared for school, active intervention on her part can make a difference. As Rutter's 1979 study showed, where teachers actively encouraged children, conscientiously set and marked homework and encouraged children to participate in all activities of life, pupils did better than their peers at schools where teachers were less pupil-centred.

Another important implication is this: it should be realised that children from upper-class homes do not perform better in general because they are born brighter. They perform better because their homes provide a better match to the skills needed at school than do the homes of less advantaged children.

Does the sex of the child make a difference to cognitive performance?

It is sometimes suggested that there are sex differences in intellectual ability and that girls excel at verbal tasks and boys at tasks requiring the ability to analyse shapes (spatial ability). Yet cross-cultural surveys show that such conclusions are often drawn from consideration of only one culture (usually from British and American data). Reading studies show that whereas in Britain and America girls usually do score better than boys at reading, this sex difference does not hold in other cultures. For example, in Israel (Downing, 1979) no difference is shown between the sexes, and in Germany and Nigeria boys have been shown to score higher at reading tests than girls (Good and Brophy, 1977). With respect to spatial ability too, research shows that the same pattern of sex differences is not found across all cultures. Working in Zambia, one of the present authors showed that sex differences in spatial ability were related to the cultural expectations of what girls and boys would be interested in.

In working life too, sex differences are not the same in all cultures. In some cultures such as Britain and America, women architects and engineers are seldom found. Yet in others, such as Egypt and Eastern Europe, they form a far larger proportion of these professions. Similarly in some areas in Africa like Zambia and Malawi women seldom take part in commerce and trade, whereas in other African territories like Nigeria and Ghana women play a most important part in trading.

How do we account for these contradictory findings? We must surely view the different patterns of abilities seen as sex-appropriate in any culture as relating to the expectations and stereotypes that the culture holds about sex roles. (By *stereotypes* we refer to a standardised opinion held by the members of a group, usually of an oversimplified nature.)

To return to the sex differences in reading, Downing (1979) has argued very persuasively that sex role stereotypes about literacy vary from culture to culture. For example, the fact that Nigerian boys tended to score higher than Nigerian girls on tests of reading was related by Abiri to the fact that school attendance was seen as less important for girls than boys in the local environment. In Britain, on the other hand, girls' higher scores on tests of reading are probably related to cultural stereotypes that see reading as a less appropriate leisure-type behaviour for boys than girls.

As Mia Kelmer Pringle points out, the influence of expected sex differences in any society is felt right from the moment of birth (1974, p. 16):

> ' One of the first questions asked about a baby is whether it is a boy or a girl and from then onwards parental attitudes and expectations become different according to the answer given: both in major and minor ways, the child will be treated, and expected to behave, differently. Clothes, toys, subtle differences in words, play, hugs, rewards, punishments and parental example, surround the child with a world which clearly distinguishes behaviour expected from boys and girls.
>
> Those psychological characteristics considered appropriate will be developed by about the third year of life; and throughout childhood the 'assigned' sex role will be practised in social relations, in play and in fantasy, and will be continually reinforced by the responses and expectations of others. Finally it will be reinforced at puberty by the various physiological changes. '

Many studies point to the immense social significance of learned sex role: that is, that children learn to behave in the way their own society expects their sex to behave. Some studies have indeed shown that where children are born with such abnormalities of the sex organs that doctors have difficulty in deciding what sex to label them, as they grow older their gender development (which sex they consider themselves to be, or which sex they model their behaviour on) is more similar to what they have been labelled than to their final physical sexual development.

In the section on adolescence we return to this topic. However, it is important to state here that, particularly in the primary school age-group, any sex differences in achievement at school will relate to the societal norms regarding how children of each sex should perform, as well as perhaps to the teacher's expectations in this area.

But once again individual family background factors are important. Nowhere has this been more clearly shown than in Joy Mbilinyi's work on traditional attitudes to women in Tanzania. By contrasting Muslim areas with other areas in the territory she shows how ingrained attitudes are to the intellectual inferiority of women in certain areas and how the girls themselves internalise such attitudes.

It is quite surprising to discover how early on in life mothers start behaving differently to children of different sexes. In a very interesting study in West Bengal in India, Graves (1978) has shown that even in their second year infants were treated differently by their mothers. For instance, mothers were both more responsive to boys and were less attentive to girls than boys. Graves suggests that this is not due to innate (inborn) differences in behaviour between the sexes, but is due instead to cultural attitudes.

Thus any teacher must examine for him- or herself whether he or she holds any deep-seated attitudes to the differing ability levels of the two sexes and whether the homes of their pupils reflect such attitudes. It is only by thinking objectively of their own society's generally held attitudes to sex roles that teachers will be able to rid themselves of any stereotyped thinking in this area. Further, by bearing in mind that there is no *physical* basis for expecting different levels of intellectual achievement for either sex, they will be able to help individual pupils (in all probability, girls) who feel they cannot achieve at high levels in a particular intellectual area because of the physical fact of their sex.

In concluding this section on factors in the home that might influence children's level of school performance, we see again and again how important are those environmental influences bearing on the child. These environmental influences spring both from the home and the parents and from the wider society. We have not, however, as yet examined the particular contribution of the genetic constitution the child is born with and the last two sections in this chapter are concerned with this.

Temperamental Differences

When a child is conceived he receives twenty-three

chromosomes from each parent. We term this his genetic constitution or, more technically, his 'genotype'. However, as we have seen, even during pregnancy the child may be affected by the intra-uterine environment provided by the mother. Thus when the baby is born it is difficult to distinguish those elements of his behaviour that are directly due to his physical make-up and those that may be due to the factors that operated when his mother was carrying him. The older he grows, the more difficult it is to distinguish the effects of what are commonly called 'nature' and 'nurture' (environment). We shall discuss this in some detail in Chapter 11 when we deal with the concept we call intelligence.

When we speak of a child's temperament we refer to the way he reacts at an emotional level to the varying situations he encounters. The view taken by the present authors is that it is impossible to distinguish between those aspects of temperament that spring from the child's genetic constitution and those aspects that spring from the child's environment and the child's interaction with that environment. Further, we believe that it is a mistake to regard temperamental propensities as fixed for life.

Nevertheless it is undeniable that babies show individual differences at birth – some cry more than others, some are more alert than others, some adjust more easily to change and some show more rhythm in their bodily functions than others do. In a study done by Thomas and his associates in 1970, they examined closely the progress of 141 children whom they measured at birth on nine variables similar to the ones we have mentioned. They then divided the children into three groups whom they labelled easy, difficult and 'slow to warm up'. They claimed that the same children remained in each group over the whole period of the study – fourteen years. What is equally important to note, however, is that 35 per cent of the original sample could not be so classified, so their finding remains a very tentative one.

Thus we would argue that this study presents very limited evidence for the stability of temperamental factors. A more direct challenge to the study of Thomas is that offered by Kagan (1976). He studied first-born babies from 4 to 27 months of age and measured them on variables such as motor activity and how much they cried. He reports that 'Very active eight-month old babies were not highly motoric [active] twenty months later; extremely fretful four-month old babies were

not the most irritable two-year olds' (p. 121). In general there was not much continuity of behaviour.

We consider that more important than the permanence or not of these differences is the influence on the child's temperament at birth exerted by his caretakers. The *match* between parent and child is what matters. The placid mother may, for instance, be less able to deal sensitively with a very alert child than she would be able to deal with a child who is more like her. Again, she may be better able to deal with a child who cries a lot at birth. Similarly, the baby who cries a lot at birth may persist in that pattern if his mother is nervy and lacks confidence, whereas if the selfsame baby has a more placid and confident mother, he may soon settle into a more contented pattern of behaviour.

It is important to remember that we all change with time and, further, that we often become what people expect us to become. Both these factors should make teachers very distrustful about confidently making assumptions about a child's temperament or what they may refer to as 'personality'. They should be very careful indeed about labelling children 'excitable' or 'withdrawn' or 'disruptive'. Teachers should also beware of placing too much importance on other people's perception of children. For example, a new teacher may be told by a child's previous teacher that the child is 'aggressive'. This may affect the new teacher's treatment of the child and may in fact precipitate more 'aggressive' behaviour. It is quite clear that we all behave in different ways at different times and therefore we do not believe that the teacher should make any firm judgements about the temperament or personality of his pupils, particularly at the primary school stage.

We shall return to this topic in Chapter 5, but at this stage we should like to remind readers that it may be both inaccurate and counter-productive to make any firm and inflexible judgements about a young child's personality or temperament.

Developmental Rate

As we have mentioned before, children develop intellectually at different rates. As with the physical rate of development, some of these differences may be due to the child's constitution. But the work we have reviewed in this chapter should convince you that other factors that may affect the developmental rate may lie both in the individual home and in the social environment. Thus work done in Liberia with Western tests that are supposed to give an index of development correlate better with the number of years the child has been at school than they do with the child's actual age (Cole and Scribner, 1974).

Nevertheless, in both nursery and infant classrooms teachers will find that some children cope well with new cognitive tasks and others less well. While all the home background factors we have reviewed thus far undoubtedly play a part, it is also clear that some individual differences are partially due to differences in developmental rate which are related to genetic factors. As far as the teacher is concerned, it is important to remember that while such individual differences clearly exist they are by no means fixed. And the child who finds learning to read a slow and arduous task may, once he has mastered the skill, show little difficulty in keeping up with the rest of the class. It is vital not to dismiss such children when they first show such difficulties. Instead, as we shall argue throughout this book, such children should be supplied with additional help and more important (see Chapter 5) should not be allowed to feel inferior to their peers, thus forming an academic self-concept of very negative nature; this feeling of inadequacy – should it become reinforced – will be very difficult to reverse.

Summary

In this chapter we have tried to explore some of the factors that may influence a child's behaviour at school. We have discussed the vital contribution home background factors make at both the social and emotional level and at the motor, perceptual and cognitive level. We concluded that there is no difference in the intellectual potential of the two sexes but noted how important social and familial expectations are in this area. Finally, we discussed temperamental and developmental differences. We pointed out how difficult it is to distinguish the contribution of 'nature' and 'nurture' in these areas. We reminded readers that it is important not to assume that such individual differences are fixed and immutable.

Chapter 2: Selected Bibliography

As we have cited mainly papers in journals in this chapter, we are not able to cite any particular books except a book already recommended at the end of Chapter 1: Durojaiye's *A New Introduction to Educational Psychology*. In addition, the Clarke and Clarke book also recommended at the end of Chapter 1 may be found useful. A book that is rather more theoretical but that may be found interesting is Mallory Wober's book *Psychology in Africa* (London: International African Institute, 1975).

LANGUAGE DEVELOPMENT AND THE FUNCTIONS OF PLAY

3

'Just as an appropriate diet is essential for normal physical growth, so it is for mental development. The most vital ingredients of this diet are play and language. Through them, the child explores the world and learns to cope with it; this is as true for the objective outside world as it is for the subjective internal world of thought and feelings. Thus too are motor skills, perception and concepts developed.'

(Pringle, 1974, p. 43)

Introduction

In Chapter 1, when we discussed the need for new experiences, we mentioned that the most important avenues of development related to this need are play and language, and in this chapter we discuss both of these important aspects of child development. In the first part of the chapter we shall briefly outline the normal process of language development and, in doing this, we shall consider cross-cultural research in this area. In the second part of the chapter we shall consider the functions of play, within a cross-cultural context. (See Figure 3.1)

Language

The course of language development
An enormous amount of research was generated in the 1960s and early 1970s into language acquisition in young children. But much of this research neglected the environment in which the child develops and the interaction the child has with others, and concentrated instead on the way the child learned to master the grammar of his own particular language. In this brief introduction to language development we shall concentrate on the communicative nature of speech development.

As we stressed in Chapter 1, the young child enters the world pre-programmed for communication with his caretakers. Even before the child utters his first recognisable word, he is well able to communicate with his parents or whoever is caring for him. How does this communication come about?

Pre-linguistic (pre-language) communicative development. Before interaction can begin a child must be able to both give and receive messages. Anyone who has ever cared for a young infant, even for a short period of time, will know that babies' cries are very effective at gaining attention, and so in another way are babies' smiles. Thus right from the beginning the infant is equipped to give messages. We have already summarised research, in the first chapter, which shows that babies are well equipped to receive messages because they pay selective attention to sounds within the human voice range, to images that are similar to the human face and because they appear to move in sympathy with human conversation. But how do caretakers interpret the babies' communication intentions? Bruner (1974–5) differentiates three major ways in which caretakers are able to interpret, sometimes rightly and occasionally, of course, incorrectly,

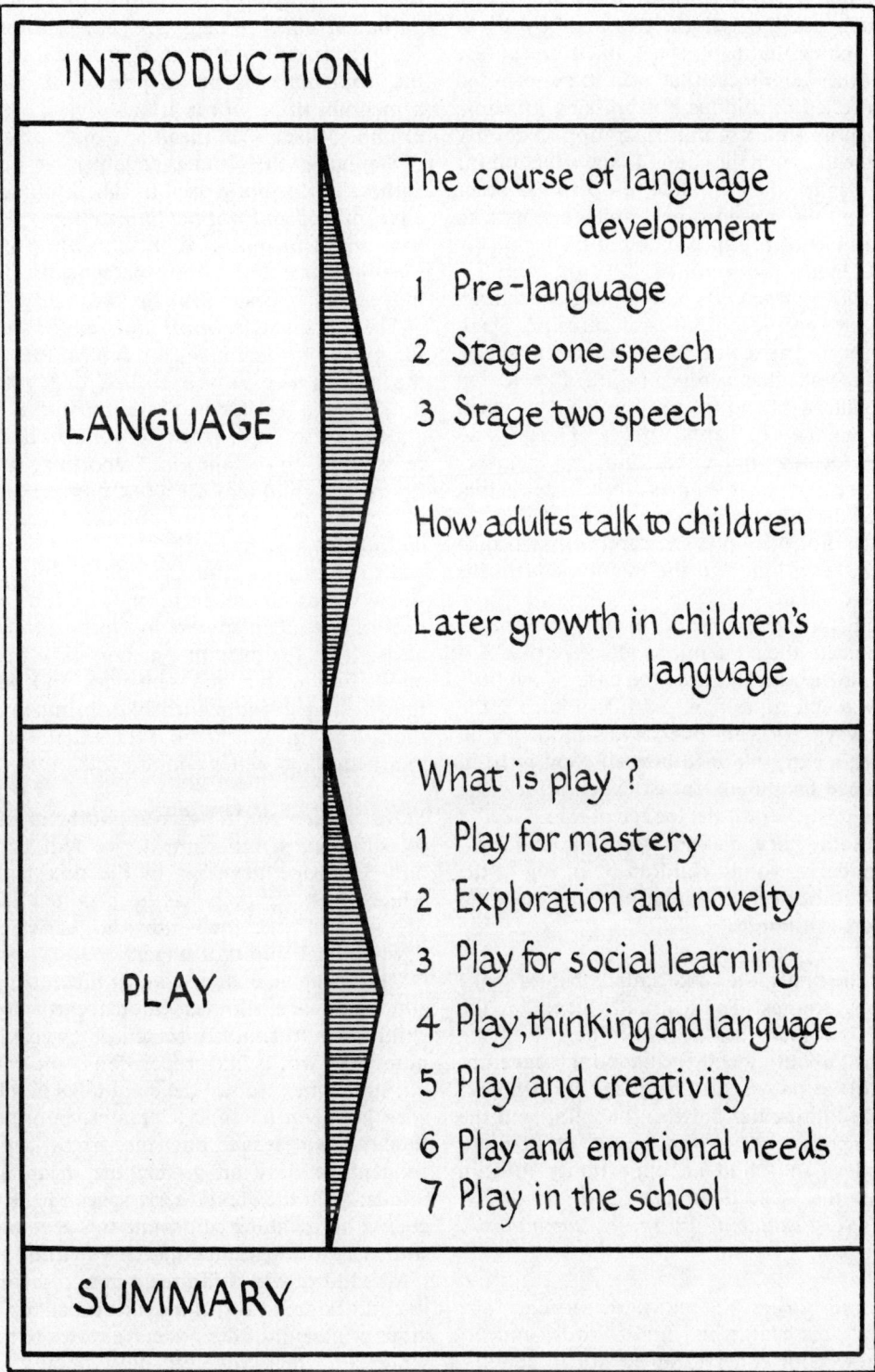

INTRODUCTION

LANGUAGE

The course of language development

1 Pre-language

2 Stage one speech

3 Stage two speech

How adults talk to children

Later growth in children's language

PLAY

What is play?

1 Play for mastery

2 Exploration and novelty

3 Play for social learning

4 Play, thinking and language

5 Play and creativity

6 Play and emotional needs

7 Play in the school

SUMMARY

Figure 3.1   Structure of Chapter 3

babies' intentions. To begin with, there are aspects of the utterances themselves. Research by Ricks (1975) has shown that parents are able to recognise cries and other utterances that were tape-recorded under controlled conditions – expressing greeting, pleased surprise, request and frustration. Not only are they able to match the sound to the situation for their own babies, they are able to do so for other babies as well. So it seems that caretakers learn to identify the sort of pre-speech sound babies make. Secondly, there is another set of cues – *accompanying movements* – pointing, searching, playing with specific objects and refusing. And, when babies are carried on their caretakers' backs, research suggests that caretakers are able to tell from the pattern of the babies' movements when they are hungry (Richards, 1974). Thirdly, no interaction occurs in a vacuum, so another important set of cues comes from the actual situation or the *context* in which the interaction is taking place. For example, the caretaker will take into account how long ago the infant was fed, his position, and so on.

So, long before speech proper begins, babies start to communicate their intentions effectively; Clark and Clark, for example, quote the case of the little boy who was able to 'ask for' a drink of juice in the following way. 'He went over to his mother who was holding a cup, stationed himself right in front of her, opened his mouth, thrust his chin forward, and then stared at her till she looked at him, asked if he wanted some juice, and held the cup out' (1977, p. 313). Similarly, young children often tug at the hands or clothes of their caretakers, and stare till they get some response.

Babbling. The first speech-like sounds babies make are babbling sounds. These usually begin in the middle of the first year of life. There is some controversy about whether babbling develops evenly into the baby's first language, or whether there are discontinuities between babbling and the first words spoken; but two facts seem clear. First, babbling gives the child an opportunity to gain control of the speech organs and, secondly, *babbling is very similar in all speech communities all over the world.*

One-word utterances. Somewhere around the child's first birthday, his first words appear. Usually these refer either to objects or to actions, like ball, doggie, give, byebye. They are not very often function words like 'what' or 'for'. Of course the most common first words tend to refer to particular kinds of objects – people. Thus a baby's first words are often 'mama' or 'dada' or whatever the equivalent is in his native language and sometimes these words are used very broadly. For example, 'dada' can mean any male person.

Similarly, the young daughter of one of the authors of this book used to call anything that was alive, moved and was not human 'kitty'. Her family have vivid memories of her crawling in anxious pursuit of an ant, calling pathetically (because it moved rather faster than she did) 'kitty, kitty'.

These first single words are used for a number of functions. For example, for description – as when the father's shoe may be labelled 'daddy' to indicate it belongs to the father; for command, as when the child may say 'up', when he wants to be lifted; for refusing – 'no'; and for reporting, when, for example, a child may see a bird and say 'bird', track it across the sky by pointing and when it disappears, say 'byebye'.

So it seems that for the young child these first single words are not just isolated words and labels but are instead an attempt to express more complex ideas. It is, for example, at this stage that a child may often understand sentences and be able to follow simple commands like 'bring mama your shoe'. This, then, is another stage in the child's way to a better and better communication system.

Stage one speech. In order to put the cross-cultural speech studies into context, we will first discuss how language develops in the first language in which most research has been done, English. In doing this we will divide early language development into two stages.

Child language is, of course, much simpler than adult language. Because in his early speech the child tends to simplify sentences by leaving out a number of words like prepositions, 'the', 'a', and so on, sometimes we say the child talks in telegraphic speech. When we send telegrams, in order to save money, we leave out the extra words and concentrate only on getting the meaning across. Similarly, in the child's early speech he is intent on getting his meaning across and this accounts for the similarity to telegraphic speech – so a child will say, if asked to repeat 'I can see mama', 'see mama'. If you break this early kind of speech up into the kinds of meaning children can express in their early sentences, then you can talk about 'semantic' (meaning) relationships.

According to Dale, in his important book on

language development (1976), we can understand the semantic relationships of stage one speech reasonably well, if we analyse it in terms of *agents* (something that acts), *objects* (something that agents affect) and *actions*. So, if a child says in English 'doll come', then doll is the agent; if he says 'hit ball', then ball is the object. In the early part of stage one speech the child tends to make this kind of two-word utterance a great deal, though he can also express other sorts of meanings like possession with two words, as, for example, when he says, 'dada shoe'. Questions are also asked in English, in early stage one speech, like 'where doll?', but sometimes the fact that a question is being asked is only understood from the child's change in tone; for example, if he says 'mama dress' in a rising voice, we understand that he is asking if it is mama's dress.

As stage one speech develops, the child starts to string more words together; thus he moves from the two-word stage of 'hit ball' to 'I hit ball' and then later to four-word sentences like 'I put dollie box'.

However, at this stage the child has not yet acquired the ability to use what are called inflections (changes to the ends of words to indicate tenses or plurals) and is also unlikely to use prepositions or articles. So he will say 'I put dollie box', not 'I put *the* dollie *in the* box', and 'I take doggie home', not 'I am taking doggie home'.

Finally, in stage one speech in English we notice that children keep pretty much to the same word order. So, for instance, they always use the agent, action, object form – 'I hit ball', not 'hit I ball'.

We can sum up, then, five characteristics of stage one speech acquisition in English.

(1) Children's language is much simpler than adult language and concentrates on expressing meaning.
(2) It is often helpful to analyse it in terms of agent, action, object.
(3) Utterances get progressively longer.
(4) Children do not use inflections such as are used in mature adult speech.
(5) Children tend to use a fixed word order.

How well do these five points apply to the acquisition of other first languages? Slobin has collected accounts of early language development in forty languages and he concludes (1979) that stage one language is very much the same all over the world. If you look at Table 3.1 you will notice

that point 1 certainly holds – language is simplified in all cases. With respect to point 2 you will notice that in all the languages surveyed the agent, action, object analysis is helpful.

It is also clear, from other sources, that point 3 holds. In all languages studied there is a gradual lengthening of utterances. Further, when we look at stage one in languages other than English, it seems that point 4 holds as well – that is, children do not use the inflections of adult speech.

Finally, does word order tend to be fixed in the acquisition of other languages? The answer to this last point is 'no'. This is not surprising because in adult speech word order is important in English and this is why children, too, tend to string words together in a fixed order. In German, for example, word order is not fixed and so children use a wider range of orders. But it is true to say that where order is consistent in a language children will use it consistently. In summary, we can say about stage one speech, as Slobin (1979) does, that early utterances in the various languages studied read like direct translations of one another.

Stage two speech. The major change in stage two speech in English is that inflections start to be used. Two important points characterise the development of inflections (an ending to a word that expresses grammatical relationships). First, all children learning English tend to learn these in much the same order. Secondly, they seem to follow the same processes in learning them, that is, they tend to make the same sort of mistakes.

It is this second point that leads us to the most interesting conclusion about stage two speech and this is that children seem, in their learning about speech, to be looking for patterns. So we get the very interesting phenomenon of 'over-regularisation'. That is, the child learns a rule and then over-regularises it.

It is interesting to look at this process of over-regularisation in a little detail. In English we see it in the case of irregular verbs like come and break. (We call these irregular because they do not simply take 'ed' to form the past tense, as most English verbs do – jump–jumped, walk–walked.) The child will first learn the past form quite correctly, by imitating his parents, and will say 'came' and 'broke'. Then he will realise that there is a rule for the past tense and he will switch to saying 'comed' and 'breaked', after having got the past tense right before. Once he has 'over-regularised' in this way the errors are very resistant to change. This

Table 3.1   *Functions of two-word sentences in child speech, with examples from several languages*

Function of utterance	Language					
	English	*German*	*Russian*	*Finnish*	*Luo*	*Samoan*
Locate, name	*there book* *that car* *see doggie*	*buch da* (book there) *gukuk wauwau* (see doggie)	*Tosya tam* (Tosya there)	*tuossa Rina* (there Rina) *vettä sünä* (water there)	*en saa* (it clock) *ma wendo* (this visitor)	*Keith lea* (Keith there)
Demand, desire	*more milk* *give candy* *want gum*	*mehr milch* (more milk) *bitte apfel* (please apple)	*yeshche moloko* (more milk) *day chasy* (give watch)	*anna Rina* (give Rina)	*miya tamtam* (give-me candy) *adway cham* (I-want food)	*mai pepe* (give doll) *fia moe* (want sleep)
Negate	*no wet* *no wash* *not hungry* *allgone milk*	*nicht blasen* (not blow) *kaffee nein* (coffee no)	*vody net* (water no) *gus' tyu-tyu* (goose allgone)	*ei susi* (not wolf) *enää pipi* (anymore sore)	*beda onge* (my-slasher absent)	*le 'ai* (not eat) *uma mea* (allgone thing)
Describe event or situation	*Bambi go* *mail come* *hit ball* *block fall* *baby highchair*	*puppe kommt* (doll comes) *tiktak hängt* (clock hangs) *sofa sitzen* (sofa sit) *messer* *schneiden* (cut knife)	*mama prua* (mama walk) *papa bay-bay* (papa sleep) *korka upala* (crust fell) *nashla yaichko* (found egg) *baba kreslo* (grandma armchair)	*takki pois* (cat away) *Seppo putoo* (Seppo fall) *talli 'bm bm'* (garage 'car')	*chungu biro* (European comes) *odhi skul* (he-went school) *omoyo oduma* (she-dries maize)	*pa'u pepe* (fall doll) *tapale 'oe* (hit you) *tu'u lalo* (put down)
Indicate possession	*my shoe* *mama dress*	*mein ball* (my ball) *mamas hut* (mama's hat)	*mami chashka* (mama's cup) *pup moya* (navel my)	*täti auto* (aunt car)	*kom baba* (chair father)	*lole a'u* (candy my) *polo 'oe* (ball your) *paluni mama* (balloon mama)
Modify, qualify	*pretty dress* *big boat*	*milch heiss* (milk hot) *armer wauwau* (poor doggie)	*mama* *khoroshaya* (mama good) *papa bol'shoy* (papa big)	*rikki auto* (broken car) *torni iso* (tower big)	*piypiy kech* (pepper hot) *gwen madichol* (chicken black)	*fa'ali'i pepe* (headstrong baby)
Question	*where ball*	*wo ball* (where ball)	*gde papa* (where papa)	*missä pallo* (where ball)		*fea Punafu* (where Punafu)

Source: Slobin, 1979.

tendency to pay attention to rules indicates the child is searching for patterns as he acquires his language.

Are these two points we have just described shown in the early acquisition of other languages besides English? That is, do children tend to learn inflections in the same order and do they show over-regularisation? If you are interested, you can perhaps follow up the references at the end of this chapter to the intensive study of the acquisition of Russian, the other language whose acquisition has been studied in great detail. These studies do show that the two points hold in Russian language acquisition as well – all children seem to learn inflections in much the same order, and the phenomenon of over-regularisation is also found. Perhaps you yourself might like to make a small-scale observational study in the acquisition of your own first language. You might arrange to monitor language acquisition in two children to see if they do learn the structures of your own language in the same order and you might, if you have irregular verbs in your own first language, or irregular plurals, check to see if you too notice the phenomenon of over-regularisation.

In summarising stage two speech, then, two aspects of child language become very clear. First, function – the child is continually striving to 'express his own ideas, emotions and actions' (Dale, 1976, p. 36). Thus the early communication skills that we saw even at the pre-speech stage become more and more effective. Secondly, the *structure* as well as the function of language becomes important.

By saying the structure becomes important we are referring to the fact that the child starts to learn the structure of his mother tongue in a rule-governed, systematic way. (This is particularly evident in the process we have described of 'over-regularisation'.) We see in the development of language skills the child's search for, and eventual mastery of, the grammar of his own language.

How adults talk to children

When people talk to one another, their general aim is to get the other person to understand what they are saying to him or her. This applies whether the listener is an adult or a child, but when we talk to children, especially young children, we know that their understanding of language is more limited than our own and so we tend to talk to them rather differently.

Adults seem to alter their speech when talking to young children in three ways – they slow down, they use short, simple sentences and they repeat themselves frequently. If you are interested in this area of language acquisition, you will find an interesting section on it, with respect to English, in the Clark and Clark book *Psychology and Language* (1977). But does this apply to other languages as well? In a study done in Kenya, Sara Harkness (1977) shows that Kenyan mothers and older children do modify their speech in similar ways when they speak to young children. And indeed, Ferguson (1977) summarises a number of studies from all over the world – ranging from Morocco to Greece – that indicate that adults everywhere do take into account the fact that young children have less language experience and so need a more specialised kind of communication than other listeners do.

Later growth in children's language

So far in looking at the acquisition of language we have been struck by the similarity displayed in all languages studied. We have seen that communication is a basic need, and that children start communicating long before they start speaking. We have also seen that adults are sensitive to children's need to communicate and help them to acquire language by using suitable speech patterns. Further, we have seen that the older children grow, the more the structure of their speech becomes like adult structure and that in this learning of structure they show evidence of a need to search for patterns.

These joint aspects of function and structure in language become more and more elaborated as children get older. With respect to structure, they start to add more words such as prepositions and articles to their speech. They also fill in their utterances with more and more complex inflections. Their sentences become longer and they start combining more than one proposition (or idea) in sentences as well.

Further, speech begins to fulfil other functions than communication. It begins to have an important effect on thought. We shall see in the next chapter that very often verbal labels help children to store information and there is no doubt that language plays an exceedingly important part in the process of memory. We shall see in Chapter 6 that verbal labelling can also play a very significant part in solving problems.

At this stage we should perhaps mention the particular difficulties that will be experienced by the child if he attends a school where the language used for teaching is not the same as his mother tongue. If a large proportion of his classmates are in the same position it is obviously not as bad for him, because the teacher will then be forced to take this into account in a systematic way. But, should it be only he, or a small proportion of the class, who are taught in a language different from their mother tongue, substantial problems may arise. We shall return to this subject in some detail in Chapter 10.

In summary, then, we can say that as children grow older their language becomes more grammatical (that is, more similar in structure to adult language) and their use of language extends from being mainly used in communication to becoming a very effective tool in their growing understanding of the world about them.

Play

What is play?

We are all familiar with the situation when we say

to a child, more or less crossly, 'For goodness sake, stop playing and pay attention'. Yet if we are asked to define play it turns out to be quite a difficult task. Perhaps we can make a start by listing some activities that we might agree are play – a baby shaking his rattle, a little girl playing house, some little boys making wire models of cars, some adults playing one of the board games that are common all over Africa, two little puppies tumbling over each other in the sunshine. What do all these activities have in common?

Catherine Garvey in her book on play (1977) has suggested that the following five attributes are commonly accepted as being characteristic of play:

(1) Play is enjoyable. It is something players want to do.
(2) Play has no other goals than enjoyment. It is *intrinsically* rewarding.
(3) Play is freely entered into. Players choose to play.
(4) Play is active.
(5) Play is related to other activities.

As we will see in the later parts of this section, play is linked to many aspects of our life – learning to manipulate objects, learning to play a social role, learning to solve problems, creativity and helping to resolve emotional tensions.

Play is universal; it is found in all cultures and, indeed, it is also found in primates like monkeys and chimpanzees, as well as other mammals like cats and dogs. This suggests it has a functional significance and indeed it is clear that in play the young of many species are able to experiment with different kinds of behaviour. Although adults do play as well, it seems that the capacity for play, as we have discussed it, declines with age. It seems appropriate then to look at the role of play in child development.

(1) *Play for mastery of physical activity*

As the reader will know quite well, children are very active beings. Right from early infancy their activity often serves to increase their motor skills, even though, of course, the child has not intentionally set out to do just that. For example, writing about the babies observed in an American study, Bruner notes that after the 6-month-old infant has learned to hold on to an object and put it easily into his mouth, he begins a programme of variation. After he has learned to hold it in his hand he holds it to look at, he shakes it, he bangs it on his chair and he drops it over the edge. Before long he manages to *fit the object into every activity* into which it is possible to put it.

This early tendency to play using motor skills increases with age. As mothers and teachers know, young children will sometimes climb into places that seem totally inaccessible. Older children run, jump, tumble and wrestle, and games that involve motion are often very popular. For example, Hake, writing of children in northern Nigeria, notes that 'Another popular play item for boys is an old bicycle tyre or a spokeless rim. Using his hand or a small wooden stick, a boy will run quickly after his rolling toy. The fun of this game is to keep the rolling toy from twisting crazily when it hits some uneven road surface' (Hake, 1972, p. 48). Like other games, this particular game can be less enjoyable for people who are not playing, for as Hake notes, 'Nigerian motorists must often screech their brakes in an effort to avoid hitting some rim-chasing boy'.

There is no doubt, however, that such games and activities, wearying though they may be to the adult observer, serve to increase the child's growing physical competencies and his mastery over the physical environment.

(2) *Play, exploration and novelty*

When we outlined children's needs we laid a great deal of stress on the fact that children are fascinated by novelty (new experiences). In exploring new situations, children can practise their growing understanding of the world. It does seem, following the work of Corinne Hutt, that the tendency to explore in early childhood is linked to later creativity. She designed a 'super-toy' for children of 3 to 5 years consisting of a table with a lever, buzzer, bells and counters. She assessed how deeply the children became involved in playing with this toy, and found when she tested the children four years later that on tests of creativity the children who scored highest tended to be those children who had become most involved in exploring the 'super-toy' four years earlier (Bruner, 1974).

How does exploratory activity develop into play proper? Garvey (1977, p. 50) describes what happened when a 3-year-old boy encountered a large wooden car in a playroom for the first time.

‘ (*a*) He paused, inspected it, and touched it. [exploration] (*b*) He tried to find out what it could do. He turned the steering wheel, felt the licence plate, looked for a horn and tried to get in the car. [manipulation] (c) Having figured out what the object was and what it could do, he got to work on what *he* could do to *it*. He put telephones on it, took them off, next put cups and dishes on it. These activities were a form of trying out ideas to see how they would work. [practice] ... (d) He then climbed into it and drove back and forth with suitable motor and horn noises. [play] '

However, children do not need to have toys in order to explore. For example, the Gikuyo boy in Kenya, according to Kenyatta, roams the countryside and 'learns to distinguish a great variety of birds, animals, insects, trees, grasses, fruits and flowers. His interests bring him in contact with these things, since they constitute the furnishings of his play activities' (Leacock, 1976, p. 467, quoting from Kenyatta).

Whether children come from the kind of environment that produces 'super-toys' or the kind described by Kenyatta, it is essential that adults accept that they need the opportunity to explore their environment and learn how to find things out for themselves. By catering to children's need for new experiences and by allowing them the freedom to manipulate things and explore their environment, we lay a good foundation for an intellectually alert adult. For example, children in Zambia observed by Leacock demonstrate great ingenuity in the way they manipulate play material and the experience they gain from this manipulation will be of benefit to them when they begin to do elementary science at school. They explore their play objects and experiment with them. Leacock writes of children she watched in an urban area, 'They also rummage in garbage bins for tin cans. A boy described how he and his friends stacked them up as high as they could before they fell. Little girls play filling them and pouring water and dirt back and forth' (1976, p. 470).

(3) *Play for social learning*

In traditional societies play was often an important part of the informal education that characterised such societies. For example, Castle in writing of East Africa (1966, p. 41), notes:

' Imitative play was an important part of informal education. Boys played with wooden spears, bows and arrows and shields made from banana bark; they built model huts and cattle pens, for these would be tasks

for them when grown up. The girls made dolls, played at 'husband and wife', plaited baskets of grass, ground corn like their mothers, made little pots of clay and cooked imaginary meals. '

Such descriptions of preparation for adult life through play are very common in the cross-cultural literature. For example, Fortes, writing about the Tale in West Africa, traces the developmental phases of play, noting as he does the close interaction of the content and type of play with the cultural demands. 'There is, in all Tale children's play, this feature of looking ahead, as it were, experimenting tentatively with what lies just beyond the present psychological horizon' (1976, p. 478).

Fortes describes how groups of girls aged between 6 and 10 and boys aged between 5 and 6 formed together to play at housekeeping. Each girl 'cooked' for herself, but they lent each other utensils and firewood. Older girls took the lead with smaller girls assisting them in the pattern of daughter helping mother in real cooking. Infants became 'our children' and the small boys were said to play the role of husbands.

Older boys in Taleland spent their time improving their skill with bow and arrow, as they went about in small groups practising marksmanship. By the age of 11 to 12 they were accompanying their fathers or older brothers on real hunts though they remained onlookers for the most part. In this way the playful activity of hunting shaded gradually into the real activity for which it was a preparation.

However it is not only the *activities* of adult life that are foreshadowed in play. Play is also the medium, particularly in traditional societies, through which children acquire the values of their culture and are absorbed into its spiritual life. In Taleland, for instance, at the time Fortes was there (the 1930s), 'ritual was men's business'. He observed that from a very early age boys prepared for this important aspect of their adult life by building shrines in the cattle yards and pouring libations on these shrines before they went away on their hunting games.

Play also reflects the dominant values of societies. We can see this with reference to three very different cultures. Let us look at the Tangu of New Guinea (Burridge, 1976). The Tangu children play a game called *taketak* which has a formal rule structure that is very like the co-operative pattern of adult Tangu society. In this society, personal relationships are dominated by an idea of moral equality. For example, in the exchange of foodstuffs it is the aim that exactly equivalent amounts should be exchanged. Similarly, in the game of *taketak* (which involves spinning tops into the spines of coconut fronds that have been placed in position), play goes on until the two teams playing are in an equivalent position.

In Nigeria, Uka describes a game that children play called *ekak* (1966, pp. 62–3). This game is played by burying a ring in the sand. The ring is hidden in such a way that it cannot easily be found and children take it in turns to look for it. Each time a child finds the ring he receives a point and may then bury it for the next round. 'The child with the largest score is declared the champion. The king or champion is empowered to administer a knock with his fist on the foreheads of other children in the group as a mark of his authority.' Uka continues that should a child rebel against this, he may be excluded from the group and in this way Uka considers that the game 'engenders a sense of *obedience to established procedure* and encourages the spirit of give-and-take' (our italics).

Finally, let us turn to Britain and look at a board game which has been popular for some years. This is Monopoly, and it involves the buying, selling and developing of property. Board games come and go in Britain with great speed, but Monopoly has remained the most popular of its type for a long time. Like most board games played in Britain, it is competitive and it could be argued that this emphasis on competition is itself typical of Western values. However, perhaps the continuing popularity of Monopoly lies in its reflection of another aspect of British society – an emphasis on the acquisition of personal belongings and property.

(4) *Play, cognition (thinking) and language*

We have already described how the Zambian children observed by Leacock played in such a way as to increase their knowledge of the physical properties of their play material – water, dirt and tin cans. And there is no doubt that this manipulation and exploration of physical objects adds to the child's increasing knowledge and mastery of the external world. Thus we find a fashion in the West for 'educational toys' that are designed to promote the development of, for example, children's spatial ability (the ability to manipulate shapes mentally which is of importance

in the study of mathematics and physics). However, children can gain their knowledge of shape and form just as effectively by being encouraged to play with materials at hand in just such a way as Leacock's children did – pouring water back and forth, stacking cans, and so on.

Can play increase children's reasoning skills? There is no experimental evidence in this area but we imagine that the custom reported in many African societies of asking riddles must help children to think analytically. Thus the practices reported by Castle (1966, p. 40) in East Africa are of undoubted value in the cognitive development of the child, not only in the area of reasoning but in the area of language development as well.

> ‘ By the evening fireside tribal legends and proverbs were told and retold; there were riddles to test childish judgement and myths to explain the origins of the tribe and the genesis of man and the heavenly bodies. These tales, told with care and with much repetition, were the African child's education in what was often a complicated and beautiful language. There were no grammar books, no writing, but correctness of speech, so characteristic of illiterate Africans, was learnt by imitation of their elders. ’

Garvey, writing about young children in America, also describes how language is an integral part of their play. The chanting of nonsense syllables or the repetition of jokes, particularly those containing puns,* not only provides great enjoyment, it also helps children get a mastery of their own language.

In the last section of this chapter we present an appendix on the kind of play that can be used with young children to promote thinking and language development.

(5) *Play and creativity*

All children like to chant rhymes, dance and sing. In many traditional societies, dancing and music were very much part of life and children joined in as they grew older. For example, writing about the Gikuyu of Kenya, Kenyatta notes that children 'merge insensibly into the dances of later years, and it is amazing to see how a small child can capture with his or her feet and bodily movement the

---

* Puns are ways of playing with the double meaning of some words, for example:
Q.   When is a door not a door?
A.   When it is a jar (ajar means open).

complicated, difficult rhythms which have been learned by merely watching their elders and imitating them' (1961, p. 104).

Sometimes chants and rhymes are woven into children's games. For example, Iona and Peter Opie (1976), writing about children in Britain, describe street-games which have been handed down from one generation of children to the next; many of these have rhymes and chants which are an indispensable part of the fun. For example, a particular chasing game may be chosen in preference to others, because children enjoy the chant that precedes it (p. 395).

'Sheep, sheep, come home.'
'We're afraid.'
'What of?'
'The wolf.'
'Wolf has gone to Devonshire
Won't be back for seven years,
Sheep, sheep, come home.'

In Britain children often decide who is to play an unpopular part in a game by counting out. The players form a circle and count along the circle the number of counts found in the accented syllable of the rhyme they are using, pointing at one child in the circle at every count, until reaching the child the last count falls on, who has to play the part. For instance, the following rhyme, quoted by the Opies, has fifteen counts:

Ee'rie, orr'ie, round' the ta'ble,
Eat' as much' as you' are a'ble:
If' you're a'ble eat' the ta'ble,
Eer'ie, orr'ie, *out*'.

In West Africa Fortes reports that organised games involving dancing and singing, are part of the traditional play of early childhood (1974, p. 479).

> ‘ The games are traditional, and often built round themes derived from the cultural idiom – farming, hunting, marriage, chiefs etc. But their value is predominantly recreational. Children play them for the pleasure of collective singing, rhythmical physical activity, and sensory and bodily stimulation. ’

Encouraging children to express themselves in rhymes, dance and music can pave the way for creative work in this area. Children who are too inhibited to use their bodies and their voices in play will find self-expression in music and dance very

difficult. For this reason, it is perhaps counter-productive to ban certain kinds of music such as popular (pop) music or dances that owe more to rock and discos than to tradition. Sometimes the imitation of pop stars can lead the child into a world of make-believe and it is very important that children should be encouraged to withdraw at times into a make-believe world where they can imagine what it feels like to be other people – whether those other people are their parents, their teacher, astronauts, famous football players or even pop stars.

Garvey reports that there is evidence linking fantasy and make-believe play to a high level of creativity. She writes that although anthropologists have reported some cultures in which there is virtually no make-believe play, in those societies where it has been reported it is linked, not surprisingly, to the activities important to that culture. For example, in Hopi Indian settlements children conduct pretend rabbit hunts and we have already described other cultures where children make believe that they are adults and in this way practise adult roles. In this way, make-believe games allow for role-playing and also for children to project themselves into the future. But make-believe games and fantasy have another important role in child development and it is to this that we turn now.

(6)   *The interaction of play with emotional needs*
Very often, the child is the smallest and most inexperienced person he knows. Compared to adults and older children he has very little power. So make-believe can offer an imaginary world where he is important and powerful and where everyone does what he says. Fantasy, of course, is not confined to children, and this particular aspect of fantasy is often indulged in by adults as well. Perhaps you can think back to an incident where someone was rude to you, and later, perhaps at night, before you fell asleep, you consoled yourself by imagining various unpleasant fates for the individual concerned. Adults, of course, seldom relate such fantasies to others, although they may come to terms with such fantasies in their art if they are creatively inclined. Children, however, sometimes come to believe, just for a while, in their own fantasies. Because of this we should not dismiss as lies the incredible stories that children may tell us about themselves. They may not be the objective truth but, on the other hand, they are not necessarily invented in order to deceive.

Make-believe can also help a child to relive or anticipate exciting or emotionally important experiences. For example, after a child has paid his first visit to the city, he may act out again all the new things he did – travelling on the train, going to the cinema, meeting new people. Similarly, a child can anticipate new experiences that he may be a little nervous of, such as his first day at school.

This aspect of play is sometimes used therapeutically (to cure) children who are emotionally disturbed. Sometimes a therapist will try to get a child to come to terms with an unpleasant aspect of his life by means of what is called play therapy. The underlying idea is that by representing a traumatic (very disturbing) experience or situation symbolically, and by returning to it and perhaps reversing what happened, the child will be better able to deal with the problem in real life. To do this, the therapist very often uses doll figures to represent the people involved in the problem.

A cross-cultural application of this Western technique was used on Pilaga Indian children in the Argentine by Jules and Zunia Henry (1974). They were interested in studying sibling rivalry (jealousy between brothers and sisters) in this particular culture because, when a new baby is born amongst the Pilaga, the next oldest child tends to be ignored by the parents and relatives in favour of the new baby. The Henrys named dolls for the children and members of their families and gave the children concerned these dolls to play with. The children kicked and hit the dolls and displayed considerable hostility towards parents and siblings and even themselves.

While not all psychologists accept the technique of play therapy or feel that it is very useful, there is no doubt that in play children can help themselves come to terms with emotions that are disturbing them.

We have described six areas of child development that are intimately involved in play. If you are interested in this area, you will find a select bibliography at the end of the chapter. Before summarising the material of this chapter, we would like to consider the role nursery and infant schools can play in stimulating constructive play. Unfortunately, as Ayonrinde, Ashem and Ugwuegbu (forthcoming) describe, not all nursery schools make the most of the opportunities open to them. For example, in a survey of nursery schools in the Ibadan area of Nigeria, they found that many offered very restricted activities to the children. In some nursery schools, the children do very little except chant nursery rhymes and practise letters. The principal of one such nursery school told one of the authors of this book that this was because money for equipment was in short supply, but we feel that with a little ingenuity an exciting play environment can be provided at relatively little expense. For this reason we offer some practical suggestions about the way in which language and intellectual development can be encouraged in the nursery school.

Encouraging language and cognitive development through play in the early years at school
It is possible for the teacher to provide, without too much expense, a learning environment for young children as they enter nursery school. In such an environment children will be able to meet different experiences which will help with the development of language and thinking. They will be able to discover the concepts (ideas) of likeness and difference, sorting, matching and organising experience. In this section we list some play areas that the teacher can use. In each area the teacher should structure the play material with care, knowing what she wants the children to gain from that area at any particular time. She must also be prepared to intervene with language which will help to clarify (make clearer) the children's thought. We suggest seven possible 'corners' or areas.

(1) *A house area.* This is a corner provided with old household articles such as dishes, cooking pots and pans of different sizes, dolls of different sizes, with dolls' clothes (if these are available), a small table, and any other spare furniture. This area can be used for make-believe play in which children can enter into the minds of others.

(2) *Glueing and working with paper and cardboard scraps.* This is an area in which such scrap materials are placed in sets or packets, matching shapes as closely as is possible with such scraps. Here the child may work freely, sticking things together to make models. He may start by sticking things together without any system but he will progress to the stage of looking at the shapes, seeing one that interests him and saying, 'This is the shape of a wheel. So I will make a car.' The next stage may be 'I *want* to make a bus – can I find the right shapes?'. At this second stage he has moved

on to a more developed way of making models because he has an idea in his mind and he is actively going to look for the material to carry out the idea.

It is important to limit the materials provided and present them in such a way that the children can see, think and then select what they want. The teacher can then intervene with words that help the child to organise his thoughts about what he has been doing, like sticky, heavy, smooth, thick, thin.

(3) *Sand, water, buckets of different sizes, jugs, tubes and funnels (if possible).* Experiences with these materials are very valuable. Apart from the fun the children experience and the enjoyment they get from simply filling, pouring, emptying and transferring, they can lead to the beginnings of understanding of such important concepts (ideas) as volume and capacity.

Dry sand can also be provided and if tools similar to those given with water and sand are offered, the children will discover the properties of dry sand that are like and different from those of damp sand: 'I can't make a cake with this sand – it's too runny.' 'I can pour this sand through the tube like water.'

(4) *Building bricks.* It is expensive to buy sets of building bricks but it may be possible to persuade woodwork teachers to get their classes to make some for the nursery school. Bricks are very valuable play materials for young children and even those up to 7 or 8 years of age.

Different shapes and sizes should, if possible, be offered to the children, and they should be stored in sets so that the children may select what they want. Tidying them away is obviously valuable too: 'Where does this go?' 'Will it fit in here?' 'Is it the same shape, the same size as that one?'

Some building materials might be placed nearby, on a low table, so that children can build at eye level. Linked to this, the teacher might provide, if these are available, doll's houses and furniture, soldiers, small cars, and so on.

(5) *Sewing.* Children (of both sexes, of course), will gain a great deal here, if materials are carefully thought out, presented and looked after. Thick, thin, long and short needles and thick and thin thread can be provided. It is also useful for the material scraps provided to be of different textures. Buttons are also useful. By using these sewing materials the child can gain a good understanding of words like 'thick' and 'thin' as well as experience of the physical properties of the material he is using: 'This thread is too thick to go through this button.' 'This material is very thick and this needle is not strong enough to go through it.'

(6) *Clay.* Clay is a very helpful material for language and cognitive development. As the children make objects they are thinking; they have an image which they copy and the teacher through discussion can make them speak of this, helping them to clarify their thoughts: 'This is a very fat piece of clay – if you roll it out it will become thinner.'

(7) *Dressing-up materials and other scraps for 'make-believe' games.* Any material which encourages imaginative play – boxes for building, materials for dressing up, art materials – offer good opportunities for language development. For example, if a child has a long cardboard tube or a stick to 'shoot' with when playing soldiers, he realises that this represents a gun. He will later realise that the printed or written word 'gun' represents a gun as well.

When a child dresses up as mother, acts and speaks like mother, he is projecting himself into the feelings of someone else. This can lay the basis of creative writing. In a similar way, when a child paints a picture or makes a model with clay or scrap materials, he has an image in his mind. He is expressing what he has felt or seen or experienced. In a way he is telling a story without words. The teacher can intervene and discuss what he has produced and, in answering her questions, the child will begin to put his story into words.

We hope this description of seven possible play areas will provide you with some practical suggestions if you are dealing with young children. It should be stressed that in all of this the thinking of the teacher is of great importance in the way she plans and structures the material and then intervenes with the correct language and helps the child to organise his own thinking about his activities.

Summary

In this chapter we looked at two aspects of children's lives – language and play – that contribute in an important way to children's mental and social development.

(1) We looked briefly at four stages of early speech development.

    (*a*) We noted that children can communicate even before they can speak (pre-linguistic communication).

    (*b*) We noted the similarities observed all over the world in the way babies babble.

    (*c*) We discovered that the earliest ways of stringing words together (stage one speech) are markedly similar in all cultures studied. We also noted that the chief characteristic of this phase of speech development is the simplification of language with the emphasis on the communication of meaning.

    (*d*) In the next stage of speech development, stage two speech, we discovered that children seek patterns in their acquisition of their own language and so the structure of their language becomes increasingly under their control.

    (*e*) We described the way adults speak to children so as to maximise the children's understanding of what they are saying and we noted the similarity in this across different cultures.

    (*f*) Finally, on language development, we noted that as children grow older, there are simultaneous changes in both the structure and function of speech. With respect to *structure*, their grammar becomes more and more similar to adult grammar. With respect to *function*, the primary function of communication becomes joined by another important function – the contribution of speech to the processes of cognitive development.

(2) We then looked at play.

    (*a*) We attempted to define some of the characteristics of play – that it is enjoyable, done for its own sake, freely entered into, active and bears some relation to other activities of life.

    (*b*) We then outlined the role of play in six areas:

      (i) in the mastery of physical activities

      (ii) in exploration

      (iii) in the learning of social skills, social roles and social values

      (iv) in cognitive and language development

      (v) in creativity

      (vi) in the interaction with emotional needs.

    (*c*) Finally we introduced some practical suggestions on introducing stimulating play activities into nursery schools at relatively little cost.

Chapter 3: Selected Bibliography

Language

Clark, H. H., and Clark, E. V., *Psychology and Language: An Introduction to Psycholinguistics* (New York: Harcourt Brace Jovanovich, 1977).

Dale, P. S., *Language Development: Structure and Function*, 2nd edn (New York: Holt, Rinehart & Winston, 1976). (This book will give you a summary of some of the research into the acquisition of Russian and refer you to other studies in this area.)

Play

Bruner, J. S., Jolly, A., and Sylva, K., *Play: Its Role in Development and Evolution* (Harmondsworth: Penguin, 1976).

Garvey, C., *Play* (London: Methuen, 1977).

Millar, S., *The Psychology of Play* (Harmondsworth: Penguin, 1968).

COGNITIVE DEVELOPMENT

4

' We approach the world wondering about it, entertaining hypotheses which we are eager to check. And we direct our questions not just to other people but to ourselves, giving ourselves the job of finding the answer by direct exploration of the world. In this way we build up what it is fashionable to call a *model* of the world – a kind of system of inner representations, the value of which is to help us to anticipate events and be ready to deal with them. '
(Margaret Donaldson in *Children's Minds*, 1978, p. 68)

Introduction

We would like to point out at the beginning of this chapter that it is rather more complex in content than the rest of the book. Further, in it we define and use a number of technical terms. The reason for this is that in this chapter we refer to a selection of the vast amount of cross-cultural data in the area covered by the chapter. The cross-cultural texts to which we refer are themselves very interesting and we are sure that many readers will wish to follow them up. (They are listed in the select bibliography at the end of this chapter.) However, these cross-cultural texts were written mainly for students majoring in psychology as an academic discipline and for this reason are themselves very technical. We hope that this chapter will provide a bridge to these for the more general reader, and for this reason we try to expand on some of the subject matter of the cross-cultural texts and we also introduce some of the relevant terminology.

In this chapter we are concerned with the development of children's thought – what Margaret Donaldson refers to as 'Children's Minds'. If you look at Figure 4.1 you will see that we discuss two major ways of describing children's cognitive development – a stage approach and a process approach. Finally we look at the ways in which different cultures can affect the course of cognitive development.

(1)   Piaget's approach – a stage approach

Any book published within the last twenty-five years dealing with children's cognitive development will have a considerable section on the work of the great Swiss psychologist Jean Piaget. His work has been enormously influential and has sparked off numerous studies throughout the world. He is above all concerned with the qualitative changes that take place in children's thinking as they move from infancy to late adolescence. His own children were his first subjects and from his careful and detailed observation of their development he first distinguished the major developmental stages through which he considers *all children pass, in the same sequence*. Each stage is characterised, according to Piaget, by particular behaviours and particular types of cognitive functioning.

In this short section we shall outline Piaget's three major developmental periods, pausing to give particular significance to the major concept of *conservation*. We shall then consider briefly some of the more important criticisms that have been made of his work and finally we shall attempt to

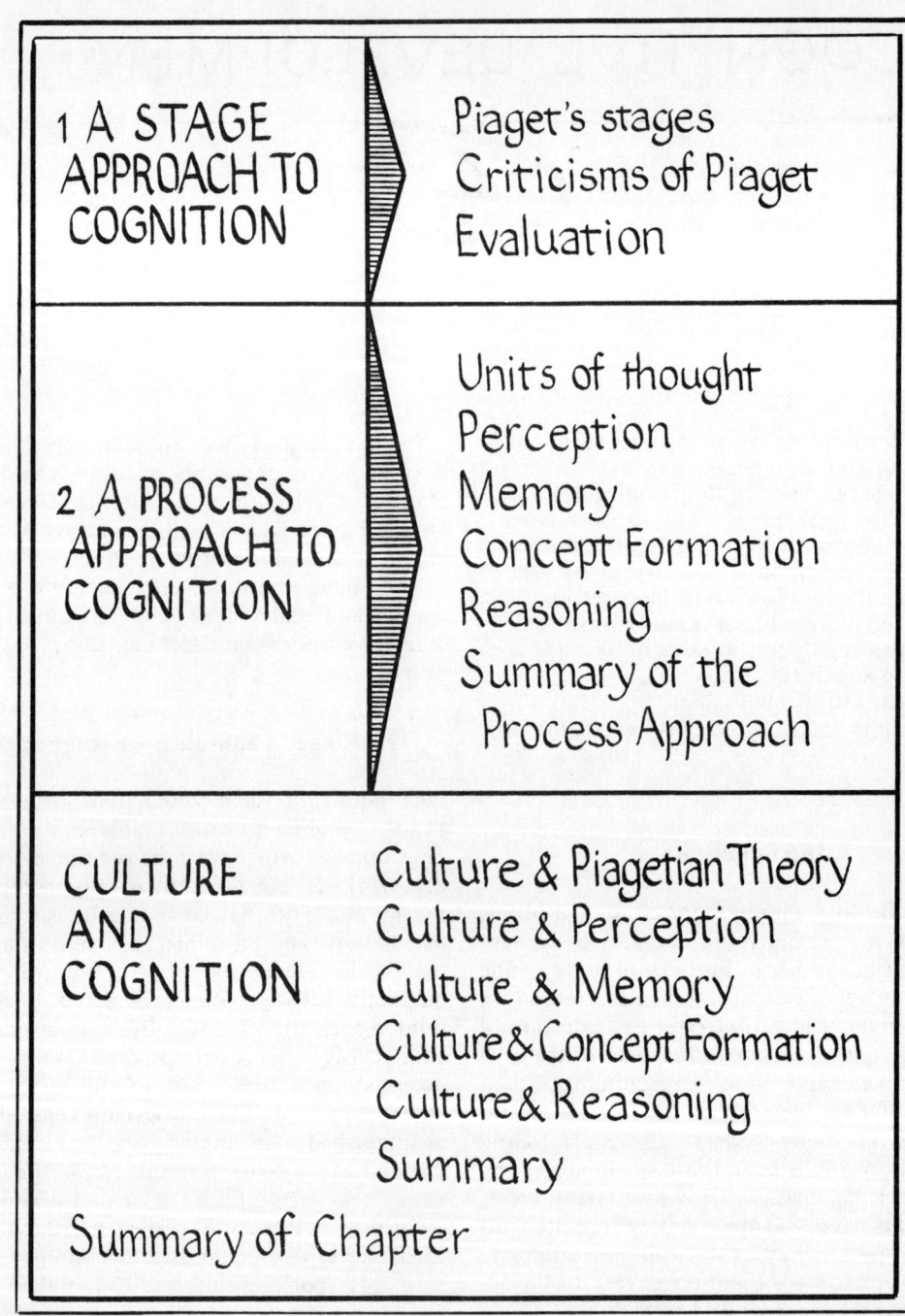

1 A STAGE APPROACH TO COGNITION	Piaget's stages Criticisms of Piaget Evaluation
2 A PROCESS APPROACH TO COGNITION	Units of thought Perception Memory Concept Formation Reasoning Summary of the Process Approach
CULTURE AND COGNITION	Culture & Piagetian Theory Culture & Perception Culture & Memory Culture & Concept Formation Culture & Reasoning Summary

Summary of Chapter

Figure 4.1   Structure of Chapter 4

evaluate the importance to the reader of his massive contribution.

However, it must be said that it is a great injustice to the monumental work of Piaget to try and present it within a few pages. If you are interested in his stages approach, you will find a select bibliography at the end of the chapter which will enable you to get a better understanding of this major and powerful thinker.

Before we describe the three major Piagetian stages, we should make three very important points about Piaget's work in general:

(1) According to Piaget, a child does not think *like* an adult only rather less effectively. Instead he believes children's thinking to be *qualitatively* different from the thinking of adults.

(2) Piaget's first work was in the field of zoology and his early interest in biological principles is reflected throughout his work. As a biologist Piaget traces cognitive development in terms of biologically inherited ways of interacting with the environment. For example, he traces the way that the reflexes the child is born with adapt to environmental experience. Here he is writing about his daughter, Jacqueline, on the twenty-seventh day of her fourth month $(0;4(27))$ and the way she is beginning to show the sucking reflex to a visual stimulus; he then shows how the reflex adapts with experience.

> ‘ *Observation* 27 – Jacqueline, at $0;4(27)$ and the days following, opens her mouth as soon as she is shown the bottle. She only began mixed feeding at $0;4(12)$. At $0;7(13)$ I note that she opens her mouth differently according to whether she is offered a bottle or a spoon. ’
>
> (Piaget, 1952, p. 60)

(3) Piaget tries to identify the thinking structures of each age level and he tries to show they become adapted by a dynamic interaction with the environment. He then tries to show how these structures combine together to form more and more powerful systems of thought. Thus we see that his approach is one in which each stage builds up in a progressive way on the preceding stage. Further, the thinking characteristic of later stages is more complex than that of the earlier stages because of the environmental experience that has been gained and because of the maturation that has taken place.

The developmental periods of Piaget

Period one: sensory-motor period – from birth through to approximately $1\frac{1}{2}$–2 years of age.

At birth the infant displays a limited number of unco-ordinated reflexes. During the next four months these are co-ordinated into simple schemes, and by the next four months, at 8 months of age, the infant is able to react to objects outside himself and to realise that they continue to exist even though he cannot see them (object permanence). By the end of this stage the child is able to carry out goal-directed behaviour and is also able to produce new solutions to problems through mental exploration. But the mental exploration, at this stage, according to Piaget, is always in terms of representing the outside world by thinking of specific sensory input (sights, sounds, smells, and so on) and specific motor actions (gestures, movements, and so on). He describes six sub-stages within the sensory-motor period.

Period two: The concrete operations period

Sub-period one: pre-operational thought – from $1\frac{1}{2}$–2 years through to 6–7 years old.

During this sub-period the child's internal cognitive picture of the world is growing and he begins to think symbolically. Some of the symbolic thinking may occur with words but not all of it; for instance, a doll may be treated as though it is a live baby, or a block of wood as though it is a car. But although the child is now thinking symbolically, according to Piaget his thinking is full of contradictions and is unstable and egocentric. By *egocentric* Piaget means that the child can only see the world from his own standpoint. This does not mean that he is selfish as it would of an older person. It means that he is completely dependent on his own viewpoint, and, according to Piaget, finds it difficult to appreciate that other people have experiences, views and ideas that differ from his own.

A well-known experiment by Piaget illustrates this 'egocentrism'. The child is seated at a table, on which there is a three-dimensional model. A doll is seated on another chair, and the child is shown a number of cards showing the model photographed from different views. The child is asked to choose a card showing what he can see and the child at this stage can do this correctly. But he cannot choose a card showing the view from the doll's side; he always chooses the view of the model that he can see. We will see in the section on criticisms of Piaget that this view of the child's egocentrism is now disputed.

One of the main characteristics in this sub-period, according to Piaget, is the child's tendency to *centration*. This concept of centration is very central to the most famous set of Piaget's experiments – those on conservation. And because we are going to return to conservation in both the section on criticisms of Piaget's theories and in the section on culture's effect on cognitive development, we shall describe these experiments.

pours the content of one glass into a taller, thinner glass and the child is asked to compare the amount of water in this glass (number three) with the amount in glass number one. In most experiments with children below the age of, say, 6½ years the child will say glass number three has more liquid than glass number one. According to Piaget this is because the child centres on the level of the liquid and does not realise that the actual amount of liquid has not changed – he fails to conserve *continuous quantity*.

Similarly in Figure 4.2 (bottom of the picture) the experimenter shows a child two sets of buttons

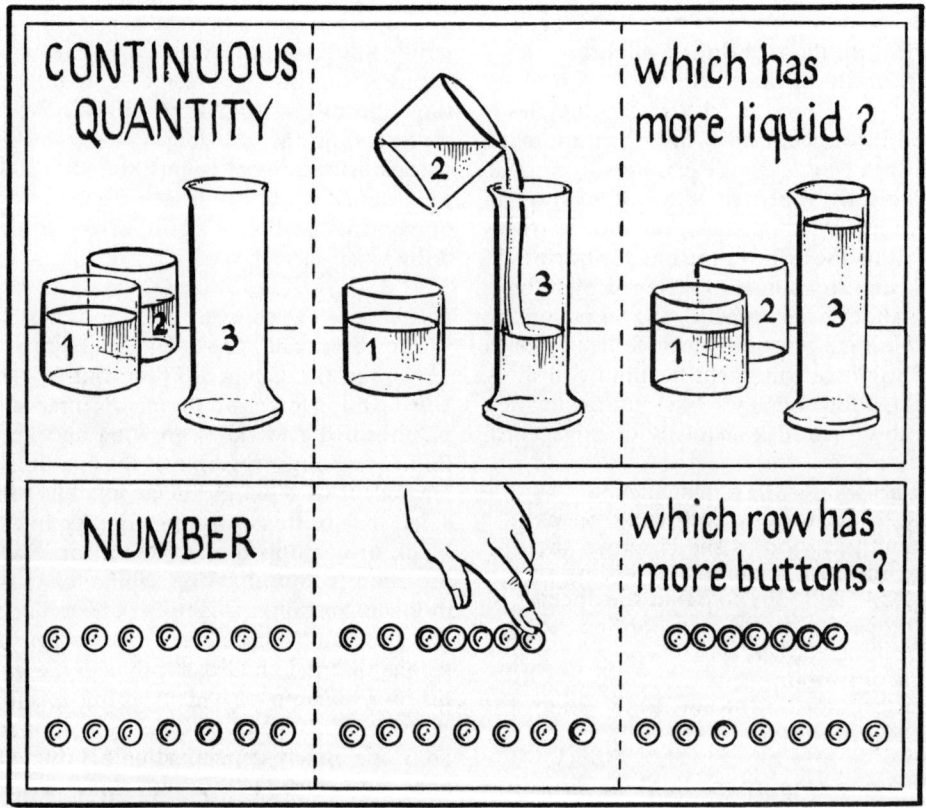

Figure 4.2　Conservation experiments

Let us first describe a conservation experiment with continuous quantity (top of Figure 4.2). A child is shown two identical glasses filled with the same amount of coloured water. The child is asked if the glasses have equal amounts of water and of course he says they do. The experimenter then

arranged in one-to-one correspondence. The child is asked if there are the same amount of buttons in the two rows and once again the child will agree there are. The experimenter then bunches the buttons in one row together and then asks the child which row has more buttons. The child below the age of 6½ tends to respond by saying the upper row has more buttons – he has centred on the appearance and has failed to conserve *number*.

This inability to conserve is typical, according to Piaget, of the pre-operational child's thought. It is not logical and is full of contradictions. If the child had been able to imagine the reverse of the experimenter's actions, say, pouring the water in the tall thin glass (number three) back into glass number two, he would have been able to conserve and would have given the correct answer. Thus the pre-operational child's thinking is also characterised by irreversibility – the lack of the ability to reverse mentally the experimenter's action.

In summary, then, in this phase the child is thinking symbolically but his thinking is not logical and is full of contradictions.

Sub-period two: concrete operations – from 6–7 years through to 11–12 years old.
The main characteristic of this second sub-period of the period of concrete operations is that the child begins to think in terms of a set of interrelated principles rather than in single bits of knowledge. He thinks in terms of systems. His thinking also becomes more logical. He believes now that number, length, mass and volume remain constant even if superficial changes are made in their external appearance. Thus, faced with a typical conservation experiment, he always conserves. By being able to imagine the reverse of the experimenter's action, he generates a stable rule – changing the appearance of an object does not change the amount of it. This is an *operation* – a Piagetian term which describes a mature mental routine. And as Mussen and his colleagues put it, Piaget considers 'that the acquisition of operations is the heart of mental growth' (1974, p. 39).

The child is no longer egocentric in his thinking either. In the experiment we described on egocentricity he can now choose the correct card from the doll's point of view. He is also, according to Piaget, more able to reason and think about classes and sub-classes. For instance, if he is shown seven blue beads and three white beads, all made of wood, he is able to answer correctly the question that the child in the previous stage cannot: 'Are there more blue beads than wooden beads?' (The child at the earlier sub-period tends to confuse 'wooden' and 'white' and answers that there are more blue beads.)

Thus, according to Piaget, unlike the child in the previous period, he is now able to think *logically* but, and this is the difference between this stage and the final period, he cannot think in abstract logical terms. He cannot generate and test a set of logical hypotheses.

Period three: Formal operations – from 11–12 years through to adulthood
In this stage the child begins to think logically, not just with reference to concrete problems, but in the abstract. He begins to appreciate that some (hypothetical) problems can be solved 'in your head', by applying the same rules as would be applied to concrete problems. He is able to think logically about a series of possible alternative solutions to a problem in a systematic fashion. A typical experiment to show this is the following. A child is shown five colourless, odourless liquids in test tubes and is asked to discover what combination of the five will produce a yellow liquid. The child in the previous period will attempt to do this by trial and error. The child in the fourth stage, however, will go about the problem systematically, for example, combining the first and second, then first and third, and so on.

In addition, with respect to more general issues, Piaget considers that whereas the younger child tends to deal largely with the present, the child in this final stage becomes concerned with the hypothetical, the future and the far away.

Throughout the child's progress through these stages, which of course Piaget believes always takes place in the same sequence, the child is seen as organising and adapting to his environment in a way that depends upon his biological maturation, his past experience and the particulars of his own situation.

Criticisms of Piaget's theories
In recent years a number of different psychologists have commented critically on Piaget's work. We will describe three sorts of criticism:

(1) *Children show the ability to be logical at ages well below those Piaget specifies.* For example Bryant (1974) has shown that children as young as 4 and 5 years old can make logical inferences whereas according to Piaget the ability to make such inferences only develops at the stage of concrete operations.

(2) *Children can be trained to solve conservation experiments correctly without actually physically handling the types of material used in the*

experiment. You will probably remember that Piaget specifies that conservation is attained when the child actually acquires an operation by realising that the experimenter's action is reversible. Siegel and his associates (1966) worked with 5-year-old children who had not yet acquired conservation of quantity with water or clay. They showed the children various objects and encouraged them to name as many characteristics as they could of the objects, for example, that oranges are round, have stems and are orange in colour. After this training which encouraged the children to realise that objects possess a number of attributes, the children were re-tested on the conservation tasks and were able to do them correctly. This is of course contrary to Piaget's theory that children attain the notion of conservation only through acquiring the reversible operation.

(3) *Children often failed Piagetian tasks not because they were incapable of the reasoning required but because the experimental conditions confused them.* In her book *Children's Minds* Margaret Donaldson summarises a number of experiments that make this point. We will describe one on the conservation of number. (If you turn back to Figure 4.2 before reading any further you will be able to remind yourself of this type of experiment.) In this experiment James McGarrigle introduced a character called 'Naughty Teddy'. This small teddy bear was taken out of his box during the experiment and moved over the buttons. McGarrigle's idea was to alter the events of the second part of the experiment so that the change in the look of the buttons seemed to occur, not by the action of the experimenter, but accidentally because 'Naughty Teddy' did it. 'McGarrigle found that this version of the task – where the transformation was ostensibly [apparently] accidental – was dealt with much more successfully than the traditional version: many more children between the ages of four and six "conserved" ' (Donaldson, 1978, p. 64).

It seems then, according to this and other experiments described by Donaldson, that sometimes children cannot solve conservation and other tasks of a Piagetian nature because the tasks are presented in such a way that the children are confused by the experimental set-up and are unable to solve the problem by reference to their past experience. If things are so arranged that the experimental set-up includes elements of their past experience – like a 'naughty' toy – then they are able to perform the task correctly. Further,

Donaldson shows that when she repeated the egocentrism experiment we described on page 43, using a situation which children had some experience of, rather than a three-dimensional model, children no longer behaved egocentrically.

Evaluation

In summary, then, it is clear that detailed as Piaget's observations were, and powerful as his theories are, major questions remain to be answered about his work. Nevertheless it seems to us that for the educator the following important points emerge from Piagetian theory:

(1) Cognitive development occurs in interaction with the environment. Thus the more stimulating the classroom environment, the more dynamic the children's cognitive development.

(2) Because, as Piaget has pointed out, symbolic thought does not always occur using language, sometimes cognitive development may not be dependent on language. Indeed it is clear that some children think in images and relationships that are not directly dependent on language. This means that teaching conducted largely through the verbal medium may not always be appropriate for all children. This is pointed out by Furth and Wachs in their book *Thinking Goes to School* (1974). This book rests largely on Piagetian theory and has a number of very stimulating games designed to encourage thinking and reasoning in ways that are not heavily dependent on the development of language. Three of these games are given below (see Figures 4.3 and 4.4). They are suitable for children between 4 and 7 years old.

The first game is a game to encourage graphic thinking. (By graphic thinking Furth and Wachs refer to an activity involving the co-ordination of arm-hand-finger and vision. They consider graphic thinking to be an important component in writing, drawing, colouring, threading and carving.) 'Dot picture' (Furth and Wachs, 1974, p. 202) is played by two children. 'The first draws "X's" on the board and the second draws a connecting line between them. When the "X's" are connected, they should form a picture, for example, four connected "X's" to form a square, three to form a triangle, many to form a circle. The first child may think of more complex designs such as a fish or a house. Both children are developing graphic thinking, and the first child is also learning how to pre-plan' (see Figure 4.3).

Another game is designed to encourage logical

Figure 4.3 Dot picture game

thinking (see Figure 4.4). Here children first collect a number of objects from their own environment – examples would be seeds, stones, feathers, leaves, buttons, food, screws, shells. Then small groups of three or four children work together with a selection of the whole class's collection. They discuss with each other which attributes they could use to classify their objects: for instance, things that were (are) living, things that are round or curved, things to eat (from Furth and Wachs, 1974, p. 227). This game helps children to think analytically about the objects in their own natural environment. They start to group things according to different criteria – form, colour, function, and so on.

Finally, here is a game that is designed to encourage children's social thinking based on the Furth and Wachs game 'Make an illustrated story' (1974, p. 260). For this game the teacher brings to class a number of photographs or illustrations from a magazine. The class decide on a theme, and come up with a story that is illustrated by the pictures. 'As the children listen to different themes and different stories based on identical pictures, they experience a variety of possible viewpoints and – what is most important – are encouraged to express their own personal bias and interest. This game can be played simultaneously by different groups.'

We hope these games serve as an example of the stimulating way a teacher can encourage children to think analytically. You will notice that all three games utilise material that is readily available in a rural classroom. Furth and Wachs describe a very large number of such games in their book. Unfortunately in many cases the games require fairly elaborate material. However, if a school were to purchase the book, no doubt local adaptations could be made of some of the material needed.

It would seem, then, that Piagetian theory encourages the educator to make the classroom a stimulating environment with plenty of material for the child to see, handle and hear. Further, through games such as those described by Furth and Wachs, the teacher can encourage children to think analytically and constructively.

Figure 4.4 Grouping game

A process approach

In the preceding section we looked at the growth of thinking within a stage approach, where each succeeding stage rested on the one before. In this section we shall look instead at the different processes in cognition. This approach does not derive from the work of one man but draws on experimental work done in different countries.

In Chapter 1 we mentioned that the optimum level of arousal is usually an intermediate one. That is, too many new experiences confuse a child and too little novelty, or too strict an adherence to routine, bores him. In doing so, we compared the human mind to a computer which actively seeks information to process, encodes it and stores it for future use. (In addition, though, unlike a computer, the human mind actively *seeks* information.) Much evidence seems to point to the conclusion that human beings attend to and learn most from events that are mildly discrepant (different) from the

current level of cognition. This has been called the 'moderate novelty principle'.

This viewpoint underlies the process approach to cognition. Human beings are motivated to extract information from the world around them. They do so by 'going beyond the information given', interpreting and constructing a model of the world so that they will be able to predict future events and thus gain competence. They are most likely to pay attention to those aspects that are relevant to their interest, help them make sense of the world and fit into their own particular 'cognitive network'. Things that fit into their particular cognitive networks are those that bear some relation to these networks but that are not too discrepant from them – that is, events that are of moderate novelty.

In presenting this view of cognition – that it is an intentional and continuous activity designed to build up a model of the outer world – we will differentiate between four units of cognition and four processes. We have already referred to these processes in Chapter 2 when we defined cognition; they are (i) perception (ii) memory, (iii) concept formation and (iv) reasoning.

(a) *The units of cognition*

We are going to distinguish between four units of cognition (thought). The first and simplest is called a *schema* (plural *schemata*). It is probably used mainly by young infants and very young children, and is the most elementary way of representing the outside world. Consider, for example, a young child, thinking of his mother – he probably has a visual impression (but not of course an exact image) of her face, an auditory impression of her voice and possibly also a sense of the way she smells and feels. Thus Ault (1977) says of schemata: 'Schemata, then, are stored conceptualizations of experiences, ways of organizing or classifying prior sensory events. They are not necessarily pictorial representations (as are images) nor are they tied to language' (p. 87). But adults also use schemata. Think, for example, of the primary school you first attended as a pupil – you will perhaps envisage certain distinctive visual features or perhaps a smell of chalk dust. Thus we might even regard a schema as a caricature because it exaggerates distinctive features.

As the child grows older he will begin to represent his mother to himself by the word mama (or whatever version of the word mother he uses). 'Mama' is then a *symbol* which stands for the mother itself. And indeed words are our most commonly used symbolic system. Symbols, then, stand for objects or processes. But they are not always verbal. For example, we all understand that the symbol ' = ' means 'equal to'. And we have already discussed the use the young child may make of symbols where, for instance, a piece of wood may represent a car. Folk tales, of course, and literature, music and art often use symbols, for example, a witch may symbolise evil, a particular sequence on the drum disaster, and so on.

Symbols generally represent one event or stimulus. *Concepts*, on the other hand, stand for a common set of attributes among a group of events or symbols. For example the concept 'cat' refers to the collection of four-legged mammals which miaow when they are unhappy and purr when they are happy, have fur and whiskers and are suitable for household pets. 'Cat' is a concrete concept and it is relatively easy to list its attributes. It is less easy to

list the attributes of abstract concepts, often because they signify slightly different things to different people. For example, take the concept 'goodness'. For some of us an event or object possesses goodness if it is potentially beneficial to mankind; for others, if it is potentially beneficial to mankind and is, in addition, linked to our religion. However, we can say that once a person has attained a concept he will be able to list some of its attributes or identify examples of it.

The fourth unit we will define is a *rule*. Rules are statements which describe a relationship between two or more concepts. Some rules are informal and not necessarily generally held. For example, a child may hold the following rule about teachers which he has generated from his experience of them – 'teachers help you learn'. This rule is usually true in his experience but he may meet a teacher who invalidates the rule and so he will say 'except for the physical education teacher who always shouts at me'. On the other hand, we soon learn that some rules are formal and always true. For example, the rules we use in arithmetic where ten times ten is always a hundred (in our number system).

In sum, then, we are going to regard cognitive processes as operating with these four basic units. In the next sections it will be seen that, as children grow older, so do these units, particularly concepts, become more elaborated.

Before continuing with the cognitive processes we would like to introduce some terminology of the distinguished psychologist Jerome Bruner, which you may come across in other psychology texts. These are the three modes of representation: *enactive*, *iconic* and *symbolic*.

Bruner regards the human brain as having three modes of representation. Firstly the *enactive* mode – this refers to events being represented in terms of the action they evoke. Thus very young children can often understand things best in terms of action. For example, children can best understand the concept of balance by referring to their experience on a balance (see top of Figure 4.5). If the child on one end is heavier, the child at the other slides back. But not only young children use the enactive mode. Most motor skills are represented that way. Think of cycling. You will see that if you wanted to describe what you do when you cycle you would have to translate it out of your enactive thinking.

Bruner's second level of representation is *iconic*. In iconic representation objects are conceivable

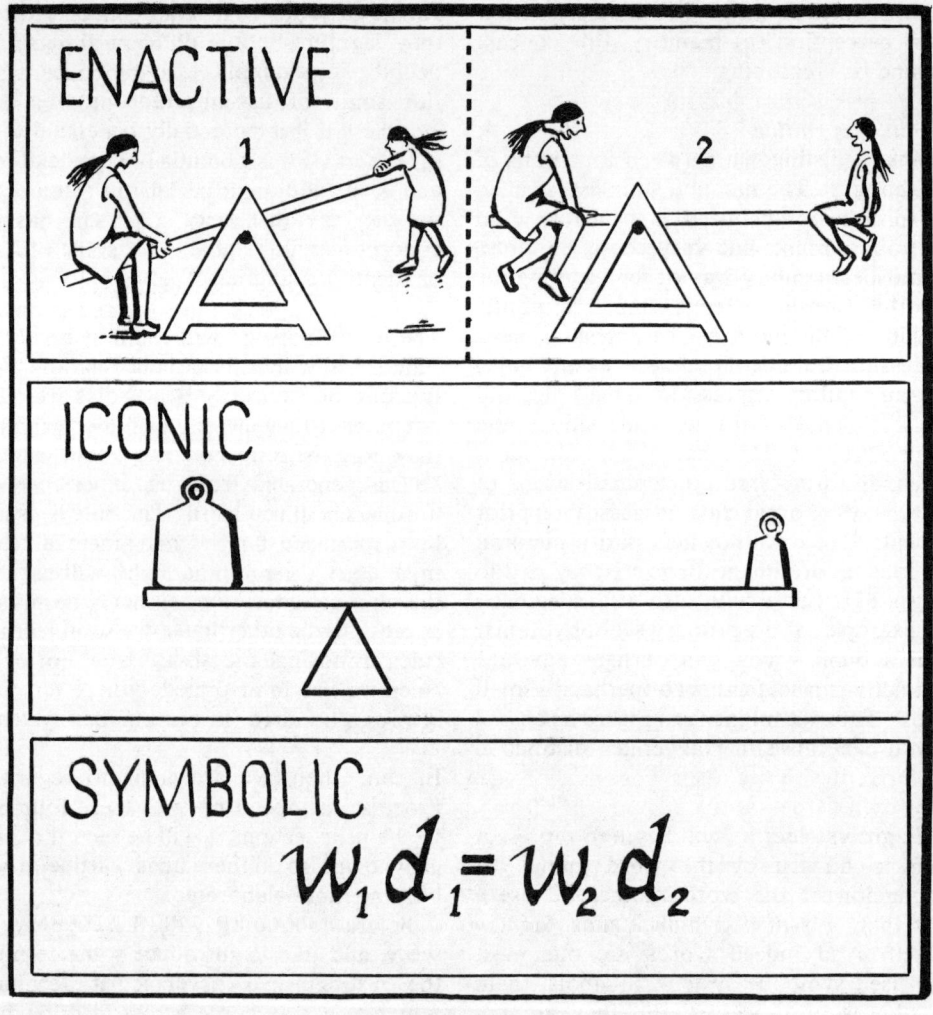

ENACTIVE

ICONIC

SYMBOLIC

$$w_1 d_1 = w_2 d_2$$

Figure 4.5
Bruner's modes of representation

without action; an object is known by means of a picture or image. Returning to the concept of balance, children may now be able to understand the concept by means of a schematic picture of a balance beam (see middle of Figure 4.5). Once again this mode of representation is not confined entirely to young children. Even students of advanced applied mathematics are often helped by iconic representation of problems (possibly by use of models).

The final method of representation is *symbolic*. Here action and image are translated into language. Thus, to return to the problem of balance – a balance beam can be explained through words alone (see bottom section of Figure 4.5).

Sprinthall and Sprinthall (1974, p. 224) summarise these three methods of representation as follows:

The wordless messages of *enactive* communication.
A picture often tells a thousand words: the *iconic* level.
Language – the *symbolic* level.

It can be seen, then, that schemata are probably represented at the enactive and iconic level whereas symbols, concepts and rules are at the symbolic level.

(b) *The processes of cognition*

Before proceeding to discuss these in turn, we would like to point out that all the four processes we are going to describe are interrelated and often overlap. The divisions between them are blurred and ideally they should all be presented simultaneously, as they often occur together in cognition. But such a presentation would be extremely complex and thus we present them separately in such a way that, in general, the more elaborated the process, the later it is presented.

(i) *Perception.* How do we see? The answer is that light waves of varying wavelengths and intensity stimulate our retina, and that messages about this stimulation are carried along the optic nerve and processed by the part of the brain known as the visual cortex. But a little reflection will indicate to you that we do not always perceive the same visual stimulus in the same way.

The classic example of the way perception may vary with the same stimulus may be seen in Figure 4.6. You may see this either as a vase or as two faces. Similarly, if you see a sheet waving on the line in your own garden at night, you will merely say 'I've forgotten to bring in the washing'. But if you are walking down an unknown street, all alone on a dark night, and you happen to pass a garden

with a sheet waving in the breeze, you might, just for a moment, see it as a ghostly figure.

In other words, when we perceive an object (whether visually or aurally) we do not simply react to the physical stimulation alone, we add something to the stimulation by relating it to our memory concerning similar sensations and interpreting it in terms of our expectations. Indeed in perception, in Bruner's classic phrase, we go 'beyond the information given'.

Thus perception may be defined as the process by which we extract meaningful information from physical stimulation. It is the way we interpret our sensations.

Bruner (1973) makes three very important points about perception:

(1) Perception is not only dependent on the stimulus attributes of what is being perceived, but is also determined by the perceiving individual's experience, intention and social needs. Thus in an experiment done with Cecile Goodman, Bruner showed that when children were asked to estimate the size of coins, poor children perceived them as larger than richer children did (1947).

(2) The perceiver is not a passive and indifferent organism but one who actively selects information and forms perceptual hypotheses in order to reduce uncertainty and decide what precisely is happening.

To illustrate this second point of Bruner's, let us look at an example taken from Mussen and his associates (1974, p. 280) who are writing about a

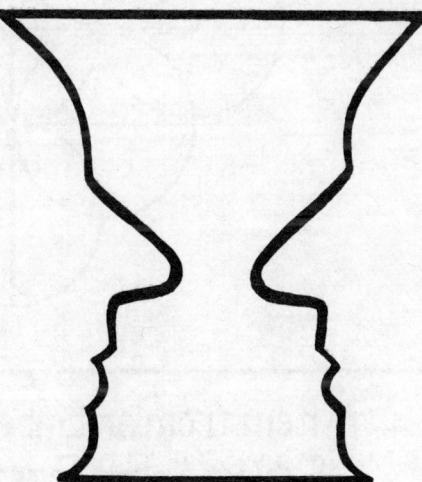

Figure 4.6
Theodore Rubin's reversible figure

child who sees a branch move in an American forest on a windless day.

> The child would begin scanning for the critical attributes of a forest animal – legs, fur, tail. If the moving branch were near the ground he might look for the tail and ears of a rabbit. If the branch were high, he might search for the wings of a bird. If our hypothetical child detected a shadow with two legs and an upright posture, his search would change abruptly, for only bears and humans have that particular form. He would now have a new problem and would look for an entirely new set of features. He would try to determine the presence of fur versus clothing and to detect the difference between the grunts of a bear and the voice of a man. If he were able to determine that the source of the movement was a hunter, he would terminate his search and turn his attention elsewhere.

(3) Perception is an activity that is fundamentally of the same nature as concept attainment and the other higher mental processes. Thus our perceptual processes help us to build up our model of the world so that we can anticipate future happenings and deal with them appropriately.

Perceptual changes with age. As we pointed out in the first chapter, very early in their lives infants start to perceive objects. For example, it seems that they are pre-programmed to be able to attend to faces rather than to disparate visual stimuli. However, it is also clear that perception improves rapidly with age. The two main areas that appear to improve perceptual ability are those of attention and prior experience. We shall deal with each of these in turn.

If you look around at the room you are sitting in you will find that there are numerous visual stimuli

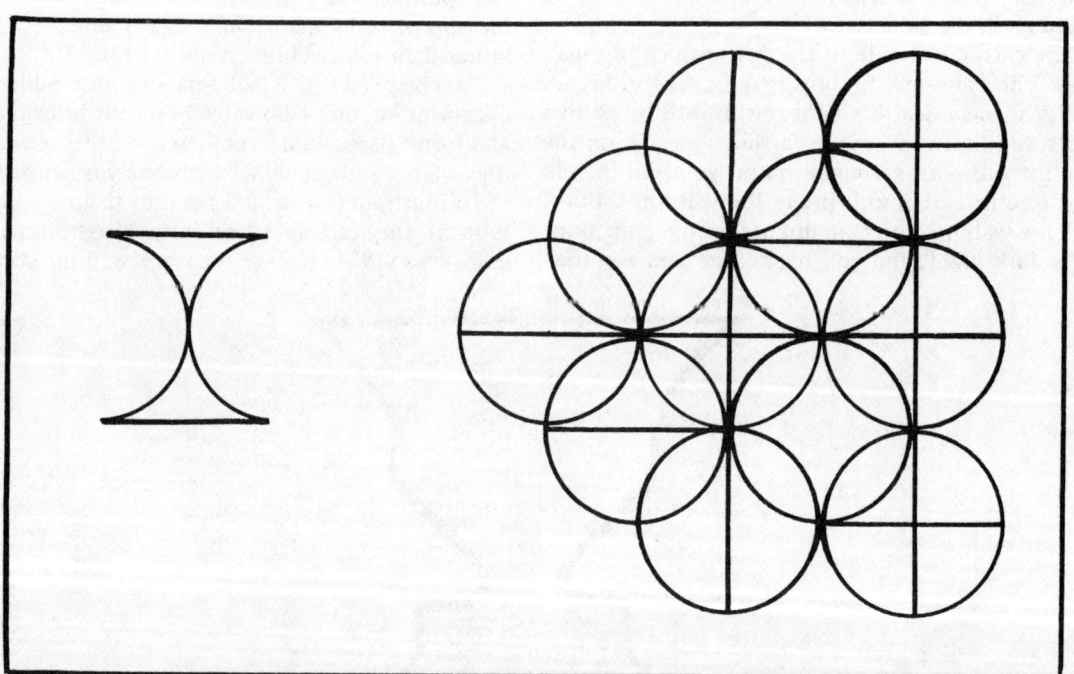

Figure 4.7   Item from an Embedded Figure Test. Subjects have to trace the outline of the simple figure on the left in the more complex figure on the right (Siann, 1972)

and, similarly, you will probably be aware, if you listen carefully, of many auditory stimuli as well – children playing outside, maybe distant traffic, a clock ticking, and so on. It would seem that our senses are assaulted all the time by an overwhelming amount of sights, sounds, odours and touch cues. Yet we actually notice only a few of them for we are able to pay attention *selectively*. An example of this is the 'cocktail party phenomenon'. This refers to the fact that even if a party is very noisy, we can listen to one conversation directed to us while managing to ignore all the other talk around us.

This ability to show *selective attention* improves with age. To illustrate this Ault describes an experiment where children were shown a list of different colours which was printed in different colours, for example, the word 'red' might be printed in yellow and the word 'blue' in green. If the child was asked to name the colour of the letters, the word that the letter spelt was a distracting cue and the cause of more naming errors in younger children than in older children.

Another aspect of attention that improves with age which you will have noticed yourself is *attention span*. The older children are, the longer the interval for which they can concentrate on one thing. Finally, another change in attention that

comes with age is the ability to *redirect attention quickly*. If you look at Figure 4.7 you will see examples of an embedded figure test (Siann, 1972). In this test children are asked to identify the smaller, simpler figure in the larger, more complex design. Among the skills needed in this test is the ability to redirect attention quickly between the part and the whole; the speed with which children can do this test improves with age.

As the child grows older, so of course does he accumulate more *experience* and, as we pointed out earlier, perception is influenced by past experience. Experience helps perception in two ways – it helps the child to enrich his schemata and it helps him to pick out the distinctive features of a stimulus. If you look at Figure 4.8 you will see that it gets more and more detailed as you move along. You could probably recognise that it was a table from the first impression but the young child will only be able to recognise it as a table at the third or fourth impression.

Thus increasing age brings improvement in perception by increasing skill at focusing, maintaining and redirecting attention and by making schemata more efficient, richer and more accurate.

(ii) *Memory*. Memory refers to the storage of

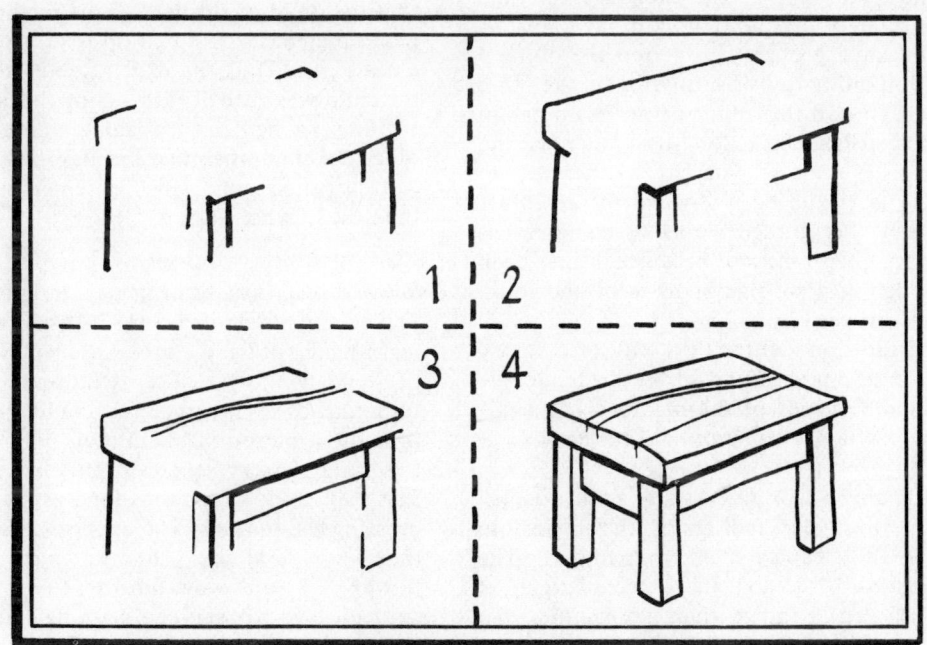

Figure 4.8 Experience aids perception

experiences for a person after they have ended. You will perhaps be able to differentiate for yourself two aspects of memory. The first is concerned with the *recall* of an event. For example, a friend may ask you to tell him all the names of the people who attended a party you recently attended without him. That is, you are asked to recall the event and must consequently retrieve all the necessary information from memory. On the other hand, he may ask you something simpler – did John Smith (a mutual friend) attend the party? Here you are simply asked to *recognise* whether an event has taken place or not. This is a much easier process. But both of course are intimately concerned with your storage of past events – that is, your memory.

Until recently, it was popular to differentiate three storage systems in memory – sensory, short term (or working memory) and long term. In discussing sensory memory we refer to the fact that we can retain a sensory, exact, picture of an event for a very short time only. That is, if you look at an object and then shut your eyes, you will probably retain an exact and vivid memory of it for only one quarter of a second. Sensory memory is probably the same for all ages. The second level of storage has been called short-term memory. This refers to a memory trace that is available for only a short period of time. Say, for example, you are going to phone a shop, you look up the phone number and dial it immediately. By the time you have finished dialling you have probably forgotten the number (provided you did not write it down). On the other hand, when you are learning for an examination you hope to consign facts to long-term memory and usually, in order to do so, you have consciously to rehearse the facts and be motivated to remember them. Latterly this storage model of memory has been less accepted; mostly because it has been difficult to demonstrate that short-term and long-term storage proceed by different mechanisms.

A more fruitful model for the study of memory now seems to be a process model. In this model we look at different stages of the memory process – acquisition, encoding, retention and retrieval.

Memory changes with age. As any educationalist will know, the older the child, the better, in general, is his capacity to remember. The improvement with age appears to occur largely at the level of *recall* rather than *recognition*. To illustrate this let us look at an experiment by Mussen and his associates. If 10-year-olds were shown twelve photos which were then put away

and they were asked to describe what the photos were of, they could typically *recall* about eight of the twelve. But if they were asked to pick out the twelve from a group of twenty-four, they *recognised* all twelve correctly. 4-year-olds, on the other hand, were only able to *recall* two or three spontaneously, although they were as good as the older children in *recognising* the twelve amongst the twenty-four they were shown. This gives us a clue as to why memory improves with age – it is in the improvement in the strategies with which memories are coded and stored so that they are then available for recall (or retrieval). We will now look at some of the strategies that aid memory.

Acquisition, encoding and retention

Verbal labelling. It seems that labelling things before we try to remember them can help retention. A very clever experiment to illustrate this was performed by Flavell and his associates (1966). They showed pictures of objects to be remembered to 5-, 7- and 10-year-old children. Seven pictures were arranged in a circle and the children had to remember the three of them that the experimenter pointed to. There was a fifteen-second delay during which the child wore a space helmet which had a visor over the eyes so that the child could not see the pictures but the experimenter (who could lip-read) could see the child's lips. Thus the experimenter could see if the child was verbally rehearsing the labels of the pictures he had been asked to remember. The older the child, the more labelling was observed. Further, those who labelled remembered better than those who did not.

Other task-appropriate strategies. In another study Flavell and his associates (1970) asked children to learn which of ten pictures was displayed in each of ten windows. The windows could be illuminated so the pictures could be seen by pressing a button. The children, who ranged in age from nursery school to 10 years, were told that they could practise as long as they liked by pressing the buttons. The experimenter then left the room and the children were observed through a one-way mirror. Four different strategies were observed – naming and labelling, testing themselves before pressing the button, length of time taken for rehearsing the task before the experimenter was called, and pointing. The older the child, the more strategies used.

Grouping into categories. In another experiment Moely and his associates (1969) asked children to remember common objects which could be grouped into categories. In general it was shown that grouping into categories occurred spontaneously only with older children and that grouping into categories improved recall, whether the grouping was done spontaneously or with help from the experimenter.

Retrieval Processes

A number of studies show that we forget things, not because they have not been stored in memory, but because we are not able to cue into the particular area where that information is stored. Perhaps an example will help to clarify this. Suppose a tutor is in his study marking an assignment. In the assignment he comes across a reference to a book he does not possess and being of a suspicious nature he decides to check up on it. Relying on his memory for the book title the tutor sets off to the library. On his way he meets a colleague and they become involved in an animated conversation about a film they have both seen recently. After this the tutor proceeds to the library, only to find he has forgotten the name of the book. He returns to his study and as he opens the door, he sees the student's name on the top of the assignment. Immediately the title of the book flashes into his mind. He has been *cued* back to the area in memory, without actually needing to open up the assignment and look up the name of the book. This indicates that part of memory lies in the ability to *retrieve* stored information. As in acquiring information, so in retrieving information, strategies are very important.

Labelling at the retrieval stage. A number of studies show that younger children can recall lists as well as older children, if they are given cues for organising the lists, not only as they learn the lists, but also before they are required to recall the lists. This seems to show that older children not only categorise information on input to memory but are also more likely to use these category systems spontaneously at recall. Younger children need to be helped at the recall stage by appropriate cues because they do not automatically call such strategies into play.

Organising by semantics (meaning). In addition, it has been shown that, the older they get, the more likely children are to organise lists by meaning and not by sound. Thus asked to remember the following list – book, nuts, magazine, bread, melons and newspapers, the younger child may tend to categorise as follows: two words beginning with 'B', two with 'M' and two with 'N'; whereas the older child may say 'three to read and three things to eat'. And in general, the second, semantic (meaning) categorisation is more efficient than the one based on sound.

Self-Awareness in memory skills. Hagen and his associates (1979) review a number of studies that show the older the child, the more he knows about how he uses his memory. Thus if you ask children of different ages whether it is easier to learn pairs of words like boy-girl, up-down, or pairs like Mary comes, John goes, the older the child the more likely he will be able to say (correctly) that opposites are easier.

In summary, then, we can see that as the child gets older so his strategies for storing and retrieving information both increase and improve. Further, the older the child, the more active and self-aware he becomes in his efforts to remember.

Before concluding the section on memory, we should of course add that in order to remember anything we must be paying attention. Also level of motivation is important. We cannot remember things in any detail unless we actually want to. Finally anxiety tends to reduce the efficiency of memory processes, as anyone who has ever tried to cram frenziedly for an examination will know!

(iii) *Concept Formation.* When we first referred to concepts, at the beginning of this section, we indicated that concepts represent abstracted characteristics of many events, stimuli or symbols. We form concepts in our day-to-day life by continually coming across members of the particular concept class and then deciding that they are all linked by unifying attributes. In this section we shall first look at the way concepts become progressively more elaborated with age and then we shall look at the basis on which children are likely to form concepts about sorting objects into groups and how this changes with age.

The elaboration of concepts with age

Abstraction. We have already referred to the difference between a concrete concept like 'cat' and an *abstract* one like 'beauty'. It is clear that the more the child is operating in what Bruner has called the symbolic mode, the easier it will be for him to form abstract concepts like justice, intelligence and so on.

Complexity. Concepts differ in the number of simpler concepts we need to define them. For example, the concept of smoke is simple for it rests on the three concepts of wispy, grey substance and rising in the air. The concept of society is *complex* for it includes the concepts of customs, laws, family structure, educational and legal institutions (Mussen *et al.*, 1974). The older the child, the more complex concepts are available to him.

Validity. The *validity* of a person's concept is the degree to which his understanding of it agrees with that of the community at large. The younger the child, the more personal and the less valid his concepts are likely to be. For example, the young child's understanding of love may refer to what he feels for his own family, whereas the adult's concept of love may be linked to religion (love others as you do yourself), politics (brotherly or comradely love for all men), sex, and so on.

Status. The *status* of a concept refers to its degree of clarity and stability in use. A 3-year-old's understanding of a half may be as a part of a whole, whereas by the time he is 6 or 7 he will know that exactly two halves make a whole and that therefore two halves are identical in substance.

Accessibility. Young children may often have an understanding of a concept, say, beauty, in that they will be able to use the word – this is beautiful – but they will not be able to tell you exactly what they mean by the use of the word. The older child, on the other hand, will be able to list some, at least, of the attributes an object must possess for him to label it as beautiful. That is, the older the child, the more *accessible* his concepts become for communication to others.

Relativity of concepts. It is sometimes difficult for a young child to see that a seed, say, is a good thing to play with, but may be a bad thing to eat. He has not learned to judge the concept *relative to its context*. Similarly, if you ask him 'which yellow is darker?' he may respond by saying that yellow is not a dark colour, because he does not understand the question is a relative one and for him yellow possesses the absolute attribution of lightness in comparison to other colours like black and brown.

The implications of these limitations in the child's use of concepts are very clear for the educationalist. She must not assume, without checking it out, that children use concepts in the same way that she as an adult does. However, this analysis rests on the assumption common to process thinking about cognition: children's thinking *is not qualitatively different from adults'*, it is just less elaborated. You will recall this is very different from Piaget's viewpoint that children's thinking is *qualitatively different from adults'*.

Changes of sorting of objects with age. In order to investigate how children form concepts, that is, how they decide on critical attributes underlying a class, a number of studies have been done in the West investigating the way children group objects. Mussen and his associates (1974) summarise a number of these and consider that, in general, the older the child, the more likely they are to use the third rather than the first or second of those listed below:

(1) Functional-locational. This is the kind of system where a child groups objects together because they are all found in the same place, for example, 'all the animals on a farm'.

(2) Functional-relational. This is the kind of system where a child groups objects together because of a relation between them, for example, a pipe and a match because the match can light the pipe.

(3) Superordinate or categorical. This is the kind of system where a child groups objects together because they all share an abstract attribute, for example, all fruit together or all methods of transport together.

In Chapter 2 we mentioned 'disembedded' thinking, and pointed out that in homes where parents are relatively well educated children are encouraged to structure their thinking in ways that are more appropriate to school. They learn, for instance, when considering a thinking problem, to isolate the *particular elements* of the problem and pay attention only to those. Thus, they learn to ignore the external appearances of, say, oranges and bananas and say that they are similar 'because they are fruit'. Clearly they are not similar in their shape or even in their taste, but a child who is accustomed to make the type of analyses that are appropriate to school learns to 'disembed' and reports in the superordinate mode that they are similar because of the abstract quality they share – they are fruit. (Incidentally sometimes the superordinate mode is called the taxonomic mode.)

It seems that children in the West move towards the third system as they grow older, because school tends to encourage the use of such superordinate systems, probably as a result of the kind of thinking needed for mathematics and science. However, as Mussen and his associates themselves note, 'It is not "better" in any absolute sense, to categorize an apple, pear, and plum as fruits (superordinate category) than to say "they grow on trees in orchards" (functional-locational)' (p. 305).

Recently Eleanor Rosch (1977, 1978) and her associates have proposed that psychologists have set up very artificial situations when they have experimented into the way people represent the real world mentally. Rosch has argued that when we think about the real world of concrete objects, we cluster our categories around objects that are most typical of their class. Thus, we all have a picture of a typical 'chair'. When we have to decide whether another object is also a chair, we see how close it is to our picture of a typical chair. So Rosch disagrees with the way other theorists have looked at the formation of concepts about concrete objects. They tend to say we look for common attributes; she argues that we look to see how well objects resemble typical members of the classes of objects we already have.

We think that the novel approach to categorisation proposed by Rosch will lead to a great deal of productive research into the way people classify concrete objects in the real world. But in the meantime it seems reasonable to conclude that when children organise their thinking, they rely on the categories and concepts that have been most useful to them in the past. Thus the particular environment in which a child lives plays a most important part in the way he organises his mental categories. We will return to the significance of environmental variables when we discuss concept formation in a cross-cultural context.

(iv) *Reasoning – generating and testing*

hypotheses. We have now considered three cognitive processes – perception, memory and concept formation – and we are ready to move on to the fourth process in which all three processes previously considered tend to be combined together. Let us consider this fourth process – reasoning – as an activity where hypotheses are generated and then tested. Before moving on to consider experiments in this area let us consider an everyday example of reasoning.

Let us assume a mother has three children aged 4, 6 and 8. She comes into a room where the 4-year-old is playing and reaching up to the top of a cupboard takes out a jar and twists the lid off and places a bag of sweets inside (see Figure 4.9), and leaves the room. The 4-year-old immediately climbs up on a chair and removes the jar. Now he generates the hypothesis that like his mother he can twist the lid. He tries to do this but his hands are not strong enough so he refines the twisting hypothesis by trying to use a cloth to help twist the lid off. This also fails so he settles down to wait until his older sister arrives from school. When he explains the problem to her she generates the hypothesis that perhaps the lid can be knocked off so she tries to do this by banging at the side of the lid with a hammer. When this does not work she refines her hypothesis by trying to lever the lid off with a coin. But once again she is unsuccessful and the two children settle down to wait until the oldest child arrives from school. On being told that neither twisting nor banging nor levering works, the third child is forced to generate a third hypothesis. He considers the dimensions of the problem and then, noting that the lid is metal while the jar is glass, decides to test the hypothesis that the lid may expand more quickly than the jar. Removing the jar to the sink, he runs hot water over the lid and is thus able to remove it as it expands. As you can see from the last sketch in Figure 4.9, the story has a happy ending for the children (until their mother discovers the crime, that is!).

Here the children have been grappling with the problem that the lid was screwed on too tightly. They first generated a 'brute force' hypothesis, then a 'tool' hypothesis and finally solved it by applying a principle of physics. So we can see that problem-solving is in general amenable to generating a series of hypotheses and then testing them systematically.

Changes in reasoning with age. Olson (1966) demonstrated that if children are given a problem to solve, their hypotheses become more specific and

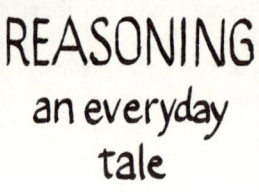

REASONING
an everyday tale

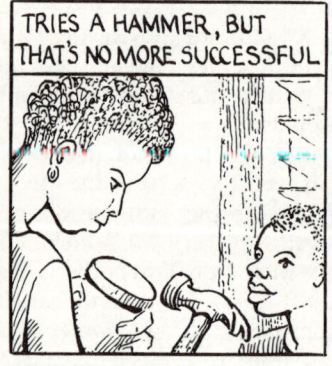

Figure 4.9

precise with age. Children aged 3, 5, 7 and 9 were shown a board with bulbs on. Some of the bulbs would light up if pressed. These bulbs formed a pattern which was hidden until the bulbs were lit up. The children were given two cards printed with patterns. One pattern corresponded to the hidden one. By pressing bulbs they had to discover which it was. This meant that the children had to go on pressing bulbs until they were able to identify which pattern was appearing. The results showed that the older the child, the more likely he was to choose to press bulbs that would give him the most information for the least amount of pressing. This was done by generating different strategies and then analysing the information gained.

In her book on children's cognitive growth, Ault reviews a number of other fairly complex experiments which show that:

(1) even the youngest children approach problem-solving by generating hypotheses, but
(2) the older the child the more likely he is to not only discard incorrect hypotheses, but, in addition, the more likely he is to keep in mind all the hypotheses that have been shown to be correct.

Another aspect of reasoning that is often tested experimentally is the ability to make inferences; that is, to bring two or more different sets of data together. Piaget, as we pointed out before, considers that the young child is not capable of being logical and is therefore not capable of making inferences. Now obviously our ability to put together different sets of data does increase with age and training but it is clear that even young children can think inferentially, as this anecdote about a child less than 6 years old shows (Donaldson, 1978, p. 55). (The child is looking at a book.)

> "But how can it be [that they are getting married]? You have to have a man too."
> (The book contains an illustration of a wedding in which the man looks rather like a woman. The child thinks it is a picture of two women.)
> Premises: (1) You need a man for a wedding.
> (2) There is no man in the picture.
> Conclusion: It can't be a wedding.

Thus we can conclude, as we did at the end of the previous section on concept formation, that children's reasoning is not different in *kind* from adults' but simply less efficient and less precise.

Summary of the four cognitive processes. Before going on to consider in some detail the influence of culture on cognitive processes, let us try and summarise what has emerged from the process approach to cognition.

(1) Underlying the cognitive processes we have looked at, we have assumed that all human beings, no matter what their age, are motivated to make sense of the world surrounding them.

(2) We have suggested that the categorisation of cognitive units into schemata, symbols, concepts and rules is an aid to understanding cognitive processes.

(3) We then differentiated four cognitive activities – perception, memory, concept formation and reasoning. Common to all four is the basic assumption that the human being, no matter what his age, does not just absorb sensory impressions or knowledge. Rather, as Ault writes, 'He constructs an interpretation of the information he has selectively attended to, based on his prior experience, his maturation, and his momentary needs among other factors' (1977, p. 145).

(4) We presented the principle of *moderate novelty*: that we are more likely to process events, facts and concepts that fit into our already existing cognitive network but that are not too discrepant from it.

(5) We stressed the fact that all four cognitive processes commonly overlap. While, for example, we are paying attention to a child reading, we may be making inferences about what the whispers at the other end of the classroom are about and we may be recalling similar disturbances from memory. Thus we may simultaneously be using at least three cognitive processes.

(6) Finally, we have shown that there are developmental changes in all areas of cognition. But we have suggested that it is not that children's thought proceeds differently from the thought of adults. Rather we have argued the processes are the same but less efficient and less elaborated.

Culture and Cognition

> The reasoning and thinking processes of different peoples in different cultures do not differ ... just their values, beliefs and ways of classifying differ.
> (Cole and Gay, 1972, p. 1066)

In the preface to this book we mentioned that much

cross-cultural work has been done in Third World countries and that much of it is very ethnocentric. By this we mean that psychologists from other areas, notably Europe and the USA, came into Third World countries with tests and experiments that tended to be more suitable for their own cultures and that had not been very sensitively adapted for use elsewhere. Thus a vast amount of data was generated that seemed to suggest that people in more traditional societies scored more poorly on tests of thinking than did people in the West. Some commentators went as far as to suggest that this was because vernacular languages are an ineffective 'medium for advanced education, communication and thinking' (Vernon, 1969, p. 231), while others suggested that more traditional cultures did not encourage 'abstract' thought and that people from such areas were more prone to think in concrete terms (for a review of this approach see Leacock, 1972). Others, on the contrary (and we agree with this view), pointed out that the experimental and test situations tend to bias the results in advance (Cole and Scribner, 1974).

In this section we shall review a necessarily small selection of the vast body of cross-cultural literature, following the same structure that was used in the first part of this chapter – namely, an examination of the Piagetian approach, followed by an examination of the cross-cultural data on the four cognitive processes we have been discussing – perception, memory, concept formation and reasoning.

The influence of culture on performance at Piagetian tasks

The largest single body of cross-cultural studies on Piaget's theories would appear to be those dealing with conservation. As we have already discussed this concept fairly extensively in the beginning of this chapter, it seems appropriate to concentrate on this aspect of his theories in evaluating cross-cultural studies on Piaget and their relevance to educational psychology in Third World countries.

One of the most extensive investigations of the development of conservation has been carried out in Senegal by Greenfield among the Wolof tribe (1966). In doing this she looked at the effect of education and urbanisation. To do so she tested children in villages who were unschooled, children in villages who had been to Western-type schools, and children living in the big city of Dakar and attending school. She found that by the age of 11 to

13 (or if they were in Grade VI) all children who had been to school, whether in the city or in the bush, had attained conservation but only half of the unschooled village children had. Thus, like many others working in this area, her results indicated the importance of *schooling* in solving conservation tasks.

However, she also made some other very interesting observations. These concerned non-conservers in the village, who responded that the amount of water in the two beakers was no longer the same because the experimenter had poured it. She reasoned that perhaps the Wolof village children thought that the experimenter had, by some sort of 'action magic', influenced the amount of water, so she repeated the experiment by letting the children themselves do the pouring. As a result of this conservation markedly increased. It seems that this result is similar to the one obtained with Scottish children, by Margaret Donaldson, who also showed an increasing tendency to conserve when the experimental conditions were adapted in such a way as to make them less confusing.

But why is it that some children, and indeed adults, in the village never learned to conserve? As Cole and Scribner write, 'Can we imagine an adult who would pour water from a small bucket into a larger one and believe that the amount of water had been decreased by this act?' (1974, pp. 151–2). Could it be that such subjects are influenced by the unfamiliarity of the apparatus and materials used? Will the number of conservers be increased if more familiar test materials are used? The answer to this question comes from the work of Price-Williams and his associates (1969) who worked in Mexico. They tested children who were matched in every way except that some came from potters' homes and some from homes with other occupational backgrounds. The children who came from potters' homes were better at conservation tasks with substance than the children from other homes. Could it not be then, that, as Margaret Donaldson demonstrated in Scotland, the unfamiliarity of both test materials and test situations handicapped the subjects who were not conservers?

It does seem clear that *ecological* factors (factors connected with the kind of environment people live in) can affect responses to Piagetian tasks. Dasen (1977) gave two types of Piagetian tasks to people from three different backgrounds – Eskimos from Greenland, Aborigines in Australia and Ebrie and Baoule Africans. He showed that hunting people were more likely to solve spatial tasks at an early age and agricultural people to solve conservation tasks.

Schooling has often been shown to have an effect on conservation tasks. We have already mentioned the work of Greenfield in Senegal in this connection but similar results have been obtained elsewhere as well. For example, Owoc (1975) showed an effect for schooling in Nigeria, as did Okonji (1971), and Philp and Kelly (1974) demonstrated an effect for schooling in Papua New Guinea.

Degree of urbanisation, or the extent to which children are in contact with modern industrial society, also affects performance at Piagetian tasks. This has been shown even within a European setting. For example, Peluffo (1967) included in his investigation of conservation children from the following three types of background: traditional (southern Italy), modern industrial (Genoa) and transitional. On the test of conservation only 35 per cent of the traditional sample could conserve whereas 60 per cent and 70 per cent respectively of the other two samples were able to conserve. Poole has shown that in northern Nigeria urban children were better at a whole range of scientific concept attainment tasks including tests of conservation. He considers that the 'paraphernalia of imported culture-schools, factories, airports, clinics, clocks and so forth' (1968, p. 62) are involved in performance at such tasks.

In much the same way Beard (1968), working in Ghana, showed that children from schools that were closest in style to Western schools did better at Piagetian tests of number and quantity. We have already mentioned, as well, the work of Lloyd (1971) who compared children of traditional homes to children of elite homes and showed the latter to be superior at Piagetian tasks.

It seems, then, that as Cole and Scribner (1974) conclude, three different constellations of factors promote good performance at Piagetian tasks: (i) the ecology and the nature of activities engaged in by members of the culture, (ii) schooling and (iii) interactions with Western culture.

Two more points remain to be made about cross-cultural studies of Piagetian tasks. First, as Heron and Simonsson (1969) showed in Zambia, with adequate attention paid to the experimental situation Third World children can score as well as European children of the same age. Secondly, as Barbara Lloyd points out, Piaget's conception of the most sophisticated kind of thinking is heavily influenced by the way Western inquiry into

knowledge has developed. Even Furth, a psychologist who has been extremely heavily influenced by Piaget, has pointed out that 'Piaget studied one limited area of life, the spontaneous growth of the capacity for *scientific thinking* ...' (1970, p. 66, our italics). Thus we think it is fair to conclude that Piaget's work is open to the criticism that it is ethnocentric – that is, it is deeply influenced by its own cultural values.

Perception

In our presentation of perception we pointed out that perception depends not only on the sensory information or impressions being processed, but also on the perceiver's intention, experience and social needs. Thus it is not surprising that much cross-cultural research has shown that different groups pay attention in their perceptual processes to different features of the visual environment. The reader who is interested in this particular aspect of cross-cultural research will find a select bibliography in this area at the end of this chapter. In this section, which deals with the influence of culture on perception, we shall deal only with the one aspect that is of immediate interest to the educationalist. This is pictorial perception and particularly three-dimensional perception. (We will refer to this from now on as 3-D perception and to two-dimensional perception as 2-D perception.)

A number of studies done in the Third World reported that people who were not exposed to *pictorial representation* had difficulty in recognising objects in pictures (Deregowski *et al.*, 1972). A second large number of reports were concerned with the difficulty experienced by subjects in interpreting 3-D cues. In particular a number of the last group of studies referred to difficulties associated with Hudson's pictures (Hudson, 1960).

Figure 4.10 shows one of Hudson's pictures. When the subject was tested on this particular picture, he was first asked to identify the items represented: man, spear, elephant, tree, hill, antelope. Next he was asked, 'What is the man doing?' If the subject reported that the man was throwing a spear at the antelope, he was regarded as having interpreted correctly the picture's 3-D cues, the chief one being that the antelope is nearer because it appears larger in the picture. Subjects who answered that the man was throwing the spear at the elephant were also those who perceived the elephant as nearer than the antelope, thus misinterpreting the 3-D cues (Hudson, 1960).

Figure 4.10   One of Hudson's pictures designed to test 3-D perception (Hudson 1960)

A number of studies replicated Hudson's finding in showing that some subjects were not able to make a 3-D inference from the 2-D representation on the paper. However, Serpell (1976), in discussing this area of investigation, points out how Hudson's wording may have biased the answers. A study by Omari and Cook (1972) showed that changing the wording increased the number of 3-D responses. Further, a study by Deregowski (1968) in Zambia, where subjects were asked to copy 3-D drawings with wire by making a model, showed that subjects could be regarded as 2-D responders on Hudson's pictures, yet nevertheless be capable of making 3-D models.

Both these findings and many others cast doubt on the two allegations that Third World subjects either cannot recognise objects represented in pictures and/or cannot make three-dimensional inferences from two-dimensional pictures (see Serpell, 1976, pp. 89–104). Nevertheless, it is clear that culture can contribute to the ease with which subjects are able to interpret 'correctly' the information a picture is intended to convey. By the term 'correctly' we mean that he can interpret what the artist or photographer is intending to represent.

To get some idea of how culture affects such responses we will look at a study by Leach (1978) done recently in Zimbabwe.

Leach argues that two important variables are involved in such studies: first, the pictorial test materials used and secondly the kind of test procedures used. First, the quality of the pictures clearly influences the responses. Thus in his own study both photographs and line- and tone-drawings produced more 3-D responses in his young Shona subjects than did outline drawings of the kind used in Hudson's pictures. Also, adapting the experimental procedure so that the experimenter pointed to the items the subjects had to identify, and conducting the experiment in a relaxed and naturalistic manner, helped to eliminate the 'excessive amount of constant error' generated by the usual artificial and restricting laboratory-type testing (Leach, 1978, p. 421). But Leach made other important findings, which are also shown in other studies. First, the more urbanised the children, the higher they scored, and secondly, training in the interpretation of 3-D cues produced higher scores.

Thus, as with the Piagetian experiment, we find

that culture may affect performance at Western-type tests because of the type of materials and the type of experimental procedure. Further we find that degree of urbanisation can affect test performance and finally that actual training in how to interpret the material will increase scores.

However, unlike the Piagetian tasks, this research has important and immediate implications for the educationalist. This is that illustrated material used in textbooks should be carefully scrutinised and the following points always borne in mind:

(a) Line- and tone-drawings should be used in preference to outline drawings where possible, and in the same way when photographs are used there should not be too much unnecessary detail in them (Serpell, 1976; Leach, 1978).

(b) Science diagrams should be carefully inspected and, where necessary, the conventions used in them fully explained. For example, in Figure 4.11 (which is a typical diagram of a beaker with a glass rod fitted into the cork and has been copied from a chemistry textbook) it seems as though the cork in the top of the beaker is transparent and that the rod can be seen through it. The picture, however, merely represents according to the accepted convention a cork, with a glass rod passing through it, at the end of a beaker. The cork is not, of course, transparent. It is important then for the teacher to make such conventions very clear to the pupil, particularly if the actual apparatus is not available for the child to see.

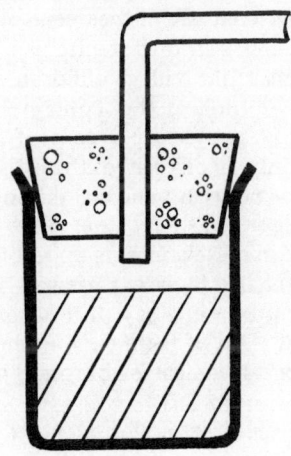

Figure 4.11
A typical chemistry illustration

(c) Cartoons may not be suitable for use in rural areas. For example, Serpell writes: 'Thus, Duncan et al. (1973) found that the small lines used by Western cartoonists to imply motion were the least understood of all the pictorial conventions they represented to rural African schoolchildren. And where the artist had drawn the head of a boy in three different positions above the same trunk [body] to indicate that he was turning his head around, about half the children concluded that the boy represented was deformed' (1976, pp. 109–10). However, as Serpell notes, Western observers have similar difficulties interpreting, for example, the art of the Nuba in the Sudan.

Memory

Quite clearly, the great majority of members of every culture can remember events and objects well enough to cope with their immediate needs. For this reason, we should not be surprised that different cultures lay stress on different memory strategies. This is most neatly illustrated in a clever and subtle set of experiments done by Cole and his associates in Liberia (Cole and Scribner, 1974) with Kpelle subjects.

They required subjects to remember lists of items that could be 'clustered': for example, plate, calabash, pot, pan, cup, which could be clustered as utensils; potato, onion, banana, orange, coconut (food); cutlass, hoe, knife, file, hammer (tools); and trousers, singlet, headtie, shirt, hat (clothes). The standard procedure was for the test list to be presented and recall asked for in five successive trials. In general it was found that whether lists or words were read out, or actual objects shown, Kpelle children performed worse than American children of the same age. However, educated Kpelle children performed better than uneducated children. In addition, American children tended to 'cluster' the words as they recalled them but the Kpelle did not. Further, Kpelle adults did not perform much better than very young children.

Does this mean that memory processes among the Kpelle are inferior to those among American children? Once again the reader might suspect that the unfamiliar nature of the task might lower the performance for the Third World children, and indeed once again this appeared to be the case.

It became clear that it was not that the Kpelle children could not remember the words, but that they did not perform well in the free recall situation. By use of the following procedure, Cole and his associates were able *to bring Kpelle performance up to the American standard.* As they were asked to recall the lists, the experimenter said, for example, 'Tell me all the *clothing* you remember' (Cole and Scribner, 1974, p. 131). Thus it was shown that the material was available in memory but was not accessible. By teaching the appropriate recall strategy, the experimenters could induce 'good recall and highly organised recall' (p. 132).

As we have said before, Western schooling emphasises certain cognitive strategies – in particular it teaches pupils to search out for underlying taxonomic or superordinate categories. This is what was particularly required in the memory task, and is why the American and educated subjects could perform better than the adults and children of rural Kpelle. But once the appropriate strategy was mastered, recall was the same for both cultural groups.

Cole and his associates were further able to show that if the Kpelle were asked to recall lists of words that fitted into a story they were able to show very high and well-organised recall. This last experiment showed that among the rural Kpelle 'recall processes [are] flexible and responsive to the structure provided in the to-be-remembered material, even when the structure is based on taxonomic categories' (p. 134).

Once again, as with perception and the performance of Piagetian tasks, we see that rural children who are unfamiliar with the cognitive demands of the test situation do not do well at Western-type tasks. But once again we note the three important points:

(1) As these tasks are close to those demanded in the school situation it has an important implication for the educationalist, who should be aware that the more urban the environment, and the more 'Western' the background, the more likely the child will be to do well at school-type tasks.

(2) However, the appropriate strategies can be taught.

(3) It is not that rural children are cognitively inferior, but that different environments or cultures stress different aspects of cognition.

Concept Formation
When we discussed concept formation earlier in this chapter, we reported that within the Western school system children are encouraged to group things, that is, induce concepts underlying sets of things, by looking for what we called superordinate categories, that is, abstract and underlying features that they hold in common; for example, to group oranges, bananas and mangoes together because 'they are fruits' rather than because 'they all grow on trees'. That is, the former, taxonomic or superordinate, category is taught rather than the latter, functional, category. But we stressed that one category system is not necessarily superior to the other, although it does fit in better with the kind of thinking demanded in school, particularly in mathematics and science.

A very interesting and sensitive experiment in this area was carried out by Maccoby and Modiano (1969). They worked with both peasant and urban samples of children aged 12 to 13 years of age in Mexico. The children were given a number of tasks but the one we shall concentrate on is 'differences and equivalences'. Here the children were asked how objects were similar and how they were different. The following items were used: banana, orange, bean, meat, milk, water, air, fire and stone. 'In each case the first two items were presented and the children were asked, "How are a banana and an orange similar?" ... After they had answered, they were asked, "How is a bean different from a banana and an orange?" and then, "How are a bean, a banana and an orange all alike?" ' (p. 24).

The responses were grouped into three different types, two of which, the concrete and abstract, were contrasted. An abstract response is one of the type 'all these are necessary for life'. Not surprisingly, in view of the evidence we have been quoting in this chapter, 32 per cent of the urban children gave this sort of response as compared to only 5 per cent of the village children.

But when we look at the 'concrete' responses, which were given by 69 per cent of the peasant children and only 30 per cent of the urban children, we see that it is not that village children cannot use superordinate concepts – *they can*. They choose not to do so because these concepts do not satisfy their ways of organising their experience. Thus a girl falling in this group can say of a banana, orange, bean and meat: 'All of them can be eaten but they are not alike because meat is not round nor is it like a banana or bean' (p. 27).

The village children preferred not to make the generalising statements of an abstract variety that are regarded as conceptually preferable in most school systems. Instead they often preferred to isolate objects in unique and often poetic detail. Thus one village child said 'Banana is like a horn, the orange a ball; and the bean, a little heart; they are not alike' (p. 27).

The 'abstract' children were so influenced by the superordinate similarities they found that they quite lost sight of objects' actual perceptible differences. In Margaret Donaldson's term, which we have used before, they were so 'disembedded' in their thinking that they no longer even considered it worthy of notice that bananas look like 'horns' and oranges like 'balls' and beans like 'hearts' – they had learned to ignore completely the perceptible (visual) differences.

Thus Maccoby and Modiano conclude that there is a continuum. At one end lie the peasant children, who are capable of making abstract categories, but prefer not to because in their own environment they are highly concerned with the concrete nature of things. At the other end of the continuum fall the urban children who concentrate on abstract formulations because these have implications for the intellectual tasks required in a more technological environment. But 'Neither end of the continuum appears to us more mature than the other. Rather, they represent different cultures' (p. 31).

Once again we reach the same conclusion. Rural environments are less favourable to inducing the kind of thinking required in schools *but* this does not mean that children's cognitive development is less mature or inferior in villages compared to towns. Different cultures stress different approaches; but we cannot say one is 'better' than the other.

Reasoning
The final cognitive process we presented was reasoning. We pointed out that all human beings employ hypotheses and inference as they make sense of the world around them, and that the older they grow the more children are able to bear a number of different hypotheses in mind at the same time. Does culture affect such processes?

Clearly, we all make inferences all the time. For example, a child may reason as follows: 'Hasan has just shared his sweets with me, I know he doesn't like me because he never chooses me to be in his team at sports. So there must be another reason. Oh, yes, perhaps he's heard my father has a new car and he wants to be invited for a ride.' This surely is inferential thinking.

Kagan and Klein (1973) showed that young rural children in Guatemala coming from very restricted backgrounds were able to solve riddles requiring inferential thinking. For example, they could solve questions like 'What moves trees, cannot be seen and makes one cold?'. Chowo (1978) too describes how common riddles are in Tanzanian rural areas. Similarly inspection of literature and folk tales reveals inferential thinking at high levels in all known human cultures. So, clearly, inferential reasoning is not confined to urban, technological culture. But on the other hand formal testing of hypotheses, within a logical sequence, is a skill that is encouraged by schooling, within a Western-type setting.

We see this very clearly in a survey of 140 children conducted by Ghuman (1975). He compared three groups of children: Punjabi boys growing up within a traditional Punjabi culture in the Punjab, India; Punjabi boys growing up in Birmingham, England; and English boys. He gave them a large number of psychometric tasks but the one we would like to consider, in this section, is Vygotsky blocks.

This is a set of twenty-two blocks which have to be sorted. The blocks differ in colour, shape, height and size of horizontal surface. The subjects are required to sort the blocks into four groups and their strategies in sorting are carefully noted and analysed to give five levels of explanation. These range from the most sophisticated hypothesis which takes into account the fact that two criteria have to be combined, to the simplest where the subject gives no explanation and cannot repeat his sorting scheme.

The results indicated there were no significant differences between the Punjabi boys living in England and the English boys, but both did significantly better than the Punjabi boys living in India. Ghuman explains this difference between the two sets of boys of Punjabi origin with reference to two factors that should by now be very familiar to the reader. First, there is the influence of the ecology. In the Punjab, children are reared in a way that does not encourage the child to analyse the environment in a formal way (note the similarity to Maccoby and Modiano's conclusion); further the technical know-how in the village is limited and confined to very few people. Secondly, in his in-depth analysis of the schools the children attended, Ghuman concludes that within the village school there was no opportunity for 'children to explore, manipulate and make things for themselves' (p. 98). Also in the village the 'authority of the teacher is supreme' (p. 98) and he considers that the Indian schools do not give scope for the kind of analytical, logical skills which are required in the tests he used.

Once again, the three types of factors that we have been considering are invoked to explain culture's effect on cognition: the ecology in which the child grows up, the degree of urbanisation – or the degree to which there is an influence of technological know-how, and schooling. Clearly of course, in all the studies we have considered the three factors tend to be interrelated.

Summary on Culture and Cognition

Thus it is clear that culture influences cognition. All cultures promote cognition, but they promote the type of cognitive analysis that suits their own demands. This has the following important implications:

(1) If a society is interested in promoting a type of education that will produce formally analytic and technologically inclined types of thinking, then the more urban the environment and the more 'Western' the school, the more children will be inclined to excel at analytic, formal and Western-type tasks.

(2) Nevertheless a number of studies, that purport to show that Third World children are poor at certain tasks, are severely to be criticised in that they are insensitive and ill-adapted to the subjects' understanding. Thus subjects fail to do well at some tasks, not because of their own conceptual inadequacies, but because of the inadequacies of the experimenter and his technology.

Summary

This chapter is the most complex and demanding of the book. This is because of the difficulties inherent in 'thinking about thinking'.

(1) First we differentiated between two approaches to cognition.

(2) Then we considered the first approach – a stage approach exemplified by the work of the great Swiss psychologist Piaget. This rests on the assumption that children pass through four distinct phases in their thinking development. Each stage rests on the other, and the thinking in each stage is *qualitatively* different from each other stage.

(3) We then presented some recent criticisms of the Piagetian approach but concluded that Piaget nevertheless has an important message for the educationalist in his claim that cognitive development is in constant interaction with the environment and that therefore the child's environment should be as stimulating as possible with the emphasis, particularly for younger children, on the active handling and manipulation of materials.

(4) We then presented a process approach to cognition, differentiating four units of cognition: schemata, symbols, concepts and rules; and four processes: perception, memory, concept formation and reasoning.

(5) Underlying the process approach to cognitive development are the following principles:

 (a) All human beings are motivated to make sense of their world.

 (b) Sensory impressions and knowledge are not just absorbed in a passive manner. Rather, humans construct an interpretation of the information they have selectively attended to, based on their experience, maturational level and their immediate and long-term needs.

 (c) We are most likely to process those events, facts and concepts that fit into our already existing cognitive networks but that are not too different from them.

 (d) All cognitive processes overlap and may take place simultaneously.

 (e) There are developmental changes in cognition; as children grow older, their cognitive processes become sharper and more elaborated.

(6) Finally we looked at some of the massive amount of data on the effect of culture on cognition. We concluded that whether we looked at Piagetian tasks, perception, memory, concept formation or reasoning, the following emerged.

 (a) Sometimes experimental results, purporting to show that Third World subjects performed worse than those in Western societies, demonstrated, on the contrary, inadequacies in the experimental methodology and approach of the experimenters.

 (b) Nevertheless culture can affect performance at cognitive tasks. On Western-type tasks, the following factors appear to affect performance: the ecology in which the subject lives, the degree of urbanisation and Westernisation and the amount of schooling received.

Chapter 4: Selected Bibliography

On Piaget
Beard, R. M., *An Outline of Piaget's Developmental Psychology* (London: Routledge & Kegan Paul, 1969).
Furth, H. G., *Piaget for Teachers* (Englewood Cliffs, NJ: Prentice-Hall, 1970).
Piaget, J., *The Child's Construction of Reality* (London: Routledge & Kegan Paul, 1958).

Criticisms of Piaget
Bryant, P., *Perception and Understanding in Young Children* (London: Methuen, 1974).
Donaldson, M., *Children's Minds* (Glasgow: Fontana/Collins, 1978).

Cognition in general
Ault, R. L., *Children's Cognitive Development* (New York: OUP, 1977).

Floyd, A. (ed.), *Cognitive Development in the School Years* (London: Croom Helm in association with the Open University Press, 1979).
Gruneberg, M. M., and Morris, P. (eds), *Aspects of Memory* (London: Methuen, 1978).
Turner, J., *Cognitive Development* (London: Methuen, 1975).

Cultures and cognition
Cole, M., and Scribner, S., *Culture and Thought* (New York: Wiley, 1974).
Lloyd, B. B., *Perception and Cognition* (Harmondsworth: Penguin, 1972).
Serpell, R., *Culture's Influence on Behaviour* (London: Methuen, 1976).
Warren, N. (ed.), *Studies in Cross-Cultural Psychology*, Vol. 1 (London: Academic Press, 1977).
Wober, M., *Psychology in Africa* (London: International African Institute, 1975).

Perceptual aspects of cross-cultural research
Lloyd, op. cit., chs 3 and 4.
Serpell, op. cit., chs 3 and 6.

PART TWO
THE PRIMARY SCHOOL YEARS

In the second part of the book we turn our attention to the primary school.

In Chapter 5 we look at the child's social and emotional adjustment to school. In doing so we examine his growing awareness of himself as an individual and we consider how this is affected both by his relationship with others – his fellow pupils and teachers – and by his perception of his own performance at school. Once we have considered these motivational aspects of the child's behaviour, we are able to move on to the process of learning.

In Chapter 6 we consider both theoretical and practical aspects of learning. In addition we look at the learning needs of special children.

SOCIAL AND EMOTIONAL ADJUSTMENT IN THE PRIMARY SCHOOL YEARS

5

' Self-concept is not some mystical abstract construct that can only be discerned by people with the right kind of eyesight, but a psychological reality that is helpful for distinguishing behavioural similarities and differences among people. '

(Hamachek, 1978, p. 221)

Introduction

In this chapter we are going to consider the child's social and emotional behaviour in the primary school within the context of self theory. Briefly, self may be defined as the knowledge we all have of ourselves that embraces our past history, our present existence and our expectations of our future life. Why do we place such an emphasis on self theory? Because it supplies a unifying framework with which we can attempt an insight into the way people perceive themselves both as private and social beings. Before we consider the practical applications we can make of self theory within the educational environment, we present a brief introduction to the topic of self.

Self Theory

Interest in self theory has been very marked in recent years. We can distinguish three different threads that led to this interest. From our point of view perhaps the most important of these emerged from *empirical* (experimental or observational) *research*. In many instances psychologists, trying to predict how people would behave under certain circumstances, found that although they were using the most sophisticated tests available another method of prediction was better. Presumably you will be curious about this method and will no doubt expect that it was rather a complicated procedure. Are you surprised to learn that the best predictor was simply asking subjects themselves how they thought they would behave? In other words, insight into other people can be gained by asking them how they view themselves.

Another source of interest in self emerged from the *consulting rooms* of clinical psychologists. Many reported that patients would sometimes say things like 'I don't feel like myself any more' or 'I really was most surprised to see myself doing that' or 'You know, I'm really not that kind of person'. These remarks indicated to psychologists like Carl Rogers that patients (as well as other people, naturally) carried around an inner picture of themselves. Rogers, in particular, became convinced that if this self-picture satisfied certain conditions, then the individual concerned could be regarded as being in a good position, psychologically speaking, to deal with all the demands of life. What were these conditions? First, the self-picture should be fairly *consistent*, that is, the individual should be able to recognise in himself both the child of the past and the adult of the present and should also not see himself as altering radically from situation to situation or from time to time. Secondly, the individual should be able to *accept within that picture of himself all aspects of his behaviour*. In other words, he should be able to integrate within his self-picture both his good and his bad points and while wanting to change those aspects of himself he does not approve of, would not deny that they are there. Thirdly, the individual, without denying his past, should view himself as moving all the time towards an *acceptance of himself as a growing, evolving being who is open to new experiences and accepting of other people*.

Another important point made by Rogers, as well as by other psychologists, is that if individuals have a healthy and realistic evaluation of themselves, if they have self-respect and in general regard themselves in a positive light, then they will be able to interact positively and constructively with other people because they will not be preoccupied with worries about their own worth as individuals.

The third thread of interest in self theory lies in the work of certain *sociologists* such as Mead. Mead (1934) describes how the child learns to have ideas about himself which are similar to those held about him by the other important people ('significant others') in his life. Through the views of these people, and the way they treat him, Mead believes the child will form various pictures of himself that will influence his behaviour in certain situations. Thus the child can have a 'home' self, a 'school' self, and so on.

If you are interested in pursuing this topic in depth, you will find a selected bibliography at the end of the chapter. In the meantime we will explore self theory under the following headings: (see Figure 5.1).

(1) The self, self-concept and self-esteem.
(2) One self or many selves?
(3) Cross-cultural validation of the idea of self concept.
(4) Are we always conscious of self?

(1) *Self, self-concept and self-esteem*
There are very many definitions of self. We have already given one at the beginning of this chapter. Perhaps one of the clearest is given by Hamachek in

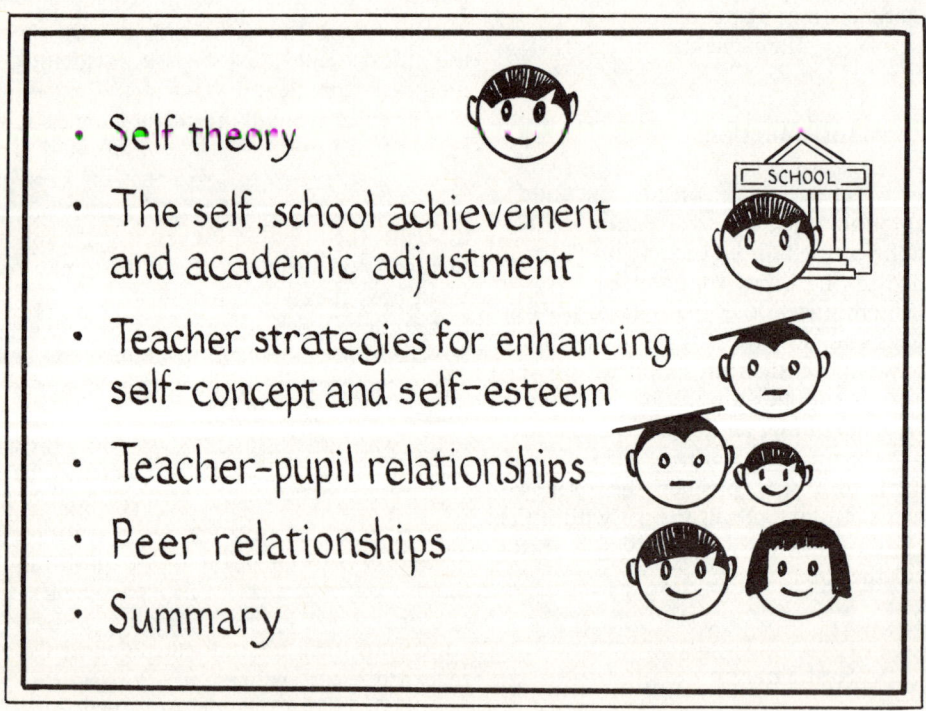

- Self theory
- The self, school achievement and academic adjustment
- Teacher strategies for enhancing self-concept and self-esteem
- Teacher-pupil relationships
- Peer relationships
- Summary

Figure 5.1 Structure of Chapter 5

his book devoted to self theory, *Encounters with the Self* (1978): self is 'that very private picture each of us has which reflects who we think we are, what we feel we can do, and how best we think we can do it' (p. vii). It is, then, that part of ourselves of which we are aware. Jersild (1952) puts it at some detail as follows:

> ❛ A person's self is the sum total of all he can call his. The self includes, among other things, a system of ideas, attitudes, values and commitments. The self is a personal total subjective environment; it is the distinctive center of experience and significance. The self constitutes a person's inner world as distinguished from the outer world consisting of all other people and things. ❜

We shall differentiate two overlapping components of self. The first is *self-concept* and this refers to the organised *cognitive* representation we have of ourselves – it is what we *think* we are like. It is the kind of person we *think* we are. You will notice the repetition of the word think – this is because it is the cognitive part of our self-picture.

Self-esteem, the other component of self, is as you might expect, the feeling or affective part of our self-picture. It is the way we feel about who we are and reflects whether we feel we are worthy or not; it is the *valuing* part of our picture of ourself.

It is a central contention of this chapter that the child who has adequate self-esteem is one who is in a good position to take advantage of education. A child who considers himself at least as good as other children and a person worthy of other people's interest is one that we might regard as having a reasonable measure of self-esteem. We think the following example may illustrate why it is important for children to have a reasonably high level of self-esteem.

We will consider the case of two little girls who are just about to start school. The first girl comes from a small family, where the parents devote a lot of time to their children and consequently her home life is happy. Her needs for love and security, praise and recognition have been met and as a result she is reasonably confident about herself and regards herself as worthy of other people's interest. Her self-concept, if she could verbalise it (put it into words), might go something like this: 'I am quite a clever little girl because I can do all sorts of things to help at home. I like playing with other children and I am very excited about going to school.' In addition, her self-esteem is quite high because she

knows her own family love and value her.

The second little girl has had a less fortunate childhood. Her family is large and no one has enough time in her busy home to pay too much attention to her. Like her brothers and sisters she has come in for a great deal of criticism from her parents. Although she is excited about going to school, she is also rather apprehensive and fearful. Her self-concept, if she could verbalise it, might run something like this: 'I'm really a bit of a nuisance – I bet my mother is glad I'm going to school – there'll be one less person at home to worry about. I hope I'll be able to do my schoolwork as well as the other children in the class because there's not much I'm good at at home.' Unlike the first little girl, her self-esteem is rather low. No one has given her the praise and recognition that all children need. Even though her parents may love their children dearly, they have been too busy and harassed to convey this to them.

Now let us suppose that these two little girls are placed next to each other at school. They have a kind and committed teacher and gradually even the second little girl begins to feel confident, happy and effective in the classroom. Unfortunately, the teacher becomes ill, and a replacement teacher is sent to take the class our two little girls are in. The replacement teacher is not very good-tempered, and her first action, on entering the classroom, is to say in a very angry voice: 'What a noisy lot! Why haven't you all got your books out?' Then, choosing at random, she points at our two little friends and says in an even angrier tone: 'What are you two staring at? I can see I'm going to have a lot of trouble from you.'

Our first little girl, sure of her self-worth and confident that she was doing nothing wrong, thinks: 'My goodness, what a bad-tempered teacher. I hope our other teacher comes back soon.' But the second little girl has her deep-seated feelings of inadequacy confirmed and she thinks: 'Oh, that teacher can see I'm not much good to anyone. I'm sure I'll never be able to do well at school. I may have been all right so far, but that was just an accident – I'm not really the type of girl who will do well at anything.'

This incident should serve to make our point clear. There are home influences which act to raise or lower a child's self-esteem in comparison with other children. Those who are high in self-esteem are better able to cope with, for example, critical remarks made by teachers or bullying incidents in the playground. Those who are low in self-esteem, on the other hand, will be easily upset and thrown into a depressed state by any critical remark by a teacher or any rejection in the playground.

It seems to us then, that understanding children's pictures of themselves, or attempting to gain insight into their self-concepts and their level of self-esteem, is a most important part of any teacher's role. For, as Hamachek says, 'It is through the door of self that one's personality is expressed' (p. 3).

(2) *One self or many selves?*

We have already mentioned the view taken by sociologists like Mead who tie self-picture to role and consider, therefore, that we may have a series of different selves – one at home, perhaps, another at work and yet a third at play. What kind of relationship do these selves have? Are they separate and dependent only on the situations we find ourselves in? The view taken by most psychologists who write on self theory, and with which we agree, is that by the time we reach adulthood we should have an underlying consistency in our picture of ourselves that helps to *integrate* the various roles we play. Of course we behave differently with different kinds of people and on different occasions – we present one facet of ourselves when we are at home with our parents, and another when we are at a party with our friends. But certain underlying values and attitudes are held in common from situation to situation and from role to role. If we can see no relationship between ourselves in different situations and at different times, we tend to feel confused and disoriented (unsure of which direction we are moving in). This state of mind is often typical of adolescence but most adults have a fairly consistent view of themselves. It seems that although we play different roles in different situations, certain threads run through our personal functioning because we remain fairly consistent in our values, attitudes and relationships. If we look back, say, on the activities of the previous year, we can relate to the way we felt when they happened. Our friendships and our personal interactions show a continuity and if we are asked to describe the kind of person we are, or fill in a questionnaire, we are able to make general statements about ourselves that indicate that we do have a reasonably clear self-picture.

At the primary school level, of course, we should not expect a child to have any clear self-picture that could be verbalised or described in any detail. Nevertheless, the child is beginning to accumulate information about himself. He does this in three important ways. To begin with, he learns about himself because people tell him things about himself: 'Aren't you a clever little boy?' or 'Isn't it surprising what good football players there are in this year's primary three class!' or 'The children in our family are always respectful to their elders'. Secondly, he learns about himself from the way other people treat him; he will note whether he is listened to or not, whether people respect his wishes, and so on. Finally, he learns about himself by relating his behaviour to the behaviour of other children and noting what he can and cannot do in comparison to them and how he compares with them on different measures. Gradually different 'snapshots' of himself form. In late adolescence he will begin to integrate and combine these self-impressions and eventually a fairly stable self-concept will emerge. Accompanying these 'snapshots' of himself will be an accumulation of attitudes towards, and feelings about, himself that we can call his level of self-esteem. These feelings will relate to the degree to which he feels he is a worthy person.

In summary, then, we note that although the primary school child does not have a clear, articulate and stable self-concept, nevertheless he does have a set of attitudes about himself that we can call his level of self-esteem, and which relate to his sense of personal worth.

(3) *Cross-cultural validation of the construct of self*

Self theory emerges from Western culture. It could be argued that it reflects a typically Western emphasis on the individual rather than the group. Does it, then, have any utility in other cultures? It seems to us that any situation which facilitates comparisons between individuals will promote concepts of self and feelings about self-adequacy. Such situations tend to occur in most schools. They also occur in many families where children draw comparisons between themselves and their siblings. It seems likely, then, that self theory will be applicable in most societies, to a greater or lesser extent, and will be of particular relevance within an institutional setting such as a school.

Of course the factors that contribute to self-concept and self-esteem will vary from society to society. Self-esteem is raised when we feel of value to other people and self-concept is related to the things we can do and the kind of person we see ourselves as being. Different cultures value different kinds of personal relationships and different achievements. For example, the Tangu of New Guinea place an importance on co-operation in interpersonal relationships, whereas in the West there is rather more emphasis on competition. Some societies value material achievement whereas others emphasise the importance of spiritual balance. So clearly, if self-esteem derives from satisfying the values of one's culture, and self-concept is shaped by the roles one plays, we might expect that the factors contributing to self will differ from society to society; but this does not detract from the validity of the construct of self. It is bound to be of importance where individuals compare themselves with others and where they are judged by others. These two conditions hold in most schools, as we have already noted, and it is therefore likely that perception of self is an important variable in pupils' behaviour, no matter where they live.

In the remainder of this chapter we shall be drawing mainly on Western research because this is an area of educational psychology that has not, as yet, received a great deal of attention within Third World settings. Two studies are, however, relevant.

The first, by Wober (1971), confirmed the point we have just made that the factors involved in perception of self will differ from culture to culture. He showed that the degree to which self-esteem derived from social rather than personal judgements varied between cultures. He defined two aspects of self-perception – those deriving from what he termed social constructs – Baptist, daughter, college student, and so on – and those deriving from what he termed individual aspects – intelligent, bored, and so on. He found that the balance of the two aspects differed between the societies he investigated (Indian, Maltese, Nigerian, British and Canadian) in a way that reflected differences in social context.

The second study showed the validity of measures of self-concept in Nigeria. It was done by Bakare (1975) with a sample of Nigerian schoolchildren. He found that his measure of self-concept differentiated between two pre-identified groups of students – 'successful' and 'failing' students.

It would seem, then, that we can usefully view relationships within schools in the context of self theory in non-Western cultures.

(4)   *Are we always conscious of self?*
We have argued that our self-picture, and in particular our self-esteem, plays a very important

part in our lives. In many situations we tend to be aware that certain outcomes will be of benefit to us psychologically and certain others will not. For example, in collecting the results of an assessment we would prefer it to be high; we prefer, on the whole, to score well at competitive sports; and, in general, we prefer new acquaintances to react positively to us and older friends to welcome our presence. All these positive outcomes confirm our sense of self-worth. But we are not always so ego- (or self-) involved. We can forget the implications for self in many pursuits – physical pursuits like eating or cycling or walking for pleasure, intellectual ones like struggling to complete a crossword puzzle, artistic and aesthetic ones like playing or listening to music, singing and dancing, looking at pictures or admiring scenery, and finally we can become oblivious (not conscious) of self in prayer and meditation. So although self is most important it is not, of course, the sum of our lives. Nor should it be.

The Self, School Achievement and Academic Adjustment

We have indicated that in order for a child to be able to turn his attention to the primary aim of school learning, he must feel relatively free of doubts and feelings of inadequacy. However, as the anecdote about the two little girls starting school illustrated, some children enter school feeling uneasy about their capabilities and self-worth. What happens to these children?

Paquita McMichael studied a group of 198 Scottish schoolboys. She first interviewed them when they entered school at between 4½ and 5 years of age. She screened them at the cognitive level by using a test of reading readiness, a concept attainment test and a test of verbal ability. In addition she attempted to measure their self-esteem in a very ingenious way. The little boys were shown pictures of other little boys performing certain actions – such as buttoning up their shirts or throwing balls (see Figure 5.2). They were asked if they themselves were similar to the little boys in the pictures and the question centred on two areas: areas of competence (this little boy can do up all his buttons every morning; this little boy can throw the ball higher than any of his friends) and areas of personal worth (this little boy is always getting

Figure 5.2 One of McMichael's pictures (1978)
'This little boy is always being
blamed for things'

blamed for things; nobody listens to this little boy when he wants them to). The child responded by posting a card into a yellow box if the little boy in the picture was 'same as me' and into a blue box if the little boy in the picture was 'not the same'. In this way she obtained measures of competence (a self-concept measure) and personal worth (a self-esteem measure).

She found that, generally speaking, boys who entered the school low on measures of self-concept and self-esteem were likely to be amongst the poorer readers at the end of the first year. However, their own judgement of their low level of competence was accurate. In fact, the children who entered school scoring low on the cognitive measures she used were the same children who both saw themselves as less competent and learned to read with greater difficulty than other children. She concluded that a vivid picture is created of a 'clumsy, inept, small boy, often in the way and ignored except when causing a disturbance, and

then, the object of criticism and possibly more deep-rooted rejection' (1977, p. 124). Thus we can see that the link-up between self-concept, school achievement and academic adjustment occurs early.

Samuels (1977), in her book *Enhancing Self-Concept in Early Childhood*, lists numbers of studies that have shown similar results – poor self-concept goes with low academic achievement. But we may ask which comes first, the chicken or the egg? Do children enter school low in self-esteem, and, unable to pay attention because of this, fail? This is the effect we proposed for our second little girl in the anecdote in the last section. Or, as McMichael's data suggests, are some children perhaps less cognitively advanced than others, therefore likely to fail and consequently to have low self-concepts? It seems that, as Hamachek notes, it is not possible to give a definite answer to this question. Possibly some children, initially quite high in self-esteem, fail because of cognitive immaturity and consequently develop low self-esteem. Other children may be so crippled with feelings of inadequacy that, even if they are cognitively well prepared, they are unable to pay attention to the learning tasks of school. In both cases a spiral is set up unless the teacher steps in and intervenes, either, in the case of the first set of children, by reassuring them and helping them to build up their cognitive skills, or, in the case of the second set, by helping them to build up their sense of self-worth.

We do know that we can experimentally induce failure by making people feel inadequate. Santrock and Ross (1975) worked with children aged 4 to 5 years and found that if some children were made to feel inferior to other children their confidence declined and they did not attend as efficiently as the other children who had not been subjected to this negative feed-back. In a similar way we can induce success by making people feel worthy. Brookover and his associates (1962) showed this in a study of 500 American schoolchildren aged between 13 and 18 years. He showed first of all that achievement was related to self-concept by asking his subjects to tick one of the following categories. Compared to others in my class, my school ability is: (a) among the best, (b) average, (c) below average, (d) among the poorest. He found that high self-concept and good achievement were associated. He then attempted to raise achievement by raising self-esteem. He did this by asking parents not to make negative remarks about their children's performance and always to give praise and encouragement. After a time this treatment resulted in an improvement in self-concept for low achievers and, more important, a rise in achievement levels.

In any event, as Hamachek notes, 'Fortunately the chicken or the egg question is more academic than practical. If we get too caught up in deciding which comes first, we may miss the real issue – namely, the student, who he or she is and where he or she is in development' (1978, p. 200). We can then turn to a far more practical issue – the ways in which teachers can increase self-esteem.

Expectation effects

Before we move on to discussing positive classroom practices that can enhance (or increase) self-esteem and a sense of personal competence and worth, we might perhaps consider some of the large body of evidence that shows that teachers can affect pupil performance by the expectations they hold of them.

The first psychologists to investigate this effect in depth were Rosenthal and Jacobson (1968), who showed that if certain children who were chosen at random (by chance) were labelled as very bright by psychologists they actually showed positive shifts on intelligence test scores. Initially they tested children in the first six years of primary school on an intelligence test and they labelled 20 per cent of these as 'bloomers' – who would show unusual intellectual gains during the year. They then returned eight months later and found that in the first two grades the children labelled as 'bloomers' had showed a significant improvement in intelligence scores, compared with those for whom no positive expectations had been set up.

This experiment has been criticised methodologically but the expectation effect has been confirmed by many others. Palardy (1969), for example, identified five primary one teachers who believed boys to be almost as good at learning to read as girls and five who believed boys to be only about half as good as girls. All the children had scored above average on pre-reading tests and there were no significant differences between the sexes. He then tested reading performance after some time and found that the boys who were taught by teachers who believed boys to be potentially as good as girls learned as well as girls, but the boys whose teachers thought boys to be below girls in reading ability scored less well than the girls in their own classes and also less well than the boys whose teachers did not hold such a negative view of boys' reading ability.

Seaver (1973) investigated something you may always have suspected, namely, that the reputation of older siblings in a school affects the way teachers treat their younger brothers and sisters. Thus, we sometimes hear a teacher say to a new pupil at the beginning of a school year: 'You're John's little brother, are you? My goodness, you look a clever little boy. I'm sure you'll do as well as your big brother'; or, on the contrary: 'Oh, so you're Peter's younger brother, are you? I suppose we'll have just as much trouble from you then.'

Seaver identified a set of younger brothers and sisters who all had older siblings who had been taught by the teacher now teaching the younger member of the family. When the older sibling had been a high achiever, he showed that the younger brother or sister scored significantly higher on eight tests than children of comparable ability in his or her class. When the older siblings had been low achievers, he showed that the younger brother or sister scored lower on these tests than children in his or her class of similar ability. Thus Seaver also demonstrated an effect for teacher expectations.

If we accept, then, that there is evidence that teacher expectations can affect pupil performance, how do we explain the effect? We suggest that it occurs because the teacher treats children of whom she holds firm expectations in such a way that the child concerned 'gets the message', and thus modifies his self-concept in the direction of the message.

Do teachers actually treat children differently if they hold strong expectations about them? There is some evidence that we interact differently on the non-verbal level with different sorts of people. Chaikin and his associates (1974) showed that this can happen in the teaching situation. They asked subjects to tutor 10-year-old boys and videoed them while they were tutoring. Only two boys were used as 'pupils' and these two boys were labelled as 'bright' for a third of the forty-two subjects, as 'dull' for another third, and were not described to the last third of subjects. The two boys were trained to behave consistently with all the tutors. Chaikin found, however, that despite the fact that the pupils actually behaved the same way in all three conditions, the tutors did not. Those who were told that their pupil was 'bright' behaved quite differently from those who were told that their pupil was 'dull' or for whom no expectation had been set up. The tutors of 'bright' pupils smiled more, had more direct eye gaze, leaned forward more and nodded their heads more. Thus, even without words being used, messages can be given.

Good and Brophy (1977) list the following ways that teachers have been observed to differentiate between those whom they regard as high achievers (highs) and those whom they regard as low achievers (lows).

(1) Teachers allow less time for 'lows' to answer questions than they do for 'highs'.
(2) If 'lows' give a wrong answer teachers tend to pass on to the next child, without encouraging the 'low' by saying, for example, 'try again'. On the other hand if 'highs' give a wrong answer, teachers tend to encourage the child to make another attempt.
(3) Teachers praise 'lows' less and criticise 'lows' more than 'highs'.

(4) Teachers pay less attention to 'lows' than they do to 'highs'.
(5) Teachers place 'highs' nearer to them in the classroom than they place 'lows'.

So it does seem that some teachers treat children in different ways and it is more than likely that children observe this treatment and that it affects their self-concepts and self-esteem. Nash (1976) showed that children do observe and interpret teacher attitudes, in a study where he asked each child in a class of thirty-four 12-year-olds to make a rank order of ability for the pupils in their class. He showed that children ranked both themselves and their fellow pupils in much the same way that the teacher did. 'It seems clear that within every classroom there is a considerable degree of shared perception among pupils and teachers' (p. 29).

To return to self-concept, one particular study unites the effect of manipulating teacher expectations and directly manipulating children's self-concepts. It was done by Rappaport and Rappaport (1975). They studied forty-five children aged between 5 and 6 years. These children were selected from a larger group of children because they all scored badly on a pre-reading test. Rappaport and Rappaport divided these forty-five children randomly into five groups of nine as follows:

GROUP ONE. These children were never seen by the experimenter and could act as controls (by controls we mean a group that can be compared to the group that we treat experimentally). These were called the *control* group.

GROUP TWO. These children spent time with the experimenter, being taken away individually to play a game with the experimenter twice a week for twelve weeks, but no attempt was made to either increase their self-concepts or manipulate teacher expectations about them. Thus they were also controls but controls who spent time with the experimenter and thus were called the *interaction control* group.

GROUP THREE. These children also spent time with the experimenter in exactly the same way as the children of group two did. In addition, the experimenter manipulated teacher expectations for this group by telling the teacher about each child who fell into this group that the child had 'strong motivation and potential'. (Of course the teachers were not aware that their expectations were being manipulated experimentally, because they thought the children were taking part in an exercise to make teaching materials.) Thus this group were the *teacher expectation* group.

GROUP FOUR. These children were also taken away in the same way as groups two and three by the experimenter. In addition they were told in very strong terms that they would do very well at school. Thus these children were the *pupil expectation* group because their self-concept was being experimentally enhanced by telling them that they were of high potential.

GROUP FIVE. These children were taken away by the experimenter in the same way as the children in the groups two, three and four. In addition they were told that they would do very well at school and their teachers were also told that they were potentially very able pupils. Thus this last group had their own self-concept enhanced (as group four). In addition teachers' expectations were

manipulated for this group as was the case for group three. Thus this group was called the *teacher–pupil expectation* group.

All forty-five children were re-tested after the twelve weeks, and their increase in test scores was computed. If expectancy and self-concept theory is correct we would assume that the greatest changes would come in group five, where both teacher expectancy and self-concept were manipulated. The next largest change should occur in group four where self-concept was directly manipulated, and the third greatest change in group three where teacher expectations were raised. We would not expect much change in either two control groups. If you look at Figure 5.3 you will see that this is precisely what happened.

It may be concluded, then, that the Rappaport and Rappaport study provides strong evidence both for the effect of raising teacher expectations and for the effect of enhancing self-concept. Further, it suggests that teacher expectations work because teachers who hold positive expectations about

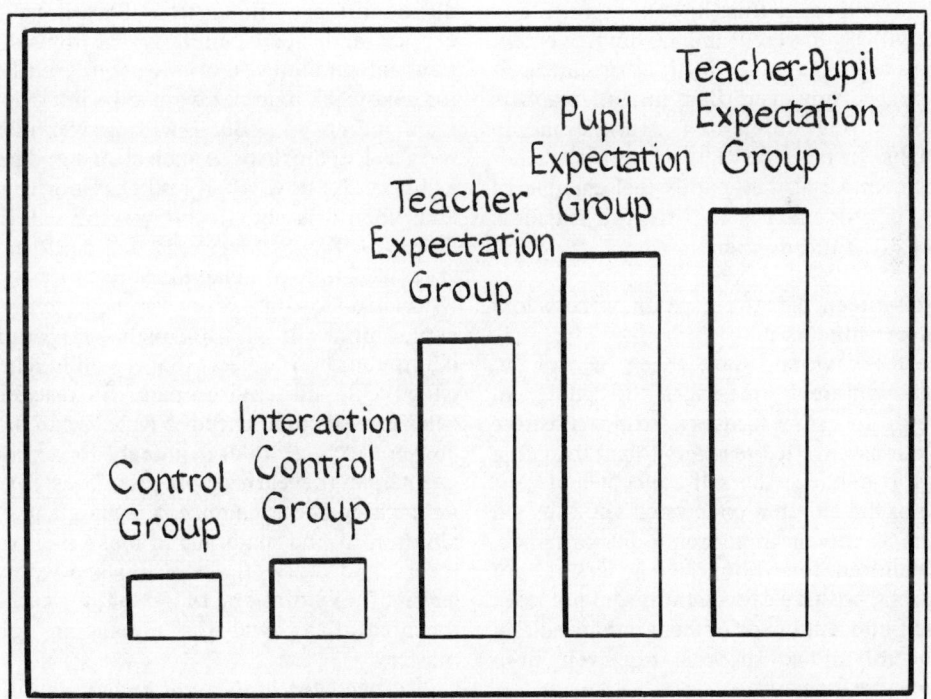

Figure 5.3   Change in test scores for five groups in Rappaport and Rappaport study

children treat them in such a way as to enhance their self-concept, thus ultimately improving achievement.

Of course, not all teachers treat children differently depending on their expectations for them. Indeed, we would want to train teachers in such a way that they treat *all* children in ways that enhance self-concept and raise self-esteem and in the next section we shall look at ways of doing so.

Teacher Strategies for Enhancing Self-Concept and Self-Esteem

So far in this chapter we have made two points. First, without an adequate degree of self-esteem a child will feel an underlying anxiety which will, in all likelihood, interfere with effective learning. Secondly, some research has shown that teachers can convey their expectations of a child's level of performance to the child, and should such expectations be high, the child's self-concept and esteem will be positively affected and the child will show an improvement in academic performance. Alternatively, should the teacher's expectations be low, the child will sense this, his self-concept and self-esteem will be lowered and no improvement will be shown in his academic performance. It should be noted, however, that not all teachers convey such strong differential expectations to different pupils. In fact, the really effective teacher should aim to make all her pupils feel capable of significant improvement in their academic performance. To sum up, then:

(1) High self-esteem aids the learning process, low self-esteem hinders it.
(2) Teacher behaviours have been shown to indicate different messages to different children. In some cases strong positive expectations have led teachers to act in such a way as to enhance the self-concept and self-esteem of the children concerned and thus led to an improvement in academic performance. Other children, for whom the teachers did not hold strong positive expectations, did not have their self-concept or self-esteem enhanced and consequently did not show an improvement in academic performance.
(3) Not all teachers convey such differential expectations. In general it is not a good thing for such differential expectations to be experienced by a class.

(4) Certain teaching strategies produce a general climate of optimism in the classroom, so that all children are encouraged to feel effective and worthy. It is with such strategies that the rest of this section deals.

You will not be surprised to learn that such teaching strategies relate to the four psychological needs that we described in the first chapter. Thus, to begin with, a great deal of research has shown that what Rosenthal has called a *warm social-emotional* mood is associated with effective learning (the need for love). Naturally teachers cannot be expected to love their pupils in the same way as a child's family love the child. Nevertheless, a warm accepting teacher provides a background that is conducive (helpful) to learning.

A teacher has also to provide *security*. By this we mean *firm standards of behaviour*. Warmth does not mean permissiveness. Children should be made very aware of what sort of behaviour is expected of them at specific times. For example, while a teacher may allow a low level of discussion while children are constructing a model, say, as a group activity, she may prefer the class to work without talking during an arithmetic test. This must be made explicit and clear. Similarly she may say: 'I am now going to tell you briefly about your homework for next week. I do not want to be interrupted while I am telling you. But I will answer questions as soon as I'm finished.' If such clear standards are set, a child will know when his behaviour is acceptable and when it is not. In this way he will internalise feelings of worthiness as he conforms to the specified kinds of behaviour.

Related to the *need for new experiences* is exploration. It is through exploration and manipulation of objects that the child learns to feel effective in his environment. So teachers should cater for the child's need to be active in his learning and not expect children merely to remain passive partners in the learning process. Thus, for example, in teaching about balance, a teacher can encourage children to find materials to make their own small levers, and derive the concepts she wants them to learn by exploration, thus making learning more meaningful as well as enhancing feelings of mastery.

The need for *praise and recognition* is basically the need for *feed-back*. As we said in Chapter 1, empty and automatic praise is not effective. Praise should be given when a child has truly made an effort. Recognition of what the child is doing is important. And therefore a key task in increasing feelings of personal worth is to get pupils to perceive for themselves the relationship between success and effort. Good and Brophy (1977) propose the following steps in teaching this relationship between success and effort.

(1) Teachers can get pupils to assess which tasks they find difficult and which tasks they find easy. For example, 'I can do short multiplication but I can't get my long multiplication sums right'.

(2) Teachers can then get the children to check the accuracy of their perceptions. For example, in the case given above, a short test in both kinds of multiplication can be given. This helps the child to set out a programme for himself: 'Since I can do some long multiplication sums right – those with just tens and units are usually right – I'll practise these and move on to hundreds only when I get every single one of the tens and units right.'

(3) The teacher can then help the child to construct a graded set of examples for himself, following on the child's own understanding of what he found easy and what he found difficult.

(4) The fourth step would call for providing the pupil with feedback about his progress on the task. The teacher should encourage the child to proceed as far as he can, and when he is stuck, ask for help. In this way, the teacher creates the expectation that assigned tasks, though appropriately difficult and challenging, can be completed correctly if the student works at them. In other words *success follows on effort*.

The final need we discussed in the first chapter is *responsibility*. One of the most effective ways of encouraging this is to get the class to help set the limits of accepted behaviour themselves. Rules are more likely to be obeyed if pupils help to set them up so they can understand the rationale (reasoning) behind them. But another equally effective way of encouraging children to feel responsible, and in this way raising both knowledge of their effectiveness (enhancing self-concept) and feelings of personal worth (increasing self-esteem) is peer teaching.

Good and Brophy have shown that getting children to tutor other children benefits both the tutor and the pupil. Further, it releases the teacher to work with individuals who are having extreme difficulty, if the rest of the class are engaged in peer work.

Naturally it cannot be done to any great extent with younger classes in the primary school, but Thomas (1970) showed that it can be very beneficial to older children in the primary school and their younger 'pupils'. He compared the effectiveness of primary five and six tutors with college students in helping primary two students with reading. He found that the primary five and six tutors were more direct and business-like. They accepted the fact that younger pupils were having problems and used the period to help them directly. It seems that this kind of tutoring of younger pupils is effective when (a) direct instruction is called for, (b) simple vocabulary is called for, and (c) 'tutors' remember their own difficulty and use their experience in teaching.

It can be seen, then, that as the parents can help a child to feel effective and worthy by the satisfaction of the four basic psychological needs we described in Chapter 1, so can the teacher. We would also like to mention three more teacher strategies for enhancing self-concept and raising self-esteem.

The first is what Good and Brophy call *interchangeable teacher comment*. By this they mean that listening to what pupils have to say, as well as always telling them what to do, makes pupils feel more positive both towards themselves and towards their teachers.

Secondly, acceptance that *each individual has his own unique pattern of learning* helps teachers react sensitively to pupils. We have discussed Bruner's formulation of the three different ways we represent the outside world mentally – enactive, iconic and symbolic representation. Clearly, particularly in the primary school, children will have different patterns of reliance on each of these methods of representation. Some children in particular may need more manipulation of the environment and direct exploration of cause and effect than others – their representation may be biased to the enactive and iconic, whereas other children may think symbolically from a very early age. Teaching should allow for such individual differences.

Finally, the use of co-operative games can change children's self-expectations. Forming children into teams to play games of this nature or to carry out tasks – like collecting money for a school outing – exerts pressure on children to become involved with working with each other for a common goal, and in this way it is possible to increase their knowledge of their own competence and thus raise their levels of self-esteem.

Teacher–Pupil Relationships

(1) Discipline in general

One of the largest investigations into how adequate levels of self-esteem are encouraged in children was undertaken by Coopersmith in the USA (1967). Although it could be argued that his findings apply specifically to the USA, at the time he undertook his survey, we would nevertheless like to discuss them as we have found that they always raise interest in the seminars conducted by one of the authors for educationalists from all over the Third World.

Coopersmith studied 1,700 primary five and six year pupils. He interviewed parents, and studied his subjects both at home and at school. The most notable antecedents (causes) of self-esteem were found to lie in the way parents treated their children. In particular, he found that when parents clearly laid down the kind of behaviour and attitudes that they would like children to display, children responded by not only conforming to these standards, thus reducing the need for high levels of punishment, but also showed high levels of self-confidence and self-respect.

From this and other studies, which we will discuss in Chapter 8, it seems that the stress we laid in Chapter 1 on the need for love and security is best interpreted in the framework we have already used of caring, warm behaviour from caretakers within a framework of clearly set out limits. Naturally, some flexibility within these limits must be allowed to give children the sense of their own autonomy (or personal effectiveness). So a parent might say: 'Yes, you can go out this evening and play in the fields, as long as you don't go near the river and provided you are home before dark.' If children are given standards of behaviour from adults, they tend to adopt these for themselves if they see the adult as caring and fair. Thus discipline should be linked, not to a system of rewards and punishments, but to an internalised set of behavioural standards.

Aronson (1976) following Kelman distinguishes three levels of responding to the demands of authority. The first occurs when the child does as he is told simply because the consequences of not doing so will be less pleasant than the consequences of doing so. (He calls this level *compliance*.) The second level is associated with obedience which occurs because the child wishes to please the adult involved. He identifies with him and his standards and because of this tends to model his behaviour on the adult's and follows his directions. (Aronson calls this second level *identification*.) The third and final level occurs when the child accepts the standards and rationale (reasons) for these standards set out by the adult. Having considered them and found them appropriate and just, the child accepts them for his own. In Aronson's terms he *internalises* them. The younger the child, the more likely he will be to accept authority at the first or second level just described. That is, he will fall in with the demands of authority either because it is inconvenient not to or because he wishes the authority figure to like him. But clearly educationalists would wish children to reach the third level, because at this stage the child is not blindly accepting but is beginning to develop a moral sense and a set of personal standards. We shall return to this area in the chapters on adolescence, when we discuss moral development.

Whichever level the child is at, he should not present discipline problems if three conditions are met. First, his psychological needs are satisfied; secondly, the limits to acceptable behaviour are clearly set out but not too rigid; and thirdly, the rules and standards he has to meet are fair and there are not too many of them. Nevertheless, some children do pose problems in the primary school and we shall deal with such problems now.

(2) The disruptive, acting-out child

It is probably fair to say that disruptive children, at the primary school level, are nearly always very low in self-esteem. Other factors may contribute to their behaviour, and we shall discuss them shortly, but the chief impetus for being aggressive and interrupting and disrupting the normal course of classroom and playground life tends to lie in the child's basic sense of inadequacy and feelings of not being valued or worthy.

In other words, the four psychological needs of the child have not been met. He may lack the kind of warm, secure and accepting home life where his efforts are praised and recognised that we have described as being most appropriate for optimum (the best) social and emotional development. However, even if his home life is emotionally satisfying, he may have difficulty at school because his needs are not met there. Thus in dealing with such a child, a teacher should ask herself if:

(a) She, and other teachers involved, are warm and basically accepting in their treatment of the child (*need for love*).

(b) Firm guidelines about the kind of behaviour that is acceptable have been laid down (*need for security*).

(c) The child has enough to keep himself occupied with. Perhaps he is developmentally quicker than his peers and is bored by the work. Or, on the other hand, perhaps he finds the cognitive tasks of school too demanding and would benefit from a more active approach to learning (*need for new experience*).

(d) The child is praised when he does make an effort. Perhaps she just pays attention to him when he is disruptive and does not reinforce his behaviour when it *is* acceptable. In dealing with such a child, the teacher should try to ignore bad behaviour as her attention is bound to be reinforcing. In other words, if a child is low in self-esteem, he needs to make his presence felt. He probably does so by behaving badly, and if the teacher pays attention to him only when he behaves badly she is reinforcing bad behaviour. You may ask, how can a teacher ignore bad behaviour such as one child being aggressive to another child? The answer here lies in the teacher responding selectively. Suppose the child who is disruptive and aggressive attacks another child. The teacher should respond by immediately going to the aid of the victim, perhaps by picking the *victim* up and talking to him, and by ignoring the aggressor. If the disruptive child perceives that disruptive attention-seeking behaviour has the reverse effect, he will attempt to meet his need for attention in other ways. The only other way left to him will be to try and win attention by being good. As soon as any evidence of such behaviour is presented, the teacher must immediately reward it (*need for praise and recognition*).

(e) The teacher should consider the effect of asking the child who is presenting problems to undertake a responsible task. In this way she will engage his energies, raise his self-esteem and help the rest of the class to see the child in a more favourable light (*need for responsibility*).

If the child's psychological needs are being appropriately met, then the cause of aggressive, disruptive behaviour may lie in two other areas. First, the child may come from a home where such behaviour is accepted. Perhaps in his family and immediate neighbourhood aggressive behaviour is acceptable. If this is the case, the teacher has to explain to the child that a different way of behaving is needed at school. It may be possible to bring the parents into such a discussion, but it is quite possible that if there is such a gap between school and home standards the parents may not wish to co-operate to any great extent. In such a case the teacher will have to proceed with great care and perhaps work with the headteacher and other members of staff to resolve the problem.

The second area which may precipitate aggressive, disruptive behaviour is the school itself. Perhaps the rules are very strict, rigid and punitively applied. The child may be rebelling against what he perceives as an unjust system. It is, therefore, always in order for the teacher to consider in which ways the school itself may contribute to anti-social behaviour. This is particularly the case where there are a number of children all behaving in the same disruptive way. We will return to this state of affairs, which is far more likely to occur at the secondary school level, in the section of the book concerned with adolescence.

(3) *The timid, withdrawn child*

Some children find the social and emotional demands of school a great trial. They may feel inadequate and inferior compared with other children and be shy and solitary. In addition, such children may attract bullying. It is often easy for teachers to forget about such children because they may not present any obvious behaviour problems in the classroom. These, too, are the children who may miss a great deal of school, because they may tend to tell their parents they feel sick in order to miss school.

Once again, by referring to the model of psychological needs the teacher may be able to help such a child to a more positive self-image:

(a) In particular, for these children, the more warmth the teacher can show, the more likely such children will be to feel relaxed and comparatively confident. Timid children need to feel that if they do make a mistake or get something wrong the repercussions (results) will not be too unpleasant (*need for love*).

(*b*) Timid and withdrawn children will not need to have the limits of acceptable behaviour emphasised. Instead they should be encouraged to see that within broad limits different sorts of behaviour are acceptable, so that they do not continue to assume that the only possible way for them to behave is to be as inconspicuous and as unnoticeable as possible (*need for security*).

(*c*) Shy children need to be encouraged to seek out new experiences. But they should be led gently in this direction, rather than forced into very unfamiliar situations. If necessary, another child who is kindly disposed to a shy child can be asked to share new activities with the withdrawn child. Perhaps the teacher can also discuss this aspect of the child's behaviour with the parents and encourage them to help their child feel less worried about the different aspects of school life (*need for new experiences*).

(*d*) If children feel unequal to the social and emotional demands of school, they need to be reinforced for any step they make in the direction of more active participation in school life. But praise and recognition must be given tactfully and discreetly, so that the children concerned do not feel that the eyes of the class are directed towards them (*need for praise and recognition*).

(*e*) Finally, a slow but steady attempt to make such children feel responsible, not only for themselves but also for co-operative activities that benefit the class or school as a whole, will help raise these children's estimates of their own competence and worth (*need for responsibility*).

With children like these, contact with their parents is a great help. Often parents may be aware that their children are unhappy at school, but may feel uncertain about the courses of action open to them. If the teacher shows that she, too, is aware of the child's difficulties, a joint plan of action may be undertaken to help the child concerned to feel more confident about his own abilities and more certain of his own personal worth.

In general, then, teacher–pupil relationships should not present too many difficulties in the primary school years if teachers are always aware of the need to enhance children's self-concepts and raise their self-esteem. Some teachers are stricter than others, some tolerate a higher noise level and some are more directive than others. These differences are often related to the teacher as an individual as well as to cultural and sub-cultural values. Such differences are bound to exist. Children are able to make the adjustment to different teacher-styles reasonably well, provided that:

(i) Teachers are concerned with fulfilling the psychological needs of individual children.

(ii) The standards of behaviour the teachers expect are clearly set out.

(iii) Some flexibility in the operation of these standards is allowed.

(iv) There are not too many rules, and the rules that exist are seen by the pupils to be fair.

Peer Relationships

When considering peer relationships in the primary school years, we can make two general observations that would seem to hold for all cultures. The first is that a large component of self-esteem is contributed by the self's perception of how others treat and value him. To this extent, then, the acceptance and liking of the child's peers is vitally important in his adjustment to school. The second is that the older the child grows, the relatively more important do peer relationships become when contrasted with adult relationships.

Both statements need some modifying. The first, that peer relationships affect self-esteem, is an oversimplification, because this process is not simply a straightforward effect of popularity creating high self-esteem. To begin with, the more confident of himself a child feels initially (and we are not here referring to those children who appear to be very over-confident, often in an attempt to hide a basic self-doubt), the more relaxed he will be in social relationships and the more likely he will be to be liked. The less sure of his self-worth a child is, on the other hand, the more reliant will he be on the feed-back given to him by others. This may make his initial contacts with other children less easy and relaxed than the contacts made by children who are more sure of themselves and the very hesitancy he shows may contribute to a less effective social style. A teacher should, therefore, keep an eye on the peer relationships of those children who are timid and unsure of themselves in social relationships.

The second statement, that as children grow older they grow more dependent on peer opinion and less on adult opinion, also needs some discussion. Although it holds to a certain extent in all cultures, because ultimately most children tend to marry one of their peers and not one of the older generation, you will immediately think of exceptions to this general rule. In many societies children still marry mates of their parents' choice and in such societies girls, in particular, remain heavily dependent on the social relationships within the family until they leave home, and then, if they move into another extended family, become dependent on the social relationships there. Thus, in societies where the extended family is organised in such a way that the older generation controls the younger, the second statement holds to a far lesser extent than it does in societies with a more nuclear family structure, and where younger people are more independent of older people.

Another qualifying aspect of the second statement relates to the extent to which different generations in the society share the same value systems. The closer the value systems of adults and children, the less there is a movement towards reliance on peer opinion rather than on adult opinion, because they tend to coincide more. Bronfenbrenner (1974) showed a striking difference in this area between Western and Russian children. He asked 12-year-olds to respond to ten 'dilemmas' (problems), for example, whether they would deny that they had damaged some property, or whether they would cheat if they could without being found out. They were presented with these dilemmas under three different experimental conditions. Under the first, called the *scientific* condition, the children were told that their responses would be revealed only to the scientists carrying out the investigation. Under the second, or *adult*, condition, their responses would be shown to teachers and parents. In the third or *peer* condition, their responses would be shown to other children. The results showed that (p. 78):

Under all three conditions, Soviet children were much less willing to engage in antisocial behavior than their age-mates in three Western countries [the United States, England, and West Germany]. In addition, the effect of the peer group was quite different in the Soviet Union and the United States. When told that their class mates would know of their actions, American children were even more inclined to take part in

misconduct. Soviet youngsters showed just the opposite tendency. In fact, their classmates were about as effective as parents and teachers in decreasing misbehavior.

Thus it is not surprising to find that, according to Bronfenbrenner, there is less of a 'generation gap' in values and behaviour in Russia than there is in the United States, and consequently not such a large shift towards peer relationships with age.

The way children behave with their peers differs from society to society, in a manner that is dependent on the organisation and values of the society's socio-economic system. Nevertheless, cultures may be grouped together in such a way that children brought up in one type of culture behave very similarly, in comparison with children from another type of culture. This conclusion was reached by the Whitings (1975) when they evaluated the results of a massive study they conducted on child development in six cultures.

Six different teams studied children from six areas – the Pacific Islands (Taira), north India (Khalipur), the United States of America (children from Orchard Town, New England), Kenya (the Nyansongo), Mexico (Juxlahuaca) and the Philippines (Tarong). Working and observing in all six cultures, they analysed children's interactions on two dimensions. The first related to what they called 'nurturant-responsible versus dependent-dominant'. A positive score on this dimension meant that children in this culture were more likely to be helpful and supportive than they were to seek help or try to dominate. The second dimension they called 'sociable-intimate versus authoritarian-aggressive'. A positive score on this dimension meant that children in this culture were more likely to act sociably to each other than they were to reprimand or assault each other.

The societies that scored high on the first dimension were the Kenyan, the Mexican and the Philippino. The Whitings related this to the fact that high scores on being helpful and low scores on being dependent or dominant were associated with a relatively simple socio-economic structure and no class or caste system and a low degree of occupational specialisation.

The Whitings related the second dimension to the type of household structure. Societies that scored high on this dimension, that is, were sociable and intimate rather than authoritarian and aggressive, were the American, the Mexican and the

Philippino, and these societies were likely to be organised on a nuclear model rather than on an extended family system.

Thus the Whitings conclude that the social behaviour of children, no matter which society they live in, relates closely to the way adult life is conducted. We have already shown that this general principle held true for play behaviour (Chapter 3) and it bears out our general contention that children are born potentially similar no matter where they live but that their development and behaviour will be shaped by cultural variables.

Summary

This chapter has rested on the contention that the child's social and emotional adjustment to school is dependent on his perception of himself. To the extent that he is reasonably sure of his competence and to the extent that he feels a worthy and valued person, to that extent will he be able to cope well with the social and emotional demands of school.

(1) We introduced self theory and covered the following points relating to it.
  (a) We differentiated between two overlapping components of self. Self-concept was seen as what an individual *thinks* about himself, and self-esteem as the way an individual *feels* about himself.
  (b) We concluded that although an adult has a relatively clear self-concept, a child builds his self-concept up slowly from the things people say to him and the way they treat him and the way he sees himself as behaving. We also concluded that the child does have a set of attitudes towards himself and feelings about himself that we call his level of self-esteem.
  (c) We decided that the construct of self has some relevance in all cultures.
  (d) We pointed out that we are not always conscious of self to the same extent. Some activities are less ego-involving than others.
(2) We presented research that shows a firm and consistent link between academic performance and self-concept and self-esteem. We decided that it was impossible to decide whether poor self-esteem causes poor academic performance or whether poor academic performance causes low self-esteem. It would seem that the direction of cause and effect differs from case to case. Sometimes a child enters school with good academic potential but poor self-esteem, and consequently cannot learn effectively because he is worried by feelings of inadequacy. At other times, a child may enter school with a low self-concept that is related to the fact that he is quite realistically aware of his lack of competence. We showed, however, (a) that performance can be lowered by artificially lowering self-esteem and (b) that performance can be improved by increasing self-esteem.

(3) We presented research that showed that some teachers have different sets of expectations for different children, and that these expectations can be conveyed to children, consequently raising or lowering performance, depending on whether the expectations are positive or negative. We decided that this 'expectation effect' works through the medium of the child's self-concept. Certain teacher behaviours raise the child's self-esteem and expectations of himself and thus cause an improvement in academic performance. Other teacher behaviours lower the child's self-esteem and expectations of himself and thus cause a deterioration in performance, or no change in levels of performance.
(4) We then described teacher strategies for enhancing self-concept and self-esteem. These embraced fulfilling the four psychological needs described in Chapter 1, using interchangeable teacher comment, accepting that different children learn in different ways and using co-operative groups.
(5) We discussed teacher–pupil relationships, pointing out that these will be best if:
  (a) the teacher is concerned with fulfilling the psychological needs of each child;
  (b) the teacher sets out clearly the standards of behaviour she expects;
  (c) the teacher allows some flexibility in the operation of these standards;
  (d) there are not too many rules and the rules that do exist are seen to be fair by the pupils.
(6) Finally we looked at peer relationships and concluded:
  (a) that the level of a child's self-esteem is related to the relationship he makes with his peers;
  (b) the older the child grows, the relatively

more important do peer relationships become;

(c) social relationships between children differ from culture to culture depending on the socio-economic and structural organisation of the culture.

Chapter 5: Selected Bibliography

Self theory
Hamachek, D. E., *Encounters with the Self*, 2nd edn

(New York: Holt, Rinehart & Winston, 1978).
Samuels, S. C., *Enhancing Self-Concept in Early Childhood* (New York: Human Sciences Press, 1977).

Expectation theory
Nash, R., *Teacher Expectation and Pupil Learning* (London: Routledge & Kegan Paul, 1976).

Peer relations in a cross-cultural context
Whiting, B. B., and Whiting, J. W. M., *Children of Six Cultures: A Psycho-Cultural Analysis* (Cambridge, Mass.: Harvard University Press, 1975).

LEARNING AND INSTRUCTION

6

Introduction

The last chapter was concerned with setting the social and emotional background to the learning experience. In this chapter we turn away from direct consideration of the areas of feeling and motivation and we look at that aspect of schooling that is commonly regarded as most important – learning.

What do we mean by learning? You may wonder how it is differentiated from language and the four processes of cognition we considered in Chapter 4: perception (and attention), memory, concept formation and reasoning. Surely learning is intimately related to these processes?

In order to answer this question, let us look at the definition given by Gagné in his recent survey of the field of learning. Gagné defines it as 'a change in human disposition or capability, which persists over a period of time, and which is not simply ascribable to processes of growth' (1977, p. 3). This definition indicates that it is a change and can therefore be measured or assessed or observed in some way. Thus, in schools, we are concerned with intervening in the processes of cognition in such a way as to change capabilities or skills – intellectual, sensory and motor. In doing so we utilise all the cognitive processes we have described so far – language, perception and attention, memory, concept formation and reasoning.

Let us give an everyday example. Suppose you are interested in growing a particular vegetable. You obtain two varieties of seeds and sow them in the same sort of soil. At harvest one variety produces a better crop than the other and you order only that particular variety for the next year. If your behaviour were observed, it could be inferred that you have *learned* that one variety of seed was superior to the other for use in your garden. In learning this you have made use of all the processes of cognition – you have *perceived* a difference in yield, you have *remembered* where you planted each variety, you have utilised the *concepts* of seed, crop, reaping, and so on and finally you have *reasoned* that if the one variety of seed was superior last year, it will be so next year as well.

Now in schools teachers are interested in facilitating the learning of particular material, or particular skills and capabilities and, in doing so, they should structure the environment to make the best use of children's language and cognitive abilities. Thus in this chapter we discuss not only the process of learning but also the different instructional approaches that are currently in use.

The Processes of Learning

In Chapter 4, when we discussed cognition, we differentiated between various processes of cognition, while noting that these processes commonly overlap. Similarly, in this chapter, we will differentiate between seven processes involved in the learning that takes place in schools (see Figure 6.1) but, as was the case when we covered cognition, we note that in any learning situation all seven processes may take place simultaneously and overlap with each other.

(1) *Association learning*

If you have studied psychology, as an academic subject rather than as an applied one, you will know that much of the work of the early psychologists was concerned with association

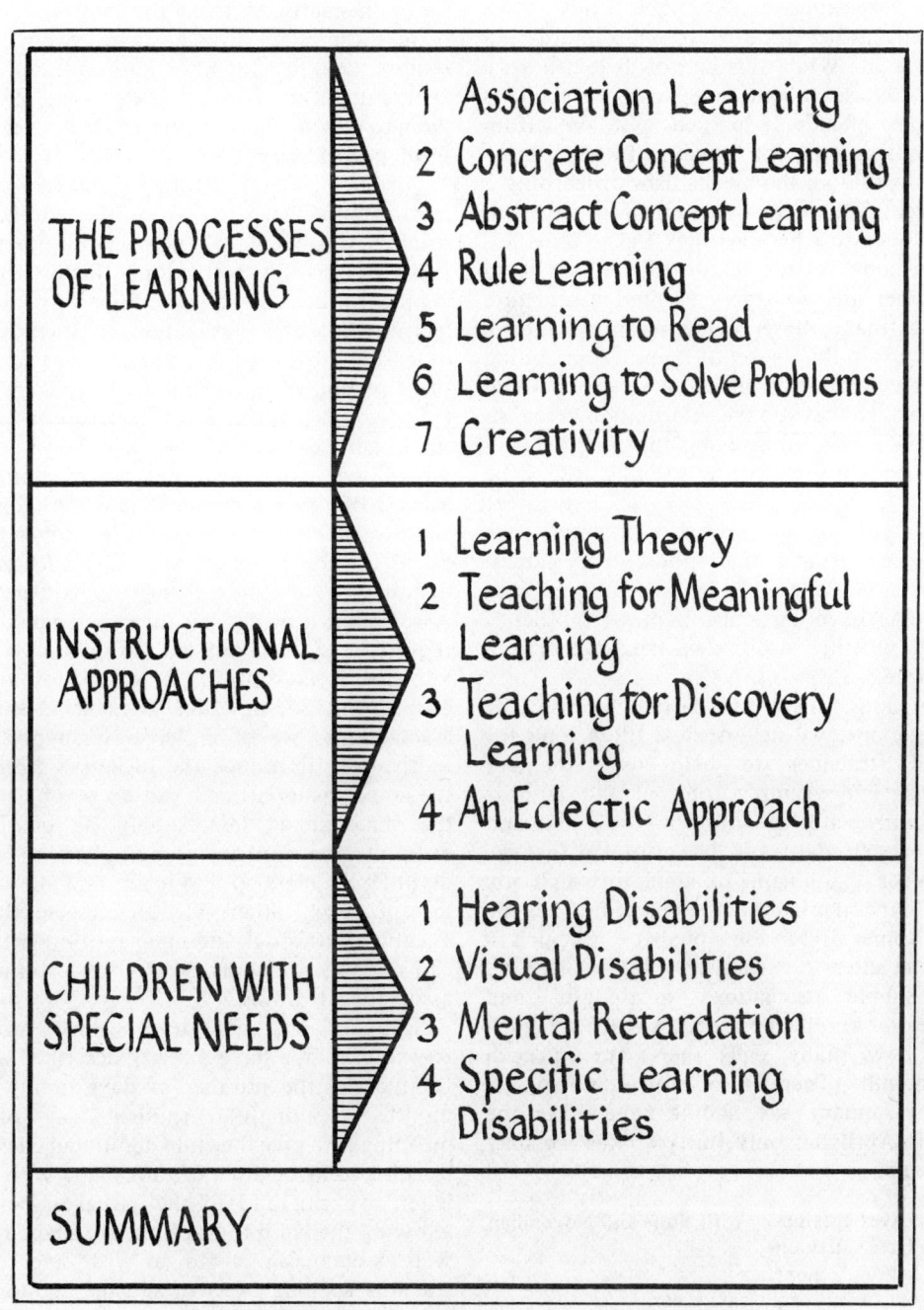

THE PROCESSES OF LEARNING
1 Association Learning
2 Concrete Concept Learning
3 Abstract Concept Learning
4 Rule Learning
5 Learning to Read
6 Learning to Solve Problems
7 Creativity

INSTRUCTIONAL APPROACHES
1 Learning Theory
2 Teaching for Meaningful Learning
3 Teaching for Discovery Learning
4 An Eclectic Approach

CHILDREN WITH SPECIAL NEEDS
1 Hearing Disabilities
2 Visual Disabilities
3 Mental Retardation
4 Specific Learning Disabilities

SUMMARY

Figure 6.1 Structure of Chapter 6

learning. They reasoned that the best way to approach the study of learning was through the simplest kind of learning, that of a simple, single association between two identifiable units – one stimulus and another stimulus; or one stimulus and a response to it. While this approach led to very specific discoveries about how such associations could be most effectively learned, it suffered from the disadvantage that, for humans at least, simple association is seldom the mechanism of learning.

In everyday life we very seldom simply learn to associate things just because they occur together. Usually we look for the reason that makes them occur together and we apply to their association our need to make sense of the world. We have already discussed this aspect of human functioning fully in our chapter on cognition, where we pointed out we tend to go 'beyond the information given' so as to integrate new information into our existing cognitive grid. However, certain things need to be associated even though they have no logical (or substantive) connection. Such, for example, are individual people and their individual names. There is no particular reason, in most cultures, why certain people have particular names. Another is vocabulary, whether in our own language or in a new language.

But even though there is no particular reason for such associations, we nevertheless often look for meaningful strategies to help us remember associations. For example, one of the authors knows a family with two sons who look alike and behave in very similar ways. The only way that she can remember which name to attach to which boy is through remembering that the bigger boy has the name that comes first in the alphabet – it begins in fact with the letter 'A'. Another example of trying to make simple associations 'meaningful' and therefore easier to remember occurs when we teach ourselves how many days there are in each calendar month. (There is, of course, no logical reason why January, say, should have thirty-one days, while April has only thirty.) Thus we may learn the verse:

Thirty days have September, April, June and November,
All the rest have thirty-one,
Except for February alone,
Which has but twenty-eight days clear,
And twenty-nine in each leap year.

In the primary school we require children to make a great many associations. For example, we ask them to attach certain shapes to certain letters, and certain other shapes to number concepts. We also ask them to learn a great number of facts. For example, we may ask them to remember how far away the earth is from the sun, or how many planets there are in the solar system. We may require them to remember dates to attach to certain events or in our language classes we may require them to attach labels to objects (that is, learn lists of foreign vocabulary).

Furth considers that there are two important implications that arise from the emphasis most primary schools place on association learning. The first concerns the motivational (factors that induce people to behave in a certain way) aspects of learning. It seems that humans most enjoy the kind of learning that requires them to take a small step in the direction of mastering a new skill or concept. (We would expect this from the principle of 'moderate novelty' that we described in Chapter 4 where we maintained that we pay attention to aspects of the environment that are close to, but slightly different from, what we know already.) Such learning seems to be *intrinsically* motivating (stimulating and interesting by its very nature). Association learning, on the other hand, does not require us to make any leap from what we already know – it is simply the acquisition of a new association. So, in order to make children learn associations, we often have to supply *extrinsic* motivation (introduce the incentive from outside the actual material). We can do this by presenting the material as interestingly as possible. For example, we can teach multiplication tables by dividing the class up into teams and allowing them to quiz each other. Or we can teach foreign vocabulary through little plays. In other words we can attempt to supply *interest* and stimulation to association learning.

Secondly, we must try to make associations *meaningful*. We have already described a strategy for making the number of days in the calendar months meaningful. Another way of adding meaning is to give the child additional cues. Thus in learning to associate a certain shape with a certain letter, we can add to the visual association by allowing the child to trace out the shape in sand as well as encouraging him to write and read it. In teaching spelling, we can add the auditory cue of chanting (or calling out loud) to the visual cue. The more different aids we can offer the child – whether they are different sensory aids or learning strategies – the more meaningful the associations will become.

To these two recommendations of Furth – that associations be made as interesting and as meaningful as possible – we can add two further recommendations that come to us from learning theory. They are that we *reinforce* (reward) correct associations or answers *as immediately as possible* by indicating to children when they respond correctly as soon as they give the right answer, and secondly that we stamp association learning in by *repetition*.

This last point may lead you to wonder whether there is any place in the modern school for what is often dismissed as 'rote learning'. Is it helpful for instance, to get children to chant their multiplication tables? It is our view that, provided it is not done to excess, it is helpful. Although this should not be the only means of teaching this very basic part of arithmetic, it will supplement more cognitive approaches like making discoveries about the nature of number by working with stones or pebbles or the specially designed number apparatus that is commercially available. If the child is able to respond automatically with 'forty-eight' when you ask him to tell you what four times twelve is, he is provided with a sound basis on which to build a thorough understanding of our number system.

To sum up, then, we can facilitate the association learning that is an important part of the primary school syllabus by:

(a) Making the learning situation as *interesting* as possible. Using little plays to teach foreign vocabulary for instance; or quizzes to teach spelling and tables.

(b) Making the material as *meaningful* as possible by imposing patterning or organisation on the material. For instance, we can point out that the five times table can be separated into alternate products ending with '0' or '5'. Mnemonics (formulae for aiding memory) are also useful. For instance, we can teach the order of colours in the spectrum by teaching the following mnemonic:

Read over your geography books in vacation.
Red orange yellow green blue indigo violet.

(c) Providing as many *different kinds of cues* as possible – for example, auditory (sound), as well as sight in learning spelling; touch (by tracing letters out in sand) as well as sight in learning letters; images as well as words in teaching number.

(d) Providing immediate feed-back when children give correct answers so that the appropriate associations can be *reinforced*.

(e) Providing a reasonable amount of *repetition* for material that is to be remembered in the form it is to be learned. For example, if you want the children to learn the capital cities of a number of countries, use quizzes and encourage children to test each other so the relevant associations are continually being made. As we have already mentioned, chanting can help, both by providing repetition and by providing auditory cues as well as written ones.

(f) Remembering, too, not to sequence similar learning tasks one after the other – for example, vocabulary in two different languages. Theorists argue over the underlying reason, but it has been shown that the association learning of similar material interferes with previously learned material if they are taught too close together in time. So never follow one language lesson with a lesson in another language. *Teach similar material after a break in time*.

Finally, remember that the key to the retention of association learning is the provision of as many cues and strategies as possible.

(2) *Concrete concept learning*

You may remember from Chapter 4 that we said a concept stands for a common set of attributes that characterise a group of objects. Therefore, before we discuss the acquisition of concepts we could perhaps spend some time looking at the process of distinguishing attributes. This is often called 'discrimination learning'. For example, suppose we wish a child to acquire the concept of the (small) letter 'd', how do we help him to distinguish its shape from a number of similar shapes like 'b' (which is just like a 'd' except that it is laterally inverted) or 'q' or 'p'?

Discrimination learning must be concerned in this case with the distinctive features of the letter. In this case, the child must learn that the letter consists of a curved shape and a line, and that it is 'd' rather than 'b', 'p' or 'q' because the curve is lower than the top of the line, and because the curve is on the left hand side of the page. Thus in teaching the shape to associate with the letter 'd', the teacher can emphasise the two parts of its shape – a curve and a line. She can teach the children to notice that the curve comes before the line and to notice that the line is taller than the curve.

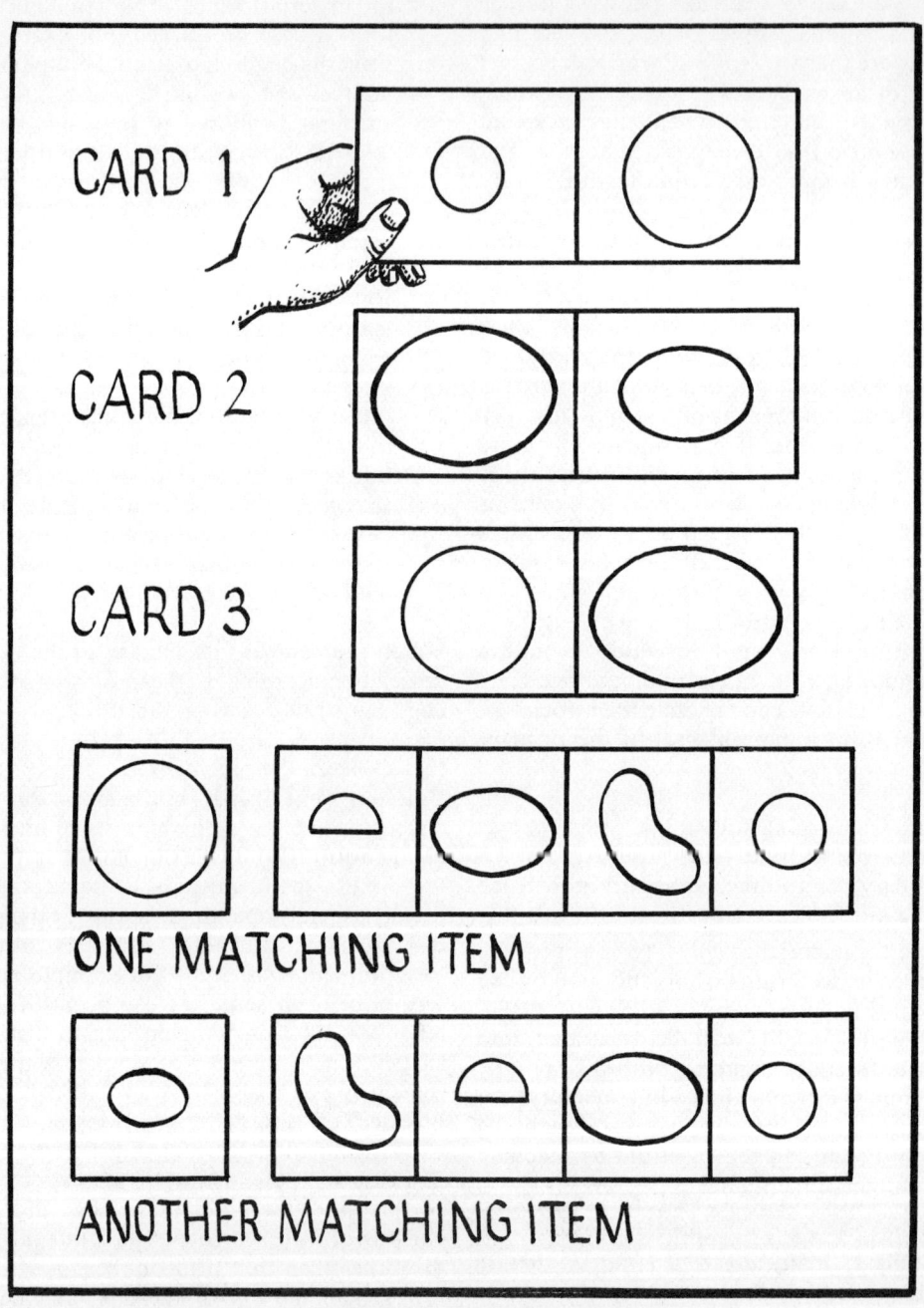

Figure 6.2 Teaching the difference
between an ellipse and a circle.

Similarly, let us consider the discrimination of a circle from an ellipse (see Figure 6.2). First the teacher may present a card containing two circles and ask if they are the same shape. Then she may present a card with two ellipses and ask the same question. Finally she may present a card with an ellipse and a circle and ask once again if they are the same. Naturally, after each response, she must indicate if the response is correct or not. After a number of such presentations, the class should be able to 'see' the required discrimination. The teacher can then check by giving a matching task in which a given figure – whether ellipse or circle – has to be matched from a set of figures. It is important that the circles and ellipses be of different sizes, so that the class learn to *generalise* the discrimination: in other words, to focus on the shape difference and not pay attention to the size of the shapes.

Let us now look at the learning of a particular concept using the stages of making discriminations and generalising. We shall consider the acquisition of the concept 'surface'. This is a concept the children will need in mathematics and refers to that which has length and breadth but no thickness. The teacher may proceed as follows.

(*a*) She may first introduce the word. Despite the fact that surface has another meaning (you only look at the *surface* of things, not at their underlying causes), the children may never have heard the word. Thus she has to introduce the *verbal label*. She may hold up a book and indicate its cover and say – 'This is a surface'. Then she may run her hand over her table and say 'Here is another surface'.

(*b*) Then she may ask for instances of other surfaces. If children are able to do this it will show that they have discriminated the criterial feature of surfaces.

(*c*) She may then move on to *generalisation* by introducing instances of the concept along with various other instances that do not belong to the concept. For example, she may hold up a box and, indicating the corners and edges, say 'These are not surfaces'; then, indicating all six surfaces, 'But all these are'. She may then point to a number of edges, corners and surfaces in the room and ask children whether they are surfaces or not. If the children can successfully identify which are, and which are not, instances of the concept being considered (surfaces), then they may be considered to have grasped the concept.

It can be seen that the teaching of such a concept which has a concrete referent is not a very difficult task. This is because we can always ensure that a child has not simply learned a verbal definition off by heart – 'a surface has length and breadth but no thickness' – by asking him actually to point out instances or non-instances of the concept. Teaching an abstract concept (or a 'defined concept' as Gagné calls abstract concepts) is a far more difficult task because in this case the teacher is teaching only through the medium of language or symbols and cannot easily use any feature of the physical environment as she can when she teaches concrete concepts.

(3) Abstract concept learning

As we have just noted, concrete concepts can be learned by active and direct interaction with the environment, whereas abstract concepts can only be learned by the use of language or other symbols. These abstract concepts are really ways of categorising objects and events, and because they do not have concrete referents they must basically be represented by definitions composed of other concepts. However, as we mentioned in Chapter 4, a person may have attained a concept without necessarily being himself able to define it completely. In order to demonstrate whether or not a person has attained a concept, we would only expect him to be able to classify instances or non-instances of the concept. Let us look at the way a teacher might attempt to teach an abstract concept, for example, the concept of a prime number.

A prime number is a number that is divisible only by itself and one. This is the verbal definition of a prime number. But in order for the child to attain the concept, he must understand the other concepts used in the definition – number and divisibility. So perhaps the teacher could proceed as follows:

(*a*) She could present a number of division sums, for example, $8 \div 3$, $10 \div 5$, $16 \div 8$, $11 \div 4$, and ask the class to tell her which of these sums gives an answer without a remainder. When they have successfully indicated which sums do this, she can introduce the word 'divisible', which means 'can be divided without giving a remainder'. From their previous work in arithmetic the children will already have the concept 'divisibility' but here she is giving them a label for this concept in order to help them attain the desired concept of 'prime number'. It can be assumed, of course, that by this stage, children have a grasp of the concept 'number'. Thus in this first step she is ensuring that the children have *attained*, and are familiar with, *the simpler concepts* involved in the desired concept.

(*b*) She may then *describe the concept* of a prime number by saying something like: 'Some numbers are special. They can only be divided exactly by themselves and one. If you divide them by anything else, they give a remainder. We call these numbers prime numbers.'

(*c*) She can then move on to the *discrimination* stage, by asking 'Is eleven a prime?' When the children respond that it is, she can check it out with them by dividing it by all the numbers less than eleven. Similarly she can ask about other primes in the same way.

(*d*) She can then move on to the *generalisation* stage, by asking children to indicate which of a list of numbers, both prime and non-prime, are primes and which are not.

(*e*) Following this she can ask the children to make up their own lists of prime and non-prime numbers. In other words, she can satisfy herself that children can *classify* instances into those that fall within the particular concept and those that do not.

(*f*) Finally, and this is not an essential requirement, but it does help children to draw the concept together, she can perhaps teach them the *formal definition* of the concept. But in doing so she must remember that just because a child can recite a definition of a concept off by heart correctly, she must not assume that he has attained the concept.

(4) *Rule learning*

In the chapters on cognition and language we argued that, in order to be able to make sense of the world, the human being tends to generate hypotheses, check them out and then formulate rules. We saw such instances of rule formulation when we described the process of 'over-regularisation' that occurs when children acquire their first language. Similarly, if you think about your daily procedure, you will realise that you operate by the use of a very large number of rules like 'If the sky is overcast, it will probably rain, so I should take an umbrella or coat with me on an overcast day', or 'People who don't smile back when I smile at them must be upset about something', or 'Children who don't keep quiet when I tell them to must be warned that I will not tolerate this kind of behaviour'.

If there is a natural tendency for human beings to structure their world by means of rules, you may wonder why it is that some of the rules you

yourself were taught in school were so difficult to remember. This may have happened because some of the rules taught at school were rote learned and not derived by pupils themselves. Other rules, even if they were at one stage derived by pupils, may have been forgotten, or remembered incorrectly, because not all the concepts involved or used in the rule were properly understood in the first place.

Let us look then at the way a teacher could teach the rule that all the angles in a triangle add up to two right angles or 180 degrees. Before doing so, let us set out some steps in teaching rules that are derived from Gagné's influential book *The Conditions of Learning* (1977).

Step i: Inform the learner about the form of the performance to be expected when learning is completed.

Step ii: Question the learner in a way that requires the recall of the previously learned concepts that make up the rule.

Step iii: Use verbal statements that will lead the learner to put the rule together, as a chain of concepts, in the proper order.

Step iv: By means of a question, ask the learner to 'demonstrate' one or more concrete instances of the rule and provide feedback as to whether these instances are correct or not.

Step v: (Optional, but useful for later instruction). By a suitable question, require the learner to make a verbal statement of the rule.

Step vi: Make sure you provide time for reviewing the rule on the days following the learning of the rule. When you do so, present new examples both for recall and for demonstration of the rule.

Let us now apply these six steps to the learning of the rule about the sum of the angles in a triangle.

Step i At this stage the teacher would inform the pupils that they are going to learn about the sum of the angles in a triangle or what they add up to in degrees.

Step ii At the second stage the teacher would ensure that each child can demonstrate an angle, and that each child can measure the size of an angle, and that each child can identify and draw a triangle.

Step iii The teacher might now ask the children to measure the angles of a triangle and add them up. After demonstrating that every child obtains an answer very close to 180 degrees, the teacher might repeat the exercise with a second set of triangles. On demonstrating once again that each individual obtains an answer close to 180 degrees, the teacher might ask the children, as a class, to formulate the rule in words.

Step iv The teacher might ask a child to come up to the board, draw a triangle and, with a blackboard protractor, measure the angles and obtain the required sum.

Step v The teacher might then ask the children to complete sentences like the following: if two angles of a triangle measure sixty degrees and twenty degrees, the third angle will measure ... Or: the three angles of a triangle add up to ... right angles.

Step vi The following mathematics periods should be used, at least in part, for revising the rule. Children can be set further examples based on the rule, both by asking them to draw triangles and measure their angles and by setting them calculations based on the sum of the angles of a triangle.

As we have mentioned before, much school learning involves the learning of rules. And, as with association learning, two important conditions for the effective learning of rules lie in making their learning as *interesting* and as *meaningful* as possible. When we discussed association learning, we recommended, in addition, that repetition and rote learning can be effective. Does this apply to rule learning? Is it effective to teach rules off by heart? We think not. Consider, for example, the rule we have just been discussing. It can be formulated in different ways:

The angles of a triangle add up to 180 degrees
OR
The sum of the angles of a triangle is 180 degrees
OR
The three angles of a triangle total two right angles.

Thus it will be seen that there is no need to learn any particular form of wording for the rule; it is more important to learn and understand the underlying concepts and their connection within the rule. For this reason the teacher should discourage a simple parroting of the rule, and encourange instead a step-by-step acquisition of the concepts which make up the rule.

As the child moves up the school there should be less emphasis on rote learning. This is because more complex learning tends to be dependent on concepts and rules rather than on simple associations. But in all kinds of learning situations the key to success lies in the three factors of maximising interest, supplying as much meaning as possible and ensuring that all underlying concepts and vocabulary are already mastered.

(5) *Learning to read*

Perhaps the most important learning task in the primary school is learning to read. While the great majority of children learn to read with a reasonable amount of ease, for some children learning to read is a more difficult task. As we have mentioned before, a slow start in learning to read does not mean that the child concerned will continue to lag behind his peers, unless the child becomes so damaged in self-concept that he can never learn to apply himself to the task because he is so overwhelmed by feelings of inadequacy. But whether they learn comparatively quickly or comparatively slowly, all children should master reading well before they leave the primary school. Studies of reading show that this does not occur 'naturally'. Teachers have to teach reading to the great majority of children. (Some exceptional children enter school already able to read in a meaningful way, and others, exceptional in another way, may unfortunately never learn to do so. We will deal with these children in the last section of this chapter.)

The area of teaching reading is covered by a vast amount of texts. At the end of this chapter there is a select bibliography of useful books; in this short section we can do no more than point to some recent approaches to the teaching of reading. However, it is worth mentioning that all reading experts agree that, for the teaching of reading to be effective, it has to be consistent, organised and thorough.

It is our view that the two principles we have relied on thus far in the chapter apply as well to the teaching of reading as they do to the teaching of associations, concepts and rules. They are that learning should be made as interesting and as enjoyable as possible, and that we should make use of the child's natural tendency to look for rules, regularities and meaning in the new material he encounters.

(a) *Making reading interesting and enjoyable*. If a child has grown up in a home where his parents

clearly derive a great deal of enjoyment out of reading, he will be well prepared for the task of learning to read, not only because he sees it as pleasurable but also because he realises that people extract meaning from print. But some children have illiterate parents or parents who, although they can read, do so seldom and with difficulty. In addition, particularly if they grow up in a rural area, they may have comparatively little experience of things to be read. Sometimes we forget, if we live in an urban area, how bathed we are in writing. Shop signs, traffic signs, advertisements, bus stop signs, newspapers, magazines and books all remind us of the importance of written communication. Children who live in outlying rural areas may have much less exposure to writing or signs or print. Indeed, their only experience of it may come from the labels on tins, bottles and boxes or the signs painted on lorries and vans. So one of the first tasks in teaching reading that should be done long before formal teaching is started is for the teacher to read stories to children out of books so they realise what reading is about; that, for example, by reading they can enjoy stories or gain information. Children must understand that *reading is about the communication of meaning between the person who has written the material and the person who is reading it*. Once the child has grasped this fundamental function of reading, and provided the material the teacher has read to him is interesting, he is ready and eager to learn to read.

A word here about the content of reading material. Children like to read about other children with whom they can identify. But, and this is where many first reading schemes fail to hold children's interest, reading material should not be tied too closely to the everyday doings of children just like the readers. The principle of moderate novelty indicates that a little divergence, fantasy or excitement will add to the interest. A recent study in Sierre Leone (Jordan, 1974), showed that the most favoured category of reading material was adventure stories. And in the West the huge comic industry shows how fascinated children are by fantasy, adventure and excitement. We are not, of course, recommending that children learn to read with comics, but it might be useful for people who are engaged in producing primers for reading to look at the content covered in the comic strips that children are so often addicted to.

Once a child has grasped what reading is about, he is ready to move on to learning to read. The most favoured contemporary approach to the teaching of reading is to regard it within the context of the child's speech and language skills (Smith, 1971). Children bring to reading a familiarity with the language they are learning to read in.* This leads them to approach reading in two ways. To begin with, they attempt to decode the symbols placed in front of them according to the rules and strategies that are taught, but more important, their familiarity with language often leads them to anticipate and guess the words that are coming on the page. They make use of all sorts of cues, and we can often see a child make an inspired guess at a word he has never encountered which is based on the sense of what he has been reading up to then. As Smith says, 'reading is a communication process in which the reader plays an active role ... all aspects of reading, from the identification of individual letters or words to the comprehension of entire passages, involve the reduction of uncertainty ...' (1971, p. 2). In other words, as Margaret Clark notes, we can regard reading as 'predicting one's way through print' (1976, p. 4).

It is very important, then, for the teacher to remember that a child does not come to the task of reading totally unprepared. He brings with him his knowledge of the language he is being taught to read in, and because of this we now see reading as a psycho-linguistic (psychological-language) skill rather than an independent learning task. This emphasis on the psycho-linguistic base of reading leads to three very important points.

(i) The language used in reading primers should be based on the natural speech patterns used by children and not on the 'see, mother, see', or 'come, Anne, come, run after me' language that used to be such a popular approach in reading primers. It is important to remember too that, as the Bullock Report on language and reading pointed out, children often use in their own speech far more complicated types of speech than are found in most reading primers; for example, longer sentences and fewer commands. Thus anyone attempting to write such a primer would be well advised to spend some time at least tape-recording children's language as they play and talk to each other.

(ii) Teachers should pay careful attention to the mistakes children may make when reading out loud. Through doing this, the teacher will be able to ascertain the extent to which the child

---

* In this section we are assuming that children learning to read are already familiar with the language they are learning to read. Of course, this is not always the case, and we shall discuss this in some detail in Chapter 10.

comprehends and understands what he is reading. The more the child is able to learn to correct his own errors in the context of gaining understanding from what he is reading, the more rapid will his reading progress be. As Clark notes (1976, p. 5):

> It is not sufficient to listen for whether the child's reading is correct or not; nor to correct him when he is wrong. It is equally important to listen to what he says when he is wrong and to ascertain the extent to which he is developing powers of self-correction when alerted to his errors. Some errors (or miscues) form part of the development towards skilled reading – indeed some may be the result of intelligent anticipation, not yet quite precise enough, but nevertheless the beginning of an awareness that print carries a message, that it is a communication in writing.

(iii) Finally we should remember that although some analysis is required in learning to read, for example, letters have to be discriminated, and sounds blended to make words, when teaching these skills teachers should not rely too much on terms like letters, sounds, syllables, words and sentences. A massive amount of research shows how confused children often are by the over-use of such terms, and perhaps it is better to rely on a single term, such as letter, rather than expect children to be able to understand what terms like words, syllables and sentences mean. As Downing says, 'Cognitive confusion is the common state of young beginners in their thinking about *units of print* (or writing) too' (1977, p. 368). For example, he cites a study with American children aged 5 and 6 who 'when they were asked to take a pair of scissors and cut off "a word" from a card with a sentence printed on it, often cut off more than one word or part of a word'.

However, it is not sufficient simply to believe that because children understand language, and appreciate that reading is a meaningful task, they will automatically learn how to read. As any teacher will know, a great deal of systematic groundwork has to be done as well so that they can match the written symbol (grapheme) to the spoken sound (phoneme). This leads us on to our second fundamental point concerning learning to read.

(*b*) *Emphasising the rules and regularities underlying reading.* We have already mentioned that children seek out regularities and rules in acquiring language. In much the same way, it can be seen that children apply rules to learning to read and write. If a language has a consistent match between the way it is written and its pronunciation, reading becomes a task to which rules and regularities can be easily applied. This is the case with some languages like Finnish and Japanese (Bullock, 1975) and Swahili (Robertson, 1979). Unfortunately it is not the case for all languages. English is a case where the pronunciation of a particular sound is seldom tied up to a particular spelling; the following is an example of the ways a particular phoneme (sound) can be written: **aisle**, **height**, **eye**, **I**, phial, **ice**, **high**, **island**, buy, **guide**, sty, rhyme.

Even if there is not a consistent relationship between sound and spelling, we still have to help children to learn to read by emphasising those regularities in reading and writing that there are in the particular language we are dealing with. We suggest that, in the case of English, the following areas can be treated in a systematic way when teaching reading.

(i) *Emphasising the orientation of letters when teaching letters.* As we have already discussed in the section on discrimination learning, we can help children to learn which letters to attach to which written shapes by presenting the letters in such a way that the children are directed to the criterial features of the shapes. An important aspect of teaching this is to realise that for children beginning to read *orientation* (or the way things are positioned) is not always an important feature of what they look at. For the first few years of his life a child learns that objects remain the same, no matter in which direction they are positioned. For example (see Figure 6.3), a doll is a doll, and a train is a train, no matter in which orientation it is presented. On the other hand, when a curve is joined to a line, it can form the letters 'd', 'b', 'p', or 'q' depending on which orientation is presented. This is something that must be made very clear to children: the direction of the shapes used for letters is very important. As Bullock (1975, p. 81) puts it:

> It is not that children have particular difficulty with orientation as such. They can see as well as any adult that b is p upside down, just as well as they can see that the doll or train is upside down. Where they have trouble is in learning to recognise these reflected and rotated forms as entirely different letters. They would regard it as very

Figure 6.3   Orientation changes letters
but not real-life objects

odd if a doll had to be called Betty instead of Susan according to which way it faced, or a train was called a motor car when it reversed.,

So it can be seen that teachers must pay attention to ensuring that children do see that the direction or orientation of letters is very important.

(ii) *Emphasising the direction in which writing and reading take place.* Another important lesson a child has to learn for any language is that writing is sequenced in a particular way. For some languages we read from left to right, in others from right to left, and in yet others reading is up and down rather than across the page. Each child has to learn the particular convention for his language and as this is not something that comes 'naturally', the learning set has to be taught. As Bullock writes, 'as with the orientation of a single letter, this conflicts to some extent with "learning sets" the child has already acquired. [By learning sets psychologists mean a learned tendency to approach similar kinds of

material in a particular way.] ... Little wonder, therefore, that many children are bemused [confused] by "on" and "no", "was" and "saw", "won" and "now", "stop" and "pots" etc.; and these are only the more obvious examples' (1975, p. 89). The teacher, then, has to ensure that the child is in a position to start making the analyses required in reading by being in possession of the required learning set for his language for processing the letters in the right order.

(iii) *Helping the child to build up a phonic analysis of his language.* Even if the first words a child learns to read are acquired by 'look-and-say' methods, at some stage his teacher will attempt to introduce him to the phonic (sound) system underlying his particular language. In English, at the moment, the method recommended by many experts, including the Bullock Report on language and reading skills, is to concentrate on teaching children the relationship between morphemes (the smallest unit of language that has a grammatical function) and sounds. Such experts consider that it is not particularly effective in English to use letter-sound approaches. For example, to teach a child that 'Kuh – a – tuh' says cat, Bullock notes, is 'simply incorrect'. Another phonic method that they do not recommend is emphasising syllables, because they consider this approach can lead to difficulties. For example, if we teach 'basket' as bas-ket, the child will have difficulty with 'walked', because he will tend to pronounce it as 'wal-ked'. Instead, Bullock and his co-writers recommend that the most helpful approach is to teach the child morphemes (*the most basic meaning units of language*) as sounds. If, for example, the child encounters *hear*, we should show him that this is the base word in *hearing* and *hears*. Similarly, when a child encounters *look*, we can extend his knowledge to *looked*, *looking*, *looks*, and so on. In this way, as Bullock says, 'by attending to whole words and their pronunciation, and over a period of time learning to make intuitive generalisations about phonemegrapheme relationships', the child will steadily acquire a sound basis of phonic knowledge (1975, pp. 87–8).

However, other experts recommend that the morpheme-based approach recommended by Bullock should be supplemented by a great deal of other phonic drill that is based on common letter clusters and the way they are usually pronounced in speech. For example, they recommend practice in common word endings, like 'ing' in walk**ing**, runn**ing**, stand**ing**, etc., and '**tion**' in atten**tion**, posi**tion**, subtrac**tion**, etc.; in letter blending like 'tr' in **tr**ain, **tr**y, sub**tr**act, etc., and 'nd' in ble**nd**, fou**nd**, rou**nd**ed, etc.; in common vowel combinations like 'ea' in **ea**ch, s**ea**t, l**ea**n, etc., and 'oa' as in r**oa**m, m**oa**n, gr**oa**n, etc.

In this short section on the teaching of reading we have tried to introduce you to some of the more recent approaches to this subject. Naturally such a brief treatment does little justice to this important topic and at the end of the chapter you will find a select bibliography dealing with the teaching of reading. We should emphasise, once again, that in this treatment we made an assumption that the child already has a thorough spoken knowledge of the language he is being taught to read. This is not, of course, always the case and we shall deal with the difficulties encountered when it is not the case in Chapter 10. Again, it should also be emphasised that the references made are nearly all to teaching children to read English. Clearly, then, some of the recommendations we have made do not apply to the same extent to other languages and in particular, to those where there is a more consistent relationship between spelling and pronunciation.

(6) *Learning to solve problems*

Problem-solving and creativity may be regarded as the most complex of the cognitive behaviours that we expect from children at school. In the next section when we discuss creativity we shall argue that much of our most creative behaviour takes place outside the formality of the educational setting but, in general, this is not true for problem-solving which, in the sense we shall use the term, is linked to the kind of situation where we expect the student to find out how to do something within a learning setting.

Precisely what do we mean by problem-solving then? Many psychologists have pointed out that definitions of problem-solving vary enormously. We shall use the term to cover behaviour where a student *has to go beyond the application of a rule or rules he has learned in order to answer a question.* In other words, as Ausubel and Robinson write, in problem-solving 'there should be a gap between where the student is and where he has to get in order to attain a solution' (1971, p. 69). The student is required, not just to apply or even generate a simple rule, but to reorganise the material he has been given to attain a novel solution of a type he has not encountered before.

Although other subjects in the school curriculum may cover topics that are concerned with the solution of problems – for example, in social studies students may discuss a real life dilemma facing a certain individual – we shall confine ourselves to the type of problem that appears to give the most difficulty in school: mathematics and science problems.

In the section on rules we spent some time discussing the rule that the angles of a triangle add up to 180 degrees. If, after he has been given the rule, we were to give a student the sizes of two angles of a triangle and ask him to calculate the third, that would hardly be a problem, but merely the application of an already mastered rule. If, however, we were to set him the following problem, he would have to go beyond the simple application of the rule, and would have to close a gap between something he already knows how to do and a new solution. In this problem we assume that the student has learned two rules of geometry, first the one we have discussed, that the three angles of a triangle add up to 180 degrees, and secondly that opposite angles are equal.

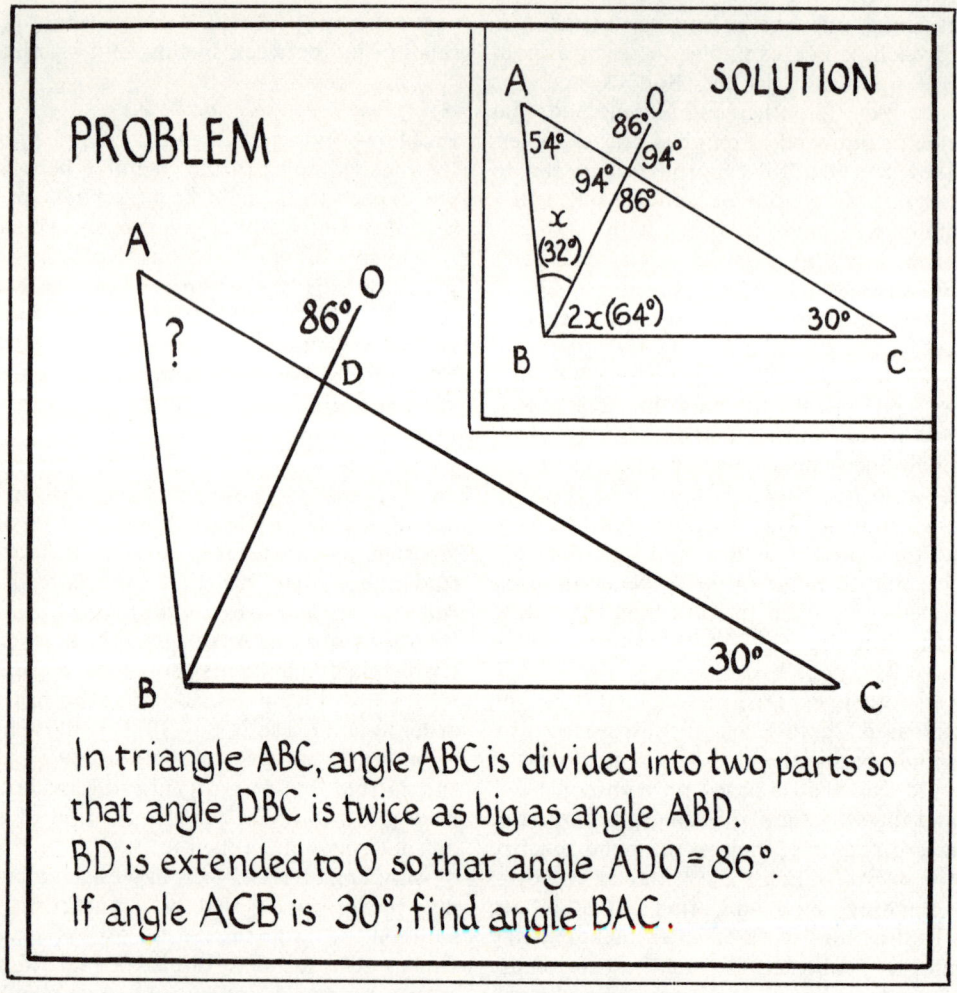

PROBLEM

SOLUTION

In triangle ABC, angle ABC is divided into two parts so that angle DBC is twice as big as angle ABD.
BD is extended to O so that angle ADO = 86°.
If angle ACB is 30°, find angle BAC.

Figure 6.4 A Geometry problem

In triangle ABC (see Figure 6.4) angle ABC is divided into two by line BDO so that angle DBC is twice as big as angle ABD. Angle ADO is 86 degrees and angle C is 30 degrees. Find angle A.

What are the steps the child has to go through to solve this problem? According to Ausubel and Robinson, there are three major steps: (a) definition of goal and present position, (b) gap-filling process and (c) post-solution verification (or checking out).

(a) *Definition of goal and present position.* At this stage, the student has to relate the problem to what he already knows. That is, he has to have mastered all the concepts used in the problem. In this case, he has to understand what we mean by an angle, a triangle and the size of an angle. Secondly he has to

be quite clear what he has been asked to do – in this case, calculate the size of a particular angle. From the point of view of the teacher, then, she has to ensure that all the underlying concepts used in a problem are well understood and she has also to make sure that the nature of the question asked is understood.

(b) *Gap-filling process.* This consists of three processes.
(i) Relevant background information. The student has to ask himself what he knows that could be helpful in this problem. He will probably remind himself of all the rules he knows about that concern angles and in doing this he may jot down that angles of a triangle

add up to 180 degrees and that opposite angles are equal. He may also of course recall rules about, say, parallel lines, but if he inspects the figure he should see that they are not particularly relevant as there are no parallel lines.

(ii) Rules of inference. By this we mean that the student should be prepared to apply simple reasoning. For example, if he finds angle DBC, then he should be able to reason that by dividing it in half, he will obtain angle ABD.

(iii) Strategies. What strategies can the student apply to the solution of such a geometric problem? It is here that previous teaching will count. If the teacher has encouraged students to write into the diagram each angle size as they discover it, this will be a very helpful strategy. If the teacher has taught students to jot down rules that are possibly relevant (see above) this will be another useful strategy. Finally, if the teacher has asked the students to think backwards this will be a third useful strategy. By thinking backwards, we mean that the student has been taught to ask himself, what do I need to know in order to work out angle A?

(c) *Post-solution verification.* Once he has found a solution the student should check his calculations and reasoning. He should also check the validity of his solution; for example, if he obtained an angle in a triangle that was greater than 180 degrees, he should be able to reject this solution.

In exploring this problem in some detail we hope we have pinpointed some of the necessary conditions for solving problems:

(a) A full and complete understanding of the concepts used in the problem, and the precise nature of the question asked.

(b) (i) A thorough understanding and knowledge of the rules that underly the solution of the problem.

(ii) Practice in using logic and reasoning to arrive at answers.

(iii) Direct teaching of strategies relevant to problem-solving.

(c) Training in inspection of the answers to problems to see if they are appropriate.

As with the other processes of learning, motivation is very important. An endless set of similar problems can be very boring and therefore if the teacher can make the content of problems relate to areas of interest, for example, perhaps using football results for problems concerning calculating averages, she can raise the intrinsic interest of arithmetic. Another constructive way of adding interest to problem-solving is to divide the class into groups and see which group can find the solution to a problem first.

(7) Creativity

'Creativity' is a word that is used a great deal in educational circles. You can probably think back to a number of times when you were encouraged to 'teach creatively' or to 'encourage children to think creatively' or to 'promote creativity in composition/drawing/painting lessons'. You would probably also list the term 'creative' as one of the qualities you would like to see your pupils described as having. But what precisely do we mean by 'creativity' and 'creative'?

It is not really possible to be too precise in answering this but we all probably recognise creativity when we meet it. In general we tend to refer to some of the following things when we talk about being creative: thinking in unusual ways, producing unusual and different uses for things, seeing things in unconventional and unique ways, solving problems using unexpected but effective solutions, producing original work in subjects like composition (often, indeed, called 'creative writing'), drawing, painting or modelling, responding to new situations in novel ways.

It is quite obvious that it is an essential part of any educator's job to encourage this quality and, indeed, no educational psychology textbook could be considered complete that did not attempt to do just this. Nevertheless, we consider that providing direct instructions as to how to promote this quality is a very difficult task because creativity in any situation, whether educational or otherwise, is so much a matter of a particular response to a particular situation. Some teachers may produce original and creative work from their pupils by their own fresh and enthusiastic approach to the learning situation, while others may encourage it by first analysing with their pupils work that they consider creative and then helping their pupils to produce original work using these analyses as guidelines. Yet other teachers may argue that it is not possible to teach creativity directly. In this section we try to provide an introduction to the area of creativity by considering some of the issues involved but, aside from providing references at the end of the chapter to some useful texts, we shall not attempt to provide a blueprint for teaching creativity.

It seems to us that the important issues in the area of creativity are the following:

(a) A history of interest in creativity.
(b) Tests that have been used to rate creativity in children.
(c) Are highly creative people different from other people?
(d) Creativity and culture.
(e) Classroom variables that may aid creative work.

(a) *Creativity – a historical perspective.* Ever since the early 1950s the study of creativity has been a very active field of psychology. A major cause of the interest was the growing conviction in the USA that intelligence tests (which we will discuss in Chapter 11) were not measuring all the most important aspects of cognitive ability. As the world entered the 'space age', American educators became concerned that their selection tests were not always selecting for advanced education those children who would potentially be of most use to society. As one of the foremost workers in the area of creativity, Paul Torrance, notes, 'The Space Age is taking us places where old and comfortable ideas no longer apply. Much will be required of the creative potential of today's school children' (1963, p. 3).

In 1950 J. P. Guildford gave his presidential address to the American Psychological Association and in the course of this he gave direction in the area of what he called 'divergent' thinking, but what became commonly referred to as 'creativity'. He argued that intelligence was not one-dimensional, and claimed that intellectual functioning can occur in different ways. One of these ways he called divergent production and he contrasted this with what he called convergent production. He argued that convergent production is a thinking process whereby people search for a particular answer to a problem which most people would agree is the logically correct answer. Divergent production, on the other hand, is a search for a number of different answers. For example, when Guildford asked his subjects how many uses they could think of for a brick, '*convergent*' responses would relate to its use as a building material, whereas '*divergent*' responses would be, for example 'make a doorstop; make a red powder; make a paper weight; make a bookcase; drown a cat'; and so on. Guildford considered that people who gave a number of divergent responses were more flexible and creative than those who could only give convergent responses.

Guildford's ideas sparked off a great deal of research. Among the most influential of the earlier work in this area was the study done by Getzels and Jackson (1962). In this study they suggest that creativity is different from intelligence. They tested children at a private school by giving them tests of intelligence and tests on five measures of creativity, partially adapted from Guildford's measures of divergent production. They then divided the children into four groups as follows: high creativity + high IQ, high creativity + low IQ, low creativity + low IQ, low creativity + high IQ. They concentrated on the two groups high creativity + low IQ (whom they call 'high creativity') and low creativity + high IQ (whom they call 'high intelligence'). (It will be seen that they ignored children who were both highly intelligent and high in creativity and also those low on both their measures, and their work has been severely criticised for this.)

Getzels and Jackson claim that highly creative children are very different from high intelligence children in that the high intelligence children tended to concentrate on stereotyped meanings, judge success by conventional standards, model themselves on their teachers and conform. On the other hand, high creatives tended to move away from conventional responses, produce original fantasies and judge success by unconventional standards.

As we have already noted, there were criticisms of Getzels' and Jackson's methodology and a number of studies, particularly one done by Hasan and Butcher (1966) in Scotland, failed to show a distinction between the two types of children. A particularly interesting study by Hudson (1966) showed that boys who gave convergent responses on tests could be manipulated into giving divergent responses by changing the experimental instructions. Similarly, boys who normally gave divergent responses could be manipulated into giving convergent ones. This of course suggested that 'creativity' could be very specific to situations.

On the other hand, a number of studies did show a distinction between children based on their scores on tests of creativity and tests of intelligence. A study that has received a great deal of attention was that done by Wallach and Kogan (1965). They gave their tests in a relaxed atmosphere to 151 schoolchildren, presenting them as 'games' because they felt that such an atmosphere would be more likely to favour the appearance of a 'creative' trait. They concluded from their results that children who are high in intelligence and low in creativity fit in well in most school situations as they regard success at school as important. On the other hand children who are low in intelligence but high in creativity have great difficulty in fitting into the conventional school situation.

What can we conclude from this short historical summary? First, that although a distinction is sometimes made between divergent thinking and creativity, most classroom studies have tended to treat these as roughly the same. Secondly, that some, though not all, studies show that on tests of creativity and on tests of intelligence some children may score well on intelligence but low on creativity and vice versa. In Chapter 11 we shall look critically at 'tests of intelligence' but here we may perhaps remind readers that what all these studies are measuring is behaviour in the test situation. The studies do not deal with 'creative' or 'intelligent' behaviour outside the test situation and so perhaps the results of the studies are contradictory because the tests are not valid (appropriate) measures of the qualities we have called 'creativity' and 'intelligence'. We shall return to this very important area in Chapter 11.

(b) *Tests of Creativity.* Leaving aside for the moment whether tests of creativity are valid or not, we should like to introduce the reader to some of these tests so that he or she may judge how appropriate they seem.

One of the most important names in the field of creativity-testing is Torrance. Some of the tests he uses are the following: Product Improvement Test in which children are asked, for example, how to make a toy more attractive; Ask and Guess Test in which children are required to guess, by asking questions, what led up to a particular event shown on a picture; and the Just Suppose Tests in which children are asked, for example, what would happen if all circular-shaped objects, like, for example, all wheels, suddenly turned square.

Guildford's tests of divergent thinking include tests like 'Plot Titles'. In this children are required to give titles to stories they have been told. For example, one item requires the subject to give a title to the following story: a missionary is captured by cannibals and is given the choice of marrying their princess or being eaten; he refuses and is boiled alive. Responses taken as divergent are of the nature *Pot's Plot*, *Stewed Parson*, *A Mate Worse than Death*, while less divergent responses are of the nature *Eaten by Savages* or *The Princess*. Incidentally, this item provides revealing insight into the culturally biased nature of some items in standard tests, a subject to which we will return in Chapter 11.

In their study Getzels and Jackson used five measures of creativity: *word association* – the subject has to give as many definitions as possible to words like 'bolt', 'bark', 'sack'; *uses for things* – the subject is required to give uses for things like bricks, paper-clips; *hidden shapes* – the subject is asked to find simple figures in more complex ones (rather like the test item shown in Figure 4.7 on page 52); *fables* – the subject is required to provide a 'moral', a 'humorous' and a 'sad' ending to four fables or stories; and *Make up problems* – the subject is presented with a numerical statement, for example, about the cost of building a house, and asked to make up mathematical problems from the statement.

Among Wallach and Kogan tests of creativity are the Incomplete Drawing Tests in which children are shown incomplete drawings which do not depict anything at all and asked to tell the investigator what the 'pictures' look like.

It is hoped that this short description has given you some idea of the type of thinking that has been labelled 'creative' or 'divergent'. You may perhaps consider two important questions. First, could divergent or creative responses be 'coached' without necessarily changing a child's basic approach to the classroom situation? Secondly, do you consider that those children who produce the most original work in your own experience would necessarily score highest at such tests? The second question is one that you could perhaps attempt to answer for yourself by producing a test along the lines just described and seeing whether those pupils that you have always considered 'creative' are the highest scorers.

(c) *Are highly creative people different from other people?* To answer this question we have to consider carefully what we regard as causing creative/divergent behaviour. Do we consider this to spring from the particular personality of the person concerned or do we see such behaviour as arising from specific environmental factors like the type of teaching received, the field of work involved, or the type of behaviour encouraged by the particular group to which the person concerned sees himself as belonging?

To answer this question let us turn first to studies made of creative adults. This is a good way to begin because most people feel confident in deciding who creative adults are. They are those individuals who have made new and original contributions to their own discipline and, particularly in the case of scientists and architects, it is relatively easy to differentiate productive and original workers from those who, though they may work consistently, seldom come up with new and effective ideas, compositions or designs.

A number of such studies have been made in the USA (these are covered in some detail in Joanna Turner's book *Psychology for the Classroom* which has a very thorough and lengthy section on Creativity). Such surveys come up with a list of characteristics for creative scientists that usually contain the following characteristics:

(i) A high degree of ability to direct their own work.

(ii) A preference for thinking about abstract, intellectual subjects rather than about interpersonal relationships.

(iii) A tendency to be emotionally stable.

(iv) A liking for being exact and precise.

(v) A tendency to be inhibited and controlled in their emotional life rather than uninhibited and impulsive.

(vi) An ability to tolerate uncertainty in their thinking. They do not need to have complete understanding of all the details of problems but are able to cope with some degree of ambiguity. Nevertheless, they like to try and embrace all aspects of the subject they are interested in.

(vii) An ability to be independent of others in their thinking, without needing to conform to group pressures.

(viii) Superior general intelligence and an early interest in intellectual activities.

Studies of creative writers and painters show rather different characteristics. For example, both these groups were shown in surveys to be more mature, dominant, adventurous, emotionally sensitive, radical, self-sufficient and energetic than the general population. Interestingly, they also score higher (as you will remember the creative scientists did) on intelligence.

MacKinnon (1962) studied architects. He compared two groups: a number who were selected by five experts as being the most creative in the country and a number selected to match these in other characteristics like age, education and area of residence but who had not been named as particularly creative* The creative architects were found to be independent in their thought, more open to experience, more flexible and spontaneous. Like the creative scientists they were able to tolerate more ambiguity than less creative people. But unlike the scientists and like the creative writers and artists, they were inclined to reject inhibiting their impulses and were also less inclined to repress their thoughts and feelings than the control group. Unlike both the scientists and artists and writers, they did not show higher levels of academic (intellectual) achievement than those who were less creative.

What can we conclude from these studies of creative adults? First of all, we should note that they were all done within one culture and therefore any conclusions we draw should perhaps be limited to that culture, or to very similar cultures. Secondly, it seems from these studies that creative people tend to be creative because something in their own approach interacts with the particular demands of the field they are working in. For example, in the case of scientists, precision and exactitude were important but this quality was not essential for creativity for either of the other two groups. Intelligence and intellectual achievement was an important characteristic of creative scientists and writers but was not a characteristic that was important in the case of creative architects. Even in terms of characteristics that are more central to the personality of the people concerned, the findings were not consistent. For, while creative scientists were found to be relatively controlled and inhibited in their emotional functioning, this characteristic was not found in the other two groups of creative people studied. It seems, then, that we cannot characterise what is associated with creativity without reference to the field in which people are working. Different kinds of characteristics tend to be associated with different

* We call such a procedure selecting a control group – a group that is matched on all characteristics, except the one we are experimenting with, to the experimental group. Here the experimental group (creative architects) was matched on all possible characteristics with another group of architects who were not creative (the control group). You may remember that control groups were used in the Rappaport and Rappaport study described in the last chapter.

fields of endeavour. Perhaps the only characteristic that was consistent for all groups was the ability to be independent of others in one's work. Aside from this, it seems from the studies that, broadly speaking, scientists are creative in a different way from those working in humanities and the arts.

This conclusion agrees with the work of Hudson (1966). He notes that divergent production or thinking (that is, doing well on the type of tests we have described in the last section) is not characteristic of scientists. On the whole the scientists he studied were more likely to be convergent in their thinking. He concludes, therefore, that divergent thinking is not the same as creativity but is a quality more associated with artists, writers and architects. Creativity, in the case of scientists, is not, then, the capacity to do well at tests of divergent thinking, which are the tests that are usually used to measure creativity. It seems that the quality of creativity must be related to the discipline under consideration.

Perhaps you have observed this yourself. If you think of the people you consider to be creative, do they all show very similar characteristics? On the whole, you may find that scientists or mathematicians, because of their training and their own particular subject matter, tend to be more controlled and convergent in their approaches whereas people in other fields may be more intuitive and less controlled in their work. We would argue, then, that teaching creativity, if it were possible, is not simply a matter of training children to give more divergent responses to tests of the type described in the last section. Indeed, as we already noted, children who score high on convergence can be made to score high on divergence if we manipulate the experimental proceedings. Hudson did this by asking boys who were studying science to answer the tests on divergence by pretending to be a writer with an unconventional life-style and answering the questions as though they were that writer.

Suran and Rizzo (1979) come to very similar conclusions as well. They consider creativity is not an all-or-none quality. Everyone is capable of some creativity and whether people produce very creative work or not depends on the field they are working in, how interested they are in it, how their particular pattern of abilities suits the field, and whether they possess personal qualities (for example, precision in the case of scientists, divergent thinking in the case of writers) that are consistent with the demands of the field they are

working in. One characteristic does seem important, though of course not everyone who possesses this characteristic is creative, and that is confidence in one's own approach and the ability to withstand the pressures of others.

(d) *Creativity and Culture.* Some writers about Third World countries have argued that because creativity is associated with the ability to think independently, cultures which require children to be respectful to their elders within the home setting are bound to lower creativity in the classroom. They argue that within traditional societies, certain child care practices are associated with lowered creative potential. Both Kuppuswamy (1974) and Ghuman (1977) claim that this is true for India, and Vernon (1969) claims this is so for African cultures.

Torrance (1963) conducted a study of what he calls the 'creative potential' in a number of different cultures. He measured this by tests that, according to the last sub-section, we might more properly regard as tests of divergent production or thinking. In his book describing this study, he reports the results from the Samoa in some detail. He notes that, overall, the Samoan sample showed the lowest 'creative potential'. In the main he sees this as springing from the demands of the Samoan culture. Like the writers mentioned in the last paragraph, he associates low creative potential with the need to conform and accept without challenge the instructions of elders and superiors. He claims that Samoan teachers value in their pupils the characteristics of being quiet, liking to work alone and being prompt, and that they rate lower than teachers in other cultures the characteristics in their pupils of being adventurous, a self-starter, curious, determined and independent in judgement.

What are we to make of this? Two conclusions seem possible. First (and quite erroneously in our opinion), we could conclude that traditional cultures prevent creativity being shown and suppress original thinking and independence of judgement. Secondly, we can conclude with Castle who worked in Uganda and Leacock who worked in Zambia that, on the contrary, traditional cultures have produced and continue to produce creative work in both the artistic and the technological spheres. However, *some* Third World classrooms do tend to lower creative responses because they require a great deal of conformity and intellectual submission to the teacher. These characteristics *are not* the result of traditional values, because, as can be seen from many descriptions of the informal education systems that preceded formal schooling in traditional cultures, children learnt within the traditional culture in an active way. Instead such conformity is more likely to spring from the type of education that was introduced with the appearance of Western education systems when missionaries tended to impose their own educational values in an authoritarian, even if in many cases kindly, way.

Castle sums it up well when he writes about artistic and cultural creativity in Africa (1966, pp. 198–9):

> ' The cultivation of manual, artistic, musical, literary, vocal, dramatic, rhythmic skills are rooted in African experience ... The exuberantly creative talents of African children are as yet barely tapped, as has been proved by those few schools and teachers who have given children the freedom and encouragment to express themselves in paint and clay. The growing point of a child's creative gifts is his innate urge to use his fingers and imagination in the material and familiar life of his home and neighbourhood ... '

Similarly Leacock, writing on Zambia, notes that it is the dependence on the rote learning that was introduced by missionary educators to Africa that is primarily responsible for practices in classrooms that do not encourage creative and original thinking in scientific and technological subjects.

Torrance too, writing about Samoa, notes that while part of the tradition of conformity he describes in Samoa comes from cultural values, much has been contributed by an acceptance of authority that was imposed by 'the influx of missionaries and German traders' who, he writes, placed the 'emphasis on submission either to God and his "special representatives" or to the traders who needed submissive workers on the plantations' (1963, p. 83).

We would argue then, that if Third World classrooms do emphasise conformity, rote learning and submission to authority, (a) this is not a result of traditional culture and (b) if indeed such practices are common in Third World classrooms this has not prevented Third World countries from displaying a most impressive body of creative work.

(e) *Classroom variables that may aid creativity.* It does seem clear that creativity is associated with an independence of judgement and with the ability to be self-directing in one's work. It also seems clear that all children are capable to some extent of creative behaviour. (Some teachers may be convinced that in the case of the more unruly pupils, such creativity is all directed into disrupting the teacher's best efforts!)

What are the implications, then, for trying to promote a classroom atmosphere that will encourage creative work? It seems to us the following apply:

(i)   While, as we have noted earlier in this chapter, rote learning has a limited though important part to play in association learning in the early years particularly, too much emphasis on passive learning of this nature destroys creativity. As Ekimo Njau, a Ugandan artist teacher, said about the subject of simply copying or learning in a passive and repetitive manner: 'Do not copy: copying puts God to sleep' (Castle, 1966).

(ii) Children should be encouraged to express their own individual ways of learning. Not everyone learns in the same way. Some children need to ask a lot of questions and follow up things that interest them individually. They should not be made to feel different from and therefore inferior to others. It should be made clear to classes that differences between class members in their learning behaviour do exist and this spread of behaviour adds interest and strength to the class.

(iii) Children should be encouraged to explore their environment and, if possible, resources should be provided for them to test out any original ideas they may have. Children who present unusual and unconventional answers to problems should be helped to test out their solutions and to evaluate how effective these solutions are.

With the end of this sub-section on creativity we have come to the end of our section on aspects of learning and we now turn our attention to instructional approaches.

Instructional Approaches

One of the most common criticisms the general public tends to make of educational practice is that it is very liable to sudden swings and changes. You've probably heard someone say 'never run after a bus or an educational theory, there is always another one round the corner'. There is indeed much substance in this criticism if one looks at books on educational psychology over a period. Sometimes the very thing that most psychologists are enthusiastically recommending during one decade is dismissed with total contempt in the next.

But educationalists are usually much more realistic. They seldom copy or take over a particular fad in its entirety. Instead they are far more likely to examine such psychological fashions in the light of their own practical experience and knowledge of psychology and extract what seems to them valuable in the new approach.

In discussing instructional processes we are going to present three approaches. Each approach springs from a particular set of assumptions about the nature of learning and all three, not surprisingly, as they are all based on the observation of learning behaviour, overlap to some extent. Few teachers would wholeheartedly accept all the assumptions and recommendations of any particular approach. For this reason, in our concluding sub-section, we present what we call an *eclectic* approach, in which we try to extract from the three approaches the most useful and realistic recommendations.

The first approach we present is one whose theoretical basis was laid during the first half of this century; the second two approaches, while they owe a great deal to the educational thinkers of the more distant past, are characteristic of the cognitive psychology of the 1960s and 1970s.

(1) Learning theory

In this book we have not taken up a position that is in line with what has been called 'behaviourism'. This is because we believe that it is important to try and discover how different people perceive the world and process their perceptions. We consider that it is only when we have some insight into this that we can understand the behaviour of other people. This viewpoint would be most unacceptable to a convinced behaviourist. He, or she, would argue that all we can really observe is human behaviour and this behaviour should be the only raw material of our psychological theory; anything else, like trying to understand the perceptions and thought processes of others, can only be speculation and guessing.

The behaviourists based their approach on learning theory. They observed the learning process in great detail, using both human and non-human subjects (commonly rats and pigeons). They considered that the most fruitful approach was to try and understand as fully as possible the most elementary processes of learning and from there build, step by step, a comprehensive theory that would embrace the whole field of human endeavour. In order to do this, they concentrated on associations between stimuli (the plural of stimulus which refers to anything perceived by the sense organs – i.e. anything seen, heard, felt, tasted or smelled) and responses, stimuli and other stimuli and, later, responses and responses.

The first experimental work that was absorbed in their theory was that of Edward Thorndike (1874–1949). He believed that learning was the result of associations between stimuli and responses that occurred through trial and error. For example, he would place a hungry cat in a box which had a lever that could be pressed for the cat to be able to get out. He would then place food outside the cage where the cat could smell and see it. Naturally the cat would begin to move around seeking to get out. Eventually, in its movements, it would press the lever. This lever pressing would be by sheer accident. The cat would then be replaced in the cage, and once again, it would move around until it pressed the lever and obtained release. This procedure would be followed until, by trial and error, the cat learned to press the lever as soon as it was placed in the box.

Thorndike considered that the cat had to be hungry for it to learn. He analysed what happened as follows. The cat had learned an association between the lever (the stimulus) and pressing the lever (the response). This association was learned because the response was rewarding (it led to food). The rewarding aspect of the association was called the *reinforcement*. Further, Thorndike claimed that *practice* helped to stamp in the association.

Another influential set of experimental data came from the Russian laboratories of Ivan Pavlov (1849–1936). He worked with dogs and was interested in the association between different stimuli. He showed that if you sounded a tone each time you fed a hungry dog, the dog, who originally salivated only at the sight of food, would eventually learn to salivate to the sound of the tone even if it was presented without food. The dog had learned an association between two stimuli – the sight of the food and the sound of the tone. The sound of the tone, which was called a 'conditioned stimulus', now acted as a signal. If, after you had taught this association, you continually presented the tone without food, the association would be weakened and the dog would no longer salivate at the sound. The association was said to be *extinguished*.

Another set of data on which the behaviourists based their theory was that of Clark Hull whose main work was published in 1943. Hull developed an elaborate system in which he tried to predict how well associations could be learned by manipulating motivation (for example, how hungry the animal was), incentive (how rewarding the reinforcer was – for example, to a rabbit a carrot is more likely to be reinforcing than a chocolate) and how often the animal was reinforced (called the schedule of reinforcement).

The final and most influential experimenter in this field has been B. F. Skinner who was born in 1904. He worked with rats and pigeons mainly and he formulated four basic laws that underlie learning theory as we know it today:

(a) *Reward or positive reinforcement*: responses that are rewarded are likely to be repeated.
(b) *Negative reinforcement*: responses bringing freedom from unpleasant or painful situations are likely to be repeated.
(c) *Extinction (non-reinforcement)*: responses that do not lead to reinforcement are unlikely to be repeated.
(d) *Punishment*: responses that lead to painful consequences will be suppressed but can reappear if the connection – response–punishment – is not always kept up.

Skinner's work in particular had a massive influence on classroom practice in the USA because, following the four principles outlined, he supplied a very simple formula for shaping behaviour in the classroom. Reward (reinforce) the habits you want to build up and ignore (or fail to reinforce) the habits you wish to get rid of.

We will consider current classroom practice that is based on the learning theories of the behaviourists in three areas: learning associations, behaviour modification and social learning.

Learning Associations Behavioural learning theorists consider that the learning of associations is the basis of all learning. Like most psychologists who are more influenced by cognitive theory, we would not agree with this viewpoint because we consider that learning involves the *active restructuring* of perceptions and concepts and is not merely a system of linked associations. Nevertheless, we would not deny that some learning is concerned with the linking of associations, though we would argue that such learning is not very common except, perhaps, in the learning of vocabulary, names and other verbal labels. (The reader who wishes to remind himself of this area might perhaps look again at the summary at the end of Chapter 4, points 4 and 5, and the section on association learning in this chapter.)

Even if we do not accept that the learning of associations is at the root of all learning, we have to accept that the conditions for the learning of associations have been very clearly laid down by behaviour theorists and the following pointers (that we have already mentioned in our section on association learning) are useful for all educationalists:

(a) Reinforce all correct learning of associations as soon as possible after they have been made.
(b) Use repetition to stamp in the learning of associations. Some learning theorists like to recommend the practice of 'overlearning' by which they mean that once association tasks are mastered, and further practice no longer brings any improvement, practice should still continue because such 'overlearning' makes the material more resistant to forgetting.

A major extension of learning theory techniques in the classroom has been to programmed learning. All programmed learning texts have two characteristics in common: they shape learning by reinforcements and they require active responses. An example of a programmed learning text can be seen in Figure 6.5 and you will notice that basically the learner is required to read a question, supply the answer he thinks is the correct one, check to see if he is right or not, move on to the next frame if he is right or move backwards in the text for revision if he is not right. Some programmed learning texts supply special revision sections depending on which incorrect answer was shown. Thus the two characteristics mentioned above, immediate feedback and active learner participation, can be seen.

The major advantages of programmed learning lie in the fact that it is self-paced or under learner control so that each learner can proceed at his own speed, that it supplies built-in revision, often of a

<u>To consolidate your ideas so far:</u>

Transform the following numerals into
base ten numerals, and check your answers
against those on the right.

<u>Answers</u>

10_{three} = ——— ten   3

10_{nine} = ——— ten   9

10_{six} = ——— ten   6

10_{two} = ——— ten   2

10_{twelve} = ——— ten   12

Now try these:-

20_{three} = ——— ten   6

30_{nine} = ——— ten   <u>If you have any</u>   27
                               <u>trouble with the</u>
50_{six} = ——— ten   <u>examples on this page,</u>   30
                               <u>read p.10 and then</u>
And then:-   <u>return to this page.</u>

21_{three} = ——— ten   7

32_{nine} = ——— ten   29

55_{six} = ——— ten   35

And then:-

123_{five} = ——— ten   38

204_{six} = ——— ten   76

333_{four} = ——— ten   63

111_{nine} = ——— ten   91

<u>Conversely</u> ......

15_{ten} = ___ nines + ___ ones i.e. ———$_{nine}$ 1, 6 i.e.
                                                            16_{nine}
7_{ten} = ___ sevens + ___ ones i.e. ———$_{seven}$ 1, 0 i.e.
                                                            10_{seven}
78_{ten} = ___ twenty-fives + ___ fives +   3, 0, 3
             ___ ones, i.e. ———$_{five}$ i.e. 303_{five}

102_{ten} = ___ thirty-sixes + ___ sixes +   2, 5, 0,
              ___ ones, i.e. ———$_{six}$ i.e. 250_{six}

If clear so far, proceed to **11**

Figure 6.5   An example of a programmed learning text
   (Calder, 1971)

very sophisticated nature, and that it is pleasant to use, as programmed learning texts are designed so that the learner is bound to get a high proportion of the questions correct. A final advantage is that the learner is always ready for the next step because the material is usually very carefully presented and sequenced in a logical order.

Although programmed learning texts have been developed from the principles of learning theory, not only simple associations are taught by means of such texts. A number of programmed learning texts aim to teach concepts as well as associations. In the case of the teaching of concepts, however, programmed texts are best used in conjunction with other methods of teaching like demonstrations and ordinary classroom techniques.

The major disadvantage of programmed instruction for most pupils lies in the absence of interpersonal relationships so that many pupils find this technique monotonous and boring. It is, however, a particularly useful technique for revision at the upper end of the school.

Behaviour modification. Let us suppose that Miss M has in her class of 5-year-olds a very aggressive little girl, Anna. Anna is always attacking other children, removing whatever toys they happen to be playing with, pushing them over and running off to another section of the classroom. Let us suppose that Miss M is aware that such behaviour stems from the fact that Anna's emotional needs have not been satisfied and/or that she has learned that such aggressive behaviour is appropriate and effective either in the home or in her own neighbourhood. Miss M will, of course, as a result discuss the case with her headteacher, attempt to uncover the emotional causes of such behaviour, see Anna's parents and in general follow the procedures that are dictated by an earnest desire to understand her pupils. While she is doing this, however, she is still faced with a management problem because Anna's behaviour is very disruptive.

If she follows the principles of learning theory she will note that if Anna did not find her behaviour reinforcing she would not act as she does. Anna probably finds such behaviour reinforcing because she gets the toy she wants, she upsets another child and she gains the teacher's attention. What the teacher now has to do is remove the reinforcement for this bad behaviour and provide reinforcement for more constructive behaviour. She can do this by following this procedure. The next time Anna starts off on one of

her battles, the teacher should make sure that Anna does not get the toy; further, she should pick up, comfort and pet the child Anna has attacked; and finally, she should totally ignore Anna. In this way Anna fails to get the desired toy, sees that the other child is petted and rewarded rather than upset and fails to obtain the teacher's attention. In other words no reinforcement is offered for her undesirable behaviour. At the same time as Miss M observes this procedure when Anna is disruptive, she can reward (reinforce) all Anna's good behaviour. She can observe which toy Anna likes best and keep it in her desk, offering it to Anna whenever she has co-operated or played in a pleasant manner with another child. She may also praise and call attention to Anna's good behaviour thus supplying more reinforcement for desirable behaviour. In general by reinforcing the responses she wants Anna to make and extinguishing those she does not want Anna to make, Miss M is shaping Anna's behaviour by using the principles of behaviour modification laid down by Skinner.

If you are interested in the further application of such principles you will find a reference in this area in the selective bibliography at the end of this chapter. It is our belief, however, that behaviour modification in the classroom is more successful with children under the age of about 8 or 9 than it is with older children. Further we believe that there are ethical considerations in attempting to modify behaviour in such a way with older children unless the procedures are explained to them and they agree to take part in the programme.

Another extension of behaviour modification springs from the work of Pavlov which we mentioned earlier. If you remember we pointed out that sometimes, by means of associations, some stimuli come to act as signs. Thus for Pavlov's dogs a certain tone was a sign that food was coming. Watson, an American behaviourist, used this conditioning procedure to make a little boy called Albert frightened of a white rat. When Watson first presented Albert with the white rat, Albert was not frightened. However, after Watson had paired the presentation of the white rat with a loud sound right next to Albert's head a number of times, the association between the two stimuli (white rat–nasty sound) was made and after that Albert cried at the sight of the white rat alone.

Now just as Albert was conditioned to fear the rat by association, we may fear swimming if we have come close to drowning, or a child may come to fear mathematics if his first mathematics teacher continually humiliates him in maths lessons. Of course no teacher would wish intentionally to condition fear into a child but he or she can unwittingly set the stage for such conditioning. For example, if a maths problem is presented and the teacher mocks the child for not getting the right answer, the child may experience fear at the teacher's action – he may start sweating, his heartbeat may rise, and he may feel very anxious. If such an occurrence happens a few times the sight of the maths text alone may induce fear and anxiety in the child and he may develop what is often called a 'set' against maths and be unable to pay attention during subsequent maths lessons because he is too overwhelmed with feelings of anxiety.

If you suspect that one of your pupils has this irrational type of fear of a particular subject, you may attempt to 'desensitise' the fear by giving him extremely easy assignments and making sure that his success at these is rewarded, thus breaking the association between the subject and anxiety.

Social Learning. An American psychologist called Albert Bandura became very interested in the fact that certain kinds of learning did not follow the laws of learning laid down by the early learning theorists. He was concerned in particular with the way children can be seen to copy the behaviour of others whom they admire or identify with even if reinforcement is not provided.

He and his co-workers have performed numerous studies on children's learning of social behaviour. They have shown, for example, that if children are exposed to the sight of another person behaving aggressively they will copy such behaviour. In these experiments the child is placed in a familiar playroom. As if by chance, in another part of a room there is a person playing with toys, sometimes a teacher, sometimes another child who is working with the experimenter. This other person behaves very aggressively by striking a large inflatable doll (called a Bobo doll), attacking and destroying toys and shouting insults. Later on the child who has been exposed to this is left alone with a number of toys including some used by the aggressive person; without any encouragement the child starts displaying exactly the same sort of aggressive behaviour he has just witnessed.

Bandura has shown that children are more likely to model the behaviour of people who have been kind to them, are similar to them, who are admired and who have high status, and this applies to constructive as well as aggressive behaviour.

The work of Bandura and his colleagues has a great deal of applicability in the classroom because it suggests that if children admire and identify with their teachers they will tend to model their behaviour on the teacher's behaviour. By this we do not mean that they will simply imitate the teacher. Clearly this would be absurd, because no classroom could operate with one adult teacher and a large number of mini-teachers. Modelling means that the children will tend to take over the attitudes, predispositions and general values of the teacher. As we mentioned in Chapter 5, once children share the values of the teacher, discipline problems tend to be reduced because both teacher and students are concerned with the same basic aim. It is, of course, very important that the teacher's aims be in the educational, emotional and social interests of the pupils or modelling can become a very destructive process.

(2) *Teaching for discovery learning*

The psychologist who is most associated with what is called 'discovery learning' is Jerome Bruner. We have already mentioned his name a number of times in this book and this is because, in addition to having a very powerful influence on educational practice, he is also a very distinguished figure in cognitive psychology.

You may remember the study we referred to in Chapter 4 when we described how poor children tended to overestimate the size of coins more than children from richer homes did. This was one of Bruner's first major contributions to child psychology and from it he concluded that values and needs affect perception. In his later work he has shown how values and needs shape other cognitive processes as well and this point of view has led to the development of a psychology of learning which places the child himself in a central role in the learning situation. For if individual values, needs and experience are important in learning and cognition, then instructional techniques must take such variables – needs, values and experience – into account in the case of each and every child.

Thus Bruner's influence on education has been to promote a child-centred approach to teaching. Specifically we can trace four major principles in his work which reflect this basic approach that sets the child at the centre of the teaching-learning process. They may be summarised as follows.

Children are, by nature, motivated to learn. This motivation springs from their inborn curiosity, their inborn need to master the world around them by becoming competent at the things that interest them and their inborn programming to interact with others which makes them respond favourably to teaching situations where they can work co-operatively with others. (You will notice, perhaps, the similarity to Pringle's needs for new experiences, responsibility, and praise and recognition.)

Structure and mode of presentation are very important in instruction. Bruner is very well known for the claim he made that any given area of knowledge can be presented in such a way as to be understood by almost any learner. Specifically he said 'any idea or problem or body of knowledge can be presented in a form simple enough so that any particular learner can understand it in a recognisable form' (1966, p. 44). Bruner considers that the structure of any body of knowledge can be characterised in three ways: how it is presented, whether by talk and chalk, demonstration or discovery, how much is presented at a time and which level of representation is being aimed at (whether it is being presented by means of actions, images or symbols). It is this structure of presentation that is the key to the learner's understanding.

The sequencing of material is very important in instruction. Bruner believes that the learner should be encouraged to move through a certain sequence when learning in a specific area. Particularly for younger learners, it is best to start at the activity level, so that the child's first mental representation is enactive. This should be followed by the use of images, through diagrams, pictures, models, and so on, so that the enactive representation will be supplemented by iconic representation. Finally, the material can be communicated using words only so that the mental representation will be symbolic. (We have already introduced the reader to the use of these three levels of representation proposed by Bruner in Chapter 4, pages 49–50, when we explained the terms enactive, iconic and symbolic.)

Feedback is most important in learning. In order to learn effectively, the learner must receive knowledge of how well he is proceeding in his learning. Thus the teacher has to be very sensitive to the learner's progress along a particular learning sequence. If there is no check on the learner's acquisition of knowledge, the learner may incorporate into his mental representation of what he is learning wrong elements which may distort the further acquisition of knowledge. However, unlike the behaviourists who would prefer learners never to make any errors so as not to practise any incorrect associations, Bruner does not believe in minimising errors. On the contrary, he thinks they may be very valuable in the learning process. Consider a child who is presented with a problem in physics; he may propose an incorrect hypothesis to account for the data. If the teacher allows him to test out this hypothesis on more data, he will not only gain a clear understanding of why he is wrong but will most probably be stimulated to propose another, and hopefully correct, hypothesis. Thus Bruner would argue that instead of leading him step by step to the right hypothesis, the teacher does best to allow the child to move through the material according to his own interest, generating ideas, testing them and finally 'discovering' the correct solution for himself.

These four principles, then, set the stage for a particular form of teaching: 'teaching for discovery learning'. We have not yet defined this term because it refers to an attitude rather more than a specific programme. But briefly *an instructional programme that promotes discovery learning is one that is based on the belief that the most valuable, deep and long-lasting learning is learning that arises from the child's own discovery of the material to be learnt.*

Discovery learning, according to Bruner, is characterised by the fact that the learner himself organises his mastery of the material. Spurred on by his innate desire to learn effectively about the world around him (principle one above), the child is presented with material which the teacher has structured so as to be interesting, not too lengthy and at the right level of representation (principles two and three). The child then proceeds through the material himself in such a way that he organises his own understanding by making, testing, and accepting or discarding hypotheses about the material he is faced with. At each stage the teacher should provide feedback on his progress (principle four).

A further important component of Bruner's discovery learning is what he calls the 'spiral' approach. By this he means that instead of the child moving through the material by first mastering the simplest step, then the next, and so on in a successive manner, the same material should be taught at different times, but each time it is taught understanding should be deepened. To give an example: suppose we consider the subject matter of biology. Very young children can be taught to label and perhaps draw different animals, and later on they may be taught the correct classification of the animals they have studied. Still later they may learn about the natural habitats and behaviour of the animals and finally, when they are much more mature, they could be introduced to material concerning the adaptations of different animals to different habitats. This example should demonstrate what Bruner means when he claims that any given area of knowledge can be presented in a form simple enough for almost any learner.

As we have noted, Bruner's contribution to cognitive psychology has been enormous. To educational practice he has brought a fresh, enthusiastic and child-centred approach that revolutionised attitudes to teaching in the USA. However, the promotion of 'discovery learning' has not had only constructive results. Many teachers, under its sway, completely abandoned any attempt to teach by more formal means and, as we have noted in the first part of this chapter, some material, by its nature, is not always taught most effectively by discovery methods. (We refer here to things like spelling, vocabulary and certain essential facts like the names of the capital cities of different countries.) The emphasis on discovery learning has led, in certain cases, to children simply being presented with material and expected to derive organisation and understanding from it. While no one would deny the importance of activity methods in teaching, and the value of concepts that have been derived by children themselves from a body of material, too much reliance on discovery learning can lead to an absence of structure, both in the classroom and in the child's understanding, which can be most confusing, and in many cases distasteful to the child. As we noted in Chapter 1, the child has a need for security and structure as well as a need for novelty. The danger with the way discovery learning is sometimes presented is that the scales are tilted too much to novelty. On the other hand, the kind of teaching that requires the child to be passive and simply act as a sponge is tilted too much to the need for security and can destroy motivation and creativity. As we mentioned at the start of this section, an eclectic approach that takes the best from all schools of psychology is much the approach to be preferred.

(3) *Teaching for meaningful learning*

In the section on learning in this chapter we made mention of learning what was meaningful to the child. We used this term 'meaningful' in its ordinary sense of making sense. The term 'meaningful learning', however, is associated with the work of a cognitive psychologist called David Ausubel.

Ausubel, whose fullest statement on teaching methodology can be found in the book *School Learning: An Introduction to Educational Psychology*, is particularly concerned with the best possible way for the teacher to *convey meaning* through instruction to her pupils. Although, like Bruner, he is a cognitive theorist, he is much more didactic in his approach. That is, he sees the teacher's role as extremely important in the learning process. Bruner, on the other hand, is more inclined to emphasise the role of the child.

Like Bruner, Ausubel assumes that cognitive processes and learning involve the active restructuring of material rather than the passive learning of associations. Unlike Bruner, however, he does not link his approach to teaching methodologies to the body of knowledge that has been produced by child and developmental psychologists. Instead he prefers to see educational psychology as a separate discipline. He believes that it is advisable to 'focus on educational phenomena as they are actually found in the schools' (1971, p. 151). It is not, therefore, appropriate to present the theoretical assumptions from which his work derives. Instead we will concentrate on his specific recommendations.

Ausubel stresses that factual information is most easily learned if it is arranged logically. Before attempting to teach anything the teacher should analyse the material in such a way that all the terminology and concepts presented in it are clear to her. Then she should ensure that her presentation is done in such a way that these are logically presented and that material which assumes prior knowledge is not taught until the assumed knowledge is thoroughly learned and understood.

As a cognitive theorist, Ausubel believes that collections of facts should be taught as logical systems rather than as random isolated pieces of information. He is most particularly concerned that wherever possible new learning becomes absorbed into prior systems of knowledge. For this reason he is very sceptical about the value of rote learning.

At the root of his work lies the conviction that it is 'meaningful learning' that is the most valuable and long-lasting method of learning. How does he define 'meaningful learning'? He sees it as 'organised and logical learning that is related to the individual's prior cognitive structure'. For meaningful learning to occur three conditions must hold:

(a) The material to be learned must be capable of being organised in some 'non-arbitrary' way. That is, there must be some structure or organisation underlying the material.

(b) The learner must possess ideas to which he can relate the material.

(c) The learner must *want* to relate his previous ideas to the new material in an organised manner.

Ausubel stresses the use of organisers. These are general concepts into which most of the material can be organised. For example, in one study he did he was concerned with the teaching of two passages about Buddhism and Zen (two Eastern religions or philosophies) to students who were Christian. Before he taught the Buddhist passage he outlined for the students the principal similarities and differences between Christianity and Buddhism, thus providing an organiser. Before he taught the Zen passage he outlined the similarities and differences between Buddhism (which the students were now familiar with) and Zen. Students who had these organisers did far better on tests on the Buddhist and Zen passages than students who only studied the history of Buddhism and Zen.

Ausubel also emphasises the role of post-lesson summaries. In these, the main content of the lesson is revised in an integrated way.

Ausubel's major recommendations can be summarised as seven points:

(1) Explain your learning objective.

(2) Start lessons with advance organisers that include general principles to help students absorb the material systematically.

(3) Alert the students to new concepts.

(4) Present the learning in systematic steps.

(5) Ensure, by asking questions, that students are actively taking part in the lesson and are mastering the material.

(6) Follow the lesson with a summary.

(7) Set questions or assignments on the material that require students to organise related material on their own.

It will be noted by the reader that the sections on learning in the earlier part of this chapter have been influenced by Ausubel's approach. While Ausubel provides a logical and coherent instructional system, many of his recommendations are those that are followed by most experienced teachers. In this sense they may appear to be common sense extended and formalised. However, this is not a bad thing, and to less experienced teachers they may provide a short cut. Unfortunately Ausubel's major book which we have referred to is extremely lengthy, over-detailed and often too concerned with attacks on discovery learning to be of a great deal of practical use to the teacher. Adequate summaries of his major points are provided, however, by most American educational psychology texts.

(4) *An eclectic approach*

In this section we have outlined three major instructional processes that are currently to be found in most educational psychology texts. The first derives, as we noted, from the work of the behaviourists, whereas the other two are cognitive in their approach.

We ourselves have already presented an eclectic approach to instruction when we outlined the different kinds of learning and recommended how we consider they should be approached in the first part of this chapter. This section was presented from a cognitive viewpoint but we did not deny the value of association learning in the case of certain material like vocabulary, the spelling of certain words and in the learning of facts where there is no underlying logical structure. While we recommended that, where possible, meaning should be imposed on such material by, for example, the use of mnemonics (like Thirty days hath September ...), we acknowledged that this is not always possible. In such cases, repetition and rote learning are obviously called for. But such rote learning need not be dull and monotonous. Quizzes, games, competitions and chanting can be used to introduce interest and variety to rote learning.

With respect to behaviour problems in the classroom we also recommend an eclectic approach. Such an approach does not deny the value of behaviour-shaping techniques (as were described in the case of Anna), while maintaining that as well as shaping behaviour we should always seek to understand what is motivating it.

As we mentioned in our section on Bruner, the promotion of discovery learning led to a revolution in attitude on the part of many school authorities. While we have cautioned against the overextension of discovery learning techniques, we would still regard ourselves as child-centred. To this extent we would support the movement towards placing the child in the centre of the teaching-learning situation. If the child is not interested and motivated to learn, even the most sophisticated instructional techniques will not be effective. Like Bruner, we believe that the child is innately predisposed to want to understand and structure his world. For this reason *all* instructional techniques should, in our opinion, require the child to play an active part.

Before concluding this section on learning and instructional techniques we should like to turn our attention briefly to the learning requirements of children with special needs.

Children with Special Needs

No parent would deny that each child is 'special' in some way. Each child has his own special and personal pattern of behaviour and his own individual view of the world. However, the term 'special' children or 'children with special needs' has come to refer to those children who are significantly different from other children in some important area of human functioning. These *special children*, because of some physical, psychological, cognitive or social factor, are the children who will find particular difficulty in reaching their full educational potential. To the educationalist and teacher such children present a challenge. In addition they can present rather more difficulties than other children, particularly in cases where educational and allied resources are scarce and financial help is limited.

In this section we consider only the learning difficulties that special children may present as it is beyond the scope of this book to cover the subject of special children more fully. In particular we cannot make recommendations concerning the educational placement of such children; whether, for example, the underlying philosophy should be to integrate them into the ordinary classroom, provide them with special facilities within the ordinary school system or make provision for them outside the school system that caters for the great majority of children. Such decisions must depend on the national philosophy concerning what education is about, as well as the financial, manpower and institutional resources available. It must also, naturally, depend to some extent on how 'special children' are viewed within the particular

culture and what variables are taken into account in defining 'special needs'.

We have noted that the way the term 'special children' is interpreted is culturally determined. In societies where education was a more informal process than it is within a school system, there was far more tolerance and acceptance of individual children whose behaviour was not particularly typical of the behaviour of other children within the culture. Many of the educational difficulties of the groups of special children we shall discuss result from their comparative inability to cope with the major communication medium of the school – the written word. Clearly in societies where literacy was not so important such difficulties were relatively non-existent and it is, therefore, likely that the adoption of a policy of universal primary school education precipitates a much higher proportion of children being regarded as having 'special' educational needs.

How the decision is made that a child has 'special' needs is also a process that varies from society to society. Within societies which have well-established and well-funded pediatric and ante- (before) and peri- (immediately after) birth services, such decisions are clearly likely to be made earlier than in societies which lack such medical resources because of a comparative scarcity of manpower and money.

Thus in many cases in Third World countries, children with special needs will only be perceived as having these when they enter school. A child may then be referred to the medical services (or psychological services if they are available) because his behaviour in the classroom seems very different from his peers.

However, whether the child is referred comparatively early or comparatively late, the specialised services will tend to follow a fairly similar process. The staff concerned will attempt to make a diagnosis by listing the symptoms that led to the child's referral, noting how often they occur, how varied they are, how severe they are, and by attempting to uncover their cause. They will also try to predict the future development of the child (his prognosis) and make recommendations on the appropriate remediation and intervention.

In making their diagnosis, prognosis and in giving their recommendations, the staff will use certain assessment techniques. This usually involves some or all of the following procedures – observing the child very carefully both at home and at school, interviewing the child, and his parents, brothers and sisters and teachers, giving thorough medical tests, and comparing the child's performance on certain psychological tests with the performance of other children of the same age and background. Such procedures facilitate general decisions about the child's future as well as specific recommendations about how the child can be helped in the learning situation.

The categories of children with special needs that we intend to consider are the following: children with hearing disabilities, children with visual disabilities, mentally retarded children and children with specific learning disabilities.

(1) Children with hearing disabilities

In looking at the problems of children with hearing disabilities we note that the type of problems they face depend on whether they have any understanding of spoken or written language. We have already noted the great importance of language in cognitive development (Chapter 3) and consequently we would expect children who understand nothing of spoken language to be very badly handicapped. This is likely to occur if the child is born with very severe hearing difficulties or loses his hearing before language is acquired. It is this group of children that we consider under (a) below. Those children who are hard of hearing, rather than completely deaf, have different sorts of problems that are not nearly so severe as they have some understanding of language, and we consider their case under (b) below.

(a) Totally, severely and profoundly deaf children.

These terms apply to the different categories of children who cannot hear ordinary spoken conversation. For the sake of brevity we will refer to them as 'profoundly' deaf children.

In Chapter 3 we described in some detail the development of speech and language, pointing out its extremely important role in communication. We also noted that as children grow older speech and language play an increasingly vital role in cognitive development.

It is the interdependence of hearing loss and language that is important. Children who have never heard speech cannot experience language development except in a very severely limited manner. If you think about the content of learning, even at the very earliest stages of the primary school, you will realise how dependent it is on language. Numbers of studies show that, even if profoundly deaf children acquire enough language through either lip reading or manual communication (by using sign language) to write language, their language is more limited, less complex and more liable to error than the language of hearing children.

This does not mean that profoundly deaf children are in any way 'mentally defective', though their lack of language may sometimes cause observers to make this assumption. Furth, whom we have already mentioned, has done a great deal of work with deaf children, and has shown that on tests of concept development that are not dependent on language deaf children perform in a very similar way to hearing children. It does mean, however, that their education must take a very specialised form. The chief aim should be to help them to gain some understanding of language in order for them to be able to communicate with others and in order for their cognitive development to be facilitated.

A major question in trying to optimise the language development of profoundly deaf children is whether to aim for speech reading (through lip reading) or to aim for communication using sign language (sometimes called manual communication and sometimes called simply 'signing'). This is a very controversial area in the education of the profoundly deaf. At the moment it seems that research suggests that signing enables the child to use his potential more fully than lip reading does. This is because some sign languages are now very sophisticated means of communication. However, the chief disadvantage of signing is that the deaf child is limited, until he can read or write or extends to lip reading as well, to communication with those who themselves know the sign language he has been taught. The reader who is interested in this area can refer to the specialised text given in the bibliography at the end of this chapter.

In conclusion, however, it should be noted that because of the very fundamental nature of the language deficiency of profoundly deaf children, those concerned with teaching them should, if possible, receive specialised training. This training should take into account not only the intellectual consequences of profound deafness that we have just outlined but also the accompanying psychological problems that accompany the loss in self-esteem and personal competence that most profoundly deaf children suffer. Profoundly deaf children consistently have more adjustment problems than hearing children and a number of studies have found them to be rigid and egocentric.

(b) *Children who are hard of hearing rather than profoundly deaf.* Children who fall into this category are not nearly so handicapped in the educational situation as the children in (a) above. This is because, although their spoken language may sound strange as a result of their difficulty in distinguishing the consonant sounds, they nevertheless do have an understanding of language. Their progress in the ordinary classroom can be optimised if the teacher follows these suggestions:

(i) The child should be seated where he can see the teacher's face as well as possible so that his lip reading can be made as efficient as possible. Similarly, in class discussions he should be encouraged to face and look directly at any classmate who is speaking. In addition the teacher should not move around too much as this makes lip reading more difficult.

(ii) Teachers should speak naturally to this kind of child, avoiding speech exaggerations, and should ensure that the child is not distracted by other things but is looking directly at the teacher while she is communicating with him.

(iii) The child should be encouraged to ask the teacher to repeat what she is saying if he does not understand but if the child misinterprets what the teacher says she should rephrase her statement as she may have used words that are difficult to lip read.

(iv) The teacher should try not to direct too much obvious attention to the hard of hearing child. In order for him to feel less different, all children in the class should be encouraged to repeat any directions the teacher gives them out loud.

(v) Finally, the teacher should see the child before the lesson if she intends to introduce some new vocabulary or terms so that the child can be better prepared for the new words to be lip read.

(2) *Children with visual disabilities*
Children with visual difficulties tend to present less difficulties in the area of learning than do those with hearing difficulties, and this is particularly true when we compare children who are badly handicapped rather than partially handicapped. As we did in the case of children with hearing difficulties, we will make a distinction between children who are severely visually handicapped (educationally blind) and those who are less severely handicapped (partially sighted).

(a) *Educationally blind children.* In their extremely comprehensive book on special education, Suran and Rizzo point out that the medical and legal definitions of blindness are not always suitable for making educational decisions. This is because visual acuity (the way a person rates on standardised tests of vision) is less important than functional visual efficiency (the way an individual uses the vision he has) in determining performance at school. Using this approach we can define the educationally blind child as the child who cannot make use of vision for the purposes of learning. Such a child must rely on the senses of touch and hearing and the most obvious result of this is that he will have to learn braille for the purpose of reading. If such resources are available, writing is best learnt through the use of a typewriter.

(b) *The partially sighted child.* Some children, even though they may be legally classified as blind, have enough residual vision to learn to read print and therefore do not need to depend on braille. To do so they may need special teaching aids (large print books and posters and high degrees of illumination) as well as exercises designed to increase visual efficiency. Nevertheless, where possible Suran and Rizzo advise that learning to read conventionally is better than learning braille and they quote a study of 14,125 legally blind children of whom 42 per cent had learnt to read print using low-vision aids of the kind just mentioned. Such low-vision aids tend to be expensive, and this suggests, perhaps, that in societies which are severely limited in terms of financial resources partially sighted children may have to be brought to special centralised schools or classes in order to economise on such resources.

Unlike children with hearing handicaps, whose fundamental understanding of language is affected, children with visual handicaps do not, on the whole, suffer such potentially severe educational risks. Their development, however, can be affected in two possible areas. The first is in the sphere of motor development. When blind children are infants they tend to have normal development in reaching such developmental milestones as rolling back from the stomach, sitting steadily alone and standing alone, but they are retarded in reaching the stages of raising themselves to a sitting position and walking towards objects. It is easy to understand why this is so. Whereas normal children are attracted by visual objects and soon learn to move towards them, blind children have far more difficulty in locating heard objects in space. In general, then, blind children tend to be more passive in this area of motor development than sighted children and are also less mobile. Occasionally too they are observed to engage in self-stimulating movements like waving their arms and swaying on one foot.

The second area in which blind children may be affected is in educational achievement. Although blind children do not differ from normally sighted children on tests of language, cognitive ability or standard tests of intelligence, American studies show that they do not achieve as well educationally as sighted children. The conclusion would seem to be that although there is no difference in the cognitive potential of blind and sighted children, the nature of the educational process, whether the blind are educated within or outside the ordinary school system, makes it difficult for most children with visual handicaps to reach their full potential. There are, of course, always outstanding exceptions to this.

Whether blind children are taught braille or whether they are encouraged to use residual vision to read print, teaching aids for them are expensive. Tape-recorders, special typewriters, braille libraries, low-vision aids like large print books, clearly require the allocation of considerable funds. It should also be noted that information acquired through recordings, braille and low-vision aids may take longer to assimilate than information acquired through normal reading and teachers therefore need to allow rather more time for visually handicapped children to do the required reading and listening than they allow for normally sighted children.

If a visually handicapped child is taught in the ordinary classroom the teacher can do a number of things to help him. To begin with, a guide or guides should be assigned to the child and the guide should provide an elbow for the handicapped child to hold rather than attempt to push the blind child around. Secondly, furniture in the classroom should not be changed around without warning the blind child. Thirdly, the teacher should provide the blind child with a special storage space near his desk, particularly if he has special equipment and materials.

(3) Children with mental retardation

Historically, within Western educational culture, a number of labels have been used to describe children and adults who display marked deficiencies in the cognitive and adaptive behaviour

that such society values. Some of these harsh terms have been feeble-minded, idiot, moron and imbecile.

Such labels sprang from the viewpoint that children and adults who did not perform within the educational process in the same way as the great majority of their peers were, by nature, very different from their peers and this viewpoint led to such individuals being segregated in special institutions for the 'mentally retarded'.

More recently two important changes have taken place. In the first case, it has been acknowledged that sometimes children labelled in the past as mentally retarded and viewed therefore as doomed for the rest of their lives to low performance in the cognitive sphere were victims of social conditions that did not allow for their full intellectual development. In Chapter 11 we will describe intervention programmes which have shown that environment may play a major role in suppressing the full development of children's educational potential.

Secondly, educational practice has shifted, particularly in the USA and Britain, to returning children who are not very severely mentally retarded back to the ordinary school and often back to the ordinary classroom. (This is often referred to in American texts as 'mainstreaming'.) There are two reasons for this practice. In the first case it has been acknowledged that certain tests used to label children as 'mentally retarded' were biased against certain social groups. (In broad terms, the working class and blacks, Chicanos and other ethnic groups.) In the second case it has been acknowledged that the 'labelling' of a child as 'mentally retarded' may have a worse effect on his educational progress than the actual handicap.

Nevertheless, the fact remains that even given the best social conditions there are some children who are so clearly different in their cognitive potential from the rest of the population that they must be considered, for educational purposes at any rate, as 'mentally retarded'. A definition of mental retardation that acknowledges this viewpoint is the following (Suran and Rizzo, 1979, p. 207):

> Mental retardation refers to significantly subaverage general intellectual functioning existing concurrently with deficits in adaptive behaviour, and manifested during the developmental period.

It is far beyond the scope of this book to deal with

the education of children who fall into this definition. A specialised text, that may be found very useful, is given at the end of the chapter. Nevertheless we would like to make the following general points with respect to the education and learning needs of such children.

(i) In view of the major environmental effects that have been shown to affect intellectual performance, great caution must be exercised in deciding whether children are 'mentally retarded' in the sense of being at a permanent disadvantage, or whether children are suffering from extreme social or physical deprivation. As we have pointed out in Chapter 2, and as Durojaiye writes about in greater detail, malnutrition may be associated with intellectual backwardness, but once proper diet is given such backwardness often disappears (Durojaiye, 1978, pp. 120–1).

(ii) Tests designed to measure 'intelligence' or IQ should be looked at very critically. We shall discuss this subject at greater length in Chapter 11 but here it must be pointed out that such tests are very often socially and culturally biased. Furthermore, if the environment of the child tested changes radically, such tests often give unreliable results from test session to test session.

(iii) If it is decided, after lengthy investigation, that a child is mentally retarded, extreme sensitivity and tact must be used in dealing with the parents.

(iv) Research has shown that the two major cognitive areas in which mentally retarded children require help are memory and attention. It has been suggested that one of the reasons mentally retarded children show difficulty with memory is that they do not 'rehearse' before trying to commit things to memory. Thus teachers should programme material to be learned in small clusters and allow a great deal of *repetition and rehearsal*. Another area of difficulty is that mentally retarded children are often not clear precisely what they are expected to pay attention to in a learning situation, and teachers should therefore help them to *focus* on the relevant aspects of the learning task.

(4) *Children with specific learning disabilities*
Experienced teachers will know that sometimes children appear to have extreme difficulty with certain aspects of the learning process, although nothing in their general behaviour indicates that they are less adaptive or intelligent than their classmates. In the past such children tended to be labelled 'slow learners' or stubborn, and sometimes

their behaviour was thought to be due to emotional problems.

Such children fall into a different category from those whom we described in the last sub-section: they are clearly not 'mentally retarded' because, except for finding extreme difficulty with certain learning tasks (most often those associated with reading), their general behaviour reveals no inability to deal adaptively and appropriately with their environment.

In order to put some flesh on the general picture, we can consider the case of Isak. At 10 years of age Isak had been at primary school for five years. In class he was a likeable and friendly child who could carry on a one-to-one conversation with an adult at a reasonable level. Standard tests of intellectual ability revealed that he was of average ability. Yet he was much slower at learning to read than his classmates. In addition, his written work was most unusual – his spelling was so peculiar that even his teacher often could not understand what he was trying to express.

If such a pattern were shown at 6 years of age, it might have been reasonable to conclude that he was one of those children who develop the particular combination of cognitive skills that are involved in reading rather later than most children. We have referred to the fact, in our section on teaching reading, that reading is a very complex task in which a number of sub-skills are combined. Consequently it is not surprising that children learn to read at different rates. We noted that if a child learns to read at a slower rate than his classmates, this does not mean that he will remain behind them permanently unless he is made to feel inadequate and inferior. We also stressed that in such cases teachers must continue actively to teach the child the skill of reading and must not assume that the skill will just develop as the child grows older. But these remarks concerned the first two or three years of reading tuition. Isak's case differs in that he had completed almost five years of reading tuition and in that his spelling is so peculiar. For example, this is Isak's attempt at a story about his pigeon.

My pigeon
My pigeons fly in the sky and has blue fere
and he fly haum forn fase and wis a ras and
my Dab ges a cup and a lot of mun and gos ta
the pud and bas bask and hes bes andmas

The following is what Isak *thought* he was writing.

This version was done by the teacher who asked Isak just what each word in his passage said.

> My pigeons fly in the sky and has blue feathers and he fly home from France and wins a race and my Dad gets a cup and a lot of money and goes to the pub (bar) and buys baskets and he buys maize.

You will have gained some impression, from this passage, of quite how poor Isak's written work was. You will notice that, like many children with his type of learning difficulties, Isak tended to leave out whole syllables – for example, 'money' becomes 'mun' and 'baskets' becomes 'bask'. In addition, he did not seem to notice the presence of some consonant sounds – for example, 'France' was written as 'fase' and 'wins' as 'wis'.

In Figure 6·6 you can see Isak's attempt at copying some standard designs. In the case of the design with the dots, not only did he fail to reproduce the slant, but he crowded the dots so close together that his copy bore very little overall resemblance to the design he was asked to copy. In the case of the other design, he had a great deal of difficulty in reproducing the curves of the standard. In both cases his difficulty with processing shape is marked. So it is no wonder that he has difficulty with 'b', 'd' and 'g'. In the passage he wrote 'pub' as 'pud' and in a spelling test spelled 'bag' 'bad' and 'today' as 'tobay'. (Of course such confusion of letters is common amongst many children in their first year or two at school, but they are disturbing in Isak's case because they occurred after five years of schooling.)

As you can see from both the written passage and Figure 6·6, despite the fact that he attained an average score on a standard test of intellectual ability, Isak had profound difficulties with the processing and sequencing of sounds and with the outline and orientation of shapes.

Isak's story is typical of a child about whom we

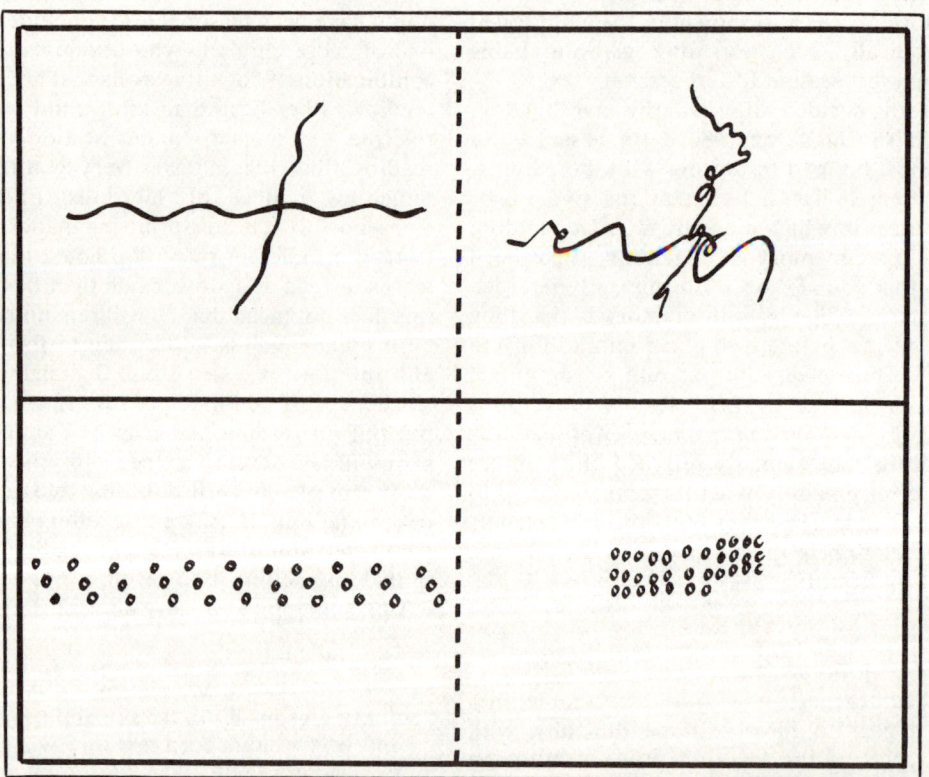

Figure 6.6 Copies of two standard shapes made by a ten-year-old child with specific learning disabilities

may say 'This child has a specific learning disability', meaning by this that while appearing to be of normal intelligence and functioning adequately socially and emotionally, the child shows great difficulty with certain aspects of learning behaviour – in Isak's case with learning to read and write. (In some texts you may find Isak's form of learning disability described as dyslexia.) With skilled and individualised tuition such children often learn to read, though they usually read more slowly than other people and continue to find extreme difficulty with spelling.

You will, of course, wonder what the causes of such learning disabilities are. The fact is that the causation of such learning problems is not, at present, very well understood. A number of different hypotheses have been proposed such as faulty learning at school entry, developmental abnormalities, visual abnormalities, minimal (slight) brain damage, difficulty in processing material in sequence, genetic causation (hereditary defects) and intellectual deprivation. Probably some, if not all, of these causes are involved. But in each case of specific learning disabilities a different pattern of causation is likely to apply.

Such cases need, if possible, skilled psychological assessment and specialised extra tuition. Where educational resources are scarce such a programme is seldom possible. However, the fact that a teacher understands something of the characteristics of such learning problems often in itself sensitises the teacher in her treatment of the child and this may lead to a slow improvement in his learning. It is particularly important that children with this sort of problem are reassured that they are not 'stupid'. It is often helpful if such children are allowed rather more time than their classmates to complete written assignments and even, if possible, tests and examinations. In some areas in Britain such pupils are allowed to give oral answers to examinations in certain subjects like history. If you are interested in this area the book recommended in the bibliography at the end of the chapter will lead you to a large number of appropriate references.

This chapter has been concerned with learning and instructional approaches. Although it has been included in Part Two of the book which concerns the primary school age-group, clearly the general principles covered extend to the secondary school age-group as well, in particular the sub-section on teaching concepts, problem-solving and creativity.

Summary

(1) Learning was defined as a relatively permanent change in disposition or capability that is not due to the processes of growth.

(2) Seven different processes of learning were covered.

(a) *Association learning.* Association learning is concerned with the learning of an associative bond between things. It was pointed out that in everyday life association learning plays a relatively small part in the way human beings learn to adapt to their environment because in most cases of everyday learning some *processing* of the learning material takes place. Nevertheless, children are required to do a fair amount of association learning, particularly in primary schools, for example, vocabulary, the spelling of certain difficult words that follow no easily taught rules, and the acquisition of certain facts. Optimising association learning requires the teacher to use some or all of the following techniques: making the material as interesting as possible, making the material as meaningful as possible, reinforcing (or rewarding) correct associations as speedily as possible, repetition of the material and using as many different cues as possible.

(b) *Concrete concept learning.* A concept stands for a common set of attributes that characterises a group of objects. Concrete concepts are concepts that can be learned by active and direct interaction with the environment. It was suggested that in teaching about a concrete concept the teacher should first introduce the word used to label the concept. Following this she should identify instances of the concept; then she should ask for as many instances of the concept as the child can give and finally that she should ensure that children can distinguish between instances of the concept and instances that are not examples of the concept.

(c) *Abstract concepts.* These are concepts that cannot be learned by direct and active interaction with the environment. It was suggested that in teaching about these the following steps should be taken: the teacher should ensure that all subsidiary concepts and terms are understood; instances of the concept can then be given; the concept can then be described; after this the children can be required to give and recognise examples of the concept and to differentiate instances that belong to the concept from instances that do not; finally a definition of the concept can be taught.

(d) *Rule learning*. The following steps were suggested in the teaching of rules: first the learners should be informed of the learning they are going to undertake; then they should be questioned to ensure that they understand all the concepts involved in the rule; following this the learners should be encouraged to derive the rule themselves from material presented to them by the teacher; after this learners can be asked to demonstrate instances of the rule; finally learners can be asked to make a verbal statement of the rule.

(e) *Learning to read*. The following major points were made.
Children learn to read at different rates.
Children must be familiar with the reading process before they themselves learn to read. That is, they must have a great deal of experience of being read to.
Children must understand that reading is about communication.
Both the language used in the reading text and the subject matter of the text must be appropriate. The language used should be based on the natural speech pattern used by children and the content should be stimulating.
Children bring to the reading process their knowledge and experience of language and the teacher should make use of this experience and knowledge.
Teachers must emphasise the rules and regularities underlying the reading process in the particular language being taught.

(f) *Problem-solving*. It was suggested that there are three major steps in problem-solving: definition of goal and present position; the gap-filling process; and checking out the solution. At the first stage the student has to relate what he already knows to the problem and has to be quite clear what he is being asked to do. At the second stage the student should be prepared to use processes of reasoning and should be able to muster strategies that have been useful in the past and any relevant experience and information. At the third stage the student should check his solution.

(g) *Creativity*. The following major areas were discussed with respect to creativity:
A history of interest in creativity.
Tests that have been used to rate creativity.
Whether highly creative people are different from other people.
Creativity and culture.
Classroom variables that may aid creative work.

In general it was concluded that it was not possible to specify how to teach creativity because the conditions for creative performance and the qualities needed to produce it are intimately related to the subject area. Nevertheless, it was suggested that creativity is associated with a strong belief in the values of one's own work and in independence of judgement and that, for this reason, teachers should encourage children to be self-directing in their approach to their work.

(3) Four instructional approaches were examined: the first behaviourist, the next two cognitive and the last eclectic.

(a) *Learning theory*. The application of learning theory was considered at three different levels – association learning, behaviour modification and social learning.

(b) *Teaching for discovery learning*. The basic propositions on which this approach is based were described and the merits and demerits of the approach discussed.

(c) *Teaching for meaningful learning*. The differences between this cognitive approach to learning and the preceding cognitive approach (discovery learning) were explored.

(d) *An eclectic approach*. It was suggested that the best instructional approach was one that extracted the most useful recommendations of the three previous approaches. It was suggested that the sections on learning that had preceded this section on instructional approaches did this, being based on a broadly cognitive position but drawing also from the insights of learning theory.

(4) Finally, the learning problems of children with special needs were considered. The following types of children were discussed: those with handicaps of hearing, those with visual handicaps, mentally retarded children and children with specific learning disabilities.

Chapter 6: Selected Bibliography

Association Learning, Concept Learning, Rule Learning and Problem-Solving
Ausubel, D. P., and Robinson, F. G., *School Learning: An Introduction to Educational Psychology* (London: Holt, Rinehart & Winston, 1971).
Gagné, R. M., *The Conditions of Learning*, 3rd edn (New York: Holt, Rinehart & Winston, 1977).
Hulse, S. H., Deese, J., and Egeth, H., *The Psychology of Learning* (Tokyo: McGraw-Hill Kogakusha, 1975).

Reading
Bullock, A., *A Language for Life; Report of the Committee of Inquiry appointed by the Secretary of State for Education and Science under the Chairmanship of Sir Alan Bullock, FBA* (London: HMSO, 1975).
Clark, M. M., *Young Fluent Readers* (London: Heinemann, 1976).
Reid, J. F., and Donaldson, H. (eds), *Reading: Problems and Practices*, 2nd edn (London: Ward Lock, 1977).
Smith, F., *Understanding Reading: A Psycholinguistic Analysis of Reading and Learning to Read* (New York: Holt, Rinehart & Winston, 1971).

Creativity
Torrance, E. P., *Education and the Creative Potential* (Minneapolis: University of Minnesota Press, 1963).

Turner, J., *Psychology for the Classroom* (London: Methuen, 1977).

Learning Theory
Skinner, B., *Contingencies of Reinforcement* (New York: Appleton, 1969).

Behaviour Modification
Fargo, G. A., Behrns, C., and Nolen, P., *Behavior Modification in the Classroom* (Belmont: Wadsworth, 1970).

Teaching for Discovery Learning
Bruner, J., *Towards a Theory of Instruction* (Cambridge, Mass.: Harvard University Press, 1966).

Teaching for Meaningful Learning
Ausubel, D. P., and Robinson, F. G., *School Learning: An Introduction to Educational Psychology* (London: Holt, Rinehart & Winston, 1971).

An Eclectic Approach to the Teaching Process
Good, T. I., and Brophy, J. E., *Educational Psychology: A Realistic Approach* (New York: Holt, Rinehart & Winston, 1977).

Special Children

Hearing handicaps
Moore, D. F., 'A review of education of the deaf', in *The Third Review of Special Education*, ed. L. Mann and D. A. Sabatino (New York: Grune & Stratton, 1976).

Visual handicaps
Suran, B. C., and Rizzo, J. V., *Special Children: An Integrative Approach* (Glenview, Ill.: Scott Foresman, 1979), ch. 6.

Mental retardation
Suran, B. C., and Rizzo, J. V., *Special Children: An Integrative Approach* (Glenview, Ill.: Scott Foresman, 1979), ch. 8.

Specific learning disabilities
Jordan, D. R., *Dyslexia in the Classroom*, 2nd edn (Columbus, Ohio: Merrill, 1977).

PART THREE
ADOLESCENCE AND YOUTH

In the second part of this book we dealt with the social and emotional behaviour of primary school children as well as with learning in the primary school. In this, the third part, we look at the behaviour of older children – adolescents. It does not seem to us to be appropriate to view adolescence solely within the context of the secondary school. This is because, although it is now less common than it was in the recent past, in some countries with scarce educational resources a number of children who have reached adolescence are still attending the primary school. Secondly, in some Third World countries, a relatively small proportion of the total age group attend secondary school. For these reasons we view the psychological development of post-primary school children within the context of adolescence rather than within the context of the secondary school.

In Chapter 7 we look at development in adolescence – physical, emotional, cognitive and moral. In Chapter 8 we consider adolescence in the social context. We examine the ways in which different societies deal with the transition from childhood to adulthood. We then consider adolescents within different social settings: within the family, with peers, at school and in the work setting. We will also look at the phenomenon of adolescent 'deviance'.

DEVELOPMENTAL CHANGES IN ADOLESCENCE

7

> ' It is fair to say that adolescence
> begins in biology and ends in culture. '
> (Conger, 1977, p. 103)

Introduction

Adolescence is the term we use to describe the period between childhood and manhood or womanhood. Most people would agree that this starts with the maturing of the sexual organs (puberty) and continues until the late teens. This fairly lengthy period (usually from about 12 or 13 years of age to about 17 or 18 years of age) has come to be regarded in the West as well as in Eastern Europe as a *particular* stage in the developmental process and so we find innumerable textbooks, as well as books of popular psychology, dealing with adolescence and its problems. This acceptance of the uniqueness of this developmental period is not new. For example, Aristotle differentiated the period between puberty and 21 years of age as 'young manhood' and saw it as a time when young people started to develop the ability to choose a course of action deliberately and rationally in contrast to the pure pursuit of pleasure that he regarded young children as following. But Aristotle regarded young people as differing from adults in that they are changeable, fickle, passionate and inclined to carry everything too far.

Not all cultures, however, have regarded adolescence as a comparatively long-lasting and distinct phase between childhood and adulthood. Many societies have prescribed a formal and extremely significant set of ceremonies to mark the transition from childhood to adulthood and once the ceremonies have been completed, there is a 'rapid role-switch' (Pelto and Pelto, 1976, p. 409) from childhood to adult life. The ceremonies serve as a period of initiation in which the young person is educated into the kind of behaviour and attitudes expected of adult members of his community. Although in some cases the ceremonies may take place over a number of years, societies prescribing such initiation ceremonies (or *rites de passage*) do not seem, in general, to regard the young people taking part in them as psychologically different in nature from either younger children or young adults. Indeed, in many cases, boys ranging in age from 8 or 9 years to their early teens will be initiated together.

In yet other societies, children move slowly and imperceptibly into the adult world in an even, continuous progression and aside from the bodily changes accompanying maturation there is not much to differentiate the older from the younger girl or boy (Mead, 1962).

We shall return to this area in the next chapter, but here we simply note that different societies have regarded the movement from childhood to adulthood in differing ways and that not all cultures have seen the adolescent as presenting particular psychological characteristics and needs.

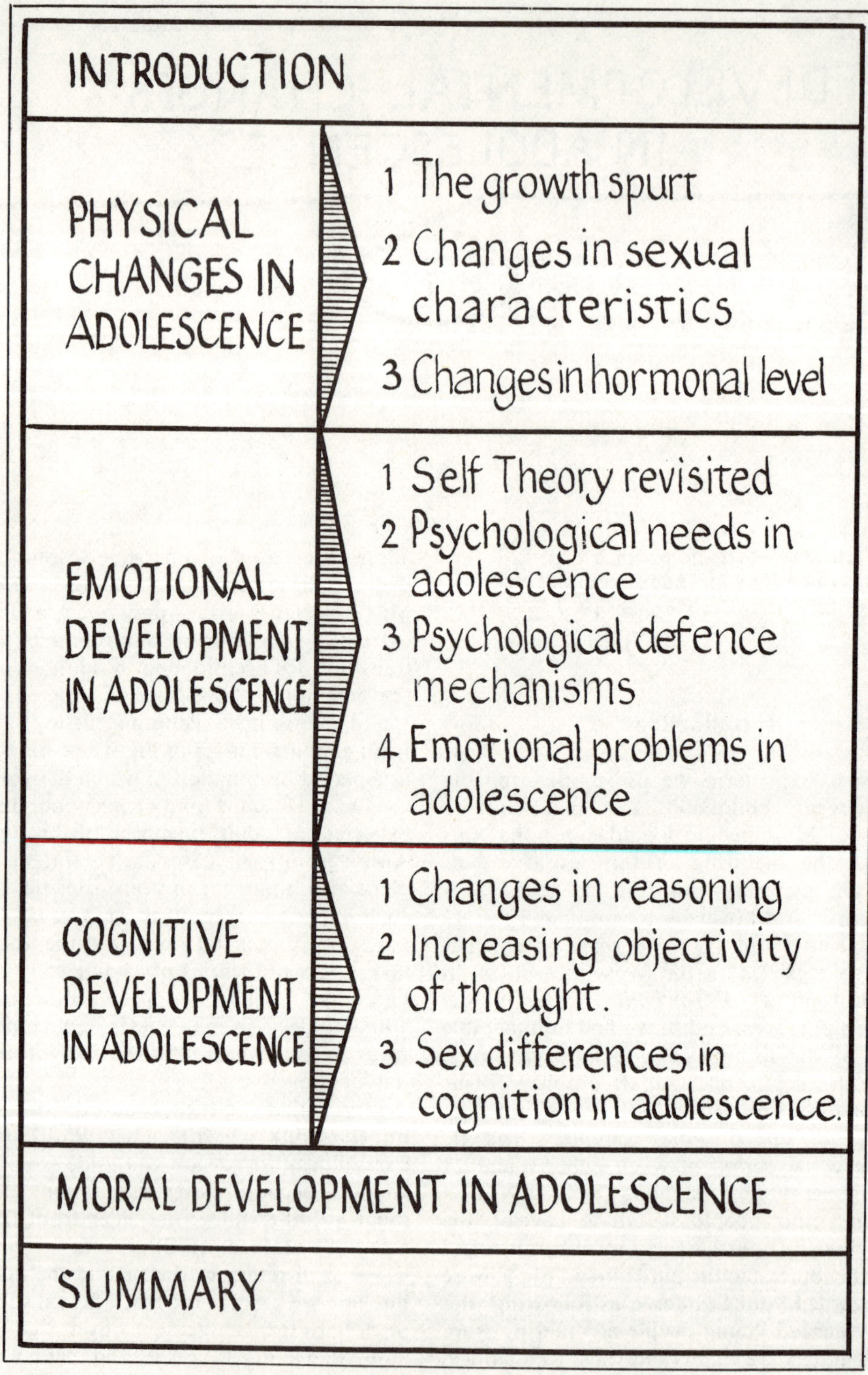

INTRODUCTION	
PHYSICAL CHANGES IN ADOLESCENCE	1 The growth spurt 2 Changes in sexual characteristics 3 Changes in hormonal level
EMOTIONAL DEVELOPMENT IN ADOLESCENCE	1 Self Theory revisited 2 Psychological needs in adolescence 3 Psychological defence mechanisms 4 Emotional problems in adolescence
COGNITIVE DEVELOPMENT IN ADOLESCENCE	1 Changes in reasoning 2 Increasing objectivity of thought. 3 Sex differences in cognition in adolescence.
MORAL DEVELOPMENT IN ADOLESCENCE	
SUMMARY	

Figure 7.1 Structure of Chapter 7.

In this and the next chapter we shall take the general view that the comparatively heavy emphasis found in many contemporary textbooks on the problems of adolescence springs *not* from the fact that adolescents have different and distinct psychological needs from younger children or adults, and therefore more problems, *but arises instead from the choices and pressures, social, emotional, academic and vocational*, that cluster around the young person as he or she emerges into adulthood.

In the remainder of this chapter we shall consider the developmental changes that accompany the movement of a child from puberty to young adulthood (see Figure 7.1). Such changes are seen as continuous and cumulative and not as sudden and disruptive. We continue to view the individual in interaction with his environment, affected by his past experience, his present appraisal of his situation, his hopes for the future, and the particular and specific environment in which he finds himself.

Physical Changes in Adolescence

In adolescence certain inborn maturational processes lead to various developmental physical changes: growth is accelerated, bodily shape changes, primary and secondary sexual characteristics become marked and hormonal levels alter. Each of these physical changes produce psychological effects and we shall consider them in turn.

Before doing so we might pause to look at the term we used in the introduction to refer to the onset of adolescence – puberty. Puberty begins with the gradual enlargment of the prostate gland and the seminal vesicles (the organs that store semen) in males and the gradual enlargement of the ovaries and uterus in females, and is accompanied by a growth spurt that usually lasts about two years. These changes are controlled largely by the sexual hormones and it is interesting to note here that both males and females have all three of what are called the 'sex hormones' but that they have them in different proportions. Thus the difference between males and females is not due to the kind of hormones they have but the proportions in which they occur.

The growth spurt
Much of the individual's growth occurs in childhood. For example, it has been estimated that on average boys reach 54 per cent of their mature growth at 3 years of age and 86 per cent at 11 years of age. Near the end of childhood, growth becomes slower and this marks a transition between the slow gradual development of childhood and the more accelerated and less regular growth of adolescence.

In boys the growth spurt may begin as early as $10\frac{1}{4}$ years or as late as 16 years but for the average boy the growth spurt begins at about 13 and starts declining again at about $15\frac{1}{2}$. In the case of girls the growth spurt usually occurs, on average, about two years earlier. These figures refer to children who are well nourished and healthy, for, not surprisingly, the timing of this growth spurt is affected by disease and malnutrition.

The rapid physical growth that accompanies adolescence means that certain strains may be imposed on the young person. Restlessness and fatigue may accompany rapid growth if adequate rest is not allowed. Similarly with regard to diet, adolescents need extra nutrition to sustain their growth, and it has been calculated that boys between 13 and 16 need 200 more calories per day than the average adult male, and the older teenager 800 more. From this it should be clear that we cannot expect good academic performance or sustained work from teenagers and adolescents whose nutritional needs are not met.

An important psychological consequence of the growth spurt is the comparisons it tends to produce among adolescents. A boy who matures later than most of his contemporaries may feel inadequate because he sees himself as deviating physically from his friends and may also, as Durojaiye points out, be at a disadvantage in athletics and games. There is not much a teacher or parent can do to stimulate physical growth in the case of a boy who is markedly shorter than his peers, aside from ensuring that he has adequate rest and a healthy diet. While most late developers will catch up with their friends, some boys will become short adults and because of this teachers and parents should try to encourage adolescents not to place too much emphasis on conforming to an idealised stereotype of physical appearance but should encourage instead a healthy interest in what people actually *are* like rather than the way they look. Of course this is far easier said than done and it is unfortunately true that in most contemporary societies adolescents who differ markedly in appearance from other adolescents will suffer lowered self-esteem.

In the case of girls, height is less likely to be important. A major problem instead may be presented by those girls who are markedly fatter than their friends. Even though obesity has not been considered a disadvantage in all cultures (in parts of southern Africa for example, plump women have been regarded as more desirable than thin ones), these days girls who are very overweight usually feel at a disadvantage. In most cases a careful attention to diet will lead to a reduction in weight. It is very important, however, that weight loss should not be allowed to go too far, as in exceptional circumstances this can lead to a neurotic compulsion to lose weight which may become an illness.

Most adolescents, however, will not deviate too much from their peers and it is useful to remember when counselling adolescents who may be concerned about their physical growth that there are wide variations in the onset of the growth spurt. It is also helpful to know that, provided nutrition is adequate, most children tend to reach a height that is close to the average height of their parents. Thus it is not really appropriate to reassure a child of very short parents that he will undoubtedly achieve average height. It is probably far better to help him to see that being a bit shorter than the average person is not very important.

The growth spurt is accompanied by changes in body dimensions, and it is to these that we turn now.

Changes in bodily dimensions

The rapid acceleration in height we have discussed above is, of course, accompanied by an acceleration in weight and also a change in bodily proportions. Nearly all parts of the skeletal and muscular structure take part in the growth spurt but they do so at different times and to different extents. The parts of the body that reach adult size and form first are the hands, head and feet; while the last part to reach adult form is the trunk. This varying rate of growth may make some adolescents feel clumsy and sometimes they may be concerned by the unevenness of their growth and worry that their feet or hands are too big. In the very great majority of cases, however, these fears will be quite unnecessary as the bodily proportions of most adults are well balanced.

Children tend to have relatively larger heads than adults in proportion to the rest of their body and in adolescence, as head growth diminishes compared to the rest of the body, this characteristic

disappears. But while the comparative growth rate of the head diminishes, subtle changes take place in the face as the nose and jaws become larger in comparison to other facial features.

At adolescence both sexes show a decline in the rate of growth of fat, but girls show this tendency less than boys and develop rather more fat on their arms and legs than boys do. At the same time the proportions of the body alter differently for the two sexes with girls' shoulders remaining slender but hips becoming rounder, while boys develop wider shoulders but retain slimmer hips. In relation to boys, as we have mentioned above, girls have a higher percentage of fat and boys normally have greater muscular strength after puberty.

These changes in physical appearance undoubtedly affect the young person's self-image because, as Conger notes, 'The young person who meets cultural standards of physical appearance and ability, and receives approval from peers and adults for these characteristics, may gain a better self-image in other respects as well, unfair as this may seem' (1977, p. 121). Conger is writing about adolescents in the USA but it is interesting to see how similar a conclusion was reached by Durojaiye writing about Nigeria. He found in a survey on the problems and anxieties of 894 children aged between 11 and 14 years that 62 per cent complained about their physical development and he noted the important psychological implications of this concern with physical growth and development (1976, p. 139).

> ' A well-matured adolescent girl knows that she can be attractive to the opposite sex. Her self-image and self-esteem are, in consequence, wholesome ... Similarly, the large boy soon gets selected at contests where size and strength are required. The experience of activity and achievement that results encourages such a boy to deeds of courage and confidence which further ' his sense of maturity and success.

This relationship between self-concept and the bodily changes at puberty was also shown in the studies made at Baroda Department of Child Development in India where it was found that 'early maturers are at an advantage of having a deeper, better self-concept than late maturers' (Kuppuswamy, 1974, p. 210).

But while physical appearance is important, it is not, of course, the only component of self-esteem. We all know people of both sexes who are attractive and popular despite the fact that they do not conform to our particular cultural ideal of physical beauty. As Hamachek writes, 'Healthy, balanced people will build their feelings of self-regard on a variety of grounds, among which would include achievement, creativeness, social status, moral and ethical behaviour, interpersonal relationships, and the like' (1978, p. 129). Consequently it is very important, as we noted before, for teachers and parents to try to build up a set of social values in adolescents that does not make physical attraction too important.

We have already traced the growth of self-esteem in Chapter 5 and in that chapter we claimed that the individual's perception of an interpersonal situation may be affected by the person's level of self-esteem. We illustrated this by giving an example of two little girls with differing levels of self-esteem who had an impatient teacher and we argued that the little girl, high in self-esteem, would interpret the teacher's unkind and unjustified remarks as springing from the teacher's bad mood while the little girl with low self-esteem would interpret the identical remarks far more personally, and her low opinion of herself would sink even further. The second little girl would not see the world objectively but would view it from her own perspective which would be shaped by her low self-concept. Similarly the self-perception of adolescents in relation to their bodily appearance is very often not objective and a child with a low self-concept may view himself as weak, unattractive or badly proportioned even if he is none of these things. Similarly an adolescent who has had a relatively fortunate upbringing and whose emotional needs have been met may be able to be quite philosophical and relatively unconcerned by not meeting the ideal cultural expectation of physical appearance.

We conclude, then, that although all adolescents would like to fit in with the cultural standard of physical appearance, it is important for adults to emphasise that physical appearance is but one aspect of a person's individuality. Further, we must remember that if we treat adolescents in such a way as to optimise their self-concepts by meeting their emotional needs, the relative importance of this aspect of their life will diminish. Finally we should remember that very often adolescents' perception of their appearance is not objective, so that if a relatively slim girl comes to us complaining of her weight problem or a boy who is quite average in size appears to be preoccupied with his height, we

should not dismiss them as fussing unnecessarily, but spend some time trying to see why their self-image is so slanted.

Change in primary and secondary sexual characteristics

There are two types of changes in the reproductive system during early adolescence. First, there are those related to the genital organs: boys secrete live spermatozoa and girls ovulate fertile eggs and their breasts become mature. We call these primary sex characteristics. Then there are also changes in what we call the secondary sex characteristics: both boys and girls show changes in bodily hair, sweat glands and sebaceous glands, and boys' voices alter and deepen.

For girls, the onset of menstruation marks a change that they cannot ignore. In some societies, menarche (or the onset of menstruation) has been marked by elaborate ceremonies. For example, amongst the Arapesh of New Guinea, the first menstruation is traditionally an occasion of great importance. Margaret Mead, writing about Arapesh life in the first part of this century, describes it as follows (1962, p. 172):

> ' Among the Arapesh, first menstruation occurs several years after a young betrothed girl has gone to live with her husband's kin, where he and his kin will hunt and garden to provide food to make her grow. Her first menstruation is occasion for ceremony; her brothers come and build her menstrual hut, placing it safely beyond the edge of the village to keep the village safe from the dangerous supernatural strength attached to menstruating women. The girl is cautioned to sit with her legs in front of her, her knees raised. Her old grass skirt and her old armlets are taken from her and either given away or destroyed. Older women of her family attend her and instruct her ... The girl fasts for five or six days, and then emerges to be painted and decorated. '

On the other hand other New Guinean cultures placed very little emphasis on menarche and this illustrates the tremendous variation, even within fairly restricted geographic areas, in the way menarche has been treated. But, as we shall point out in the next chapter, the elaborate ceremonies associated with initiation and, in this case, with menarche, have tended to become modified because most young people attend schools during puberty and cannot therefore be withdrawn from everyday life for long continuous periods of time. Thus it is not likely to be the experience of many girls these days that menarche will be celebrated in quite such a distinctive way as it was described above.

Nevertheless, even if menarche is not treated ceremonially, to most girls the occasion of their first period will be one that they remember, because it is the symbol of sexual maturity. It is of course crucial that girls be prepared for this so that their initial experience may be as favourable as possible. It is thought that a number of symptoms associated with the first years of periods such as headaches, cramps, backaches and severe abdominal pain may be, in some cases at least, partially due to negative attitudes to menstruation which may spring from fear and ignorance as to the precise nature of the process. For this reason great care must be taken to prepare girls for their first period so they are not taken by surprise.

The average age for menarche in the West is just before 13 years of age, but the range is large – it may occur anywhere between 10 and 16½ years of age. It is interesting to note that the age of menarche has declined consistently over the last century in a number of countries (Norway, Germany, Finland, Great Britain, Denmark, Sweden and the USA). This is thought to be associated with improvements in living standards and with improvements in medical care. It is not thought likely, however, that it will decline further in the West because it seems there are physiological limits. However, it is likely that in some developing countries, where nutrition is not currently high and medical services are not widely spread, the same trend will be noticed with improvement in health services. Durojaiye reports that the average age of menarche for Baganda secondary schoolgirls was 13·4 years and for Yoruba girls 13·8, and these averages are slightly older than those reported in the West, bearing out the finding that age of menarche may be related to nutritional and health standards.

If a girl is prepared in advance for the onset of her periods, and if she is reassured that this is an entirely natural happening, then there is no reason to suppose there should be any psychological effects for the menarche. Unless it occurs at an exceptionally late or early age, the age of menarche has not been shown to have any psychological effects and the Baroda study of child development in India showed no association between age of menarche and self-concept.

In boys, changes in the primary sexual characteristics (genitals) usually start rather earlier than changes in the secondary sexual characteristics such as growth of facial hair and changes in the voice.

For most boys these changes are not associated with any psychological distress. There are, however, three sets of circumstances that may cause distress and concern. First, if these changes are mocked or ridiculed by adults, even in a friendly fashion, the boy may feel embarrassed and shy. Secondly, as we mentioned earlier, late development in boys, if it causes them to appear markedly different from their peers, may give rise to feelings of inadequacy unless it is sensitively handled by parents and caretakers. Thirdly, some boys, early in their sexual development, may show a tendency to slight breast development and fattening of the lower torso. This may cause a great deal of unnecessary anxiety and even misery, although in the absence of any specific illness these conditions are not associated with future abnormality and will disappear as the boy gets older. It is important that an adolescent boy should have some adult in whom he can confide, should any of these three sets of circumstances happen to him, so that he can be reassured.

Alteration in hormonal levels

As was mentioned at the beginning of this chapter, it is the change in the secretion of hormones that is largely responsible for the physical changes of adolescence. This rise in the level of sex hormones undoubtedly contributes to a greater awareness of sexual potential as well and this is true for both sexes. It is likely to present more difficulties for adolescent boys, because a sexual response on their part may be visible to others.

The developing boy is likely to be relatively easily aroused sexually during adolescence. As Conger notes, for him 'almost anything can take on a sexual meaning'. Consequently he may worry about his ability to control his sexual response. Another disturbing feature of male adolescence may be nocturnal emission when spontaneous ejaculation occurs during sleep, usually accompanied by dreams of a sexual nature. Once again we would stress the need for some sex education so boys are prepared for this to happen and do not regard the ejaculation of seminal fluid as harmful or a sign that something is wrong.

The way that different cultures have handled sexual behaviour has varied enormously. Although there are some almost universal similarities, for example, some form of incest taboo (restriction of sexual behaviour between close relatives), there have been marked differences between cultures not only in the amount and type of sexual behaviour that is socially accepted, but also in the consistency with which sexual behaviour is regarded as children develop. A society may view sexual behaviour restrictively throughout the whole life-span, or it may be permissive to it at all ages, or it may be highly restrictive during childhood and adolescence and then more permissive towards sexual activity during adulthood.

Let us look at sexual behaviour before adolescence. The Chewa of Africa and the Lepcha of India both believe that sex play before puberty is extremely important, and among the Lepcha girls of 11 or 12 regularly engage in sexual intercourse. On the other hand the Ashanti of Ghana believe sexual intercourse with a girl who has not undergone puberty to be so harmful to the community that both partners should be put to death. Similarly the Cuna of South America believe that children should remain so ignorant of sexual matters that they are not even allowed to watch animals give birth (Conger, 1977).

In the West, sexual behaviour has not been tolerated before adolescence for either boys or girls. At adolescence, however, a marked difference in attitude to sexual behaviour is usually shown to the two sexes in that boys are permitted to experiment sexually but girls are expected to remain chaste until marriage. Recently, as less differentiation is made between the sexes in social expectations, this difference in attitude is less noticeable in many Western countries.

It can be seen, then, that whether young people are permitted or are not permitted to take part in sexual behaviour varies from culture to culture. However, whether the society is, or is not, permissive to sexual behaviour in adolescence, it still has to take account of the fact that the rise in the level of sex hormones during adolescence commonly leads to an awareness of sexual potential in the adolescent. Thus some form of sex education should be provided, whether in the home, in youth groups, in school or in traditional ceremonies, so that the young person learns to reconcile his growing sexual awareness with the cultural expectation of social behaviour. In earlier times, in many societies, such information played an extremely large part in initiation ceremonies. In urban areas these days such important aids to the young adolescent are not always available and consequently some form of sex education is advisable.

Durojaiye recommends, in the absence of initiation rites and other cultural practices, that sex education programmes have the following aims (1976, p. 242):

‘ (a) To give correct and adequate factual information and understanding of sex, its development, its function and its expression.
(b) To cultivate correct reactions to sexual experience.
(c) To prevent the child from acquiring a sense of guilt, horror, disgust or fear of sex.
(d) To teach children continuing and widening sublimatory or socially acceptable expressions for sexual thoughts, feelings and acts.
(e) To cultivate in children self-respect and self-control, without blocking or repression, but with growing consideration for others.
(f) To introduce children to the role of parents. ’

We have mentioned that research suggests that females have, potentially, very similar levels of sexual response to males. The practice of circumcision, which is still common in Africa, in Oceania and amongst the Indian people of North and South America may, in the case of female circumcision, lower the interest and pleasure that women are able to obtain from sex. For this reason, and because the operation may be a very painful and frightening experience for a young girl, and because it is potentially very dangerous, sometimes leading to medical conditions like haemorrhage, urinary infections and gynaecological complications, many young people from areas which have traditionally practised it are very critical of the operation. Esther Ogunmodede writes in a recent issue of *People*, ‘Let us all mount a campaign against the evil that impairs the health of our women and puts their lives in danger, as well as their babies’ (1979, p. 31). A recent survey in Sudan amongst university students showed that only eight out of 153 young men were in favour of the operation. Nevertheless the practice remains widespread because it is seen as a part of traditional heritage and culture (Epelboin and Epelboin, 1979).

It would seem, then, that sexuality cannot be

looked at except in the context of the specific culture within which it occurs, as attitudes and practices vary so much between cultures. Whether or not the adolescent experiences psychological problems with respect to sexual behaviour depends largely on the degree to which he or she has been prepared for sexual maturity. In some societies, for example, in areas of central Africa, conversation about sexual matters between parents and their children is not regarded as proper. In other societies, for example, in parts of the USA, parents do not approve of any adult other than themselves discussing sexual matters with their children. Clearly, who provides help and counselling in the area of adolescent behaviour will vary from culture to culture. But it does seem that adolescent problems concerned with sexual behaviour and attitudes can be helped if sympathetic and tolerant adults are able to provide information and guidance.

Emotional Development in Adolescence

In looking at emotional development in adolescence we shall refer back briefly to self theory, then we shall look at the psychological needs of adolescence, following this we shall consider how emotional development may be affected by the use of psychological defence mechanisms and finally we shall look at some of the emotional problems of adolescence (see Figure 7.1).

Self theory revisited

In Chapter 5 we discussed emotional and social development in the primary school years within the context of self theory because we suggested that trying to gain some insight into the way other people view themselves helps us to understand why they behave the way they do and helps us to see how they come to hold the views they hold. We pointed out that a person's picture of himself is built up slowly and is shaped largely by the way other people treat him and his observations of his own behaviour and the effect his behaviour has on others and on the external environment.

To begin with, the young child does not have a stable self-concept; he sees himself as a member of his own family, as a schoolchild, as a friend and at the same time has aspirations for the future, perhaps visualising for himself glory, fame and riches or perhaps seeing himself as following the same life-pattern as someone he admires and

identifies with – a parent, teacher, older sibling or older friend.

Many theorists regard adolescence as the time when young people merge these multi-layered and diffuse self-pictures into a more stable identity. Pre-eminent amongst such thinkers has been Erik Erikson, who regards adolescence as a period when young people go through what he has termed an 'identity crisis' during which they strive to find something to be true to in all areas of their lives – emotional, social, vocational (with respect to work) and ideological. Erikson goes rather further, however, than most self theorists in seeing the acquisition of identity as being primarily rooted in a particular stage of development – namely, in adolescence. He sees it (see below) as a 'unique product' generated to meet the crises of adolescence rather than seeing the acquisition of identity, as we do, as occurring because the self-concept is slowly being unified. Further he sees the acquisition of identity as a response to the pressures and needs generated in adolescence, rather than seeing it as we do as part of the individual's attempt to make sense of the world by structuring his own attitudes, feelings and behaviour into a unified sense of self. Thus Erikson (1968, p. 87) writes:

> ' Young people must become whole people in their own right and this during a developmental stage characterized by a diversity of changes in physical growth, genital maturation and social awareness. The wholeness to be achieved at this stage I have called a *sense of inner identity*. The young person, in order to experience wholeness, must feel a progressive continuity between that which he has come to be during the long years of childhood, and that which he promises to become in the anticipated future; between that which he conceives himself to be and that which he perceives others to see in him and expect of him. Individually speaking, the identity includes, but is more than, the sum of all the successive identifications of those earlier years when the child wanted to be, and often was forced to become, like the people he depended on. Identity is a unique product which now meets a crisis to be solved only in new identifications with age mates and with leader figures outside the family. The search for a new and yet reliable identity can, perhaps, best be seen in the persistent adolescent endeavour to define, overdefine and redefine themselves and each other in often ruthless

competition while a search for reliable alignments can be recognized in the restless testing of the newest in possibilities and the oldest in values. Where the resulting self-definition becomes too difficult, a *sense of role confusion* results.'

In order for the young person to resolve this identity crisis, Erikson considers that ideally there should be a 'psychosocial moratorium' by which he means an extended period in which the young person may take some time off, before making any major future decisions about his life, to experiment with different roles and explore varied avenues of behaviour. Such a situation is, of course, ideal and may be possible within societies where there are enough resources to allow each young person to choose how to take this period of retreat and then come back to an educational system or the type of employment he desires. In practical terms, for most young people in most countries such luxury is not possible – there are limited choices and restricted periods in which they have to be made.

We have not, until this stage, presented Erikson's model of development in which he differentiates life into eight stages, each stage being characterised by specific areas of conflict. His stages and their areas of conflict are:

infancy: oral sensory stage – basic trust versus mistrust
early childhood: muscular anal stage – autonomy versus shame and doubt
middle childhood: locomotor-genital stage – initiative versus guilt latency – industry versus inferiority
puberty and adolescence: identity versus identity confusion
young adulthood: intimacy versus isolation
adulthood: generativity versus stagnation
maturity: ego integrity versus despair.

It can be seen that the infant years are regarded as being chiefly characterised by trust or mistrust; by this Erikson refers to the child's relationship with his caretakers. Early childhood is characterised by autonomy or shame; by this Erikson means that the child begins to view himself as a being independent of others. The primary school years are seen as being characterised by the resolution of initiative versus guilt and industry versus the inferiority stage; and the child is seen as developing competence in both social and technical spheres. Adolescence is characterised by the conflict

between identity and identity confusion and the need for fidelity, that is, something or someone to be true to. Thus Erikson in the emotional sphere, like Piaget in the cognitive sphere, has an 'ages and stages' approach to emotional development.

As the reader may remember, when we discussed cognition in Chapter 4 we preferred to view it using a process approach, rather than a stages approach. Similarly, with emotional behaviour we have not used the Erikson developmental model because his stage approach conflicts with our own approach which regards development as a slow cumulative process in which different ways of behaving are observed at all ages. We do not regard it as particularly useful to try and characterise different age levels by specific area of conflict. However, it must be said that Erikson's stage approach to emotional development, particularly his work on adolescence, has been very influential in the USA, and if you are interested in his approach you will find a reference in the select bibliography at the end of this chapter.

In contrast to Erikson's stage approach, self theory sees the gradual acquisition of a relatively unified self-concept as continuing throughout life and in such a way that, although self-concept and identity are always rooted in the past, they are continually sensitive both to what is happening in the present and to the appraisal of what is likely to happen in the future.

As the child enters adolescence, he is beginning to draw together all that he knows about himself and he starts to merge into one picture his behaviour at home, at school, with friends and when he is by himself. For him to deal in a satisfactory way with the social and emotional pressures that will occur as he moves towards adulthood, these different sets of behaviours and his appraisal of them must start to merge.

Is there any evidence that self-concept becomes more unified and relatively more stable as adolescents grow older? Engel tested adolescents between the ages of 13 and 15 and found a relative stability of self-concept; interestingly, those with a positive self-concept showed more stability than those with a negative self-concept. Carlson, too, found that self-esteem stabilised between the ages of 12 and 18 (Cockram and Beloff, 1978). The work of Tome with French adolescents showed that not only do adolescents have a relatively consistent view of self but they are also capable of describing the way they appear to others. Tome asked his subjects to describe themselves both as they saw themselves and as their parents saw them. He also asked their parents to judge their children as they thought their children would judge themselves and he found that the children were closer to the mark in their task than the adults were – that is, children were pretty accurate in describing how their parents saw them (Elkind and Weiner, 1978).

What kind of self-concept will enable adolescents to deal most adequately with the emotional and social pressures of moving from childhood to adulthood? To answer this question we return to the assertion we made in Chapter 5 that an adequate self-concept is dependent on a healthy but realistic degree of self-esteem. The self-concept must be free of both neurotic pride and unrealistic fears. The individual must feel at least as good as other people in dealing with life. Quite clearly this degree of self-esteem cannot arise unless the person has shown himself equal, thus far, to others in dealing with life. Whatever a child's abilities and attitudes are, this feeling of adequacy can be given to him if his needs have been satisfied. In the first two chapters of this book, as well as in Chapter 5, we suggested that there were four basic psychological needs, and if these were met a healthy degree of self-esteem would be generated.

We argued that if, during childhood, a child has been reassured that others love him and will protect him if necessary (need for love and security), if he has been allowed to learn about the world and to gain competence in dealing with other people and acquiring academic and other skills (need for new experience and need for responsibility) and if he has been encouraged to view himself as an effective and independent individual (need for praise and recognition), he will enter adolescence well able to deal with the social and emotional aspects of his life. This will be because he will have acquired a level of self-esteem which will enable him to meet the challenges of growing up and entering adulthood with confidence and faith in himself.

During adolescence the four basic needs continue to be felt, but the need for love and security becomes modified to some extent, differing from culture to culture, by the need for autonomy – the need to move away from the protection of others and towards *independence*. We will now consider the four basic psychological needs in adolescence in rather more detail.

Psychological needs in adolescence

Like the young child, the adolescent too *needs love and security*. He continues to need a safe emotional base from which he can emerge to deal with the pressures of growing up and to which he can make a temporary retreat if the pressures begin to loom too large. In the next chapter we shall consider parent–adolescent relations in some detail but here we would like to mention that most recent surveys in a number of different countries have shown that, contrary to the stereotyped view many people have of the 'generation gap', most adolescents remain on good terms with their parents and continue to value their parents' interest in, and influence on, their lives.

Naturally the relationship between parent and child changes as children grow older and, as we shall discuss in greater detail in the next chapter, this relationship must be responsive not only to the adolescent's changing perception of himself and his role but also the fact that the young parents of the small child are now growing older and are themselves beginning to deal with the emotional problems generated by moving from young adulthood towards middle age.

Western surveys of adolescent relationships with their parents seem to indicate that adolescents continue to need the reassurance of their parents' love within a parental acceptance that their children are moving towards adolescence and require, therefore, more independence. As Conger reports, after summarising a large number of studies, adolescents 'reared in homes where parental love is evident though not cloying, and where the child is given considerable age-appropriate autonomy, are likely to emerge as more active, outgoing, socially assertive, independent, friendly, creative and lacking in hostility towards others and the self' (1977, p. 224).

As we have mentioned before, the tendency in many cultures which are affected by customary values has been to expect younger people to defer to older people in their behaviour and in their attitudes. It has been suggested by a number of writers, including Kuppuswamy, Ghuman and Vernon, that such an approach to child-rearing tends to stifle emotional and cognitive development in children. However, despite these claims for the negative effects of obedience within the home, there is no evidence to suggest that adults from cultures which emphasise obedience from younger people towards older people are in any way inferior in their social and emotional behaviour to adults from cultures where adolescents are allowed more autonomy. Consequently it is probably not appropriate to generalise Conger's conclusions (above) to non-Western cultures. Clearly the degree of autonomy and independence that should be encouraged within the home is related not to adolescent needs in the abstract but to the behaviour expected from adolescents in the culture in which they live. As Professor Majasan of Nigeria points out in writing about cultures which stress indigenous values that are based on traditional practice (1976, p. 134),

> ⸢ It is a time-honoured principle and practice in almost all African societies that no individual has the right to exist unto himself alone. Everybody has to develop within the society and interact with others for the well being of society in general ... Right from birth, the child is made to realise that his lot is tied on to that of the community which includes himself, his mates, the elders, the souls of the departed and generations unborn. ⸥

Thus we would argue that until large-scale investigations are made into adolescent–parent relationships within a broader cultural range than is covered by studies done thus far, it is advisable to treat those conclusions emerging from particular cultures with caution.

It seems, then, that while we can conclude that adolescents will continue to need the love and affection supplied by their parents, their need for independence will be tempered by the particular culture they find themselves in. If they see their peers being allowed more freedom than they are allowed, they are bound to feel resentful. If, on the other hand, within their society there is an emphasis on social cohesion and the majority of adolescents move imperceptibly into adult life without the need for an open and clearly recognised period of independence, then what American and British writers tend to call the need for independence will not loom particularly large.

Where the adolescent is most likely to differ from the younger child, with respect to his need for love and affection, will be in his increasing need for the companionship of his peers. During adolescence the need to belong to, and identify with, a group becomes very strong. Indeed, some writers see the influence of the peer-group as the most important determinant of the adolescent's self-image. While others dispute that peers are the most important determinant, there is no doubt that a young person who has no friends or companions of his own age will feel inadequate and inferior even if his home is warm and loving. However, as we mentioned in Chapter 5, this is not likely to occur frequently because it is precisely those children whose home has reinforced the self-concept who will find it comparatively easy to make and keep friends.

But, as we have stressed before, it is always possible to compensate to some extent for a poor and deprived past environment. And sometimes an adolescent who is low in self-esteem because of an unrewarding home background can form a friendship or friendships which enable him to see himself in a more positive light. Thus Conger notes (1977, p. 326):

> ⸢ adolescence may provide an important opportunity, sometimes the last major opportunity, for repairing psychological damage incurred during the years of early and middle childhood and for developing new and more rewarding relationships both with one's self and others. A mature, warm, interested and above all non-exploitative adolescent peer may play an important, sometimes crucial, role in helping a boy or girl to gain a clearer concept of self, problems, and goals, a feeling of personal worth; and renewed hope for the future. ⸥

It is clear, at any event, that the need for love and affection remains as strong for the adolescent as it does for the younger child although those supplying this need will probably extend from the immediate family to include peers. The need for security will be more tempered by a growing need for independence although this latter need will be modifiable itself by the cultural expectations of the degree of autonomy that is appropriate for the adolescent.

In adolescence the need for what we call *new experience* is also very crucial. As the young person's cognitive development proceeds he is able to deal with more and more stimulation and information and he is likely to seek out as many new experiences as possible to help him to structure and make more meaningful his understanding both of the world around him and of himself. In the next chapter, in the section on deviance, we will expand on this important aspect of adolescent behaviour but we may just mention at this stage that much of the adolescent behaviour like vandalism and rowdiness that is sometimes labelled as 'deviance' or 'delinquency' can be averted if there are sufficient interesting hobbies and occupations to satisfy this growing need. Young people who have absorbing and rewarding activities to take part in are most unlikely to seek out destructive activities. But if young people are faced with idleness and enforced unemployment, it is not surprising that their need for adventure and novelty will drive them to seek some sort of relief from boredom and this relief may not always be pro-social or constructive in nature.

The third need we quoted at the beginning of this book was the need for *praise and recognition*. This need is probably as strong in adolescence as it is at earlier ages because, although adolescence is often a period of intense sociability, for most young people it is also often a period of intense loneliness during which the adolescent wonders whether he can cope with the many demands of adult life. In the simpler societies of the past, roles were clear-cut. Girls could look at their mothers, or even their grandmothers, and visualise their own future; boys could see their future life mirrored in the day-to-day activities of their fathers. In the rapidly changing world of today such an easy transition to adulthood is seldom possible and it is no wonder that many young people feel unequal to the tasks before them. They need to feel that they can cope, and this inner conviction that they will be able to master the tasks they are asked to do can only be obtained if they are reinforced whenever they do accomplish something. Recognition of their efforts is all-important, otherwise they may feel that no matter how hard they try they will never be able to deal effectively with the pressures surrounding them.

The final need we considered was the need for *responsibility*. Fulfilling this need is even more crucial for adolescents than it is for younger children. The feelings of mastery and competence that we would wish to engender in young adults can only come through the practice of responsibility. If our primary aim is to ensure that young people have healthy self-concepts then we must provide the material from which they can build these. An adolescent who can look back at the successful completion of tasks, academic, social and physical, that required him to exercise judgement and care is bound to feel that he is worthy of other people's respect and consequently his level of self-esteem will be raised.

It sometimes takes courage on the part of a teacher or parent to allow adolescents to organise and carry out projects that have previously only been done under tight supervision, but as Hargreaves points out in his sensitive study of interpersonal relations in education, a basic assumption in flexible and caring teaching must be a trust in the pupil that is rooted in the belief that all young people should be given the chance to demonstrate their capacity for responsible and autonomous behaviour. He continues: 'there is little point in trusting the pupil if the pupil does not realise that he is trusted, or if the teacher's trust is shortlived' (1975, p. 228). The adult has to *convey* to the young person both that he trusts him and that he is prepared to act on that trust by allowing the young person to show initiative and take responsibility.

In discussing traditional attitudes to adolescents in African societies, Majasan (1976) points out that it is at this stage, when the child has learned about the expectations of his own society, that he can be encouraged to take up innovations himself. It does certainly seem to be the case that in societies which utilised initiation ceremonies in the transition from childhood to adulthood there was an assumption that young people could take on and carry out responsible tasks, and it may have been this acceptance and trust in the judgement of young people that largely contributed to the absence of strife between the younger and older generations that was so characteristic of such societies.

That self-concept is enhanced after initiation has been shown by Hertzog (1973) in a study to which we shall refer again in the next chapter. He found that Kikuyu youths showed enhanced self-concept some time after initiation rather than immediately after and concluded that this was due to the fact that after initiation the youths gradually started to interact with older and more mature youths and as a result of this took part in the more responsible behaviour that was now appropriate for them. He regards this gradual assumption of *responsibility* as being very important in increasing the boys' self-confidence and self-esteem.

In this section on emotional development in adolescence it has been argued that the needs model outlined in Chapter 1 of the book is applicable to the adolescent period as well as to the periods of early and middle childhood. It has been suggested that, if these needs continue to be satisfied as the child matures, the child's emotional development will continue smoothly because from a secure base of realistic self-confidence he will be able to react sensitively to others and will be able to respond to their emotional and psychological needs as well as his own.

Psychological defence mechanisms

In Chapter 5 and in this chapter we have viewed emotional behaviour in the context of self theory by focusing on the picture of self which is gradually being built up throughout the child's life. We have noted that an individual's self-picture may be regarded as having two major components: the *cognitive appraisal* he has of self – the *self-concept* which, we have seen, is gradually constructed out of the different impressions he gains of self in the home, at school, with friends, at work and when he is on his own; and the *feelings* he has about himself – his level of *self-esteem*. Sometimes he may need to use certain psychological 'defence mechanisms' to protect this self-esteem system.

Because the term psychological defence mechanism is not one with which most people are familiar, let us give some illustrations. For example, a student who fails an examination may 'project' the blame for this on the unfairness of the examiner rather than accept that his performance was not up to standard. A student who cheats in an examination may 'rationalise' this by persuading himself that 'everyone else cheats too' rather than face the fact that he has done something that runs counter to accepted moral standards. A teacher who is treated unfairly by his headteacher may 'displace' the hostility he feels towards the headteacher by being unnecessarily severe to his pupils rather than challenge the headteacher and thus jeopardise his position.

We now describe some of the more commonly used defence mechanisms. Bear in mind that the use of such mechanisms is universal and an essential part of the way we protect our self-esteem. They are only destructive if used in excess to avoid taking responsibility for one's own destiny, or to manufacture excuses for persisting in immature behaviour.

The use of defence mechanisms to protect self is a normal human reaction because each person's self is the integrated core of his personality, threats to the adequacy or worth of self are very disturbing and, as the examples given above illustrate, it is often easier to disguise reality than to face it head on. It should also be noted that when we utilise defence mechanisms to protect our self-image, we do not do so consciously. We are not usually aware of using them unless we are looking critically at our

behaviour and what motivates it.

If you are interested in pursuing this aspect of self theory in some detail you will find a reference in the select bibliography at the end of this chapter. In this sub-section we shall confine ourselves to listing briefly some of the defence mechanisms psychologists have identified. Each serves the purpose of safeguarding the integrity and worth of self. They are clearly necessary if the individual is to preserve a relatively consistent self-system, but used in excess they can blind him to objective reality and prevent his coming to terms with changes in the interpersonal environment. Some defence mechanisms are more easily seen in children while others depend on a fairly advanced level of cognitive functioning and are, therefore, more commonly seen in adolescence and adulthood.

We shall now consider six defence mechanisms in a little detail.

(1) *Denial of reality*. Sometimes we manage to ignore unpleasant realities by simply refusing to acknowledge that they are happening. This can often be seen in everyday behaviour when we may prefer not to talk about unpleasant topics, or look at unpleasant sights. We may observe this behaviour in an adolescent girl who, although clearly having difficulty with seeing the blackboard, may deny it because she does not want to be taken to an optician with the probable result of having to wear glasses which she fears may spoil her appearance. Teachers may sometimes see this behaviour in parents who may refuse to acknowledge that their children are behaving in a way that is very different from other children. This mechanism does guard us from painful experience but if used to excess may result in our failing to deal effectively with situations. Thus, if a parent accepts rather than denies that an adolescent child is, for example, far too withdrawn and turned inward, she may be able to embark, with the teacher's help, on a constructive programme to help her daughter. If she chooses to deny it on the other hand, her daughter may become even more estranged. (See Figure 7.2.)

(2) *Fantasy*. Sometimes not only do we deny unpleasant reality, but we also represent reality to ourselves in a more attractive light. Perhaps you can remember attending a social gathering and being very shy and tongue-tied and feeling very embarrassed and inadequate, but consoling yourself as you lay in bed that night by imagining

Figure 7.2 Three psychological defence mechanisms

being invited to another similar party and instead of repeating that day's depressing performance you see yourself holding everyone spellbound by your brilliant conversation.

Such fantasies are ready-made for us very often in books, magazines and films when we can imagine that we are the hero or heroine who is dealing so well with all the problems of life. Naturally such fantasies can be very valuable because they not only add some excitement to life but they can often stir people on to renewed efforts. However, an individual who consistently deals with failure by daydreaming and fantasising is unlikely actually to deal very effectively with the failures that dog him. As Hamchek puts it, 'It is when we use [fantasy] as a permanent not a temporary escape that we are apt to get into trouble. It is one thing to build a castle in the sky; it is quite another to try to live in it' (1978, p. 25). (See Figure 7.2.)

(3) *Projection*. Projection can best be understood by the English proverb 'The bad workman blames his tools'. It refers to the tendency we all show at times to attribute our own failures to the shortcomings of others. Thus, for example, at a fairly simple level we sometimes hear a 6-year-old asserting 'It's not my fault, he started the fight'. Or the captain of a football team may try to excuse the defeat of his team by complaining that the referee was biased.

At a deeper level we sometimes find adolescents projecting the blame for their own anti-social behaviour on to others. For example, a youth may feel envious of a classmate because his classmate is more successful than he is himself and as a result he may behave in a very hostile manner to his rival. He may excuse his own aggressive behaviour by claiming that the other boy hates him and is always getting at him. Similarly, a girl who is threatened and worried by her own strong sexual feelings and her response to them may complain that she is trapped into sexual relationships by men who are always pursuing her.

Such projections maintain self-esteem because they enable us to excuse the fact that we are not conforming to our own ideals of acceptable behaviour by placing the blame for our shortcomings on others. Without a certain amount of projection we would find ourselves continually plunged into self-criticism, but if projection is carried too far we may never move on to more mature levels of behaviour.

(4) *Rationalisation*. Rationalisation is a very comforting defence mechanism because we use it to give a socially acceptable excuse for doing something we feel to be wrong. For example, a student may miss a lecture because he is too lazy to get up in the morning but he may say that he missed it because he knew the lecturer was going to go over work he knew perfectly well already. Or, for example, an adolescent may omit to tell his parents that he failed a test because he 'doesn't want to upset them'.

At a more serious level, a teacher may sometimes lose her temper and punish a child severely and perhaps unfairly but excuse herself by saying that she did this 'for the child's own good'.

If we did not indulge in rationalisation occasionally we would probably be paralysed by feelings of guilt and inadequacy. On the other hand, like all defence mechanisms, if used to excess it may lead to self-deception and the inability to deal constructively with reality.

(5) *Displacement*. When we refer to the use of displacement as a psychological defence we indicate the shift of emotion from the person to whom it was originally felt towards a more neutral or less threatening person or object. For example, an adolescent who is just starting a new job may be most unjustly criticised by a foreman. Rather than answer back, he may suppress his hostility until he gets home that evening when he may vent his pent-up feelings on a younger brother.

But displacement can be rather more subtle and complex than this example. Envy can sometimes be responsible for displacement. Perhaps a girl is very envious of a more popular classmate. She may realise that an open expression of her negative feelings to the more popular girl may rebound on her, and she may instead start a whispering campaign against the more popular girl on the lines that 'someone should tell her for her own good that a girl who goes out with as many different boys as she does can easily be regarded as having low morals'. Interestingly, the girl who starts the whispering campaign may not even realise that it springs from jealousy and may herself believe that she is acting from the kindest of motives.

While displacement is a valuable mechanism in that it helps us to deal with strong emotions in a way that does not necessarily involve any risk to our position or self-esteem, too much reliance on it results in us blanketing our minds to our real feelings. On the whole it is much better if we can learn to be more open about our emotional responses and teachers and parents can encourage this openness by showing an accepting and understanding attitude to the psychological doubts and dilemmas of adolescents. (See Figure 7.2.)

(6) *Withdrawal and regression.* Sometimes adolescents are so plagued by their inability to deal with emotional problems that they may refuse to acknowledge their existence at all. In *withdrawal*, or as some writers call it emotional insulation, the individual does not even try to confront his needs and fears, but retreats instead into a state of passivity. Thus an adolescent boy, badly hurt by his first relationship with a girl, which has left him feeling not only rejected, but completely inadequate with the opposite sex, may refuse to get emotionally involved with girls again and may cultivate a hard, cynical, exploitative attitude to women. Or a child who has always done badly at school, and whose academic self-esteem is extremely low, may refuse to pay any attention in lessons at adolescence, and may withdraw into silent, passive attendance at school, making hardly any attempt at all to submit work for fear that it too will be met with out-and-out rejection.

Naturally we all use withdrawal to some extent in order to cope with disappointments in aspects of life that we cannot do well at. For example, a girl may state 'I am useless at games' and may, as a result, treat physical education very lightly. This is hardly a major emotional problem. On the other hand, too much withdrawal, and isolating oneself from many aspects of everyday life, can lead to a very shallow and superficial participation in life and, as Hamachek says, 'When we "dare not hope" we cease to grow' (1978, p. 31).

Regression involves a retreat when we are faced with emotional difficulties to behaviour that is more appropriate to earlier developmental levels. For example, a young child may regress to bedwetting when he is deeply upset by a continuing problem like a parent's chronic illness, or an adolescent may start playing again with younger siblings if he finds he cannot get on with his peers, or a young wife may run back to her parental home if she cannot cope with the stresses of marriage.

Regression can be viewed as an attempt to reduce the demands of the world that we behave independently by a retreat to a more dependent way of behaving. Regression, however, does not only consist of behaving in childlike or immature ways, but is more complex because it usually means that we replace relatively mature goals with less demanding ones. For example, the adolescent who becomes anxious that he is not fitting in with his friends may not confront the situation and adjust his behaviour to that of his contemporaries but may reduce his anxiety by reassuring himself that his younger brothers and sisters still love him.

In this short introduction to psychological defence mechanisms, you may have recognised some patterns you have noticed in the past in your own behaviour and in the behaviour of others. It is most important to remember that in themselves defence mechanisms are a valuable way of protecting our self-esteem. It is only when there is an excessive reliance on them in order to avoid facing reality that they pose any psychological danger. In the next sub-section, which deals with emotional problems in adolescence, you will notice that too consistent a use of defence mechanisms is often characteristic of disturbed adolescents.

Emotional problems in adolescence

Minor emotional problems. As we shall see in the next section, one of the major developmental changes that occurs in adolescence is the tendency to think more deeply and analytically about issues external to the individual himself. And, as we have already noted, another developmental change occurring in adolescence is the increasing self-awareness that arises. Both of these changes may lead to sudden mood changes in adolescence as the individual struggles to deal with both the demands of the external world and anxieties about the future, not only of himself, but of mankind in general, and with the pressures of presenting to the world a confident and competent image.

In a study of 14-year-olds done in Britain, Rutter and his colleagues reported that nearly half said that at times they felt so miserable that they cried and felt they just wanted to retreat from the world. One-quarter reported that they felt people were watching them and talking about them and about one-fifth that they were very self-critical and felt that they did not matter very much to anyone (Cockram and Beloff, 1978). These feelings of misery and worthlessness seem to be quite common in adolescence when young people are faced with a number of conflicting demands and uncertainty about both the way they should behave in the present and what will happen in the future. Thus Yulisa Amadau Maddy (1977) describes the feelings of a teenager from Sierre Leone, Joe Bengoh, who feels he has transgressed against his own code of honour:

' Joe Bengoh lay awake all night. He was restless and unhappy.
"I am responsible for it all. I am the one who has destroyed everything for them. They were happy before I came. There is a curse on me! God, what have I done to deserve this? Padre must know about what happened between Mary and me and Ade. God! But I will only make it worse. Maybe there is a curse on my family. Generation upon generation yet unborn will suffer." Joe wept and wept. "But why? Why? Why?" he shouted, hoping the answer would come from somewhere, anywhere. He felt dizzy. He lay back on the bed and started to repeat [a prayer] to himself. '

For most adolescents such feelings, though intense, and perhaps relatively common, are short-lived. Severe emotional problems do not just appear in adolescence 'out of the blue' but are likely to spring from either very disturbed early childhoods or from very demanding external pressures. If (1) outside pressures are not too severe and conflicting, (2) his level of self-esteem is adequate and (3) he does not rely too much on the blanketing of reality by too much dependence on psychological defence mechanisms, the adolescent is unlikely to suffer from deep-seated emotional problems.

Undoubtedly teachers and parents can contribute to the lessening of minor emotional problems in adolescence by acting so as to enhance self-esteem and by trying to help young people to deal with the pressures exerted on them by external demands – such as academic pressures, financial constraints and problems concerned with finding work. A knowledge of specific areas that worry young people can also help, though these will of course vary from situation to situation. Some insight into the areas causing particular emotional distress to young people is given by the survey of 400 young people who were referred to the counselling programme in Lagos. Shaikh (1974) reported the following psychological items as occuring most often in his secondary school sample.

For boys: I wish I had more confidence in what I can do (54 per cent).
For girls: I feel that my teachers do not like me (60 per cent).

I wish I could overcome my fear of making mistakes (58 per cent).

Shaikh's survey showed that there was considerable variation in the kind of problems cited by boys as compared to girls. He considered that his data indicated that for his sample girls found greater difficulty in adjusting to school than boys did. This result runs counter to the general finding in Britain and America that boys have greater problems in adjusting to schools than girls do. But this very contradiction illustrates a general point about emotional problems in adolescence, which is that these are often related to specific pressures and demands exerted by the environment as well as to generalised feelings of inadequacy. Thus, if the cultural expectations are that it is more important for boys to be educated than it is for girls, then schools may be run in such a way as to make adjustment easier for boys than for girls. Presumably this was the case for the Nigerian sample. In the West, however, as Conger says, ' it is typical in our culture for adolescent boys to be more highly motivated by needs for autonomy and independence than girls' (1977, p. 375). So it is not surprising that they are more inclined to show emotional problems with regard to schools than girls do.

We can conclude, then, that the incidence of emotional problems in a particular adolescent's development will depend on a number of factors:

(1) How many external demands he is facing with respect, for instance, to domestic problems, financial difficulties, academic pressure and peer relationships.
(2) How compatible his aims and attitudes are with cultural expectations.
(3) How high his general level of self-esteem is.
(4) How able he is to confront his problems rather than attempt to suppress them by the use of psychological defence mechanisms.
(5) How supportive the adults in his life are.
(6) How able he is to discuss his problems in an open and confiding way with his peers or with concerned adults.

However, even if adolescents do suffer from depression, feelings of inadequacy or feelings of rebellion, for most of them such problems will be short-lived. For a few adolescents, unfortunately, problems will loom so large, and self-concept will be so impaired, that severe depressions or abnormally disruptive behaviour will result.

More serious emotional problems. Acute depression in adolescence seems to have its basis in long-standing, repeated experiences of defeat. Frequently the last straw leading to protracted bouts of very severe depression is the loss of a relationship, whether with a parent or friend or someone the adolescent was in love with. The depressed young person may try to escape from his feelings by the excessive use of defence mechanisms like withdrawal or regression. Sometimes he may turn to drink or drugs or a long series of unsatisfactory sexual relationships. But such solutions *are* clearly unsatisfactory and any young person who is observed to be following such behaviour patterns is obviously in great need of skilled and concerned intervention by caring adults or perhaps by older friends.

A young person who is extremely anxious and very depressed may, sometimes, make a suicide attempt. Fortunately, a large proportion of such attempts are forestalled before death can actually result. Nevertheless, any attempt at suicide, even though it may not appear very determined, must be regarded as a 'cry for help' and the young person concerned must be persuaded that others do care for him. Occasionally, unfortunately, young people do succeed in killing themselves. A survey of the processes which lead to this tragedy has been outlined by Cockram and Beloff (1978) as:

(1) A long history of emotional problems dating from early childhood.
(2) Encountering rather more external pressures than are encountered by other young people.
(3) A worsening of these pressures with adolescence.
(4) An inability to cope with the emotional problems encountered except by retreating into isolation and withdrawal.
(5) A complete lack of any meaningful social relationships in the days and weeks preceding the suicide.

In dealing with extremely depressed or suicidal youngsters, our aims should be twofold: first, and most important, to try to repair the damaged self-image of the young person and reassure him that we do care for him and wish him to share his anxieties with us; and secondly, to deal with any immediate problems that may have led him to this state, such as extreme academic anxiety or severe financial or domestic problems. But in most cases a young person who is as badly disturbed as to attempt suicide or lapse into complete withdrawal will benefit from professional psychological help. If you are interested in the kinds of psychological help (or psychotherapy) that may be used with young people you will find a reference at the end of the chapter.

Adolescents who become severely depressed or even, in extreme cases, turn to suicide are internalising their anxieties. Other adolescents may 'act these out' instead, and may attempt to distract themselves from their feelings of inadequacy and inferiority by disruptive and aggressive behaviour. Thus, bullies frequently suffer from low self-esteem, and in his rigorous study of violent individuals in the USA (both those continually in trouble with the police because of their violent behaviour and those policemen who were most violent in their treatment of offenders) Toch found that all his subjects suffered from deep-seated feelings of rejection and inferiority. Similarly a study of the most violent boys in an institution for young offenders done by Millham and his colleagues in Britain (1976) showed these to have very low self-esteem.

Like extremely depressed adolescents, young people who are very aggressive and disruptive need professional help and once again you may wish to follow up the reference at the end of this chapter in order to discover how such psychotherapy may proceed. But, as we stressed at the beginning of this section, although most adolescents who live in today's complex and demanding world will on occasion show signs of emotional distress, in the great majority of cases this distress will be short-lived and in all cases it can be helped by a sensitive attention to the young person and his problems and by a determined attempt to bolster his self-confidence both by reassurance and love and by encouraging him to undertake responsible tasks that he can complete successfully.

Cognitive Changes in Adolescence

In this section we will look at the growth in the powers of reasoning, at the increasing objectivity in thought and at sex differences in cognitive ability (see Figure 7.1).

Changes in reasoning
In Chapter 4 we described cognitive development

and, in doing so, we indicated that the major developmental changes in cognition are that cognitive processes become sharper and more elaborated with age.

In the school setting adolescents are able to handle abstract concepts and complex rules more easily than younger children, and their capacity to solve mathematical problems and to consider abstract propositions increases. This is partly due to maturational processes and partly due to the increasing practice and experience in these areas that occurs as children move up the educational ladder.

The increased elaboration in thought processes that is found in adolescents attending school is probably affected by five factors:

(1) An increasing vocabulary of abstract words.
(2) More elaborate concepts (see page 56 for a detailed description of this change).
(3) An increased capacity to function in the symbolic mode so that thinking is not heavily dependent on concrete props (see page 50).
(4) More sophisticated techniques for encoding material into memory and more awareness of schemes for retrieving material from memory (see pages 54–5).
(5) More experience and a growing system of cognitive structures so that new material can be related to a greater variety of past experiences.

These five factors, contributing as they do to the more elaborated thought processes, promote a growing capacity for reasoning so that adolescents become capable of solving complex mathematical and scientific problems. They also become more capable of formally testing hypotheses. This ability to manipulate hypotheses and test them is called propositional thinking.

Piaget investigates propositional thinking with tasks that are considered to test whether individuals have reached the most sophisticated cognitive stage, the stage of formal operations (see page 45). If adolescents are tested on formal operations, it is sometimes found that those who do not stay within an educational setting cannot succeed at these tasks. Psychologists may then state that such individuals 'have not attained the stage of formal operations' and therefore are not capable of sophisticated propositional reasoning. We would not accept this, but would argue that this incapacity to do Piagetian tasks is because the tasks are not appropriate.

Therefore statements that you may encounter that in some cultures adults do not reach Piaget's last cognitive stage must not be interpreted as meaning that adults and adolescents in those cultures are not capable of abstract thought and reasoning.

Clearly adults in all cultures are capable of abstract thought. If this were not the case we would not find as we do in all cultures the use of symbols in art and in folk tales. Even when individuals do not remain within an educational setting, they show changes in thought processes as they move from childhood to adolescence and adulthood. They become, for instance, far more skilled in understanding human relationships and interpreting what lies beneath the surface of conversation. If they move into areas like trading and commerce their ability to conclude profitable deals increases, if they become farmers their skill at predicting probable harvests improves, and if they take employment within the industrial setting their ability to use tools in a skilled manner grows.

It can be stated that, except in the cases of individuals who are mentally retarded in the sense in which we defined the term on page 118 of the last chapter, as children move from childhood to adolescence and on to adulthood, their thinking becomes more elaborated and more sophisticated in response to the particular demands made by their way of life.

Increasing objectivity of thought
Although adolescents, like adults, use fantasy and daydreams as an escape from the sometimes depressing realities of life, unlike younger children they are conscious of the difference between wishful thinking and the objective world. The kind of behaviour that Elkind describes younger children indulging in seldom occurs with adolescents. For instance, Elkind describes how Paul, aged 8, would 'periodically spend days digging in the yard to find buried treasure – "jewels" and "olden days things". He dug up several pieces of china, which he carefully washed and tried to fit together, convinced that they were fragments of ancient pottery and probably of great value' (Elkind, 1974, quoting Davidson and Fay). Adolescents seldom carry fantasy to such lengths; they are aware of the difference between their fantasy life and reality.

In early adolescence, before the ages of about 15 or 16, some adolescents spend a great deal of time not only thinking about themselves but also imagining how they appear to other people.

According to Elkind, the adolescent at this stage may behave as though he is 'reacting to an imaginary audience'. He considers that this tendency in the younger adolescent accounts for the power of the peer-group because the adolescent is continually trying to project a particular image of himself to his friends. Elkind also considers that 'adolescents' feelings that they are always on stage may help to explain some of their attention-getting maneuvers, such as eccentric clothing and behaviour' (Elkind and Weiner, p. 552).

But towards the end of adolescence this type of self-involved thinking dies down. The young person comes to realise that other people are thinking more about themselves and their own problems than they are about him. This realisation enables the young person to feel freer of his peer-group and more confident about acting on his own initiative.

As young people grow older, they become able to look at themselves more objectively. They become more introspective; that is, they no longer think about themselves in the egocentric way we have just described, but become, instead, more capable of self-analysis and self-criticism. When they do this, they realise that they are not unique and they become capable of 'empathy', that is, they start being able to imagine themselves in the place of other people.

Whereas younger children live in the here-and-now, and younger adolescents are preoccupied with their particular problems and the way they appear to other people, the older adolescent as he moves towards adulthood starts to compare his situation to that of other people in an objective and analytical manner. He starts to look at his own situation in relation to the situation of others in his culture, to others in other cultures, to those who lived in the past and those who will live in the future.

He moves into the world of ideals, of theories and of possibilities. He starts to become aware of political and social realities and may, if he rejects the values of his community, be moved to try and change the conditions that hold in his community.

Thus, adolescence is sometimes an age of rebellion. But this is by no means a general rule. As we shall see in the next chapter, in most surveys the great majority of adolescents are found to be in general agreement with the values of their parents and their society.

However, whether he endorses the values of his school, or his parents and of his community or not,

the adolescent differs from the younger child in that these abstract social and political issues concern him. He differs also in that when he thinks about such issues he is usually able to do so objectively, that is, he is able to consider them independently of his own particular needs.

Sex differences in cognition in adolescence

In Chapter 2 we noted that sex differences in behaviour, cognitive ability and academic performance are related to the expectations of the culture regarding the appropriate behaviour for the sexes.

In adolescence most young people become very conscious of their sexuality. Even if they are not particularly anxious to 'fall in love' or find a boy/girlfriend, they become conscious of the fact that society (and this has held for most societies until very recently) expects that the young adult will marry. The institution of marriage, in most societies, even those where arranged marriages are the rule, imposes, particularly on women, stereotypes concerning 'desirable' characteristics in young people wishing to marry.

In many societies, women who compete on an equal footing with men at academic tasks, particularly those of a technical and scientific nature, are perceived to be 'less feminine', and there is a great deal of evidence to suggest that, whether there are physiological reasons or not that cause boys to excel at scientific and technical tasks, girls are discouraged from trying to compete in these fields because they have been influenced by an attitude which regards being good at science and technology as unfeminine and therefore undesirable.

In a survey done by one of the present authors in Scotland, she found that sex differences in the ability to do certain technical tasks, mainly concerned with manipulating shapes, only started appearing at 14 years of age. After this age boys increased in ability at these tasks but girls decreased in ability. This suggested that the differences in ability were social in origin because, unless we are to suppose that parts of the girls' brains actually deteriorated as they got older, we can only explain their decrease in performance in terms of the fact that as they get older girls become more influenced by the stereotype that being good at these tasks is more suitable for boys than girls. Some evidence for this was shown by asking the subjects to indicate how much they enjoyed doing these tasks. In general, it was found that as girls grew older they reported less enjoyment, but boys' enjoyment remained at much the same level as they grew older.

A further feature of this survey that suggested that sex differences at such tasks are a matter of expectation and differing opportunities for practice was provided when subjects of both sexes were coached. Girls' performance after the age of 14 years was comparable to boys' when they were coached.

Such results seem to suggest that social rather than physical variables account for sex differences in performance at technical tasks. But the fact remains that in general, in the West, girls do tend to fall behind boys at the later stages of the secondary school in scientific subjects. Writers in this area have related this to the general feeling amongst older adolescent girls that it is not feminine to be too 'brainy', particularly at technical subjects. More recently, with the growth of the women's movement, such stereotypes are beginning to disappear, and in the West a growing trend is appearing for girls to take and excel in such subjects as engineering. Further, more girls are beginning to study subjects such as medicine, law and architecture which have long been regarded as more appropriate for men.

This bias against girls excelling in academic areas appears in non-Western societies too, particularly in Muslim ones. This was shown in a study done in 1978 by the other author of the present book. He used 457 Nigerian university students as subjects and gave them a questionnaire regarding, amongst other questions, education for women. The subjects came from three regions of Nigeria, one of which was the northern area which is strongly Islamic in tradition. He tested the theory that subjects coming from this northern area would, because of its Islamic tradition, regard education as not particularly important for women.

His results confirmed his theory and showed that northern subjects were more likely to show traditional bias against Western education for women than other students were; they agreed with the statement that women with more than eight years of formal education would not be good home-makers. Further, students from the north in education and social sciences thought that education for girls was not important and that it was not good for a family if a wife had a higher education than the husband. We have already mentioned that there is very little evidence to support any innate (or physiological) reasons for

sex differences in adacemic performance. Nevertheless, girls tend not to do as well as boys in a number of subjects at the latter end of the secondary school and at university, and this is a tendency that is observed in numbers of different countries. There seems to be little doubt that this disparity in performance is at least in part due to very widely held expectations that, in most marriages, the chief wage-earner is the man and the chief home-maker is the woman, and that this expectation is held in a wide range of cultures.

Moral Development in Adolescence

By moral development we refer to the child's acquisition of an internal set of standards which he uses to guide his behaviour. In Chapter 5 when we discussed discipline we noted that 'discipline should be linked not to a system of rewards and punishments, but to an internalised set of behavioural standards'. We continued that three levels of responding positively to authority can be distinguished: compliance, when the child responds because he fears the consequences of not responding; identification, when the child responds because he wishes to please the authority figure; and internalisation, when he responds positively because he accepts the demands of authority as just.

In that discussion we were concerned with behaviour and, particularly in schools and in other social situations, moral behaviour must be a major concern. But to understand what motivates such behaviour we also have to look at the individual's perception of any given situation and his interpretation of it within his moral framework.

Thus, in this section on moral development, we turn to a theory which attempts to chart the individual's moral reasoning. This theory deals with the development of a set of principles which guide moral interpretations. You will notice that this theory is concerned with judgements and with cognitions about how people *should* behave; it does not predict, however, that people *will always behave* in accordance with their moral judgements because in any given situation there will be many other factors that may sway people from their principles.

Kohlberg's theory of moral reasoning
Kohlberg has studied the moral reasoning of children over a wide age-range from a cognitive-developmental point of view. He rests his theory on

a number of assumptions which are in general agreement with the perspective of this book. They are:

(1) Moral development depends largely on the cognitions an individual has about the world.
(2) The basic motivation for morality is a generalised motive to enhance self-esteem. That is, we wish to be moral in order to satisfy our needs to see ourselves as worthwhile individuals.
(3) Major aspects of moral development are culturally universal because all cultures are concerned with social interaction.
(4) Basic moral principles arise out of experiences of social interaction between the self and others.
(5) It is the overall environment that is important in promoting moral development rather than single specific experiences of reward and punishment.

In general, then, this perspective is based on the assumption that throughout the world children develop similar moral principles and standards because they are in interaction with other people and wish their interactions with other people to be of the type that will make them feel that by their behaviour they are contributing to the general good, thus enhancing their own self-esteem.

The six stages proposed by Kohlberg are as follows.

Pre-conventional level. This level can be regarded as the stage when children are *compliant* to authority. At this stage conduct is determined by external factors. It is loosely thought of as holding up to about 10 years of age.

Stage 1 The child is only influenced by whether his action will result in punishment or reward.
Stage 2 The child is still only influenced by the consequences of his actions but realises that sometimes he has to bargain so he takes up the attitude of 'You scratch my back and I'll scratch yours'. For example, he may share his toys or sweets with others, but not because he is sorry that they have less, rather because he expects them to share with him next time.

Conventional level. This level may be regarded as the stage when the child *identifies* with authority. It is loosely thought of as holding until middle adolescence.

Stage 3 'Good-boy/good-girl orientation.' Good behaviour is that which pleases or helps others who are important to the individual; but the child does not have a generalised idea about the overall good of society.
Stage 4 The individual believes that moral behaviour is that which upholds the social order. Laws have to be upheld because society has determined them.

Post-conventional level. This level can be regarded as the level when the child responds positively to authority only if he agrees with the principles upon which the demands of authority are based; that is, if he has *internalised* its standards. It can be loosely regarded as commencing during adolescence.

Stage 5 At this stage the individual is aware that people hold a variety of values. Values are relative to the group to which you belong. Nevertheless, rules should be usually upheld because they contribute 'to the greatest good for the greatest number'.
Stage 6 At this stage the individual follows self-chosen ethical principles. Principles are usually universal principles of justice, equality of human rights, respect for the dignity of human beings as individual persons. It is at this stage that an individual would agree that it would be better for him to go to gaol for his principles rather than comply with demands of society that he considered wrong.

You may wonder what Kohlberg based these stages on. For twelve years he studied the same group of seventy-five American boys and in addition he has explored moral development in a number of different cultures including Great Britain, Taiwan, Canada, Mexico and Turkey. His general procedure has been to outline a problem which calls for a moral decision, then ask for a moral decision and then ask for the basis on which the decision was made. For example, a person may be asked 'Is it better to save the life of one important person or a lot of unimportant persons?'

Or an individual might be asked 'Why shouldn't you steal from a store?'.

Kohlberg claims that even in small and isolated villages in Turkey the same developmental stages are shown as are shown in the other (mainly rural) Western cultures he has studied. Muhammad Maqsud has used Kohlberg's six stages in a study done in Nigeria in 1978. He adapted Kohlberg's items so that they were relevant to northern Nigerian culture and tested Kohlberg's assumptions that the more interaction adolescents have with other people who are prepared to discuss moral issues, the more likely they will be to move up the developmental stages. He concluded that Kohlberg's work was of relevance in Nigerian culture.

Kohlberg's work may be criticised on the same grounds as those on which we have criticised other stage theories, that different levels of development may occur at different ages. But, unlike Piaget's stages, Kohlberg's stages are seen as arising through social interaction; Piaget, as you may remember, sees his stages as depending on the attainment of logical structures that exist and must be internalised. Kohlberg is not concerned with building up a grand theory that embraces the philosophy of knowledge, but he is interested in studying the way people perceive moral issues as a result of their interaction with other people and the way this interaction allows them to put themselves in the place of other people. Thus, and most important from our point of view, Kohlberg concludes (1968, p. 30):

> The social worlds of all men seem to contain the same basic structures. All the societies we have studied have the same basic institutions – family, economy, law, government. In addition, however, all societies are alike because they *are* societies – systems of defined complementary roles. In order to *play* a social role in the family, school or society, the child must implicitly take the role of others toward himself and toward others in the group. These role-taking tendencies form the basis of all social institutions. They represent various patternings of shared or complementary expectations ... In our studies, we have found that youths who understand justice act more justly, and the man who understands justice helps create a moral climate which goes far beyond his immediate and personal acts. The universal society is the beneficiary.

In this section we have considered moral development at a cognitive level. As we pointed out earlier, holding a particular moral viewpoint does not always mean that an individual will follow the path his theoretical point of view dictates. In any situation that demands a moral response, it is not only the cognitive appraisal that a person makes that will determine his behaviour. He may not even have the time to think his actions out, he may be swayed by the people he is with, he may be too timid to take a stand that is different from other people's, he may be reluctant to draw attention to himself and finally, his judgement may be clouded by sickness, drugs or drink. Another important variable is level of self-esteem. A number of studies have shown that if you lower subjects' self-esteem by causing them to fail a number of times at a series of tasks, they are far more likely to cheat than other subjects who have been allowed to succeed in the preliminary tasks (Wright, 1971).

In the next chapter we shall be concerned with adolescent behaviour within different social settings. In discussing punishment, discipline and deviance we shall attempt to show that behaviour in moral and ethical areas is multi-determined by, amongst other variables, the social climate, the specifics of the situation and the value system, as well as the moral development of the individual concerned.

Summary

This chapter has been concerned with development in adolescence.

(1) We first discussed the physical changes that occur during adolescence and their psychological effects.
   (a) We outlined the nature of the growth spurt during adolescence and we discussed the psychological implications for children who do not conform, in their physical growth, to the majority of their peers. We stressed the importance of adequate nutrition and rest and the necessity for adolescents to have a sympathetic and tolerant adult to whom they can refer with worries concerning physical growth.
   (b) We also looked at changes in primary and secondary sexual characteristics: we

described these changes for the two sexes and stressed again the importance for young people of both sexes to have adequate information about physical changes.

(c) In discussing changes in hormonal level we pointed out that this brings with it a growing awareness of sexual potential. It was pointed out that cultural attitudes to sexual values and practice vary greatly but that, whatever these are, some guidance must be supplied to young people so that they can handle their sexual feelings in a way that is appropriate to the demands of their culture.

(2) We then discussed emotional development in adolescence.

(a) We viewed adolescence as another stage in the continuing development of self-concept and self-esteem, and rejected the idea that it is a unique period in which a permanent identity is forged.

(b) It was pointed out that the four psychological needs outlined in Chapter 1 apply to adolescence, as well as to early and middle childhood. We discussed the growing need for independence and related it to cultural expectations concerning the desirable level of autonomy for young people.

(c) We introduced the term psychological defence mechanisms and outlined the part these play in preserving the integrity and worth of self. We also stressed, however, that too great a dependence on these can lead to the evasion of reality and withdrawal from social life.

(d) In discussing emotional problems in adolescence, we indicated that for most adolescents these are of a transitory nature. Adolescents who suffer from severe and long-standing emotional problems are likely to be facing a great many external demands such as financial trouble, domestic strife, academic pressure and social inadequacy. They are also more likely than other young people to suffer from low self-esteem and to rely on the excessive use of psychological defence mechanisms.

(3) In discussing cognitive changes in adolescence we referred to three areas:

(a) We described the growing elaboration of cognitive processes and pointed out that this occurs whether or not the young person remains in the school setting. But the nature of this elaboration will be such as to match the society's needs.

(b) It was pointed out that the older the individual grows the more he is able to be objective in thinking about himself and the more he is able to consider social and political as well as personal issues.

(c) In discussing sex differences in cognition, we stressed that sex differences in academic performance are closely related to cultural expectations of desirable behaviour for the two sexes.

(4) In considering moral development in adolescence, we presented the six stages outlined by Kohlberg and related these to the three processes outlined in Chapter 5 of compliance, identification and internalisation. We stressed that responses to a moral situation are not dependent only on the level of cognitive moral development but are influenced by other factors relating to the specific situation and general moral climate.

Chapter 7: Selected Bibliography

Physical changes in adolescence
Conger, J. J., *Adolescence and Youth: Psychological Development in a Changing World* (New York: Harper & Row 1977), ch. 4.
Durojaiye, M. O. A., *A New Introduction to Educational Psychology* (London: Evans, 1976), chs 5–7.

Erikson's stage theory of emotional development
Erikson, E. H., *Identity, Youth and Crisis* (New York: Norton, 1968).

Self theory and adolescent development
Burns, R. B., *The Self Concept in Theory, Measurement, Development and Behaviour* (London: Longman, 1979).

Psychological defence mechanisms
Hamachek, D. E., *Encounters with the Self* (New York: Holt, Rinehart & Winston, 1978), ch. 1.

Psychotherapy with adolescents
Conger, op. cit., ch. 15.

Moral development in adolescence
Wright, D., *The Psychology of Moral Behaviour*
  (Harmondsworth: Penguin, 1971).
Cognitive changes in adolescence
Conger, op. cit., ch. 5.

THE ADOLESCENT IN SOCIETY

8

Introduction

In the last chapter we discussed adolescent development in the areas of physical, emotional and cognitive growth. In doing so we were concerned, in the main, with those aspects of development that spring from growth and maturation. We did not focus to any great extent on the adolescent in the social world. In this chapter we shift attention to social aspects of adolescence and discuss the adolescent in relation to his family, his friends, his school and his attitudes to work. Finally, we look at adolescents who are in conflict with society. (See Figure 8.1.) However, before we explore these social aspects of adolescence we should like to return to the subject we introduced in the last chapter – differing perspectives on adolescence that can be related to the customs and values of different societies.

Two Perspectives on Adolescence

Perspective 1

In many societies there comes a time when young people are formally initiated into their adult roles. Such initiation ceremonies often involve the separation of the young people to be initiated from the rest of the community. They also often involve, or did involve in the past, scarification. By scarification we refer to the ritual of indicating that a young person had been initiated by some physical sign such as filing the teeth, marking the face or cutting the hair.

It has seemed to most social scientists who have studied initiation rites that male initiation rites are, in general, found in societies where there is a sharp sex role differentiation; that is, where adult men and women function in very different ways and there is little sharing of tasks between the sexes. This led many anthropologists to believe that the chief function of male initiation rites is to separate young boys symbolically (and in many cases physically, while the ceremonies are taking place) from the women's circle in which they have spent their earliest years. Thus, Burton and Whiting, writing about societies they studied where there was an early strong mother–son bond, noted that 'initiation rites serve psychologically to brainwash the initial feminine identity and to establish firmly the secondary male identity' (1961, p. 90).

Some evidence for this is found in the work of Margaret Mead, when she shows that in four New Guinean societies that she studied there was a strong relationship between the kind of initiation rite carried out and the type of male–female relationships that were characteristic of the society. In each of the four societies where she investigated male initiation in great detail, there were superficial resemblances to the initiation rites of the other three, but the particulars of the ceremonies of each society related to the overall social patterning. Thus each of the four societies had a men's house or houses where males gathered for ceremonial purposes, but the way this house was utilised in initiation ceremonies differed from society to society.

The Iatmul, for example, during the initiatory ceremonies, surrounded the men's house with a great enclosure of leaves. After a period of bullyings, scarification and humiliation, during which their previous passive feminine-like state was stressed, the young Iatmul initiates were led with great and solemn ceremony through the leaves

INTRODUCTION

DIFFERING PERSPECTIVES ON ADOLESCENCE
- Perspective 1
- Perspective 2
- Reconciling the two perspectives

THE ADOLESCENT IN RELATION TO HIS FAMILY
(i) General aspects of this relationship
(ii) Within an extended family setting
(iii) Within a nuclear family setting
(iv) Principles concerning such relationships

THE ADOLESCENT IN RELATION TO HIS PEERS
(i) The importance of peer relationships
(ii) Peer relationships and social adjustment
(iii) Peer relationships within a cultural context

THE ADOLESCENT IN RELATION TO SCHOOL
(i) The adolescent's perception of school
(ii) School climate and adolescent response
(iii) Individual factors and adolescent response to school

THE ADOLESCENT & HIS ATTITUDES TO WORK
(i) Problems of vocational choice
(ii) School curricula and the demands of work

THE ADOLESCENT IN CONFLICT WITH SOCIETY

SUMMARY

Figure 8.1 Structure of Chapter 8.

and into the house. Mead relates this rigorous initiation experience to the patterns of sex role behaviour that were characteristic of Iatmul life. Men in this society were required to be very active in their behaviour, always asserting their domination over women and never showing any display of passivity. Thus the initiation ceremony concentrated on removing any desire on the boys' part to identify with women in their behaviour.

Among the Tchambuli, however, there was far less difference in the overall behaviour of the sexes. Women were as active as men in everyday life, and were, in fact, far less inferior to their men than the Iatmul women were to Iatmul men. This comparatively slight status difference between the sexes accounted, according to Mead's analysis, for the comparatively low-key nature of Tchambuli male initiations, where, 'Instead of the great collective initiations of the Iatmul, Tchambuli small boys are initiated and scarified one at a time in a family ceremonial, in which the emphasis is upon the ceremonial exchange of valuables, not upon them' (1962, p. 106).

But, of course, in most cultures which practise them, the male initiation rites served other purposes aside from the function of emphasising role differences between the sexes. They were (and as we will note, in many cases still are) associated with education in both practical and ritual activities, and in most cultures, after the ceremonies, the young initiates were expected to take part in food production activities.

Hertzog (1973) describes the initiation ceremonies that held among the Kikuyu in Kenya as including adoption by ritual parents, circumcision, anointment with white earth, much singing and dancing, eating of special foods and a symbolic race to a sacred fig tree. Each boy to be initiated chose one or several sponsors, who were slightly older than him, to support him, care for him and advise him during the initiation period.

After the circumcision ceremony and its ceremonials were over, the young Kikuyu boy was regarded as having changed in status. From this time on he would be treated by the members of the community with more respect, because he would be regarded as having left behind him his childish ways to enter into the community of adult men.

Among girls, initiation ceremonies often centre on the onset of menstruation. In most cases the ceremonies include special instruction from older women on matters pertaining to sex and marriage, social customs and childbirth. Where such ceremonies were or are held, there was or is the same emphasis on seclusion that we noted held for the New Guinean and Kenyan boys. But this seclusion is not always absolute. For instance, describing female initiation rites in Lesotho, Gay (1979) notes that during the daytime the young initiates, or *bale*, are allowed to go about the surrounding areas, collecting firewood, vegetables and seeds. As they do this they have the traditional right to stop any passerby and demand gifts. Indeed, the giving of gifts is often an important part of initiation ceremonies, emphasising the fact that after their emergence from the ceremony the girls (or boys) will require a new set of clothing and possessions in order to enter into their new adult status.

It is clear that in those societies where such ceremonies are held they serve very important functions both in the education of the young persons into the ways, values, behaviour and attitudes expected of them as adults, and, perhaps more important, psychologically, in confirming the self-worth of the young persons. As Hertzog notes about male initiation rites in Kenya in the early 1970s (1973, p. 481):

> These initiation procedures, however attenuated in modern form, are regarded as absolutely indispensable by the eligible boys and their families. I know of no young man in the village, over twenty years old, who has not been circumcised. The boys say that initiation gains them increased respect from others, both younger and older, as well as privileges such as staying out at night and sexual intercourse with initiated girls. They feel that their general behavior improves after initiation, and that they leave off cursing, fighting, and childish games. A smaller number claims to experience an increase in self-confidence. An older boy (nineteen or twenty) who remains uncircumcised runs the risk of being thought unnatural or cowardly, unless he and/or his father are known to be delaying the operation until the boy's completion of Standard 7.

This last sentence of Hertzog's brings us to a very important consideration which is the extent to which schooling, in the formal sense, interferes with these most important customs. In the paragraph just quoted it is noted that, even in 1973, for the group of Kenyans that Hertzog studied, who lived approximately eighteen miles north of Nairobi, 'initiation procedures are regarded as absolutely indispensable'. And in the article from which this quotation is taken he describes how initiation is usually timed so as to take place after primary school is completed, and to allow enough time for the circumcision wound to heal before those who will be attending secondary school are required to start this. After the obligatory period of withdrawal following the circumcision, the initiate will start to 'roam' with his age-mates but he will only do so for a short while if he is to return to school.

It can be seen, then, that this very important customary ceremony has been adapted to suit the demands of formal schooling for these Kenyan boys. Similarly in the case of the Liberian girls studied by Gay, the traditional time of withdrawal of about three or four years has been in many cases cut down to the two-month dry-season holiday period in order that initiation does not conflict with schooling.

Another effect noted by Gay is the shifting of initiation from puberty, or the period just shortly before puberty, to early childhood. Thus she writes that in 1974, in the area where she was working in Liberia, girls of 5 and 6 were initiated in a ceremony that had once been regarded as appropriate for teenagers only. At the other end of the age-scale, both in Lesotho and in Liberia, she noted cases of adults being initiated with adolescents because due to starting work at adolescence, or because of schooling, these adults had missed the opportunity to be initiated during the more usual age-period.

Among the North American Indian people the previous elaborate female puberty celebration has recently become more likely to take place as a group ceremony rather than, as had been the case, individually for each girl, at the commencement of her menstruation. Pelto and Pelto note that sometimes these group ceremonies take place on 5 July as part of the more general American celebration of 4 July.

It would seem, then, that in many areas the traditional ceremonies are observed, but in a form which has been modified to fit in with changing social conditions. It is possible that the shortening of the initiation period means in many cases that the amount of information that can be transmitted is reduced. And it is possible that where the initiation period is drastically shortened, or is amended to include initiates of widely different age-ranges, that the initiation becomes largely symbolic. If this is the case, then, as Durojaiye recommends, care must be taken to ensure that young people are able to obtain the guidance, information and advice, that was so much part of the original initiation ceremonies, somewhere else. In some cases this function can be served by the parents, in other cases by the school or youth group, or in yet other cases by the religious advisers.

In societies in which it has been the custom for young people to undergo initiation ceremonies, there does not seem to be a general feeling that the years between puberty and early adulthood are ones in which young people are very different in temperament from both younger children and adults. This period is not seen as one in which the individual is particularly at risk psychologically. In the second perspective on adolescence, which we will examine now, adolescents are seen as peculiarly vulnerable in their psychological make-up.

Perspective 2

As we noted in the introduction to the last chapter, this second perspective – that adolescents are markedly different in their psychological make-up – has been characteristic of many Western societies. Even in some Western cultures where there has been some symbolic *rite de passage*, like confirmation for some Christians and *bar-mitzvah* for male Jews, these ceremonies have been concerned largely with religious and spiritual values, and have not been regarded as conferring on those who take part in them a new adult status. Instead adult status is seen, in this perspective, as coming only after the young person has lived through the 'storms and stresses' of the adolescent period. Those who take this viewpoint see these 'storms and stresses' as deriving primarily from within the adolescent – both from his rapid fluctuations in mood and from his comparative inability to deal psychologically with the physical changes that are taking place. Thus Anna Freud writes:

    ‘ The atmosphere in which the adolescent lives, his anxieties, the height of elation, the depths of despair, the quickly-rising enthusiasms, the utter hopelessness, the burning – or at other times sterile – intellectual and philosophical preoccupations, the yearning for freedom, the sense of loneliness, the feeling of oppression by the parents, the impotent rages, or active hates directed against the adult world, the erotic crushes – whether homosexually or heterosexually directed – the suicidal fantasies etc. These are *,* the elusive mood swings. *'*

(Quoted by Cockram and Beloff, 1978)

Throughout this century popular ideas in the West have included ideas of this sort, and even as recently as 1975 we find Meyerson noting:

' Why adolescence becomes a time of crisis?
The problem for Jane and Peter (children from a 'usually co-operative family') is that adolescence becomes a crisis because of the clash between what is happening to them in their animal bodies, and the kind of behaviour demanded of them as social beings by their family and wider social environment. The explosive fantasies embodied in Peter's chemistry experiment, and the explosive sounds of Jane's pop-music, reflect not only their psychic state, but also the explosive body-state which underlies it. Adolescents are exploding with sexuality and sexual curiosity, and with animal aggression which is a necessary accompaniment to the animal's need to seek a *,*
mate, and for survival. *'*

(Quoted by Coleman *et al.*, 1977)

Despite the widespread and long-standing nature of this viewpoint of adolescent behaviour in the West, there is little empirical evidence to support it. In fact, on the contrary, numbers of studies of adolescents have indicated that adolescents do not regard their lives as filled with crises. Coleman and his associates (1977) summarise five large-scale surveys which concluded that there was little evidence to support the view that adolescents are more psychologically disturbed than other age-groups. In a similar vein, Conger quotes an investigation in this area which came to the conclusion that the typical teenager 'is a reasonably well-adjusted individual whose daily functioning is minimally marred by psychological incapacity' (1977, p. 28).

How is it, then, that such a stereotype has arisen? It seems to us that there are four possible causes of psychological disturbance in adolescence, and that some adolescents are so disrupted by one or more of these aspects of adolescent life that adults observing them allow the behaviour of these particular young people to colour their view of adolescents in general. The four possible origins of this stereotype about adolescence are:

(1) Some adolescents have to face a large number of *external* demands – financial, domestic, academic or related to work and unemployment. If, in addition to having to face these problems, they lack confidence and self-esteem, they may suffer from severe psychological disturbance.

(2) Sometimes adolescents are not clear about the *roles they will be expected to play* as adults. In more simple societies, as we noted in the introduction to the last chapter, children could look at the older generation and use them as a guide to the way their future life would take shape. But in a rapidly changing society, such continuity is not always so apparent. Further, the world the young person lives in may be radically different from the one his parents grew up in. As Margaret Mead notes: 'Even very recently, the elders could say "You know, I have been young but you have never been old". But to-day's young people can reply "You never have been young in the world that I am young in, and you never can be" ' (quoted in Cockram and Beloff, 1978).

Thus another cause for the stereotype may lie in the excessive confusion and bewilderment shown by some (but clearly not all) adolescents who have no coherent ideas about what is expected of them, what is likely to happen to them and no firm expectations of the way their own particular corner of the world will develop. Naturally such role confusion is more likely to occur in those societies undergoing rapid changes – perhaps a general movement from rural to urban life for the great majority of the adolescents' acquaintances, or a rapid movement from a culture of low technology to one of high technology.

(3) Some adolescents appear to be *alienated* from the world around them. As we mentioned in the last chapter, one of the cognitive developments in adolescence is the ability to view the environment objectively, and thus there is an increasing tendency to become interested in ideological, moral, religious and social issues. Sometimes, in looking around them, adolescents judge their society as unjust and consequently they become inclined to reject the values on which they consider it to

be based. In their desire for change, they become alienated from the point of view held by the great majority of people around them and they may turn to other viewpoints based on books they have read, or the opinions of others who share their rejection of their own society, or occasionally to ideological approaches that underlie social functioning in other countries. (But here it should be pointed out that research shows that adolescents who hold such radical perspectives on social and political issues, often have parents with very similar viewpoints.)

(4) Some adolescents *reject the life-style of the older generation*, including their parents'. Unlike the adolescents in (3) above, they are less concerned with underlying values and attitudes than they are with behaviour. They may replace the mode of behaviour of adults with a youth culture which has its own expectations of behaviour and which explicitly rejects their parents' way of life. Thus we get the phenomenon of adolescents dressing, not just unconventionally in their parents' terms, but in extremely odd and divergent ways, listening only to very special kinds of music and regarding everything their parents' generation does as boring and out-of-date. This way of behaving is sometimes referred to as evidence of 'a generation gap'.

But although each single young person may be affected by all four of the dispositions we have just described to a minor extent, few adolescents are affected by one or more of these to any substantial extent. This has been made clear by the surveys we described above, which show that only a few adolescents regard themselves as having serious emotional disturbances, and by other investigations that indicate that most adolescents do not reject parental values except perhaps in relatively unimportant areas like dress and hair-styling and general grooming. (We shall return to these investigations in the next section.)

In summary, then, in the West, despite the popular belief often fostered by the press that adolescents are emotionally disturbed creatures, continually in revolt and preoccupied with rejecting the values of the world they live in, research indicates a very different picture. True, a few adolescents are seriously emotionally disturbed, but in most cases this is because they have serious objective problems to deal with and/or have been the victims of childhoods where their needs were not satisfied. True, some adolescents are confused, but this is not because adolescence in itself produces confusion, but because they have no clear roles to follow and no assurance of continuity in the world in which they live. Finally, it is true that some adolescents do feel alienated from the world around them, but in most cases this is because their own parents themselves have serious doubts about the values of the world in which both generations live.

It would seem that adolescence is not in itself a period of storm and stress, but if it coincides with a number of external problems, and occurs in a period of rapid social change, then adolescents will reflect these difficulties. Thus the trauma of adolescence does not arise from within the individual alone but is largely determined by external forces.

Reconciling the two perspectives

We have outlined two different perspectives on adolescence. The first sees the child moving into adult life after undergoing an often lengthy period of initiation in which he is educated into the behaviour expected of him (or her) as an adult member of the community. This initiation traditionally took place at, or just before, puberty, but more recently such ceremonies have included initiates of widely differing ages. After initiation the young person is accepted into the adult life of the community and is not regarded as being particularly at risk psychologically. The second perspective has seen adolescence as a disturbed and traumatic period of storm and stress. We suggest that it is possible to reconcile these apparently opposing perspectives by arguing that where society places excessive demands on adolescents, where it supplies no clear expectations of the future, and where it is changing so rapidly that the adolescent has no one to model himself on, adolescence may on occasion be a period of storm and stress, not because adolescents are, by nature, emotionally unstable, but because too much is being demanded of them. On the other hand, if adolescence occurs in a stable environment, where expectations of adult behaviour are clear and explicit and where adolescents have been well prepared for their change in status, little disturbance will be shown during the years from puberty to physical maturity.

The Adolescent in Relation to his Family

In the section in the last chapter on the emotional needs of adolescents we suggested that the need each adolescent feels for autonomy is affected to a great extent by cultural attitudes about the degree to which it is desirable that adolescents should be independent of their families.

Similarly, in general terms we would expect that attitudes towards parent–adolescent relationships would also vary with culture. Speaking very broadly, we might expect to find a set of values about such relationships in a nuclear family setting rather different from the values that are more characteristic of the extended family situation. Consequently we shall discuss adolescents' relationships with their parents separately for the two family structures; we are, of course, aware that in doing so we blur the subtleties of relationships in families which do not fall in a simple way into either of these broad categories. Before doing so we will look at some aspects of adolescent–adult interactions that seem to us to hold whenever young people on the threshold of adulthood live with members of an older generation, whether or not they are the natural parents.

(1) *General aspects of adult–adolescent relationships within the family*

Perhaps the most important influence on such relationships emerges from the growing cognitive maturity that characterises the individual as he moves through the years of adolescence. As we noted in the last chapter, this cognitive maturity leads to an increasing ability to think objectively about other people. Thus the adolescent starts to become aware that parents and other adults in his home are individuals too. Coupled with this realisation may be a tendency to find certain habits of these adults annoying. If the adolescent reacts against such habits with irritation and resentment, his simultaneous acceptance of the adults' rights as individuals may make him feel guilty for his antagonistic behaviour. This guilt may lead to even more conflict as the adolescent tries to drown it by acting in an even more negative fashion. Thus, this period of growing up is typically a period of a kind of push and pull: a push towards the security provided by the adults, and the love and respect felt by the younger person for the older; and a pull away from the adults engendered by an impatience with certain of the adults' habits, values and attitudes, and the adolescent's desire to be responsible for himself.

But, as we noted in the last chapter, while the adolescent moves towards physical and social maturity, so do the adults in his life move away from their own youth. This can lead to conflicts arising from both open and hidden resentments that the adult may feel about growing old. Some of the adults' restrictions on adolescent activities may then be due to the operation of this resentment. Thus, using the term we introduced in our discussion on defence mechanisms, the adult may behave repressively towards the younger person because he is envious of the pleasures of youth, but may *rationalise* his restrictive behaviour by telling both himself and the adolescent that such restrictions 'are good for young people and keep them out of trouble'.

Of course, such deep-seated conflicts are not typical of the everyday behaviour that occurs in most families. As we shall show, such evidence as exists points to the fact that most adolescents love and value the adults in their homes, but the potential does exist in every home for 'wires to get crossed' in this way.

In general, in most homes, even those that are relatively free from conflict, the feelings that adults and young people may have about each other are often mixed and unclear. But if both parties have a fairly reasonable level of self-esteem, the complicated feelings that occur in all homes will not result in too much friction. This is because people who have an adequate degree of self-esteem seem to be able to accept themselves, with both their strengths and weaknesses, and in accepting themselves, they appear to be tolerant in their treatment of others. As Hamachek says: 'Self-acceptance and acceptance of others seem to go hand-in-hand' (1978, p. 253). This is particularly applicable to the relationships between adolescents and the important adults in their lives.

In summary, then, it seems that there is the potential for poor interpersonal relationships between adolescents and those adults who are closest to them. This potential exists because contradictory and mixed feelings may arise on both sides as children mature into young adults and adults move towards middle age. But the potential is unlikely to develop into serious emotional conflicts if both parties are able to view themselves and each other with tolerance and sensitivity.

(2) *Adolescent–adult relationships in the extended family situation*

Throughout this book we have stressed the

advantages of the extended family system in child development. Such a system enables the growing child to have a number of loving caretakers who are acutely interested in him and his welfare. Further, it affords the child many opportunities to develop his interpersonal skills as he relates to the family members who surround him.

The presence of grandparents aids young parents in the problems that always accompany the rearing of small children. They are able to reassure the parents that their children's behaviour is not exceptional and so the new generation of parents profits from the experience of the older generation. Young children in extended families always have playmates, and particularly in cultures where initiation occurs in groups, as they grow older, young people have a stable collection of their peers to whom they can relate in the members of their 'age sets'.

Psychological needs are well catered for in the extended family. *Love and security* are always present in the form of a large family circle. *Responsibility* comes as the child helps in the care of younger members of the family or in the collection and cultivation of food for the family. *Praise and recognition* are provided by the numbers of adults and older children around. Finally, the need for *new experiences* is met as the child moves slowly into new task situations and as he is encouraged to learn about different aspects of daily life.

However, no interpersonal system is wholly without weakness. Within the extended family system the multiplicity of relationships sometimes leads to jealousies and rivalries and it is often the young adolescent who is affected by these as his sensitivity towards the feelings of others increases.

Durojaiye carried out an investigation among 4,000 Nigerian children from both primary and secondary schools. Amongst children from extended families 80 per cent reported interference from grandparents, aunts and uncles in discipline at home; 92 per cent complained of lack of clear standards to follow; 91 per cent complained that running errands for relatives interfered with their school work; and 78 per cent justified the need to lie as a means of escaping blame from others. Of his sample coming from nuclear families, he writes: 'Not more than 47 per cent of children from nuclear families reported any of these' (1976, p. 24).

This survey points to some of the difficulties young adolescents may face in the extended family situation – a feeling that too many people are concerned with their discipline, which tends to lead to a confusion in standards.

For young girls, in particular, the polygamous family situation may give rise to very conflicting feelings. If she continues with her education and ultimately expects to gain a degree or a professional qualification, she may see herself on the same academic and intellectual level as her male peers. Yet she may at the same time have to face the realisation that a future marriage within a culture where polygamy is prevalent will probably place her in a less than equal position in comparison to her husband, because she may have to face the prospect of a co-wife or wives.

A similar finding that adolescent girls may be more stressed in the extended family system than adolescent boys are comes from India. A study of the extended family system within a Hindu culture done by Khatri (quoted by Prabhu, 1976) suggested that such a system provides a less congenial climate for girls than it does for boys. This finding is probably related to the clash between traditional Hindu views on male–female relationships within the family and the increasing tendency for young Indian girls to want the same educational opportunities as their male peers.

Thus it can be seen that the extended family system, despite its strengths, may place some specific strains on adolescents. These strains relate mostly to forging an independent identity when there is a multiplicity of adult figures within the family. And for girls, in particular, there may be difficulty in reconciling expectations and values arising from being educated within the formal school setting and traditional views of the role of females in the family.

One area where adolescents in the extended family situation probably suffer from less stress than adolescents in the nuclear family situation is that of boy–girl relationships. The reason for this lies in the differing assumptions that are held about marriage within the two systems.

In the nuclear family situation, marriage tends to be seen, primarily, in terms of the relationship between man and wife. This emphasis on the one-to-one love bond leads to a preoccupation amongst adolescents with romance and male–female social contacts like 'dating' or 'going steady' or having a particularly intense relationship with a boy/girlfriend. In a society where the extended family system is the norm, marriage is seen primarily as providing a basis for the continued extension of the family by the procreation of children. Thus adolescents within an extended family system, though they may be interested in members of the opposite sex and fully expect to marry in due course, are less likely to romanticise relationships with the opposite sex and are less likely to be preoccupied with 'falling in love'.

(3)   Adolescent–parent relationships in the nuclear family

As we mentioned in the last section, there has been a tendency in the West to view adolescence as a time of storm and stress. Not surprisingly, then, much research has been generated around the idea that parent–adolescent relationships are bound to be full of conflict. While there is some built-in potential for conflict in terms of the fact that adolescents are moving towards the physical peak of their lives, while their parents are moving away from it (see page 158), as we have already noted, surveys show far less intergenerational conflict in the family than is suggested by popular stereotypes. Thus in their review of the area Cockram and Beloff note that seven studies in this field have 'all found that adolescents do not, on the whole, go through a period of rebellion and hostility to parents and the values they represent' (1978, p. 42).

In 1958 a study was mounted in Great Britain of all the children born in one particular week. When these children were 16, 14,761 of the original 17,000 were contacted for a further survey of their development. In this follow-up survey an attempt was made to investigate relationships within the family. This is a very important survey because it represents a relatively unbiased sampling of the British teenage population in the 1970s. Eighty-six per cent of the 11,045 children who answered the questionnaire used in the study reported that they 'got on well with their mother' and 80 per cent that they 'got on well with their father'. Areas of disagreement within the family were investigated and it was found that major areas of disagreement were about relatively unimportant issues like dress or hair-style (Fogelman, 1976).

This finding that, where tension exists, it centres on comparatively unimportant areas like hair-styles and clothes, reflects the general failure of most surveys to support the contention that adults and adolescents in the West hold fundamentally opposing viewpoints on life in general. As Coleman and his colleagues note, conflict centres on areas that are related to the details of day-to-day living, rather than on more general moral issues. 'The areas of conflict are not, as is sometimes supposed,

the large issues of morality or ideology, but are infinitely more mundane' (related to everyday life). They are the real issues which are involved when groups of people share living accommodation (Coleman et al., 1977, pp. 244–5).

A second major research area in the West concerning adolescent–parent relationships centres on the child-rearing techniques that parents use with this age-group. As we noted in the section in the last chapter on the adolescent's need for independence, the general conclusion reached by most investigations is that adolescents are best prepared for becoming independent and well-adjusted young adults when parents use 'democratic practices with frequent explanations by parents of their rules of conduct and expectations' (Conger, 1977, p. 240).

Interestingly, one study in this area reported that adolescents who perceive their parents as 'democratic' in their attitude to them are likely to regard their parents as happy, whereas adolescents who perceive their parents as authoritarian (that is, who impose rules and regulations regardless of the opinions of others) tend to regard their parents as unhappy.

Many of the studies on parent–child interaction reported in the psychological journals are based on data drawn from the USA. But studies from other Western cultures like Denmark, Sweden, Israel and Britain show much the same general trend, with 'democratic' child-rearing practices appearing to produce the most autonomous and well-adjusted adolescents. Nevertheless, both between and within different societies, patterns of child-rearing vary. For example, in a very large cross-cultural survey of adolescents done by Kandel and Lesser in Denmark and in the USA, it was found that within the American families mothers take much of the responsibility for both directing and disciplining adolescents, particularly in the case of girls. Where parental disagreements over this occur, mothers tend to win. In Denmark responsibility in these areas tends to be equally shared by both parents (Kandel and Lesser, 1975). In interpreting this finding, the authors attribute it to the following causes (p. 480):

> ❛ The relative dominance of the American mother may be explained to some extent by a withdrawal of the American father from social interaction. Perhaps the same need for achievement, which is expressed in other ways in the American family, keeps

American men committed to the world of work to the point where they are relatively unavailable at home. **,**

Kandel and Lesser's interpretation of this finding reflects an approach that we consider should always prevail when analysing cross-cultural data. That is, specific conclusions should not be drawn without considering the more general social context. For example, in this case, Kandel and Lesser, having discovered the relative dominance of American women compared to Danish women in this area, did not go on to generalise that American women are overall more dominant than their Danish counterparts. Instead, they looked at the finding, correctly in our opinion, within a broader social perspective.

Another set of data relating to adolescent–parent relationships across two cultural groups is concerned with the general finding in Britain that children of West Indian immigrants tend to perform less well at school than children of indigenous parents. Some investigators relate this to the matrifocal nature of many West Indian homes in Britain. (Matrifocal families are families that are run by women in the absence of fathers or other males such as uncles.) They argue that the absence of fathers contributes directly to the poorer academic performance of children. This seems to us a mistaken approach, as a great deal of evidence suggests that children in one-parent families in Britain are disadvantaged primarily because such families are usually financially badly off. In the case of immigrant one-parent families in Britain, there are added disadvantages due to the social prejudice suffered by such immigrants. It would seem that such social and financial pressures are a far more powerful influence on school performance than the family structure of such homes, particularly since throughout the world there are numbers of societies which function very adequately indeed with a matrifocal family structure.

(4) *Principles concerning adolescent–adult relationships*
In looking at adolescent relationships with the adults in their homes, it is most important to view them within the general social context. Nevertheless, it seems to us that, irrespective of the social context, there are some general principles that apply equally well across all cultures. We would argue that responsible and socially constructive behaviour is most likely to be shown by adolescents when the adults in their homes:

(a) Slowly allow the young people to take more and more responsibility while at the same time continuing to assure them of their underlying support.
(b) Indicate their approval or disapproval of adolescents' behaviour within an atmosphere of love and respect rather than rejection or indifference.
(c) Provide, by their own example, models of the kinds of social attitudes, values and behaviour that they consider correct.
(d) Acknowledge the growing cognitive maturity of adolescents by being prepared to discuss and explain their actions and moral stands, both with respect to the way they treat young people, and at the more general social level.
(e) Look realistically at their own behaviour with respect to their treatment of adolescents so that they are sensitive to the reasons for such behaviour and do not shelter behind too many psychological defence mechanisms of the type we described in the last chapter.

The Adolescent in Relation to his Peers

When we discussed peer relationships in the primary school age-group at the end of Chapter 5 we made three points.
(1) The older the child grows, the more important peer relationships become, in comparison with other relationships.
(2) The liking and the respect of peers contributes in a large measure to self-esteem and, therefore, to the child's psychological adjustment.
(3) The social behaviour of children relates closely to the way adult life in the society is conducted.
In this discussion of peer relationships in adolescence we will use the three points derived from the earlier section on peer relations as a framework.

(1) *The importance of peer relationships*
During adolescence the need to belong to and identify with a group of individuals of the same age is stronger than it is at any other period. This tendency seems to hold in most contemporary societies. Adolescents spend a great deal of time

with their own age-group, and the values and attitudes of their own particular set of friends within the peer-group become an important influence on their behaviour.

The increasing reliance on peers for social interaction and emotional support has been documented by numbers of in-depth studies: for example, by Dunphy (1963) in Australia, Willmott (1966) in London, Kandel and Lesser (1975) in the USA and Denmark and by Durojaiye (1976) in both Uganda and Nigeria. The reasons for the growing importance of peer relationships are varied but three major areas can be distinguished.

(a) To begin with, relations with both same- and opposite-sex peers serve as *prototypes* (first examples) of adult social relationships. Adolescence is a period in which learning about interpersonal behaviour in a variety of situations – social, intimate, and work-oriented – speeds up and, as you will know from your own experience, even a short period of a year or eighteen months can produce a striking change in the social maturity of the adolescent. Much of this social maturity is acquired in interactions with peers.

(b) Another reason for the increasing dependence on peers lies in the fact that *ties with adults loosen as children grow older*. For a number of reasons many parents are not able to revive their own memories of the emotions and changes of adolescence and so adolescents seek others of the same age-group to share their doubts and uncertainties about the future and their defeats and victories of the present. This is not to say that, as we discussed before and shall return to later, there are necessarily conflicts of values between adults and peers, but merely that other peers have more time, inclination and patience to share the often introspective thoughts that are characteristic of adolescence.

(c) Peers also help the adolescent in *defining his sense of himself*. No longer a child, not yet an adult, the adolescent must prepare to meet the demands his society makes of adult functioning in many spheres – social, sexual and vocational. As we have pointed out, the escalation of such demands can make adolescence a very trying period, particularly if the young person is faced with a great many possible choices. The peer-group, members of which are facing similar choices, can help the adolescent in defining his sense of self and his expectations of the future. This function of peer-groups is not only to be found within Western society. Abiola, writing about the general experience of transition 'from a traditional society to an assumed westernized mode of living', talks about the conflict of cultural values that children may face in growing up (1971, p. 65):

> ❛ a clash between a village economy and a monetary one; between an extended family consciousness and a nuclear family one; between a polygamous attitude and a monogamous substitute; between comprehensive inclusive living and occupationally oriented existence; between imported secular religion and traditional belief system; between group living with its authority and constraints and a self-oriented existence. ❜

The peer group helps in dealing with such conflicting patterns of behaviour and expectations. As Abiola continues: 'One form of adaptation to the transitional situation is the formation of "clubs", picnic groups etc., by the adolescent. The phenomenon is not specific to Africa, and it serves the purpose of providing a stepping stone from childhood to fulfilling adult functions in society' (1971, p. 66).

Thus adolescents often form their own 'cultures' that 'consist of unique values that young people subscribe to and that give them a sense of belonging to an identifiable group. For the most part, these values involve tastes in clothing, language, music and leisure-time activities that are seldom shared or appreciated by adults' (Elkind and Weiner, 1978, p. 572).

However, as we noted in the last section, because adolescents share interests and activities in common with other adolescents, this does not mean that they reject parental values, or that their values clash with parental values. Both British and American data suggest that, in societies where economic and social class differences exist, there is a greater similarity between the values of parents and adolescents of one class than there is a similarity between adolescents of very different class backgrounds. Thus, as Conger notes, an adolescent from a Catholic, working-class background, is more likely to share values and attitudes with his parents than with a young person of the same age, but from a Protestant upper-class background.

When we discussed adolescent–adult relationships we noted that disagreements between them seem to be mostly concerned with relatively minor matters. So it is not surprising to find that parents do not, on the whole, disapprove of their children's choice of friends. For example, in the large British survey we reported on, only 28 per cent of adolescents ever reported clashes with their parents over their choice of friends. Similarly, in the Danish-American survey conducted by Kandel and Lesser, it was found that there was a similarity in educational values between adolescents' parents and their friends. However, particularly in the long term, where differences existed, parental influence in this area outstripped the influence of friends.

In Nigeria, too, a recent survey shows that both parents and peers are important in shaping attitudes among adolescents and, like the other data cited, it seems that in this culture as well peers are referred to in matters concerning personal appearance and adults on more central matters. Uka (1974) administered a questionnaire to 800 adolescent boys and girls between the ages of 18 and 20 in eleven secondary schools in the east-central and mid-western states. He found that 77·5 per cent of boys and 67·5 per cent of girls referred to peers for advice on what to wear to a party and 81·5 per cent of boys and 75·75 per cent of girls referred to peers for advice on personal grooming. On more central matters adolescents tended to prefer the advice of adults, with 70·75 per cent of boys and 65·75 per cent of girls responding that they would go to adults for advice on 'personal problems' and 61 per cent of boys and 68·5 per cent of girls responding that they would go to adults for advice on how to spend money.

Where adolescents' relationships with adults are poor, not surprisingly, they tend to place far more emphasis on friendship with peers. In writing about adolescents who identify almost completely with a gang, Durojaiye notes that in his survey of adolescent children in Ibadan and Kampala young people who 'came from homes where there was social recognition and mutual understanding between parents and children and where there was free interchange of opinions' did not seek social recognition so much from their peer-group as did young people whose relationship with their parents 'could not be described in these terms' (1976, p. 66). He concludes that persistent failure on behalf of parents and adults to give approval and social recognition to children may lead to them identifying with a delinquent sub-group. Bronfenbrenner (1975) notes the same phenomenon in the USA where children who are the most peer-oriented tend to come from homes that are 'less

affectionate and less firm in discipline' (p. 489).

It seems, then, that there are valid reasons for peer relationships to grow in importance in adolescence, but that such relationships conflict with relationships with adults only, in the case of most adolescents, in relatively insignificant areas. Where adolescents tend to rely disproportionately on their peers, it seems that this springs from poor relationships with parents or other significant adults.

(2) *Peer relationships and personal adjustment*

Most of us need to feel wanted and because of this need we like to belong to groups of other people where we feel valued and where we feel our absence would be regretted. In early childhood such needs are met almost entirely within the family and in adult life many people find satisfaction for these needs within close familial and work relationships. In adolescence, however, most individuals seek the satisfaction of this need in their peers as well as in the family or work situation.

If adolescents are not accepted and liked by their peers, this tends to have extremely severe effects on their level of self-esteem. However, as we have mentioned before, this tends to be a circular process as individuals who are high in self-esteem find it easier to make friends than those who are low in self-esteem.

But aside from the confidence engendered by reasonable levels of self-esteem, what other factors make for popularity within adolescent peer-groups? We can look at this question in two ways. We can first of all consider peer relationships within the group situation and look at popularity within the group, acknowledging that for most sets of adolescents (within a school or work situation) there are usually a number of 'crowds' which differ in social status. Secondly, we can look at the friendships that are formed between one individual and another.

(*a*) Considering the question of popularity in the *group situation* first, we can turn again to the Kandel and Lesser study of adolescents in Denmark and the USA. They found that in both cultures there were different 'crowds' in the groups of adolescents they studied. Crowds differed in that membership of some crowds was regarded as more socially desirable than membership of others. They called the crowds highest in social status 'leading crowds'. In America, the leading crowds were more prominant and visible than they were in

Denmark, but in both societies young people identified certain crowds as being more socially desirable than others (leading crowds) and in both societies young people could identify which individuals belonged to leading crowds.

Members of leading crowds shared similar characteristics in both cultures. They were popular with more people, they tended to be good students, good athletes and well dressed. In addition they tended to come from homes of comparatively higher social status, and they tended to have more ambitious life-goals. Interestingly, in both cultures, although members of leading groups tended to be good students, they did not show much interest in the academic field, but instead were more interested in 'fun', companionship and sports.

Durojaiye (1972) calls this accumulation of recognition where certain individuals excel in a number of spheres – sport, academic, socio-economic, being fun to be with – 'status aggregation'. He argues that it is status aggregation that makes certain individuals more popular than others. In a study of white and coloured children (his term) in a Nigerian school, he found that coloured children, whether or not they were Nigerian, were more popular, and he attributed this to the fact that because the coloured children were the same colour as the majority of people in the country, this contributed to status aggregation for them and resulted in their being more popular.

In summarising American research on what makes for popularity in adolescence, Conger too notes that popularity and social acceptance are related to being a member of the culturally dominant majority, thus supporting Durojaiye's finding (above). Like Kandel and Lesser, as well as Durojaiye, he notes that popular adolescents tend to be popular because they possess a number of different personal characteristics. Once again the same characteristics noted by Kandel and Lesser are cited – intelligence and ability, physical attractiveness and social class status. But, in addition to these characteristics, he notes that 'adolescents who are viewed favourably tend to be those who contribute to others by making *them* feel accepted and involved, by promoting constructive interaction between peers, or by planning and initiating interesting or enjoyable group activities' (1977, p. 343).

Characteristics that are related to unpopularity seem to be derived from low self-esteem. Thus we find that there are two types of social isolates (Conger). First, those who are ill at ease, nervous, timid and lacking in self-confidence. All these characteristics stem, as we discussed in Chapter 5, from low self-esteem. Secondly, adolescents who are over-aggressive, appear conceited and are attention-seeking also tend to be unpopular. As we noted in the last chapter, these are defences that are often adopted by individuals who lack adequate self-esteem.

It seems, then, that in attempting to help adolescents who are social isolates, adults must intervene directly in the young person's perception of himself. No matter how lacking in self-confidence, all adolescents possess at least one characteristic – a particular bent for music, an ability to cook, a compassionate nature, a gift for mimicry, and so on, on which the concerned adult can start to build up a more positive self-view on the part of the adolescent. Sometimes training in social skills can help as well; that is, the adult can help the young person, whether in a group therapy situation or on his own, to develop techniques to deal with social situations by getting the adolescent concerned to role-play, or act out, common social situations. If you are interested in this area, there is a specific reference at the end of this chapter.

However, as we mentioned above, peer relationships fall into two classes. We have dealt with the first, which is peer interaction in the group situation, and we now turn to the other, which is concerned with friendships between two individuals, or a small group of individuals.

(b) Although most adolescents dream of being popular, and nearly all adolescents would like to belong to the leading social crowd, not all can achieve this aim. The majority of adolescents, then, get most of their social pleasure by one or two important and meaningful *friendships*. A few adolescents, of course, never yearn for general popularity and prefer to have one or two deep and meaningful relationships instead.

What draws people together in friendship? A great deal of research indicates that friendship is most likely to develop between adolescents who share a number of the more obvious social characteristics: age, intelligence, interests and life-goals. Though friendships are sometimes based on the attraction of opposites, similarities are usually more evident than differences (Douvan and Gold, 1966).

Adolescent friendships often have their roots in earlier years. Thus, in the Willmott study referred to earlier, two-thirds of the boys who had a particular friend said it was someone they had grown up with. This finding seems to apply to girls as well as to boys but in some other respects, in the West anyway, friendship patterns are rather different for the two sexes. For example, in early adolescence boys often go about in groups whereas girls usually prefer to have only one or two close friends (Cockram and Beloff, 1978).

Compared to the relationships in groups, friendships between adolescents are typically more intimate, more honest and more open. They afford the young person, particularly in early adolescence, an opportunity to deal with his complex feelings about the changes facing him. Furthermore, particularly in the case of the adolescent who is not very outgoing, they reassure him that, as Conger puts it, 'since [my friend] is fond of me, since he likes me, it means that I am really worth something' (Conger, 1977, p. 339).

Not unexpectedly, whether a particular adolescent is likely to rely more on group interactions or close personal friendships varies from person to person. But cultural variables also alter the balance. In their cross-cultural survey, Kandel and Lesser found that friendship patterns differed in the two cultures they studied in a way that related to overall cultural differences. Thus they report (1975, p. 475):

> Our data suggest a difference between American and Danish friendship patterns in the extent of close, mutually recognized bonds. In a number of ways – including relative frequency of visiting of friends ranked as 'best', 'second best', and 'third best'; the smaller number of reciprocated friendship choices; and the greater similarity of attitudes among reciprocated and non-reciprocated friendship choices – American adolescents form several friendships of about the same intensity, while Danish adolescents form one very close tie and then maintain several other more distant relationships. These characteristics of friendships among American and Danish adolescents support Lewin's interpretations of American and European adult social life. Lewin suggested that Americans participate in many friendships, each of which engages a rather superficial level of personality, while Europeans engage in fewer friendships, each of which penetrates more deeply into their personal sphere.

This interaction between cultural values and adolescent behaviour brings us on to our last section on adolescent–peer relationships.

(3)   *Peer relationships in adolescence within a cultural context*

In Chapter 5 we described the large-scale survey of child-rearing practices that was conducted by the Whitings in which six different teams of social scientists studied peer relationships in the six different cultures concerned. The overall conclusion was that the way children behave with their peers differs from society to society in a manner that is dependent on the organisation and values of the society's socio-economic system.

We do not know of any comparable survey of peer relationships at a later developmental stage, but clearly the same principle, that interpersonal relationships are shaped by societal values, will apply to older, as well as younger, age-groups. In this short section we shall discuss some relevant material in two interpersonal areas – first relating to co-operative as opposed to competitive behaviour, and secondly related to heterosexual relationships (or relationships with the opposite sex).

(a)   *Factors affecting co-operative/competitive behaviour*. A fair amount of research has been done in a wide range of countries, looking at the extent to which individuals co-operate or compete in specially set up game situations. We must make two initial reservations about this data. In the first instance, such research conducted in the cross-cultural context usually involves asking the subjects to behave in a manner that is far removed from any behaviour they will have engaged in in the past and as a result it is possible that the subjects do not necessarily display any behaviour other than the kind of behaviour they think the experiment wants to see. Secondly, we are going to group together studies that include subjects over a wide age-range, even though we are discussing this under the heading of adolescent peer relationships. We do this because the conclusions, which commonly show an interaction between game behaviour and the social context, are seldom confined by the authors of the studies to the age-range used in the specific study.

A number of studies in this area have looked at sub-cultural differences or differences between two social classes or ethnic groups within a particular culture. Thus Madsen found that in Mexico both rural and urban poor children were 'dramatically' more competitive than urban middle-class children, and Shapira and Madsen found that Israeli children who grew up in a kibbutz (where child-rearing is communally based) were far more co-operative than Israeli city children. It was particularly interesting that the kibbutz children, who had grown up as a closely knit group in an atmosphere where competition is frowned upon, organised their play techniques as a group and tried to work as a team rather than as individuals (Shapira and Madsen, 1975). Shapira and Madsen conclude from both the Mexican and the Israeli findings that peer relationships in this game situation were related to the atmosphere in which the children grew up. In the home backgrounds of both the Mexican urban middle-class children and the Israeli urban children, children are encouraged by teachers and parents to achieve and competition is an acceptable way of arriving at high levels of achievement.

Madsen, in another study, looked at competitive and co-operative behaviour amongst children in South Korea coming respectively from rural and urban backgrounds. In reporting the results, Madsen and his co-worker, Yi, (1975, p. 273) write that the results of the experiment,

> taken together with the results of previous studies in which the same techniques were used, lend support to the hypothesis of greater cooperative and less competitive behaviour in rural primary group societies. That these results appear in an oriental society as well as those occidental societies previously studied would seem to justify the speculation that an increase in competitive behavior, at least as measured by these tasks, is an inevitable concomitant of the world-wide trend towards urbanization.

Bethlehem (1975), working in Zambia, supports this general statement with a study in which his subjects were 'traditional' Tonga men and women and Westernised Tonga men and women and Asian students. The traditional group played the game he used more co-operatively than the other two groups, and even when their partners had made a competitive response the traditional subjects responded with a co-operative response, whereas in the other two groups competition was met with competition.

In general, it does seem that the majority of studies in this area show that co-operative or competitive behaviour in a game situation is related to the degree to which social background encourages such behaviour, but as Meeker (1970) points out from her work in Liberia, the differences in behaviour in these studies are complex and there are probably more dimensions than can be measured by the techniques used.

We have cited these studies on co-operation and competition in the game situation in this section on peer behaviour in adolescence in order to indicate that interpersonal behaviour varies from sub-culture to sub-culture and society to society in ways that reflect the underlying values and attitudes of the community. Because of this, readers should be careful, when they look at the behaviour of specific adolescents, to relate such behaviour not only to general texts of psychology but also to the normative values of the adolescents' background. What may be regarded as intensely unco-operative behaviour in a rural situation may be quite appropriate in an urban one. Thus teachers and educationalists faced with children and adolescents who have made sudden transitions from rural to urban situations or from urban to rural situations must always consider whether the adolescents concerned may be facing a cultural conflict.

(b) *Heterosexual behaviour in adolescence.* As we mentioned earlier in this chapter, assumptions about marriage differ greatly from culture to culture and, speaking very broadly, it is possible to distinguish two basic ways of looking at this institution. These underlying assumptions about marriage obviously affect social relationships between adolescents of different sexes.

The first approach is perhaps more characteristic of societies where the extended family is the norm. Here *marriage is regarded as part of an elaborate kinship system*, and the marriage between any individual couple is seen as fitting into the already existing framework of the family group that the young couple join. Within such a framework, arranged marriages are common.

Indeed, in some societies where arranged marriages took place at an early age, there was no period that could be regarded as adolescence. Thus Kuppuswamy notes (1974, p. 196) that where early marriage was prevalent in India,

> adolescence as a stage in the growth of the individual is hardly recognised. For example, with early marriage, the girl starts her life as a wife even when she is only thirteen or fourteen years old. Probably she becomes a mother by the time she is fifteen years old. Even the boy has hardly any period of adolescence ... Early marriage makes him

a husband before he is
fifteen or sixteen years of age. '

Even though early marriages in India are now outlawed, the traditional approach to sex role in Indian society must colour the thoughts of young people, in that they will be aware that even where parents allow them considerable freedom in their social life, they will be expected, eventually, to marry in accordance with the wishes of their family. Thus, even as recently as 1974, Kuppuswamy writes (p. 204):

' In general, wifehood and motherhood is the universal norm for women in India among all the cultural and religious groups and arranging the marriage is the responsibility of the parents of the girl ... Spinsterhood as well as bachelorhood is looked upon as a misfortune. '

Early marriages, however, are not a necessary part of an extended family system. Nor, indeed, are arranged marriages. But the existence of an extended family system has usually meant that marriages are regarded as part of the overall family structure, and therefore marriages have not been regarded as being the exclusive affair of the two partners. Because of this acceptance of the interests of people other than the couple directly involved, adolescents growing up within an extended family system are unlikely to have very romantic views of marriage and are unlikely to expect marriage to provide all their personal happiness and emotional satisfaction.

However, within the second approach to marriage, which is more characteristic of a nuclear family system, *marriage is regarded primarily as a bond between a particular man and woman* who have made an emotional commitment to one another. Not surprisingly, then, adolescents who grow up within this second tradition tend to take heterosexual relationships in adolescence extremely seriously and any book published in the West on adolescence will have a great deal of space devoted to personal relationships between the sexes. This is because in the West boys and girls view each other, not just as peers, but as potential 'boyfriends' or 'girlfriends', and, particularly in late adolescence, it is comparatively rare to find opposite-sex friendships that are not affected, to some extent at least, by the knowledge that love or romance is possible between the two young people concerned.

Patterns of heterosexual relationships in societies which allow boys and girls to mix freely with each other have been studied in both Britain and the USA in some detail. The general finding has been that in early adolescence there may be indifference to, or even avoidance of, members of the opposite sex, but that a year or two after puberty there is a marked upsurge in interest in the opposite sex, and that this interest is likely to be shown at an earlier age by girls than by boys. Schofield's large study of British adolescents in 1965 showed that there were wide individual variations but most adolescents started dating and kissing between 13 and 16 years of age.

During these mid-adolescent years, boys and girls tend to rely on the support of their same-sex friends to help them through the conflicts and anxieties of their early heterosexual relationships. But by their late teens, Western adolescents start to develop mature and often long-lasting emotional commitments in their heterosexual relationships and, indeed, some older adolescents make stable and successful marriages.

In discussing the first approach to marriage, we indicated that adolescents within an extended family system are less likely to romanticise marriage than adolescents within a nuclear family system. But this does not mean that adolescents in societies where the extended family system is common show no interest in the other sex. On the contrary, recent work reported by Durojaiye in Uganda and Nigeria shows adolescents in these countries following very similar social patterns to the one we have just described for British and American adolescents. He writes (1976, p. 213):

' In early adolescence boys and girls remain in separate groups, but the group of girls will talk and walk with the boys if opportunities permit. Later, at the age of 15 onwards, pairing of boys and girls is common; 81% of the mixed-sex day secondary schools' pupils in Ibadan and Kampala, who were aged between 15 and 19, had regular friends of the opposite sex. Only 27% of the 13–14-year-olds had regular friends of the opposite sex. '

It would seem that two conclusions can be drawn from material on opposite-sex friendships in adolescence:

(*a*) In any society where informal opposite-sex relationships are permitted in adolescence, these are bound to generate some worries, conflict and anxieties. Girls may worry because they do not have any boyfriends; or they may worry that they have too many and may, thus, be thought morally loose; or they may worry because their romances do not last a long time and that therefore they are not capable of sustaining a boy's interest for long; or they may worry that the wrong sort of boys are attracted to them. Boys may feel too shy to approach girls or, having approached them, may worry that they have nothing to say to girls, or they may worry that they are less attractive to girls than their friends are. Both sexes may have conflicts if their parents do not approve of their current boy/girlfriend and both sexes may feel guilty that their friendships with the opposite sex are distracting them from school work. These worries and anxieties are likely to occur irrespective of the types of marriage prevalent in their society.

(b) If, in addition to permitting informal sex relationships between the sexes, a culture regards marriage as primarily the culmination of a very special relationship between two particular people, adolescents from that culture, as well as having to deal with the worries and anxieties outlined in (a) above, will be inclined to place a great deal of stress on emotional commitments. This is because each boyfriend or girlfriend is potentially the ideal partner whom ultimately they might marry. But, if a culture views marriage in a rather broader context than the romantic union of two particular individuals, young people from that society will be rather more relaxed about heterosexual relationships, because they are aware that their marriage, when it takes place, will not stand or fall entirely on the emotional bond generated, but will depend as well on other factors not so central to their inner selves, such as the social and financial status of the two individuals concerned as well as parental wishes.

The Adolescent in Relation to School

(1) *The importance of focusing on the adolescent's perceptions of school*

From the beginning of this book, we have stressed that each individual has his own particular perceptions of any situation or environment in which he is involved. No two children will evaluate, or react to, any situation in an identical fashion, and even where behaviour may look comparable the underlying reasons for behaviour may be very dissimilar.

Take, for example, the subject of non-attendance at school. We might find that two young adolescents in their first year at secondary school both consistently fail to attend school, even though they are in good physical health. The first may do so because he has something he prefers to do, say, collecting old bottles and returning them to a bottle depot for their deposits. He may have decided that school offers him little he wants to know or do. Consequently, because his parents wish him to attend school, he may consciously set out to deceive them by pretending to go off to school every morning while he is, in reality, starting off on his bottle collection. We would label such behaviour as truancy.

The second boy may not attend school for very different reasons. He may be very interested in the work he is doing at school and he may really wish to do well at school; he may in fact feel school offers him a great deal. His non-attendance may spring from the fact that he is terrified by a bully in the class and he may lack a sympathetic teacher or parents in whom he can confide. So he may tell his mother, morning after morning, that he feels too ill to go to school, or he may wander around the streets pretending to his parents that he is attending school.

In these cases we have non-attendance springing from very different reasons. Let us take another example: this time, two girls who are rude and disruptive in class. The first may behave in this way because she is deeply unhappy and feels that no one cares for her or values her. Her unco-operative manner and attitude springs from a desire for attention, even of a negative nature. The second girl may be reasonably well adjusted emotionally, and may have an adequate amount of self-esteem, but she may feel that school offers her nothing that she really cares for and she may long to be able to leave school, and move into the job market. Because she perceives school as irrelevant to her own interests, this second girl may start to withdraw from any active participation in class. If she is challenged by an insensitive teacher in a belligerent manner, she may herself react aggressively and in a disruptive fashion. Once again, then, we encounter behaviour that looks superficially similar, but springs from very different attitudes and values both to the self and to school.

So, it seems to us, in looking at the interaction between the school and the adolescent, we must take into account the growing cognitive maturity of the young person and acknowledge that he or she is not a passive recipient of whatever the school offers, but an active participant in a social situation who may, or may not, decide that he or she wishes to co-operate at the level required. In order to clarify this viewpoint, we will look in some detail at two studies that are concerned with adolescents and their responses to school.

The first study was conducted by Hargreaves in 1967 in a large boys' secondary school in England. Clearly the details of this only properly apply to the particular place and time in which this study was done, but in his methodology and analysis Hargreaves displays the emphasis on the adolescents' perceptions of school that we consider should inform any attempt to understand this area. The second is an analysis of social psychological mechanisms affecting high school drop-out in Nigeria and was done by Ogionwo in 1970 (Ogionwo, 1972). This study demonstrates how drop-out rates from high school can be explained by looking in detail at the way young people perceive their futures, and the extent to which they see schools as contributing in a positive way to those futures.

In his study, Hargreaves looked at fourth-year pupils attending a secondary school that was streamed into high and low ability classes. In the A stream he found that boys subscribed to a distinctive set of pro-school values (1975, pp. 232–3).

> They valued academic achievement and hard work; 'fooling about' and other methods of failing to work hard and pay attention to the teachers were strictly forbidden. All of them wanted to do well at school and to pass their examinations. They also valued smart appearance, approving the wearing of sports jacket, tie and trousers. All wore their hair in a short well-groomed style. Since they were keen about school, these boys pressured one another into attendance. Boys who were ill were encouraged to return as soon as possible and playing truant for an afternoon was frowned upon. None of these boys smoked or had been involved in delinquency.

Boys in the C stream, on the other hand, had a very different set of values. Most of them shared a 'culture' that was the opposite of the dominant culture in the A stream.

> The central value of these boys was to 'have fun' in school. It was normative to avoid work as far as possible, to 'mess about'. If work was demanded then the easiest way was to copy from someone who had worked. Clothes were an important aspect of this culture, but here it is the wearing of jeans that is normative. Hair was worn long, in the style promoted by ... pop groups. Any boy who came to school in a tie was ridiculed. Since they did not show any enthusiasm about school ... members were free to absent themselves from school whenever they wished; it was assumed that most boys would truant from time to time. Most of them smoked, most indulged in regular petty thieving and most had a court record.

Hargreaves relates these attitudes and values held by the boys to the expectations maintained by the teachers about the ability of boys within each stream. Boys in the A stream were expected to do well at school, the better teachers were assigned to them, and all the boys soon became aware that some of them, the A stream boys, were destined for academic success at school, and others, the C stream boys, were destined for academic failure. It is not surprising then, that boys adapted to these expectations in an appropriate manner and became supportive of the school values, if they could foresee success for themselves in school, and adopted an entirely different set of values if they foresaw failure for themselves within the school setting.

Hargreaves considers that because A stream boys were more conformist to teachers' values a cycle was set up whereby these boys were more likely to be taken on visits by teachers, and given special attention in the school, thus reinforcing their pro-school values, and increasing the perception of the other boys that school was not a place in which it was worthwhile expending any effort.

The Hargreaves study showed that it is more appropriate to view behaviour within the school as an outcome of pupils' perceptions and evaluations of what school could offer them, rather than to view behaviour within a context of some children, the better-adjusted ones, showing pro-school values, and other children, the less well-adjusted ones, showing anti-school values. We shall return to this subject in the last section of this chapter when we shall discuss what we shall call 'sociological deviants' that is, young people who get into trouble with authority, not because they are vicious or destructive, but because they belong to a sub-culture which does not share the normative (generally held) values of the majority of the members of their society.

Looking at a rather different area, Ogionwo shows the same sensitivity to the way in which an adolescent's assessment of what school can offer him may affect his behaviour. He conducted a study into drop-out rate among Port Harcourt academic high school students in Nigeria. By academic high schools he meant schools where there was an emphasis on learning and education as of value in itself and there was no clear link-up with getting on in the job market.

He used both questionnaires and open-structured interviews to get information about students, their families, the students' attitudes to school and study, vocational plans, future expectations, peer-group activities, status within peer-groups and expectations about peer-group membership. He compared two groups, those who dropped out and a control group who were matched by school ability and social class.

He found out that, broadly speaking, there were two types of drop-outs. First, those who dropped out because they did not aspire to high 'social mobility' (by which he means they did not expect to succeed socially at a higher level than their families). It is not difficult to see why this group dropped out. They did so because they did not regard themselves as 'high fliers' and therefore saw no need for advanced educational qualifications. On the other hand, there was another group with very high mobility aspirations, but who either came from medium socio-economic classes or were girls, who also dropped out. How was it that people with such a high desire to succeed dropped out of school?

Ogionwo explains the reasons for their drop-out as follows. Both these groups, boys with comparatively poorly educated fathers, and girls, would not perceive the lesson content of 'academic' high schools as relevant to getting on in the world; therefore, in their haste to succeed, they would leave school in an attempt to come to grips with practical situations where they could express their need to achieve and get on in life. He ends his report on this study with a plea that high schools amend their curriculum so as to fit 'certain students' short range planning and enable them to make a smooth and direct transition into the labour market after graduation' (Ogionwo, 1972, p. 366); in other words, to amend the content of their lessons in such a way that students will perceive them to be useful to them in their desire to get on in life.

We have discussed both these studies in some detail to make the point that, particularly during adolescence, students evaluate the school and what it can offer them in much the same way that teachers and educationalists continually evaluate students and their performance.

(2) *School climate and adolescent response*

We have already referred in the earlier part of this book to the large study of secondary schools in London conducted by Rutter, in which the major finding was that the general climate or 'ethos' of a school can contribute directly to both academic performance and social adjustment. We will now look at this study in rather more detail.

In 1970 Rutter had done a comparative study of children in a London suburb and children in the Isle of Wight, in which he showed that primary schools in London differed widely in rates of the behavioural difficulty observed in children, and in reading performance. From this study it could not be conclusively established whether these differences were caused to any extent by the schools or whether they were due solely to differences in pupil intake.

About two-thirds of the London sample went on to one of twenty non-selective schools in the London area and Rutter decided to follow these children up. He already had details about the children's previous academic attainment, social adjustment, scores on tests of verbal reasoning, and family and home background. Thus he could, in his subsequent analyses, judge whether or not the twenty secondary schools had markedly different intakes, in terms of home backgrounds, previous academic performance and behavioural difficulties.

He used investigators who had no knowledge of the details of children's previous performance and they studied schools by observation, by interview with the teachers, by pupil questionnaires and by becoming thoroughly familiar with each school as a total organisation. In 1974 he reinvestigated the children on four key outcome variables: attendance at school; behaviour, observed in school by skilled researchers; delinquency − having been officially cautioned by the police or appearing in a juvenile court; and examination results.

The results of the study indicated very clearly that some schools were more effective than others in that their pupils had better attendance records, were observed to behave better in class, had lower deviancy rates and scored better at examinations. These differences in school outcomes were not related to differences in intake, in that schools with the most advantaged intakes did not necessarily score better on the four outcome variables.

This finding that intake variables did not account for outcomes was clearly obvious in the area of examination results. You will remember that Rutter had data on the children's verbal reasoning at an earlier age, and from these test results he divided the children into three bands on intake into secondary school (naturally neither the children nor the teachers knew into which band any particular pupil fell). Secondary schools made such a difference to pupil performance that the average score for band 3 children (the lowest band) in the most successful schools was as good as that for band 1 children (the best band) in the least successful school.

Of course, intake variables did matter, to the extent that children with poor academic records and relatively disadvantaged family backgrounds continued to score lower than children with better academic and family backgrounds, *within* each school. But two children who were equally disadvantaged on intake could show marked differences in outcome four years later depending on whether they went to one of the best or one of the worst of the twenty secondary schools studied.

What made some schools 'the best' on the outcome variables and others 'the worst'? Rutter and his team saw three elements in the life of a school: its physical and administrative features, the effect of its environment and its own internal climate which they called 'school processes'. We shall look at each of these in turn.

(*a*) *Physical and administrative features* made no difference. Neither size, nor whether schools were single sex or co-educational, seemed to matter. Buildings and degree of overcrowding did not seem to matter either. These conclusions are similar to those of Jencks and his associates (1972) who, after reviewing numerous American studies, reported that the amount of money spent on equipment and buildings did not seem to have any direct effect on how well pupils did at school.

(*b*) *Environmental factors* or where the school was situated seemed to matter only to a very limited extent. Rutter showed, and this is in line with other British research, that schools with poorer in-school behaviour were not admitting a larger proportion of pupils from areas with high rates of delinquency. Similarly, the schools with the poorest attendance and the poorest academic records were not the schools that served the most disadvantaged areas.

(*c*) The most significant determinant of outcome seemed to be what Rutter and his team called '*school processes*'. They found that there was a cluster of variables which together helped to produce a school climate that had a strong influence on the four outcome variables – attendance, behaviour in lessons, rate of deviancy and academic performance. These variables were:

Academic emphasis This variable was measured by observing how conscientiously teachers marked and set homework, the expectations held by teachers of pupils' examination success, how much the pupils' work was displayed, and use of libraries. Those schools that showed the greatest academic emphasis tended to show the best performance on the four outcome variables.

Teacher action in the classroom Rutter and his team did not look directly at the personal qualities of teachers. Instead they observed how teachers handled their classes. They found that frequent disciplinary interruptions were associated with worse behaviour. Of course, it is difficult to disentangle cause and effect here, but it did seem as though continual stoppages of lessons in order to reprimand pupils served to intensify behavioural disturbance. Another important aspect of teacher behaviour that was associated with good outcomes was whether the teacher started the lesson on time and devoted the major part of the lesson to the topic that she was covering rather than to classroom management.

Rewards and punishments Self-discipline, encouraged by clearly understood guidelines, emerged as the most effective kind of discipline. Overall there was a tendency for high levels of corporal punishment to be associated with rather worse behaviour. Frequent public praise was associated with better pupil behaviour and so was positive feedback, such as displaying pupils' work on walls.

Pupil conditions The provision of school outings was associated with examination success and schools where pupils reported that they were willing to consult teachers about personal problems showed better attendance records and better academic attainment.

Responsibilities and participation As we reported in Chapter 1, a striking association was shown between giving pupils responsibilities and encouraging them to participate in school activities, and better pupil performance on all the outcome measures.

Stability of peer-groups An interesting finding was that low deviance or delinquency rates were found in those schools that kept the same pupils in the same groups (in the same English class) since they started school. Low delinquency was also associated with schools where pupils made friends outside their own class as well as in their own class.

Staff management The schools with the best outcomes seemed to be those that combined decision-making by senior staff with preliminary consultation with junior staff.

Rutter and his team performed numbers of sophisticated statistical analyses of the data and all the analyses seemed to point to a *causal* influence for schools. Those schools that produced a climate that promoted self-discipline, self-esteem and responsibility in pupils, and where teachers worked conscientiously using the minimum of punishment and frequent praise and encouragement, appeared to provide the kind of atmosphere that made the pupil identify with the school values, and thus optimised pupil performance on all four outcome measures.

The type of school climate that was shown to be effective with English adolescents in this study is very similar to the one advocated by Fagbongbe (1973) in Nigeria, who recommends as the result of interviewing 800 Nigerian students and secondary school pupils that there should be a 'decline of the old authoritarian tendency in discipline' which 'is based on the humiliation of the erring child' and recommends instead a discipline which 'recognizes the inherent dignity and rights of every human being' (p. 405).

We have devoted some time to this study by Rutter because it is, from the point of view of the teacher and educationalist, a very encouraging one, in that it shows that if a school bases its approach to adolescence on an understanding of the emotional and social needs, a climate or 'ethos' will be produced which will encourage optimum pupil performance at behavioural, social and academic levels.

Once again, the concept of self-worth is applicable. Rutter and his team considered that the most successful schools were ones whose climates encouraged a feeling of self-worth. They stressed, as we have throughout this book, that children's self-perceptions play a major part in their desire and ability to perform well academically. Similarly, a study by Isaacs (1976) in Jamaica showed that pupil performance at mathematics was affected by the student's perception of his ability to do mathematics. Self-esteem was also implicated in the study of Kikuyu youth, done by Hertzog, to which we made reference in the last chapter. He argued that as the time spent in informal education declines and the time spent in the more formal school system increases, so educators should realise that schools must supply the reinforcement of self-worth that was previously supplied by the lengthy periods of initiation that used to take place in Kenyan society. All these studies stress the importance of the school climate in stressing self-worth; all these studies agree that self-worth is promoted by conferring responsibility and by giving generous but realistic praise and recognition. Finally, all these studies agree that schools can causally affect pupil performance by following these guidelines. As Rutter concludes, schools do matter because his study established 'that schools can do much to foster good behaviour and attainments, and that even in disadvantaged areas, schools can be a force for the good' (Rutter *et al.*, 1979, p. 295).

(3)   *Individual factors and adolescent response to school*

In the last section, we argued for the importance of group processes in the adolescent's response to school. We claimed that a school's overall climate can cause a pupil to identify with the values of the school, and we noted that a pupil's self-esteem can be enhanced by working with others in schools with a participatory atmosphere and in which praise, recognition and responsibility are generously given.

However, in the final analysis, schools do consist of individuals and, irrespective of his degree of personal identification with the school's values, or the type of group interactions occurring in the school, each pupil brings to the school certain individual qualities. Similarly, each teacher makes her own particular personal contribution to the school which depends largely on her personal characteristics. We would now like to discuss these individual factors, grouping them broadly into four areas: the pupil's demographic characteristics, his level of cognitive skill, his degree of emotional and social adjustment, and the teacher's personal style.

(a) By the term 'demographic' we refer to characteristics of the pupil over which he or she has no personal control – like socio-economic class, sex, and whether he or she lives in a rural or urban area.

As we discussed at some length in Chapter 2, certain home background variables make a major contribution to the degree to which the child is well or ill prepared for school. We listed these as physical environment in the home, parental attitudes to school, child care practices and preparation for the kind of thought helpful in the school situation. We also mentioned that, generally speaking, homes that have been called 'elite' in some Third World countries and that are referred to as of higher *socio-economic class* in the West tend to provide the particular type of physical environment, parental attitudes, child care practices and manner of thinking that are appropriate to success in the primary school years.

These home background factors are also relevant to adolescents in the school setting but, by the time a pupil has reached adolescence, they matter much less than they did in the earlier years. The exception to this general statement lies in parental attitudes which continue to be very important, as Ogionwo points out in discussing the roots of 'drop-out' from Nigerian secondary schools. He argues that the comparatively lower drop-out rate shown by children from 'well-to-do middle class homes' where parents themselves have a high educational standard is due to the similarity in values between such parents and most secondary schools.

It is not only with respect to drop-out rates that parental values are important. Parents who are in sympathy with the aims and objectives of secondary schools, and who regard high school education as a useful preparation for later life, are far more likely to encourage their children to prepare their homework conscientiously, attend school consistently and prepare for examinations in a responsible manner.

However, as the reader will know, not all successful secondary school pupils come from homes of the type we have just described. In many Third World countries, the most academically motivated children sometimes come from traditional rural backgrounds. But the more entrenched the 'elite' are in an educational system, the more difficult it becomes for children from rural or poor homes to succeed in the system. In general,

the more a country moves towards the social class stratification of the kind that is so characteristic of most Western developed countries, the more difficult it will be for children from poorer homes to succeed at secondary schools.

We have just said that not all successful secondary school pupils come from elite homes or homes of a higher socio-economic class and the converse holds true as well, as most readers will also know from their own experience. Not all children from elite homes or homes of a higher socio-economic class are successful secondary school pupils. Sometimes, as Conger notes, 'a parent may possess academically useful characteristics, but his child may not find identification with him rewarding or, worse, may find it self-defeating or destructive' (1977, p. 391). In other words, sometimes a child may deliberately reject what his parent values but as we have noted already in this chapter, such parent–child conflicts are the exception rather than the rule.

We have already discussed *rural/urban* differences in Chapter 2, when we pointed out that children from rural areas tend to have more difficulty with academic modes of thought than those from urban areas at the primary school level. But, of course, even within one country, rural areas differ in the values and attitudes that are characteristic of them. This has recently been pointed out in a study done by Wilson in Papua, New Guinea (1976). He compared school-leavers in two rural areas, one in a remote highlands area, the Tambul sample, and the other in a coastal area, the Kara sample, where many of the subjects' parents had themselves been to school. He found that in general the coastal subjects made more use of their education and also were more discriminating in their evaluation of the educational system. These differences are probably related to the fact that schooling had been established longer in the coastal area. However, subjects in both groups considered that 'there should be more practical, village oriented activities in the school curriculum'.

In the last chapter we explored the role of *sex differences* in cognitive performance in adolescence and pointed out that such differences are intimately related to cultural values about sex role. This observation about sex differences in cognitive performance extends, of course, to sex differences in social behaviour in the school situation as well. For example, if women within a certain culture are expected to be less dominant than men socially, it will be unlikely that girls at secondary schools in that society will play a major role in organising school activities. Thus it seems that certain characteristics that the adolescent pupil has no direct control over, such as home background factors, sex and the area he comes from, may influence both his expectations of, and his attitudes to, school.

(b) When we talk about the pupil's 'level of *cognitive skill*' we refer to the degree of preparedness the pupil shows for the academic tasks of school. Some people might have preferred to talk of 'intelligence'. This is a term we have not used up to now, partly because we intend to discuss its use fully in Chapter 11, and partly because we think 'intelligence' is normally taken to refer to a constant and unchanging amount of cognitive ability that an individual possesses. It seems to us that this assumption that cognitive ability or potential is unchanging is not justified. We shall cite other evidence in Chapter 11, but here we should merely like to remind the reader of Rutter's finding that measures of verbal reasoning were not the sole predictors of academic performance in secondary schools in his large study. You will remember that he found that children who had scored at the band 3 level when measured on verbal reasoning on entry to secondary school sometimes scored far better in later years than children who had scored at the band 1 level on entry. It seems to us that, disregarding children with special needs, the vast majority of pupils are capable during adolescence of the academic tasks of the secondary school.

Of course, performance at school does depend to some extent on the innate characteristics each individual is born with (his genotype), but at adolescence this has been so affected by the home, primary school and general environment that it is not particularly helpful to think in terms of inborn or 'innate' intelligence. Academic performance at adolescence is related to many other factors besides genetic inheritance – home environment, primary school teaching, social environment and the young person's own perception of how important it is for him to excel at such intellectual tasks. Thus young people do vary in their cognitive preparedness for academic tasks, but it is important to remember that such preparedness is as affected by the previous environment as it is by inborn characteristics and, more important, it must always be borne in mind that, as the Rutter study showed, 'schools matter'. That is, irrespective of the pupil's level of cognitive preparedness, secondary schools can, depending on

their approach and the pupil's response to it, either build on and improve cognitive skills, or cause such skills to remain static, or, exceptionally, to deteriorate.

(c) In the last chapter we spent some time discussing emotional adjustment in adolescence, and when we did this we emphasised the relationship between emotional adjustment and self-esteem. The young person's adjustment to school will of course also be related to his level of self-esteem. Thus a young person who has a healthy self-concept is far more likely to be able to cope with the social and emotional demands of school than the adolescent who is crippled with self-doubts.

But it must be remembered that if the adolescent does not subscribe to the values of his school, or does not see his attendance at school as serving any useful function, from the point of view of his own personal development, self-concept within the school setting will not be important to him. In other words, if an adolescent does not care about how well he does at school, or what his teachers think of him, he will not attempt to fit in at school or adapt to its social and academic demands. This will not mean that the adolescent concerned is, in general, not socially or emotionally well adjusted.

In sum, adolescents who are well adjusted socially and emotionally, and who have healthy levels of self-esteem, will not have difficulty in coping with the social and emotional as well as academic tasks of the secondary school, always provided they want to identify with the goals and values of the school and its teachers.

(d) Obviously adolescents, in general, like and respond to some teachers rather than to others. In any school some teachers tend to be popular and others less so. But again, in any school, certain teachers may be greatly admired by a minority of pupils while the great majority of pupils are indifferent to them, and the converse can obviously hold as well. There are some teachers who are 'hated' only by a minority of pupils, while other pupils feel relatively indifferent to them. Is it possible to distinguish any *teacher characteristics* that are universally liked or disliked?

Such evidence that we have on this tends to come mostly from British and American studies which seem to show that adolescents favour teachers who are warm, confident, enthusiastic, adaptable, able to display initiative and sensitive to pupils' needs. They tend to dislike teachers who are domineering and autocratic and this latter finding holds more strongly for girls than it does for boys.

Numerous studies exist on teacher style. These are often conflicting and many seem to reflect the prejudices of researchers rather than any objective evidence. It is probably fair to say that different teacher styles are more appropriate for different school conditions. A teacher who believes in a relaxed, warm approach may find it easier to teach in a school where the other teachers hold similar views than she would in a school where pupils, other teachers and parents see a teacher's role as more directive and less informal. If you are interested in this area, you will find the second section of the Hargreaves book on interpersonal relations in education very helpful (see the select bibliography at the end of this chapter). We shall return to teacher–pupil relationships in the next chapter.

This section on individual factors in the school situation concludes our discussion of adolescents in school. As before in the book, we have tried to show that in any social situation the previous experience of the participants is important in that it shapes their expectations and values. We have also laid stress on the dynamic nature of any social interaction – schools can change pupils, and teachers and pupils respond in different ways to shifting situations. In addition, we have tried to point out that when an adolescent does not respond to the school situation in the way that teachers would like him to, the reason for this may lie as much in the institution and its values as it does in the personal characteristics of the young person.

The Adolescent and His Attitudes to Work

In many earlier societies, both Western and Third World, the vocational problems of adolescents were much simpler than they are today. Such societies did not offer so many work choices as are now offered to many young people. In earlier days, when both geographic and social mobility were more limited, most young people grew up likely to have observed adults performing the kind of work they would be doing in the future. In societies with informal educational systems most young people were slowly absorbed into the working life of adults. The Arapesh youth in New Guinea, for example, was able to take over from his father responsibility for tilling the family garden as he grew towards adolescence. Even in Western societies with more formal educational systems,

young people in the past were able to see at first hand the various crafts and professions that their society offered. This is certainly not the case today. With the growing technological complexities of societies all over the world, numbers of different professions, crafts and skilled trades are generated yearly, and keeping up with these vocational opportunities is a major task for any vocational adviser.

This is not to say that the existence of many different kinds of vocations means that today's adolescent will, necessarily, be offered such a choice. Unfortunately, all over the world there is a growing incidence of unemployment among school-leavers.

It is beyond the scope of this book to explore the causes of this rising tide of unemployment amongst young people and it is also beyond its scope to look at the social, economic and political reasons for the shift towards the cash economy which makes finding employment often a psychological, if not an economic, necessity. In this short section we shall look only at two psychological aspects concerning work that face young people as they move towards the end of their schooldays. These are: problems of vocational choice for those young people fortunate enough to be able to go on to further education or skilled employment; and the conflict that may be experienced in schools by pupils when teaching becomes more directed to passing examinations than to preparing pupils for the world outside school.

(1) *Problems of vocational choice*

Although, as we mentioned above, there is an increasing tendency for school-leavers all over the world to be unemployed, in all countries a large proportion of young people will be fortunate enough to be able to make some vocational choices as they move towards school-leaving.

Conger suggests that there are three distinguishable stages in the maturation of vocational choice: the fantasy period, the tentative period and the realist period. If you ask children in early or middle childhood what they want to do when they are grown-up, they often respond by citing active, exciting and glamorous occupations, air hostess, football star, pilot, and so on. These choices are, of course, based on emotion rather than cognition. As the child grows older, he realises that what he would really like to do in his *fantasies* about adult life may not be possible, and he begins to work out a compromise between what he is interested in and the choices that will, realistically and practically, be available to him.

At this second *tentative* stage he will become influenced by the social status of preferred occupations. A great many studies have been done all over the world looking at the way that certain occupations rate in people's prestige. The general finding has been that as societies begin to offer occupations similar to those found in economically and technologically developed societies, so occupational prestige begins to resemble the following prestige ranking: professional, white collar, supervisory, skilled and unskilled. For example, Mitchell and Epstein (1959) found in Zambia a very close degree of similarity in the prestige-ranking of different occupations between students in three different types of educational institutions and the generally held prestige-ranking in Western Europe.

At the tentative stage of vocational choice the social status of different occupations becomes, as we have said, relatively influential in moving towards a decision, but, overriding the prestige or status of any occupation, comes the slow realisation that not all occupations are open in practice to everybody. Thus in the West social class differences in vocational choice begin to appear at this stage as adolescents start becoming aware of educational qualifications that may be needed for high status occupations, and as they begin to work out whether or not they will be in a position to get such qualifications both financially and academically. As Conger puts it (1977, p. 427):

> ❝ A lower-class girl whose parents are unable to, or uninterested in, helping her to go to college is less likely to aspire to be a doctor than one whose parents encourage such a vocational choice and who are in a position to help her. Similarly a boy whose parents expect him to go to work upon completion of the ninth grade is not likely to spend much time contemplating the idea of becoming an engineer. ❞

At the final, *realistic* stage of vocational choice the young person has probably decided upon the work area he is interested in, and should he be fortunate enough to have a choice of particular jobs offered to him he starts to balance out what he thinks the important aspects of a job are.

Studies in this area show that while money and security are often important factors, they are not the only criteria in choosing jobs. Thus Silvey, working in Uganda with a large sample of secondary school leavers, showed that, for his sample, the 'considerations put highest are those which make the job satisfying in itself for the particular person concerned' (1969, p. 146). His sample cited the following factors as most important:

1st   Interest in the job
2nd   Abilities and personality well suited
3rd   Whether it offers a chance to serve the community
4th   The pay
5th   Whether it is a secure and stable job
6th   Prospects for promotion to a senior position.

It is interesting to compare these criteria with those cited by British adolescents in the large National Children's Bureau study which we have referred to before. Fogelman shows them citing these aspects as most important in choosing a job:

1st   It should be well paid
2nd   The job should involve variety
3rd   The job should offer you chances of promotion
4th   It should have convenient hours and conditions
5th   It should give you the opportunity of helping others
6th   It should involve using your head and need thought and concentration.

Both studies show the interplay between factors to do with financial security and factors to do with personal satisfaction that is typical of the thinking of most young people as they come to make a final decision about their first job on leaving school or higher education.

(2) *The conflict that some young people may experience if school curricula are dominated by preparation for examinations*

As Ronald Dore points out in his influential book *The Diploma Disease* (1976), the curricula of secondary schools in many countries have become dominated by examinations and their requirements. As he notes, 'unfortunately not all schooling is education. Much of it is mere qualification earning' (p. ix). What Dore is referring to here is the increasing tendency in many societies, both Third World and Western, to direct teaching towards the passing of examinations rather than towards the broadening of intellectual and personal horizons.

If the majority of students in secondary schools are able to go on to further education, then this emphasis on preparation for academic examinations will not be misplaced even if it is not 'educational' in the sense in which Dore uses the term. Unfortunately, however, in many countries it is only a minority of students who will need to use the results of academic examinations. A larger number may find, when they seek work, that much of their school curriculum is not particularly relevant to the skills they will need for the actual work. It is possible, then, that particularly in secondary schools that are rigidly streamed and set in different ability groups, pupils who know they are unlikely to go on to higher education may feel that the content of much of their lessons is not particularly appropriate to their future needs. This perception may lead them to either drop out of school or form within the school a 'counter-school' culture, in which pupils who ascribe to the values of the culture may behave in such a way as to disrupt the learning of other pupils who do wish to play a more conventional pupil role.

It is not within the scope of this book to discuss these issues in detail, though we shall return to them briefly in Chapter 10. At this stage we should merely like to reiterate that educationalists and teachers must be sensitive to the possibility of such perceptions on the part of their pupils, if there is a conflict between what is taught in schools and what school-leavers actually need to know if they are to take their place in the outside world.

As Callaway recommends, as a result of his study on the employment problem of secondary grammar school leavers in Nigeria, 'The curriculum in all secondary ... schools should include practical subjects and problem-solving experience which would enable students to learn basic technical skills and to acquire new insights and interests. This would prepare students to be realistic in choosing a career' (1975, p. 23).

The Adolescent in Conflict with Society

Throughout this book we have stressed that if we wish children or young people to conform to our values and behave in a manner that we consider to be appropriate, then we have to persuade them that our values and our mode of behaviour are right.

While punishment may have a deterrent value for a while, it is unlikely to be an effective manner of controlling behaviour that we consider anti-social, for as soon as a situation arises in which the potential wrong-doer thinks he may evade punishment he will repeat his delinquent behaviour.

We have suggested that when there is a conflict between an individual's behaviour and the way we would prefer him to behave, we have to look critically at the motivations for his behaviour while, at the same time, examining our requirements of him to make sure that what we are requiring of him is something that is in his interest and society's interest as well as our own. Thus we have argued that the best method of discipline is self-discipline in an atmosphere where both young people and adults endorse the same basic moral and ethical values.

However, we all know that even the best of us often behave in a way that we know to be morally wrong according to our own value system. Why does this happen? Imagine for a while that you are a secondary school student about to take a crucial examination. Shortly before this you manage, by accident, to be in the same room as the examination papers concerned, with no chance at all of anyone discovering your presence there. What are the kinds of factors that will determine whether or not you look at those papers? We would suggest that the following variables may influence your behaviour.

(a) How important the examination is to you. You may already have the offer of a good job that is not conditional on doing well at the examination. If this is the case you will be less likely to look at the papers than you would be if the results of the examination were crucial to your future.

(b) Your home background may also play an important part in your decision. If you have a widowed mother for whom you are going to be the sole support you may be more likely to cheat than if you come from a prosperous family with the kind of connections that will always assure you of a good job no matter what your examination results are.

(c) How good a student you are. If you are confident of doing very well, you may be less likely to look at the papers than someone who is a borderline case.

(d) Whether you are alone or not. Research shows that peer pressure can be very important in such dilemmas. If you are with a companion he may sway your judgement one way or the other and you may make a decision which would be the opposite of the one you might make on your own.

(e)   Your sex may also be an important variable. In Western countries girls are far less likely to offend than boys because, on the whole, they seem to need their behaviour to be such as to predispose to general social approval. In Nigeria, one of the present authors showed that, faced with an imaginary dilemma like this, girl secondary school pupils were less likely than boys to agree that they would take advantage of gaining access to the papers (Ugwuegbu, 1975a, 1975b).

(f)   The general value system concerning the moral issue of cheating in this way. If cheating at examinations is a fairly common happening you will be far more likely to do so yourself than if such behaviour is extremely rare and generally condemned.

(g)   Self-esteem can be an important factor. As we mentioned before, studies show that people are less likely to take advantage of the opportunity to cheat if they feel secure about their general level of competence. If, on the other hand, an individual feels unsure of his ability to achieve in the normal manner, he may resort to ways of behaving that he does not really approve of but sees as necessary in order to win some kind of recognition.

(h)   Finally, your own moral reasoning that has developed in the way we described in Chapter 7 will come into play. Such reasoning may indicate that cheating is wrong because it goes against the basic ethical principle that everyone should have the same basic opportunities in life, and by looking at the papers you will place your peers at a disadvantage. On the other hand, from the same ethical principle you may conclude that it is morally acceptable to cheat because you may think that you come from a disadvantaged section of society and have had less chance than your peers to succeed at school and looking at the examination papers will redress this imbalance.

We think that this imaginary dilemma may help to clarify the statement we made in Chapter 7 that 'behaviour in moral and ethical areas is multi-determined by, amongst other variables, the social climate, the specifics of the situation and the value system and moral development of the individual concerned'.

If one deviant act is susceptible to the influence of so many different factors, we should not be surprised to discover that young people who persistently offend against the rules of society by cheating, stealing, being aggressive, and so on, do so for many different reasons.

Not surprisingly, a great deal of research has been done on the causes of delinquent behaviour. All such investigations seem to point to the fact that in general the young person who persistently commits delinquent acts, and who continues to do so in adulthood, suffers from a number of disadvantages which tend to interact with each other. Amongst the variables that have been shown to be involved in persistent adolescent offences are the following:

(a)   Poverty, overcrowding, homelessness and poor physical home conditions.

(b)   Poor academic attainment and a history of poor school adjustment.

(c)   Low self-concept and a general lack of social skills and the ability to get on with others. Children who feel that no one cares about them are likely to draw attention to themselves by misbehaving.

(d)   Poor relations within the home. Sometimes broken homes are quoted as predisposing to delinquent behaviour but research tends to show that it is not the broken homes, as such, that contribute to this behaviour. Rather it is the friction that often precedes the break-up and the consequent financial and social strain that often follows the break-up. Unhappy, quarrelling parents who remain together but who do not devote any time to satisfying their children's psychological needs may also contribute to a child's delinquent behaviour.

(e)   Lack of facilities to satisfy the psychological needs for recognition, responsibility and new experiences. As we mentioned in the last chapter, if young people are unemployed and lack both work to confirm their self-worth and to provide them with money, as well as recreational facilities to satisfy their need for new experiences, it is no wonder that vandalism and rowdiness result.

(f)   Finally, some young people who commit offences may be regarded as what Elkind and Weiner call 'sociological delinquents'. These young people may be emotionally well adjusted and come from warm and loving homes but they belong to a peer-group who, as a whole, hold values that are at variance with those of society in general. These sub-cultures may grant prestige to the successful law-breaker and, as Elkind and Weiner note, 'In such a context, then, delinquent youths experience a sense of self-esteem and belongingness, while non-delinquents feel outcast and unworthy' (1978,

p. 669). However, research shows that in general such sociological delinquents tend to grow out of their persistent tendency to offend if, and when, they get good jobs and/or steady girlfriends.

As we noted above, deviance usually occurs because of the interaction of a number of the factors we have listed above. In dealing with such young people, it is clearly important to establish what the precipitating factors are. In doing so, three objectives must remain paramount. The first is to restrain the young offender so that he no longer is a menace to innocent people, the second is to try and repair the damaged self-esteem that is always, with the exception of what we have called 'the sociological delinquent', so characteristic of the young offender, and the third is to provide him with an alternative set of behaviours and skills, and to make sure that such alternative behaviours and skills are more rewarding than his previous delinquent way of behaving.

Summary

In this chapter we have tried to look at the adolescent period within the social setting. Throughout we have attempted to show quite how important the cultural values and attitudes are in adolescent development. We have also emphasised the dynamic nature of the young person's interaction with those around him. Not only do they influence him directly, but by his appraisal of, and response to, their behaviour and attitudes, he interacts with them and causes them to shift in their own behaviour and attitudes. Consequently it should be clear that individual adolescent behaviour should only be considered within a social and cultural context.

The following areas were dealt with in this chapter:

(1) Two different perspectives on the nature of adolescent development were presented. Within the first perspective the adolescent years are not regarded as differing in major ways from the periods preceding and following them. Within the second perspective the adolescent is regarded as peculiarly susceptible to emotional stresses and strains.

(2) We then considered the adolescent in relation to his family. We made the point that, contrary to the commonly held view, most adolescents do not experience much stress in their relationships with their family and, on larger issues, they tend to agree with the views held by adult members of their family.

(3) In considering the relationships of adolescents and their peers we discussed both social relationships in adolescent groups or crowds and friendships between two or three adolescents.

(4) Following this we looked at adolescent behaviour in school. In doing so we stressed the importance of always paying attention to the adolescent's own appraisal and perception of school and its value to him.

(5) In considering adolescents in relation to work, we looked at how young people make vocational choices. We also discussed the effect on the adolescent's adaptation to work if school curricula are dominated by examinations.

(6) Finally, we looked at adolescent behaviour when it is in conflict with the values of society in general. We concluded that such behaviour, if it is persistent, is multi-determined.

Chapter 8: Selected Bibliography

Different perspectives on adolescence
Kenyatta, J., *Facing Mount Kenya* (London: Secker & Warburg, 1961).
Mead, M., *Male and Female* (Harmondsworth: Penguin, 1962).

Adolescents in relation to their families
Conger, J. J., *Adolescence and Youth* (New York: Harper & Row, 1977).

Adolescents in relation to their peers
Conger, op. cit., ch. 9.

Improving social skills in adolescence
Trower, P., Bryant, B., and Argyle, M., *Social Skills and Mental Health* (London: Methuen, 1978).

Adolescents in school
Conger, op. cit., ch. 11.
Hargreaves, D. H., *Interpersonal Relations and Education*, revised student edition (London: Routledge & Kegan Paul, 1975).
Rutter, M., Maughan, B., Mortimore, P., and Ouston, J., *Fifteen Thousand Hours* (London: Open Books, 1979).

The adolescent in conflict with society
Conger, op. cit., ch. 14.
Oloruntimehin, O., 'Some factors related to juvenile delinquency in Nigerian children', *West African Journal of Education*, vol. XVIII, no. 2 (1974).

PART FOUR
SCHOOL AND SOCIETY

In the last part of this book we look at the effect on the school of social variables. In Chapter 9 we examine the social psychology of the school. First we consider the social system of the classroom, looking in turn at the behavioural dimensions of the teacher–pupil role relationship, at the teacher's leadership style and at group interactions between pupils. Following this we examine the way in which the organisation of the school can affect relationships between teachers and between teachers and the headteacher.

In Chapter 10 we consider the school in its social setting, discussing in turn how parental and community values may influence what goes on in the school, how different approaches to the nature of knowledge interact with what is taught in schools, how the major linguistic medium used in schools can affect learning and social behaviour, and how important it is to locate schools and what goes on in them in a broader social perspective.

Finally, in Chapter 11 we look at the ways educationalists make decisions about students' progress in schools, discussing in turn how intelligence and achievement are defined and measured, and we relate such definitions and measures to cultural values and social expectations.

THE SCHOOL AS A SOCIAL SYSTEM

9

Introduction

In the last chapter we discussed the social climate of the school, and we argued that this climate has an important influence on pupil behaviour. In this chapter we look at the way this climate is affected by the social system that obtains in the school. By the term 'social system' we refer to the more formal aspects of the social relationships of the school.

The formal aspects of these relationships are very much influenced by the ways in which those who take part in such relationships perceive their *roles*; that is, by the way the participants perceive their rights and obligations. For example, the child, on entering school, soon learns that teachers and other pupils hold certain firm expectations of the ways in which it is appropriate for pupils to behave. Pupils are expected to accept that teachers have the authority to tell them what to do. They also learn that teachers themselves are subject to the higher authority of the headmaster. Thus they learn that both teachers and pupils have certain *obligations* to respect the authoritative positions of others. But they also learn that they have certain *rights*: for example, that teachers will be concerned to teach them, and that headteachers will be concerned to organise the school in such a way that teachers may get on with the job of teaching them.

If teachers and headteachers are not seen to concern themselves in this way, pupils, particularly at the secondary school level, may sometimes become so angry that they may resort to strikes and occasionally, as has occurred in some African schools in the recent past, to riot.

But, in general, most schools run fairly smoothly, and this is because those who participate in the social relationships of the school are aware of the type of social behaviour that is expected of them. Similarly, they find that others behave in the ways that they expect them to behave. In other words, there is usually a consensus of opinion about the rights and obligations of pupils, teachers and headteachers which stem from their role relationships.

The child in school is thus caught up in a web of interpersonal role relationships and expectations, and the purpose of this chapter is to examine the more formal aspect of such relationships. We shall now consider the teacher–pupil role relationship and the pupil–pupil relationship in the classroom, and following that we shall consider the way in which the organisation of the school can affect relationships between teachers and between teachers and the headteacher (see Figure 9.1).

(1) Behavioural Dimensions of the Teacher–Pupil Relationship

In Chapters 5 and 8 we discussed some aspects of the teacher–pupil relationship. In doing so we stressed that teachers, particularly at the primary level, may, by their interaction with the pupil, act in such a way as to raise or lower the child's self-esteem. We also pointed out that teachers who appear to be well disposed towards their pupils and who show warmth, enthusiasm and concern in their interactions with pupils are more likely to be positively perceived by pupils than teachers who do not show these qualities. In this section, following

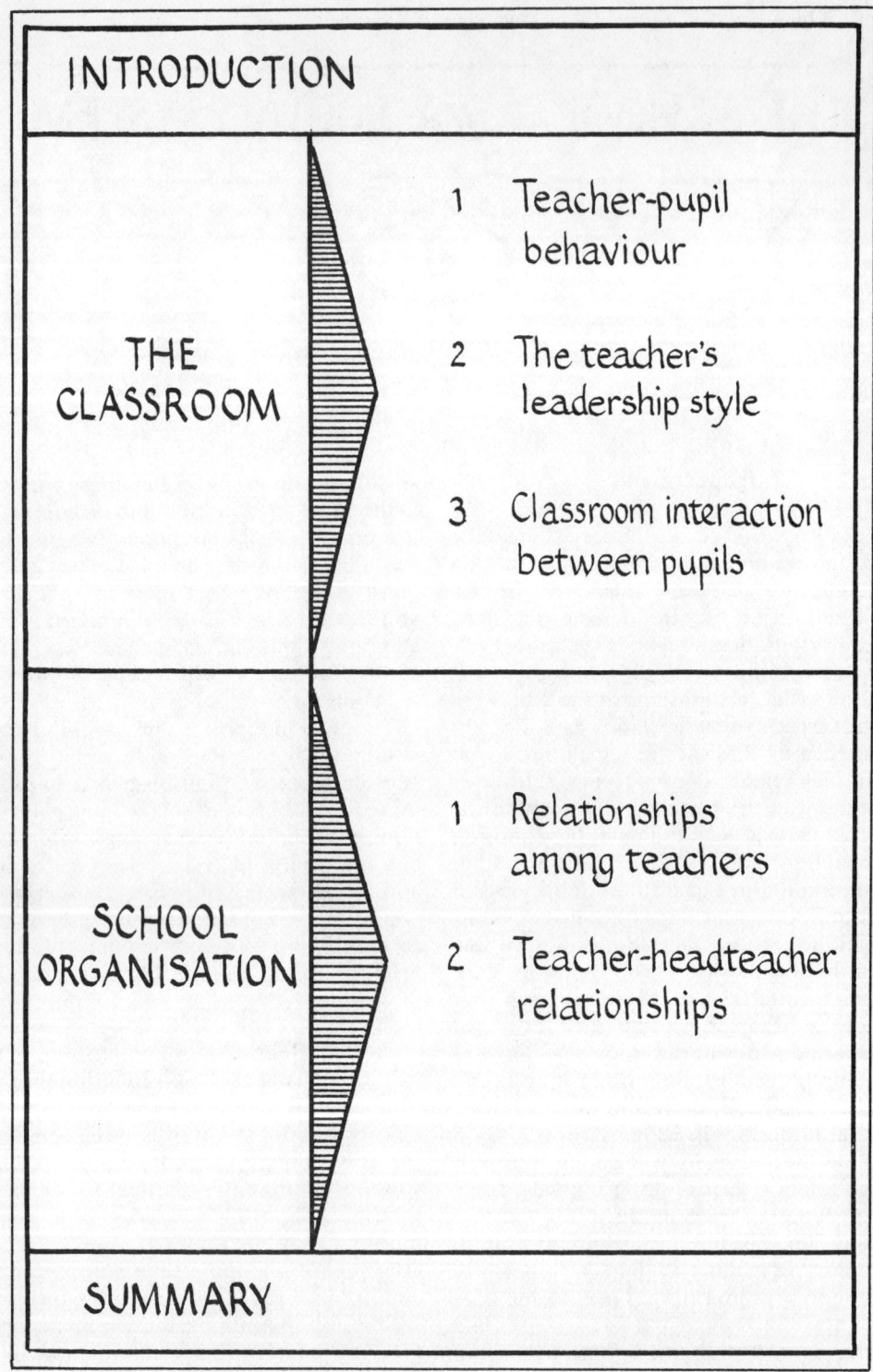

INTRODUCTION	
THE CLASSROOM	1 Teacher-pupil behaviour
	2 The teacher's leadership style
	3 Classroom interaction between pupils
SCHOOL ORGANISATION	1 Relationships among teachers
	2 Teacher-headteacher relationships
SUMMARY	

Figure 9.1 Structure of Chapter 9

Goslin (1965), we look at four behavioural dimensions which may reflect these teacher qualities. They are:

(a) the child's physical position in class
(b) the frequency and type of interaction between the teacher and the taught
(c) the extent to which the child participates in the interaction
(d) the extent to which the relationship involves some emotional dimension as opposed to being affectively neutral.

(a) The child's physical position in class

In many classrooms children are allowed to choose where they sit; indeed, in a number of classrooms such positions are not constant but may change from lesson to lesson, as a result of pupil decision. But in other classrooms pupils are assigned particular positions by the teacher, according to a particular criterion the teacher may have in mind.

In many primary schools in Third World countries seating arrangements are often based on performance on tests in various subjects. Children are tested weekly and the members of the class are rank-ordered on the results of the tests. Allocation of seats is then based on each child's order of merit. In other words, the child who scores the highest in order of ranking is seated at the front bench nearest the teacher. He is followed by the next child in order of rank and so on down to the lowest ranked child who sits at the end of the last bench in the class. Some teachers go further than this; they exhibit on a merit notice board the names of three or four children who scored the highest marks on the test and a corresponding number of children who performed worst.

Such practices have obvious psychological implications for the pupils concerned. Some of the implications are discussed by Stones (1969). He writes (pp. 339–40):

‘ whenever children are placed in rank order the success of one child is dependent on the failure of the other. The positive reinforcement and corresponding affect state of the child at the top of the list has its obverse in the negative reinforcement and adverse emotional state of the child at the bottom. ’

Only one child, the top child in the whole class, can possibly experience a feeling of success, while the rest of the children will experience differing degrees of failure. While the child at the bottom of the list develops feelings of rejection, the child at the top of the list has his need for love, security and recognition enhanced.

Some teachers argue that such practices encourage children to strive to be 'top' and, in this way, they contend, educational standards are raised. We would argue that, on the contrary, such seating arrangements reinforce only the unhealthy aspects of an extremely competitive approach to education, which is not necessarily a constructive approach to the learning situation. Indeed, Sprott (1958) claims that competition is one of the least important educational needs. Discussing educational practice obtaining in China some time ago, he shows that deliberate efforts were made to train children in co-operative rather than competitive interpersonal relationships in education. As a result, when English children who had experienced Chinese education returned to England they usually found it difficult to adjust to the competitive English atmosphere. Further, Sprott gave instances of Chinese students at the university level who would spend a part of their holiday at the university in order to help one of the students who was ill during some part of the session so that the whole class would be sure to pass their examinations. A failure in the class would bring loss of face not only to the person who failed but to the whole class.

This attitude of co-operation differs from the attitudes that are sometimes shown in some Third World countries at present. For example, one of the present authors, Ugwuegbu (1979a and 1979b), showed that in Nigeria examination irregularities and cheating on the West African School Certificate can be ascribed to the nature of the educational competition to which Nigerian children are conditioned. The results of his studies show that Nigerian high school students are motivated to cheat to avoid failure or enhance their good performance position, even if such behaviour involves threats of individual or collective punishment such as cancellation of the students' final examination results. So we can see that children subjected to extreme competitive striving to be top may fail to develop the 'we feeling' necessary for the building of a healthy interpersonal relationship in any group or society, and we would argue that seating arrangements that reinforce such competitive striving are unlikely to contribute to a constructive educational environment.

(b)   *The frequency and type of teacher–pupil interaction*

We expect a child's impressions of the teacher's personality to influence the child's interactions with the teacher. A teacher who is perceived by the pupil as understanding and encouraging will generate more frequent interaction with the pupils than a teacher who is perceived as not caring about the needs of the pupil.

A teacher's behavioural patterns vary from child to child as well as from one moment to the other. We pointed out in Chapters 5 and 8 that teachers treat children differently. One teacher may be friendly and encouraging, another may remain aloof from the children and may institute many rules designed to maintain discipline. Some teachers often praise the pupils' efforts and some use ridicule and sarcasm. Children, of course, observe teachers' different ways of behaving.

Previous feedback from attempted interaction with a teacher may determine whether a child in a class will attempt future interaction with the teacher or not. A child will ask a question or participate in an oral discussion in class when the consequence of such an interaction is expected to be positive in terms of the child's need satisfaction. When the consequence of an interaction is expected to be negative the interaction will be avoided.

The teacher may use the same principle to determine the frequency of his or her interaction with a child. Who does the teacher ask more questions of in the class? Who does she smile or frown at? A teacher interacts more with a pupil when the pupil's classroom participation is rewarding to the teacher (McDonald, 1965). Some teachers persistently call on one or two pupils in their class because these are the pupils who are perceived by the teacher as being able to give the right answer. As we indicated in Chapter 5, the studies of Good and Brophy show that teacher interactions at these verbal and non-verbal levels may have profound implications for children's perceptions of their own ability and self-worth.

(c)   *The degree to which each child participates in the interaction*

The degree of each child's involvement in an interaction with the teacher will depend on the child's perception of the teacher's personality and the extent he *feels* that such interaction will enhance his self-esteem. The child's perception of the interaction situation will be influenced by his or her previous direct experience with the teacher or a generalisation from this experience. It could also be based on direct evidence, such as somebody else's judgement (for example, 'Chidi, you are in Mrs X's class? Too bad you won't like her.').

The interaction situation may be one-way as in television presentation or large assembly hall presentation as when the headteacher addresses the pupils. It can also be an open interaction in which each of the participants has equal opportunities for contributing to the learning situation. Some social psychology studies in the area of attitude change indicate that the recipient of a communication designed to change his attitudes is more likely to be influenced when he actively participates in the interactive system. Results obtained by one of the present authors in Nigeria (Ugwuegbu, 1979a and 1979b) support this conclusion.

Two other factors that may affect the extent of the pupil's participation in the classroom interaction are the teacher's leadership style and the class size. We shall discuss the effect of leadership style later; for the moment we turn our attention to class size.

The amount of pupil participation is limited in a large class. Small classes should therefore, theoretically, offer advantages over large classes, when it comes to the amount of classroom interaction. Supporting this viewpoint, Goslin (1965) notes that 'it is a longstanding educational principle that small classes with discussions are better than large classes with little or no discussion'.

However, not all educationalists would agree that it is quite as straightforward as this. For example, Blair and his associates claim that class size, in itself, is probably of less importance than other factors such as 'the type of instructional method, the grade level of pupils, and the personality of the individual teacher' (1975, p. 322). Sufficient research evidence exists to support this contention that class size should not be studied in isolation. Problems related to educational goals, curriculum, teacher leadership style, teacher experience and skills, and class procedures must be considered in determining the effects of class size on the degree of learner–teacher effective interaction.

Pupils' active participation in an interactive system serves as feedback to the teacher. It informs the teacher how well the pupils are processing the information being presented.

If a teacher is anxious to finish her syllabus she will attempt to reduce the level of pupil participation in the interaction system. On the other hand, if a teacher is concerned about learner growth she will create more opportunities for her pupils to participate in the interaction system.

(d) Degree of affective relationship

We have argued throughout the book that the teacher–pupil relationship should show some degree of what Goslin calls an 'emotional' or 'expressive' component. While no one would disagree that the primary aim of the school situation should be the imparting of skills and knowledge, it should be clear at this stage to the reader that such learning cannot take place unless the learner feels emotionally secure enough to be able to concentrate on the cognitive tasks he is required to perform. Thus school can be regarded as a place of learning where the teacher recognises the needs of the pupils and treats every child as an individual in order to facilitate his learning. To achieve this the teacher must behave as a warm, concerned and helpful adult. Can we then say that the teacher should behave as a friend to the pupil?

The question of how friendly a teacher can be with her class pupils has long been a matter of concern for educators. What point along the teacher–pupil relationship represents the best condition necessary for meeting the child's needs and educational growth?

Within the conventional classroom situation there are some constraints which tend to decrease the degree to which a teacher can also be a friend. One such constraint is that the teacher–pupil relationship is defined in terms of 'status inequality' (Goslin). The teacher occupies a higher social status and she is rarely expected to change as a function of the interaction between her and the pupils. The pupil, on the other hand, occupies a lower status than the teacher and he is expected to change in behaviour. Another constraint is the differing socio-economic status between the teacher and the pupils. Most teachers usually occupy a higher socio-economic status than their pupils. This may be particularly true in Third World countries where many of the pupils come from poor home backgrounds. A third constraint is sex differences between the teacher and his or her pupils, especially in the secondary school. Close friendship between male teachers and female pupils or that between female teachers and male pupils may generate gossip and unwarranted rumours. Fear of such gossip may prevent some teachers from engaging in the warm relationships that best promote educational growth.

One of the teacher's functions is to present her educational values in such an attractive light that the pupil finds them acceptable. This particular function can only be served if the teacher is perceived as an admired and respected figure, whose values and attitudes can serve as a model for the pupils. Some educationalists have argued that teaching is most effective when the child regards the teacher as a superior and distant figure. In our view this approach raises some problems. While we agree that the teacher and the pupils should not be equals, we wonder how superior the teacher should feel, and how distant the pupils should perceive the teacher to be, to make him or her effective.

Carl Rogers (1969), an eminent theorist in the area of emotional or expressive understanding of learners, argues that the teacher is most effective when he or she is a real person to his or her pupils. He writes (p. 106):

> ‘ When the teacher is a real person, being what he is, entering into a real relationship with the learner without presenting a front or a facade, he is much more likely to be effective ... It means that he comes into a direct personal encounter with the learner, meeting him on a person-to-person basis. It means that he is being himself not denying himself ... Seen from this point of view it is suggested that the teacher can be a real person in his relationship with his students. He can be enthusiastic, he can be bored, he can be interested in students, he can be angry, he can be sensitive and sympathetic. ’

If the teacher's responsibility is to educate, he cannot be effective unless he is trustworthy. Children can only imitate and identify with the values of a teacher they can trust, a teacher who can understand their needs and one who is real to them; not a person who is a faceless and distant superior.

(2) The Teacher's Leadership Style

Consider a visit to a neighbouring primary school. As you visit the classes you may notice a considerable number of differences between the ways the teachers go about their classroom management. In one class you may notice that the children are seated 'properly', with folded arms on their desks. They have no books or other school materials on the desk. The teacher has firm control over the class. She dominates the learning activities. She sets the goals and the means of accomplishing them. The general atmosphere in this class is very tense and the pupils are denied opportunities for interaction. In another class you may notice that the learning is less rigidly organised. Children are busy with different learning materials. They interact freely with each other and with the teacher in their goal-oriented activities. The atmosphere in the second class you visit is quite relaxed.

The differences noticed in the classrooms you visit may be due, partly, to the type of leadership provided by the teachers. The kind of leadership role the teacher assumes has significant impact on the learning situation in the classroom. The school characteristics also affect classroom leadership. The larger the school, the greater the likelihood of there being a number of leaders (Krech, Crutchfield and Ballachey, 1962). Like any other organisations the school leadership is, however, arranged in a hierarchy with the principal, or headteacher, as the leader of leaders.

In this section we shall consider the kind of leadership role that teachers may take in the classroom.

What is Leadership?

Psychologists are not agreed on the precise meaning of leadership. One early definition of the leader is the *individual in a given office*. This definition covers the president of a country, a principal of a school, or the chairman of a company. Worchel and Cooper (1976) say: 'While this definition is empirical and can easily be applied to groups where definite offices exist, it has a serious drawback because many groups lack a clearly defined position or office of leader.' A good example of leaders without defined position or office can be cited from the early activities of nationalistic leaders in Third World countries like Dr Nnamdi Azikiwe of Nigeria, Julius Nyerere of Tanzania, Osagyefo Dr Kwame Nkrumah of Ghana and Mahatma Gandhi in India. These leaders had far greater powers as leaders than that which derived from whatever office they held in the early days of struggle for independence.

The definition that has enjoyed more acceptance in social psychology is that which identifies leaders as individuals who 'influence the activities of the group' (Fiedler, 1971). A teacher may thus be regarded as a leader because he or she has the *power effectively to influence the behaviour of others*. The teacher can motivate and direct

children's activities in a desired channel. Children follow the teacher's direction, identify with her and use her as a model.

A third approach to the definition of leadership has been suggested by the University of Ohio Leadership Studies Group. Their approach has been to describe leadership on the basis of the individual's behaviour, functions, or goals. The Ohio group identified two important dimensions of leader behaviour – *initiating structure* and *consideration*. Initiating structure refers to leadership behaviour which is oriented towards goal attainment, while consideration refers to leadership behaviour that emphasises group maintenance.

In the classroom situation, if a teacher leans towards the 'initiating structure' aspect of leadership, she will tend to emphasise task-related behaviour; that is, she will focus her attention mostly on the learning tasks of the school. Conversely, a teacher who inclines towards 'consideration' will focus not so much on the learning tasks as on satisfying her pupils' emotional and social needs. Most teachers will, of course, use both dimensions of leadership behaviour.

In addition, of course, most teachers will vary their type of leadership behaviour from class to class and from school to school. For example, younger children on the whole seek more emotional fulfilment from their teacher than older children do. Thus a particular teacher may incline towards the 'consideration' aspects of leadership with a class of 6-year-olds who are in their first year of school, but may incline towards the 'initiating structure' aspects of leadership if she is preparing a class of 12-year-olds for a secondary school entrance examination. Similarly, if a teacher is teaching in a school where teacher–pupil relationships are good, she may be able to emphasise mainly the 'consideration' aspects of leadership. But should she leave that school, and enter another where teacher–pupil relationships are poor and where pupils continually challenge her, she may find it necessary to change her leadership style and, presenting what Cortis (1977) calls a 'strong' image, emphasise the 'initiating structure' aspects of leadership.

Some psychologists differentiate between what has been called the 'democratic' style of leadership, what has been called the 'autocratic' style of leadership, and what has been called the *laissez-faire* style of leadership. Thus a *democratic* classroom may be described as a class where the teacher uses a warm and expressive approach in her interpersonal relationship with the pupils; it is child-centred. In the words of McDonald (1965, p. 520), here the teacher uses 'a large degree of permissiveness in the teacher–pupil relationship'. She shares planning and decision-making in the class with the pupils, who are encouraged as individuals and as groups to participate in learning activities. The teacher praises and criticises objectively. In contrast, an *autocratic* classroom may be described as teacher-centred. The teacher uses an extremely directive approach in her interpersonal relations with the pupils. She expects complete conformity to all rules which she achieves by relying on the use of punishment, often relying a lot on corporal punishment. A third leadership style is the *laissez-faire* style. A classroom is dominant in *laissez-faire* leadership style if it is marked by lack of clear goal orientation and if the teacher–pupil interpersonal relationship is guided by the teacher's belief that children should be left alone.

How does a teacher's use of the democratic, autocratic or *laissez-faire* leadership style affect the learning behaviour of children? An early attempt to answer this question was made by Lewin, Lippitt and White (1939). They observed four comparable groups of 10-year-old boys under democratic, autocratic and *laissez-faire* adult leaders. The experimental leaders were trained to respond to the children in one of these styles:

(*a*) as an *autocratic* leader, who determined the policy of the group, dictated all the steps and techniques for attaining the group goals, assigned tasks and task partners and remained aloof from the group;

(*b*) as a *democratic* leader, who allowed the group to determine policy, offered suggestions as to procedures and tasks, allowed members to choose their own tasks and task partners, was objective in praise and criticism and participated in the group tasks;

(*c*) as a *laissez-faire* leader, who allowed the group complete freedom and did not participate in the group activities.

The group task was to engage in hobbies such as making masks for theatre or building objects. The experimenters also kept a detailed record of the behaviour of the boys under each kind of leadership during the study.

The results of the study showed marked differences as a function of the type of leader under which the boys worked. As measured by the amount of completed work, the level of identification with the group, group morale and 'we feeling', and friendly interpersonal relations with the leader, the democratic type of leadership was superior to either the autocratic or *laissez-faire*. The boys under autocratic leadership expressed more hostility and aggression than children in other groups. The subjects also evidenced unwillingness to continue with the project under an autocratic leadership but not under a democratic one. Under autocratic leadership, reactions like externalisation of frustration (for example, attacking some innocent weaker group members, whom they felt were responsible for their frustration) were exhibited by the boys.

This particular study has received a great deal of attention in the psychological literature and has been generalised to support the contention that 'democratic' leadership is always the most successful form of classroom leadership. As we have tried to indicate, and as more sophisticated studies show (Fiedler, 1971), this is an oversimplification because different situations demand different leadership styles. The Lewin experiment was, after all, concerned only with after-school activities; perhaps the very same boys would have worked more effectively under an autocratic leader, if they were in a specially accelerated mathematics class who were working towards a particular difficult examination. Further, the boys came from homes where a democratic style of leadership was likely to fit in with their past experience with adults. Had they come from homes where 'strong' leadership was supplied by adults, they might have found the 'democratic' regime confusing. Finally, as Cortis notes (1977, p. 90):

> it is amazing that so much precept for practice has been built on a small-scale study in which boys were the only group participants. Girls' attitudes would almost certainly have been somewhat different then (in the 1930s) and certainly now, and perhaps mixed groups (boys and girls) – the normal unit of society – different again.

It is clearly a mistake to generalise this study to all classrooms in all societies. As should be obvious, leadership style in classrooms must take into account the expectations of pupils. Of course, most teachers prefer to work with rather than against children, and most of us find it easier to persuade rather than threaten or force. Nevertheless, there are times, perhaps when pupils are younger rather than older, when they are feeling insecure or when they hold firm expectations that teachers will be strong leaders, when teachers will find that a 'stronger' style of leadership will be more effective than a weak style which relies on indirect rather than direct influence.

Nevertheless, using a strong style of leadership, that is, being directive, does not imply that the teacher should also be completely autocratic. A teacher can be warm and understanding even when she is being directive and using a strong leadership style. Even if she does feel that her class need and expect a firm and controlling teacher, she can avoid the excesses of what Stones (1969) calls the authoritarian teacher who controls her class mainly through the threat of punishment.

Stones maintains that an extreme case of the authoritarian (autocratic) teacher is the one who relies on corporal punishment. Almost all primary school and a majority of secondary school teachers in many Third World countries employ some form of corporal punishment as an ultimate sanction. In many of these countries the adage, 'spare the rod and spoil the child' is still an accepted unwritten basic principle of education for many parents and teachers. Barrington Kaye (1962) describes some instances where teachers rely on this form of punishment in his study of Ghanaian primary schools. He writes: 'Formerly, the relations between a teacher and his pupils were dominated by fear on the part of the latter ... It is therefore common for parents to send their children to school to be punished by the teachers or to use the teacher's name as a threat to stop the children from misbehaving' (p. 185). The general belief was that punishment was required to 'discipline' the children. We shall return to this subject in the next chapter, when we discuss the effect on the school of parental and community values. Here, we would reiterate the statement that we have made before that, on the whole, high levels of corporal punishment tend to be associated with less positive educational outcomes.

In general, punitive approaches, that is, approaches in which teachers motivate children by fear rather than by more positive incentives, tend to have less than satisfactory long-term effects. This is clearly illustrated in a study by Kounin and Gump

(1961). In this study Kounin and Gump selected 174 first-grade primary school children who were pupils of six teachers drawn from three schools. Half of the teachers were classified as non-punitive while the other half were classified as punitive. Each of the children was interviewed privately about what he thought was 'the worst thing to do in school', and why he thought these misdeeds were bad. The children's responses showed that, compared with children who have non-punitive teachers, children who have punitive teachers 'manifest more aggression in their misconducts, are more unsettled and conflicted about misconduct in school, are less concerned with learning and school-unique values, and show ... ... indications of reduction in rationality pertaining to school misconduct'. In other words, children who have punitive teachers tend to develop unsatisfactory emotional adjustment to school and to life in general.

What can we learn from Leadership Studies?

Psychologists seem agreed that the following conclusions from leadership studies apply cross-culturally.

(a) Some patterns of teacher behaviour, such as the extreme form of autocratic (authoritarian) control of others' behaviour, have the same negative effects wherever they are applied.

(b) Autocratic teacher behaviour is less likely to be accepted by pupils than other teacher behaviour and generates negative attitudes towards learning.

(c) Autocratic leadership style relies on corporal punishment or its threats for maintenance of the regime.

(d) Autocratic control cuts off the communication of pupils with each other and isolates the timid child from the group, thus creating tension, irritability and aggression among pupils (Blair et al., 1975).

(e) Democratic patterns of teacher control may not always be accepted but are less likely to be rejected than extreme forms of autocratic control.

(f) The effectiveness of democratic leadership style depends on the children's previous backgrounds. Children who are not accustomed to democratic leadership practices may find such practices difficult to adjust to at first.

(g) Reward rather than punishment, example

rather than force, and stimulation rather than repetitive drilling are teacher behaviour patterns that are preferred by children in most cultures. This is because these behaviour patterns tend to fulfil children's psychological needs.

(h) Finally, while children may submit to the teacher's demands, they expect the teacher to act consistently within the pupils' expectations of desirable teacher behaviour.

(3) Classroom interactions Between Pupils

In both Chapters 5 and 8 we pointed out how important peer relationships are to young people. We also indicated that feeling rejected or isolated can lead to loss of self-esteem and, indeed,

sometimes to depression. Experienced teachers are often able to identify children and young people who are rejected or isolated by watching classroom or playground interactions. But sometimes they can learn a great deal about peer relationships within a group of children by using sociometric devices like the one we are about to describe. If the results of using such devices indicate that certain children are rejected or isolated, the teacher can then take appropriate action to try and make the children concerned more popular with their peers.

In collecting information for what is called sociometric analysis, the teacher must make it very clear to the pupils that what she is asking them to tell her will be treated with great confidentiality and that any information they give her will in no way reflect against them. She then proceeds as follows:

(a) She attempts to get information from the

Names	AUD	BEN	CHIDE	DEREK	EZE	FELIX	GAB	HELEN	IGE	JIM	KIM	MABEL
AUD		X		X								
BEN				X		X						
CHIDE		X							X			
DEREK		X				X						
EZE				X				X				
FELIX		X		X								
GAB				X					X			
HELEN						X	X					
IGE		X				X						
JIM					X			X				
KIM				X						X		
MABEL												
TOTAL	0	5	0	6	1	4	1	2	2	1	0	0

Table 9.1 *Sociometric chart of responses of children requested to list two classmates they would prefer to sit next to them*

children on an individual basis concerning their preferred peers. A simple example is to ask the child privately to list the people he likes best in his class. Many variations of this kind of question can be put to children, either individually or, provided they can be assured of recording their responses without others seeing them, in the class situation.

For example, the teacher can ask the children to 'list the person you would like to invite to your birthday party'; 'list the person you would like to sit next to in class'; 'with whom in the class would you like to study arithmetic?'; 'whom do you prefer as the class games master?'. The children may be requested to make a single choice or two or three choices. The teacher obtains different kinds of information about the pupils' preferences from these differently focused questions.

For purposes of illustration, suppose we asked twelve children to choose 'whom you would like to sit next to in class'. Each child is allowed two choices.

(b) As a second step, the teacher charts the answers she receives on a specially constructed table. You can see how this is done if you look at Table 9.1, where we have charted the answers children gave in our example of this technique. As you will see, the children's names are listed both down the side of the tables and across the top. The 'total' line allows you to get a quick estimate of popular children. In our case Derek, who obtains the most nominations, is the most popular student.

(c) Thirdly the teacher transfers the information from her table to a 'sociogram'. We have done this in Figure 9.2. If you look at this figure you will see that a sociogram allows you to see how the cliques in the class are distributed.

In our example you will note that we have represented each child by a circle, and indicated

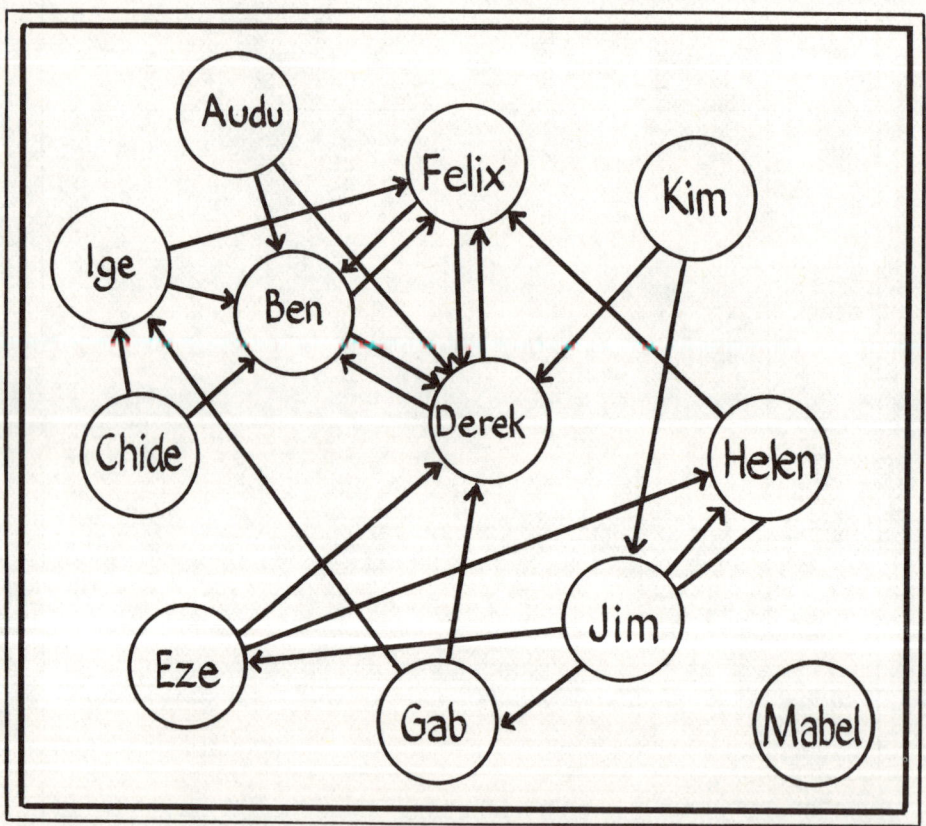

Figure 9.2 The Sociogram shows the popularity of each of the twelve pupils in a class among class-mates regarding sitting preferences (Illustrated by B. Allen-Taylor)

choices by means of arrows pointing from the child who made the choice to the child he preferred.

In our sociogram Derek, Ben and Felix are the most popular in the class. These children are designated the *stars*. Arrows pointing both to and from them show that their attraction to each other as friends is reciprocated. They also form a clique. The single arrows from Eze, Gab, Kim and Audu to Derek indicate that these children desire friendship and more interactions with Derek but their preferences are not reciprocated by Derek. Chide and Audu aspire to friendship with other members of the class but no child in the class would like to sit with them since none of the other children chose them. We could regard them as *isolates* on the basis of the question we asked. Sometimes a *true isolate* is neither chosen by anyone nor does he choose anybody. In our sociogram Mabel is a 'true isolate'.

(*d*) Finally, the teacher should ask herself how valid and significant the pupils' expressed preferences are. Frandsen (1967) suggests that the teacher should compare the pupils' preferences with other information available to her. Such information includes the teacher's classroom observations, interviews and other procedures. If these sources support the children's responses, then the teacher will know that her sociogram is valid, and if a particular child is the class isolate the teacher will be alerted to the need to provide special help to remove the causes of rejection.

Further information about the patterns of liking and disliking is provided to the teacher by the overall distribution of the children's choices. For example, Schmuck (1963) argues that a classroom peer-group that expresses comparatively widely distributed friendship choices will be characterised by a greater 'we feeling' than those marked by friendship choices that are narrowly guided by clique interest.

Modifying group interaction in the classroom
As we noted in discussing peer relationships in Chapter 8, children and young people who are popular are often popular because of what we called 'status aggregation'; that is, belonging to a particular high status category, or group of categories, contributes to popularity. The converse holds too; that is, unpopularity or rejection sometimes derives from belonging to a particular category or group of people.

Both these effects were shown in a study by one of the present authors (Ugwuegbu 1979a and 1979b). He studied Nigerian children who were in primary classes 4, 5 and 6 who ranged in age from 8 to 13 years. They were drawn from several ethnic groups. The children were exposed to several choice situations and requested to select the pupils each subject would like to (1) 'sit next to me in class', (2) 'invite to my birthday party'. The results of the study showed that ethnic sentiment influenced Nigerian primary school children's rejection or acceptance of their peers because the subjects preferred their own ethnic group peers. Secondly, the preferential choice of own ethnic group peers held for both questions that were asked. The results of Ugwuegbu's study are in agreement with a body of literature in the area of social psychology where it has been shown that dissimilarity of belief and/or ethnicity is a causal factor in social rejection and acceptance.

Another social cause of rejection in school may lie in the influence of reference group members. By 'reference group' we mean teachers, parents and ministers or other groups whose behaviour serves as a standard for the child. These reference group members (especially in a multi-ethnic society) may make derogatory remarks about other tribes (ethnic groups), thus giving the children the impression that other ethnic groups are 'strangers' who possess beliefs, values, customs and cultures as well as traits that are dissimilar to the children's. This type of reference group influence creates the type of social environment we witness in Ugwuegbu's study where preference of relationship among schoolchildren is based on tribal or racial affiliation and similarity.

Finally, socio-economic background of the children may determine whether the child will be socially accepted or rejected. Kaye (1962) cites examples in Ghana where poor men's sons are rejected as friends by rich men's sons.

If a teacher suspects that children in her class are being rejected or isolated for the reasons we have just described – because they belong to particular ethnic or socio-economic categories – what can she do?

The first step must surely be to check whether her suspicions are justified. She can do this by performing a sociometric exercise such as we have just described. Should she find that her suspicions are justified, that is, friendship cliques are based on ethnic origins, various procedures are open to her. She can, for example, try to encourage an open *discussion* of prejudices and stereotypes. In doing this she should show how inappropriate it is to make judgements about others based only on their membership of a particular group.

Regrouping, so that members of particular ethnic groups do not always work together, can be another way of helping to destroy such barriers. In doing this the teacher should not act randomly but should try to place children near those for whom they have shown some preference, even though they are of different ethnic groups. She can also use work-groups for this purpose, distributing children amongst groups who have need of their particular skills. For example, she can place a good draughtsman in a group which is not particularly skilled artistically.

Another method of breaking down such barriers is to engage the whole class in a group effort to meet some collective goal that requires that all class members be involved. (This kind of goal is commonly called a *superordinate* goal.) You may remember the Chinese students whom we described earlier in this chapter, who gave up their leisure-time to coach their classmates. Their superordinate goal, for which they were prepared to make individual sacrifices, was that no member of the group should fail.

A headteacher can use this concept of a superordinate goal to try and break up ethnic groupings. He could, for example, arrange for classes to compete against each other. For example, in a village school he can provide a trophy for the class who kept their classroom and section of the school compound neatest. In striving to get the prize, different ethnic groups in each class will be forced to work together and, in this way, barriers between such groups may be broken down gradually.

It can be seen that teachers can explore group interactions in the class by means of sociometric techniques, like the one we have just described; and that, further, members of school staffs can take active measures to restructure such group interactions if they consider such measures are necessary. Three of the ways this can be done are by discussion, by regrouping and by providing superordinate goals.

The Organisation of the School

In the previous section we examined the teacher–pupil and group relationship in the classroom. In the present section we are concerned with how the organisation of the school influences (1) the relationship between teachers in the school and (2) the relations between the teacher and the principal or headteacher.

(1)   *Relations among teachers*

In an earlier section of this chapter we said that the teacher is a leader. The teacher is also a member of a bureaucratic organisation in which the administrative officers like the headteacher expect the teacher to behave in a certain way and to perform specified duties in conformity with set rules, regulations and expectations. She is to adhere to the teaching methods, syllabus to be covered, disciplinary and administrative procedures. The students, too, expect certain role behaviour from the teacher. In addition, as we discuss in the next chapter, the community has its own expectations of what the teacher's role in the school should be.

The teacher, on the other hand, also holds certain expectations about her job. Not only does she expect to play the role of teacher but she also expects her work environment to meet some of her own psychological needs. Like anyone else holding down a job, she will, regardless of her professional level or seniority, expect the job to be rewarding, not only in the financial sense but also in the area of her own psychological well-being.

Some of her personal satisfactions will come from what happens in the classroom, if her pupils show educational progress and if they respond positively to her as an individual. But she will also expect her interactions with other members of the school staff, and in particular her interactions with her fellow teachers, to be personally satisfying. If she does not relate well to her peers this is bound to be reflected in the classroom. As Blair and his colleagues note, if favourable relationships are not maintained amongst teachers the pupils will suffer both directly and indirectly.

Ideally, then, teachers should experience little interpersonal conflict at work for the sake of their pupils and also, of course, for the sake of their own psychological well-being. In practice, as all teachers will know, such an idyllic state of affairs occurs all too seldom. Three areas in particular may provoke such interpersonal problems.

(*a*) To begin with, teachers may experience feelings of hostility which spring from jealousy about the progress other teachers are making in their careers. Thus sometimes interpersonal relationships between teachers may be affected by the manner in which promotion is decided. For example, in some cases, headteachers may promote those teachers whom they consider are doing a good job; while in other cases headteachers may promote using seniority as the basis. Whichever procedure a headteacher adopts, she should make her rationale clear to her staff, otherwise there is likely to be very bad feeling amongst her staff members.

(b) Secondly, teachers may sometimes hold very different sets of assumptions about what the teaching role involves. Some teachers may believe that, ideally, all teachers should aim at a leadership style which emphasises what we called the 'consideration' dimension; that is, they may believe that the teacher's primary aim and objective should be to educate the 'whole' child and that this education should cover all aspects of the child's life – moral, emotional and social, as well as intellectual. On the other hand, another set of teachers may be more inclined to lay stress on what we called the 'initiating structure' aspects of the teacher's role. For them, particularly if they are subject specialists, the major component of their vocation is imparting knowledge of their own intellectual discipline or disciplines.

Then organisation of a school can be structured in such a way as to cater for these two differing sets of assumptions. Teachers who are 'consideration'-oriented can be channelled into the roles of class teachers, tutors or specialists in the areas of counselling and guidance, while teachers who incline to the other set of assumptions may be channelled into more examination-oriented teaching of their particular specialities. But if this source of conflict is not catered for in the organisation of the school, interpersonal relationships are bound to suffer.

(c) Finally, interpersonal conflicts may sometimes occur in a school if a teacher is faced with two sets of expectations that differ. For example, a teacher fresh from college may be sent to a school where the headteacher tells her that she is required to prepare lesson notes and give children homework every night and mark this homework daily. The teachers in the school, on the other hand, may indicate to the new teacher that none of them complies with these demands. Here we have two differing sets of expectations, one held by the formal organisation and the other held by the informal organisation of the school, concerning how the teacher should conduct herself. If the new teacher conforms to the expectations of the other teachers she may affect her relationship with the headteacher in a negative manner. On the other hand, if she conforms to the formal organisational expectations she may be headed for animosity and hostility from the rest of the teachers.

Educational psychologists and sociologists in Third World countries have not paid much attention to role conflicts among teachers and most of the research in these areas comes from the USA and Britain. For example, Getzels and Guba (1955) studied differences in teachers' reactions to role conflicts. The results of the study show that male teachers felt more conflict than female teachers. More role conflict was also felt by teachers with more than one dependent. Getzels and Guba explain their results in terms of conflicting role expectations and the realities of the teaching profession. This explanation holds, that while teaching is a respected profession in the community, it is a profession that is not well paid. Males rather than females, and those with many dependents, are most likely to suffer from this financial handicap. But if, in order to compensate, a teacher were to take additional work to make extra money, this behaviour would come into conflict with community expectations of teacher behaviour.

In conclusion, because interpersonal relations are so complex, there can be no rule-of-thumb for preventing conflict between teachers. This conflict may be minimised, however, by improving teacher–teacher communication and teacher–headteacher communication.

Improving Teacher–Teacher Interaction. We should like to offer some suggestions for improving interpersonal interaction among teachers.

(a) The school should endeavour to engender a feeling of *esprit-de-corps* among the members of staff. Members should generously share work materials.

(b) Teachers should be encouraged to maintain open communication channels. Teachers should often discuss the problems of their pupils both formally and informally, with a view to eliciting suggestions that will lead to problem solution. In addition, teachers should be frank about what they are doing in their classes.

(c) The staff should work together:
  (i) to improve or revise the syllabus or school curriculum;
  (ii) to monitor assignments so as to prevent too much homework being given. If teachers are aware when each teacher is likely to assign some

homework to a class, a reasonable distribution of homework will result;

(iii) in marking examination papers, preparing report cards and discussing the activities and behaviour of their pupils.

(d) Regular staff meetings should be held. Ideally, these should be of two kinds. First, there is clearly a need for regular, comparatively formal discussions of the performance of the pupils. Secondly, and perhaps in a more informal atmosphere, discussion of teachers' underlying values about, and attitudes towards, their vocation and educational issues in general should be encouraged. In this way, teachers who hold different sets of assumptions about their roles as teachers can share their ideas with others and attempt to understand why some of their other colleagues hold differing viewpoints.

(e) Teachers should be encouraged to work together in a continuing effort to promote their own educational progress. Teacher education should not cease once teachers have gained their diplomas or certificates. Instead, teachers should aim to keep abreast of new directions in education and this is often best achieved in a group setting. Thus inservice workshops, training programmes and conferences should be held whenever possible and, ideally, teachers from the same school should attend in groups so that the shared nature of the educational process is emphasised. Similarly, school libraries should provide books, magazines and journals that are aimed at the teachers as well as those that are meant for the pupils.

(2) Teacher–headteacher relationships

Just as the teacher plays the role of leader in the classroom, so does the headteacher play a leadership role in the organisation and administration of the school.

Research in educational psychology shows that the type of leadership quality exhibited by the headteacher has important implications for the rank-and-file members of staff. The headteacher affects other teachers' morale, effectiveness and professional growth through his or her leadership behaviour. This in turn influences the classroom behaviour of teachers.

Getzels and Guba carried out a study of the leadership patterns of the head of schools. In doing this they identified three kinds of leadership (Cortis, 1977):

(a) The leader who is keen to stress the institution's rather than the staff's requirements. Thus such a leader will tend to judge staff on how well they keep to fixed rules and procedures. Using the term we introduced in our discussion on the teacher as a leader, he will tend to place his emphasis on 'initiating structure'.

(b) The leader who tends to emphasise the individual needs of staff rather than the rules of the institution. Such a leader will tend to focus a great deal of his attention on interpersonal relations with the staff, and will tend to be more inclined to the 'consideration' dimension of leadership.

(c) The leader who may be regarded as intermediate between the other two types of leaders. Such a leader is often called a 'transactional' leader. He tries to cater for both institutional and interpersonal requirements in his leadership style.

Getzels and Guba, working in the USA, concluded that the third leadership style was the most effective. Similarly, Ohikhena and Anam (1974), who surveyed 182 teachers in south-eastern Nigeria, came to the conclusion that for Nigerian conditions as well a transactional style of leadership was the most dominant style. They write (p. 95):

> The fact that transactional leadership has been identified in this study is an indication that in the South-Eastern State this type of leadership is likely to have more favourable consequences on teachers' effectiveness and school climate. This, in fact, has been borne out already by a more detailed study recently carried out by Anam. In it the researcher showed that the preference for transactional leadership by teachers has a significant influence on teachers' morale.

We pointed out earlier that the same teacher may adopt different leadership styles on different occasions, depending on situational factors. The same may be said of headteachers. In some schools, which have a more academically inclined pupil population (Imogene, 1979), organisational and administrative problems may be less dominant than they are in other schools, so that it may be easier for a headteacher to adopt a more transactional approach. The same headteacher in a school with massive administrative problems may favour a more 'initiating structure' leadership style.

Another important factor in headteacher–teacher interaction is the expectation of the headteacher about the role teachers should play. As we noted before, the classroom teacher is caught up in a web of expectations, which include pupils' expectations of the teacher's role behaviour, the headteacher's expectations and the community's expectations. The headteacher, too, is caught up in a complex role of expectations within the school system. He needs, for example, to satisfy the expectations of the school manager or the state or local government board who hired him. The teachers also expect him to behave in a certain way in the process of discharging his day-to-day responsibilities. Often these expectations are contradictory, hence the headteacher's problem. For example, while the manager or board of education may stress *initiating structure* as the administrative behaviour that is expected from a headteacher or a principal, staff members may tend to stress *consideration*. The headteacher is thus placed in a dilemma. Is he to adhere to superordinate or subordinate expectations?

Sometimes the headteacher may experience problems because he holds certain expectations about the teacher's role which the teachers on his staff do not share. For example, the headteacher may expect members of the staff to control their pupils without sending offending pupils to him to be disciplined. On the other hand, younger staff members in particular may expect the headteacher to deal with those pupils who give them problems. In general, the teacher's perception of the headteacher's expectations regarding the teacher's role will be bound to affect interpersonal relationships within the school. This may be particularly important in the area of parent–school relationships. If the headteacher supports the teacher's classroom authority when there are parental objections to the teacher's behaviour, the teacher will be in a better position to fulfil her obligations to the class. But if the headteacher does not support the teacher's authority, the teacher will tend to 'absorb conflict in the classroom' and thus may be more likely to adopt an autocratic leadership style (Gordon, 1957). This in turn will generate hostility between the teacher and the pupils, and the teacher and the headteacher.

Perception of the roles of teachers and headteachers varies from school to school, from person to person and from time to time. To reduce variability in perceived role expectations in any school system

the headteacher should endeavour to make his role expectations as clear as possible to his teachers. Bidwell (1955) suggests that if the role expectations are relatively clearly *communicated* and *known* by the teachers, there is greater satisfaction among them.

Finally we indicated that the teacher–headteacher interpersonal relationship is influenced by other variables such as transfer and promotion within the organisation. A headteacher ought to adopt a consistent pattern of behaviour in his recommendation of teachers for promotion as well as for assignment of teachers to classes or subjects.

Improving Teacher–Headteacher Relations. If a teacher discovers that his professional relationship with the headteacher is very unhealthy, what should he do? If he stays on in that school he will experience tensions and frustrations. The best thing may be for the teacher to seek transfer to another school. If this fails the teacher may leave teaching altogether if he finds an equally rewarding profession. If the probability of securing another equally rewarding job is low, the teacher will stay on, a frustrated, tense and ineffective teacher, unless the headteacher and the teacher take steps to improve on their relationship. How can they do this?

Myers and his colleagues (1975) suggest three different ways in which a teacher and the headteacher can actively improve their professional relations (pp. 587–8).

One way is to understand the causes of the difficulties by analysing them objectively. Naturally when difficulties in interpersonal relations arise the trouble is usually blamed on somebody else. The headteacher will select one or two teachers and blame them for the school's poor performance at the previous year's results. The teachers, on the other hand, will blame the headteacher's leadership style or his lack of organisation for such poor performance. A sounder approach by those involved in the conflict is to examine their own contribution to the problem. This *self-examination* provides insight essential for the initiation of communication necessary for resolution of the conflict.

A second strategy for improved relationship is that the teacher should be more active and become more involved in the activities of the school. Such *involvement* will bring the teacher into more working contact with the headteacher. Increased contact will increase liking as the teacher discovers that it is possible to work with the headteacher. The headteacher will also discover that the teacher is willing to contribute to the general objectives of the school and may therefore begin to appreciate the teacher's contributions.

Finally, the headteacher and the teacher should develop attitudes of 'mutual respect, co-operation and trust'. The teacher should feel able to discuss her weaknesses with the headteacher. Such trust must be reciprocated by the headteacher who should treat such matters discussed with him confidentially. If the teacher's perception of the relationship is that the headteacher is prepared to help her grow professionally, and the headteacher's perception is that the teacher is contributing to the objectives of the school by her behaviour, interpersonal relationship between the teacher and the headteacher will improve.

Summary

(1) In this chapter we turned our attention to various characteristics of the school which contribute to its operation and effectiveness as an institution.
(2) We considered certain behavioural dimensions of teacher–pupil interaction in the classroom.
  (a) We showed that seating pupils according to the results of tests may overemphasise the competitive aspects of schooling.
  (b) We indicated that positive interaction between the teacher and the pupil is more likely to occur if it is rewarding to both parties.
  (c) We showed that the frequency of such interaction does not only depend on staff-pupil ratios.
  (d) We argued that the teacher functions best when she displays some warmth to her pupils.
(3) We agreed that the teacher may be regarded as a leader because she has the power to influence others (her pupils). We discussed leadership styles at some length and concluded that situational factors may affect the leadership style a teacher adopts.
(4) We introduced the concept of sociometry and showed how it can be used to indicate group interaction in a classroom.
(5) We discussed the problems that may arise when group interactions in the classroom are based on the ethnic origin of the pupils and showed that such interactions can be modified by discussion, by regrouping and by imposing superordinate goals.
(6) We discussed interpersonal interactions between teachers, and showed how role conflicts may sometimes cause difficulties in these interactions. Following this we made some recommendations for reducing such conflicts.
(7) Finally we discussed teacher–headteacher relationships, focusing on the headteacher's leadership style and conflicts in the perception of roles. We concluded by making recommendations for reducing interpersonal conflicts in this relationship.

Chapter 9: Selected Bibliography

The social system of the classroom
Blair, M. G., Jones, R. S., and Simpson, R., *Educational Psychology*, 4th edn (New York: Macmillan, 1975).

The organisation of the school
Cortis, G., *The Social Context of Teaching* (London: Open Books, 1977).

THE SCHOOL AND ITS SOCIAL SETTING

10

Introduction

If we work as teachers or educationalists within an educational system that is largely based on formal schools, colleges and universities, then the word 'education' usually conjures up for us the whole apparatus of our own academic background – specially constructed buildings, classrooms, laboratories and lecture halls. But as we have tried to point out throughout this book, 'education' has a much broader meaning. Discussing education as it is practised, or was practised, in different cultures throughout the world, Majasan writes (1976, p. 132):

> Education is a universal process occurring in all human societies involving the interaction of the members and lasting for a lifetime. It is the process by which any society passes on its culture, that is, the aggregate of the social, ethical, intellectual and artistic attainments of the group by which it can be differentiated from any other group. It therefore goes on formally and informally and has deep roots in the environment in which it takes place.

All societies have had an educational system, whether it was formal or informal, which conserved and transmitted its own cultural heritage, and, as history reveals, such educational systems often became modified and adapted when two cultures came in contact with each other. In particular, within the last century and a half, the Western educational system has had a strong impact on many other educational systems. Sometimes this occurred because the members of that culture explicitly decided to remodel their own indigenous system. Thus in Japan, where traditional and Confucian schools had existed for many centuries, the second part of the eighteenth century saw a determined attempt on the part of the Meiji government to reorganise the schooling systems along a Western model (Kobayashi, 1976).

In India and Pakistan, on the other hand, education was affected by the Western model, not as in Japan because of a decision emanating from the local population, but rather because, in the early part of the nineteenth century, the British government decided to take over control of the 'widespread, popular, indigenous system' (Keay and Karve, 1964, p. 141). We can see the colonial attitude that such an indigenous system was inferior to the British one in the complaint made by Adams in the 1830s that the indigenous system neglected moral instruction and utilised 'unsuitable' textbooks. In this case, the British considered the textbooks to be unsuitable because, based as they were on the religious books of the Hindus, they dealt with the love of the god Krishna for his mistress Rādhā (Keay and Karve, 1964, p. 153).

There is no doubt that the Western system of schooling has, in many cases, replaced valuable indigenous educational systems in an insensitive manner. As Beeby noted in 1966, there is no difficulty 'in finding in Africa and Asia, scores of examples of curricula and educational objectives more suited to England and France half a century ago than to the crying needs of an emergent tropical country today' (quoted in Majasan, 1976, pp. 140–1).

This lack of sensitivity to the local indigenous system was particularly obvious in countries like Uganda where, as Castle notes, 'One of the saddest mistakes of early missionaries was their assumption that they brought education to an entirely uneducated people' (Castle, 1966, p. 39).

The arrogance of this assumption has already been demonstrated in this book when we looked at the way children grew up within cultures like the Kikuyu culture in Kenya. To remind the reader of the close interaction between cultural values and the practices of child-rearing in such societies, we turn again to Kenyatta, who wrote (as quoted by Castle, 1966):

' The first and most obvious principle of educational value which we see in the Gikuyu system of education is that the instruction is always applied to an individual concrete situation; behaviour is taught in relation to some particular person. Whereas in Europe and America schools provide courses in moral instruction or citizenship, the African is taught how to behave to father or mother, grandparents and to other members of the kinship group, paternal and maternal. Whereas European schools in Africa provide training in nature study, woodwork, animal husbandry etc., much of which is taught by general class instruction, the tribal method is to teach the names of particular plants, the use of different trees, or the management of a particular herd of sheep and goats or cattle. After this the child is left free to develop his own initiative by experiments and through trial and error to acquire proficiency. '

Because this book presents primarily a psychological, rather than a sociological, view of child development and education, we feel that an extended discussion of such cultural differences in the perception of educational functions, objectives and goals is not appropriate. Nevertheless we should like to emphasise that, while our discussion of schools has up to now been based on the Western approach to education, this does not mean that we are unaware of, or insensitive to, the conflict that exists in many Third World countries between the indigenous and traditional educational system and the formal school, college and university system.

In this chapter we touch on some areas where the conflict may be highlighted. First, we look at the influence on schools of parental and community values. Then we look at different approaches to knowledge. Following this we look at the use of the mother tongue in schools and the advantages and disadvantages of using it as the primary teaching language. Finally, we turn our attention, very briefly, to different national approaches to the function of education in Third World countries (see Figure 10.1).

Parental and Community Values and the School

Throughout this book we have suggested that children are active participants in school. Right from their first day at school they attempt to merge their impressions of school into their understanding of the world around them and their own place in that world. This process will be easier for those pupils whose parents hold attitudes to, and opinions about, school that are similar to those held by the majority of teachers in the school. If there is such a coincidence of values and opinions, then parents will be able to prepare children effectively for their role as pupils. For example, a mother who has herself attended school and who considers that doing well at school is a most important aspect of her child's life will be able to stress to the child the importance of being punctual, attending regularly, doing homework conscientiously, paying attention in class and in general responding to the teacher's demands and expectations. A mother, on the other hand, who has never attended school herself may be able to offer no more detailed advice to a young school entrant than 'remember to behave yourself properly'. Thus it is not surprising to discover that many studies show that one of the most important contributors to a child's academic performance is, in fact, parental attitudes to school. For example, in a study done in Jamaica, Reid (1976) found that the best predictor of academic achievement in the sixty-seven schools he studied was parental interest in education.

Similarly, community values also affect the child's perception of school and its functions. If a child attends school in an area where there is a generally positive attitude to school and where it is thought that school serves a useful function, he will be able to integrate his school and home life relatively well. But consider a child who attends

INTRODUCTION

PARENTAL AND COMMUNITY VALUES

(i)   Towards education in general
(ii)   Towards what is taught in schools, and how
        it is taught
(iii)   Towards discipline
(iv)   Towards the characteristics of good schools
        and good teachers

DIFFERENT APPROACHES TO KNOWLEDGE

(i)   A reminder about 'disembedded' thinking
(ii)   What sort of knowledge is important?
(iii)   What kind of explanations of natural phenomena
        are accepted?
(iv)   Are explanations of natural phenomena fixed?
(v)   Are some 'cognitive styles' superior?

THE LANGUAGE MEDIUM USED IN SCHOOLS

(i)   The mother-tongue as the only medium
(ii)   The mother-tongue introduced first, and a
        second language introduced some time after
(iii)   Mother-tongue and second language introduced
(iv)   Only a second language used.   together
(v)   Children whose mother-tongue is not the same as
        the indigenous language used in school

SCHOOL IN A BROADER PERSPECTIVE

SUMMARY

Figure 10.1 Structure of Chapter 10

school in an area where school attendance, whether a statutory duty or not, is poor because the people who live in that area do not consider that schools perform an essential function. He may have some difficulty in integrating his perceptions of school and home.

A very interesting study done some time ago in Jamaica by Edward Seaga highlights some of the aspects of parental and community values about school that affect parent–teacher, and consquently teacher–child, relationships. In 1953 Seaga studied parental values with respect to an elementary school. The school was in a village which was located in the foothills bordering a sugar plantation and the village was less than thirty miles from Kingston, the capital of Jamaica. A fair proportion of the adult inhabitants of this village were illiterate (22 per cent) and the primary occupations were agricultural. In some ways, then, this village was typical of many all over the Third World, and therefore Seaga's in-depth study of parental attitudes to schools and teachers is very relevant to the subject matter of this book, although, of course, the detailed conclusions he drew properly apply only to this village, which he called 'Rural Ridge' (Seaga, 1976).

We will now look at Seaga's study in some detail, concentrating on four aspects of parent and community school interactions: parental attitudes to education in general, to what schools should teach and how they should teach it, to discipline and, finally, to the characteristics of good schools and good teachers.

(1) *Parental and community attitudes towards education in general*

As Seaga comments, the question of parent–school interaction involves the wider issue of parental attitudes towards the educational system. In Rural Ridge parents generally endorsed education but there were certain qualifications. First, they did not consider it necessary for every child to have the full scholastic training offered by the school, maintaining that this should be reserved for those who were 'mentally capable' of it and who were intending to go on to professions like nursing, teaching or postal clerkship. Secondly, they considered that apart from the function of preparing the child to enter these professions, the main function of education lay in the prestige it offered. It can be seen, then, that if a teacher entered a community where such attitudes were commonly held by parents, it would have been

very difficult for her to promote the idea that education is intrinsically valuable because it broadens the mind. It might also be difficult for her to put forward the idea, which we shall develop more fully in the next chapter, that in the early years at school it is difficult to divide pupils up into those who are 'mentally capable' of secondary education and those who are not.

This particular belief, that not all children can profit by secondary education, is found in the West as well, where sometimes parents turn a blind eye to their children's truancy because they feel that education has little to offer them once they are able to read and write. Particularly within the decaying city centres, where unemployment is high, parents often feel that unless children are at the top of their classes and likely to pass the academic examinations that will gain them entrance to university or to professional training, they will profit little from continued attendance at school. Like the parents in Seaga's study, they do not see any intrinsic benefit in learning for learning's sake. It is of course very obvious that such deep-seated conflict between teachers and certain parents regarding the utility of education will affect the children concerned. They will tend to be poorly motivated to take an active part in lessons.

Community attitudes to school and its functions are also important. The reader may perhaps remember the New Guinean study of two village communities to which we referred in the last chapter. In this study we reported that Wilson found that, in a coastal area where schooling was well established, young people who had left school were more discriminating in their perception of what education offered them than were ex-pupils who came from a remote highlands village. He noted similar differences in community attitudes. In the coastal area villagers were far more likely to ask ex-pupils for help in teaching others to read and write than they were in the more remote area, thus indicating that the coastal community placed more emphasis on school-type skills. Such community attitudes tend to be conveyed to pupils. Thus if a community, as a whole, values the functions of schooling, then pupils from that community will enter school with a more positive attitude than pupils who come from a community which does not regard schools as fulfilling valuable social functions.

In the West, too, community attitudes to education are important. For example, in Britain until very recently children from 'travelling' communities (or gypsies) attended school in a very patchy way. Partially, of course, this was due to the fact that their communities were always on the move, but another reason for the poor attendance of such children has been the traditional attitude of their community to schooling, which regarded schools as useful only for teaching children the basic skills of literacy. Once this was achieved, gypsy parents did not regard school attendance as important.

(2) Parental attitudes towards what the school should teach and how the school should teach it

In his study Seaga found that the foremost criticism the parents made of what the school taught concerned the reading textbooks. In an attempt to concentrate on West Indian culture these textbooks were based largely on the adventures of characters from Ashanti folklore. Parents objected to this subject matter on at least two grounds. First, because these tales were also used in village festivities, it was thought that they were unsuitable for the scholastic atmosphere; and, secondly, because the stories often concerned the exploits of mythical characters who were cunning, like 'Anancy', the Spider King, it was argued by parents that these stories only taught children to 'lie and thieve'. Thus one parent commented, 'dem children nowadays learning stupidness. Look what dem give dem to read – Anancy stories' (p. 241).

In other cultures, too, there is often a clash between what the school teaches and what parents consider that schools should teach. Very often parents' views about these matters are shaped by their own school experience. Thus sometimes parents protest in Britain when teachers attempt to make education relevant to later life by, for example, training their pupils in the filling out of forms. Parents often complain that this is not proper subject matter for the classroom.

Seaga found that there were certain teaching methods that were popular with parents – for example, the chanting aloud we referred to in Chapter 6. The popularity of this method with parents was based on the fact that the chorus was clearly audible all over the village. As one parent remarked, he had always considered one particular teacher to be particularly effective because 'me could stay down at de coffee pice [about one mile away] and hear him drill de pickney [the children] in dem ABC' (p. 243). If a teacher was not prepared to place so large and so loud an emphasis on rote learning, in Rural Ridge, he would be bound to

have to deal with some complaints from anxious parents.

Other studies also show that sometimes parents become dissatisfied with teaching methods in the school their children attend. However, this dissatisfaction seldom becomes great enough for parents to do more than voice their complaints in interviews at the school. It is only when teaching methods conflict very markedly with community values about the appropriate methods of teaching that open clashes between schools and parents may take place. A recent example of this occurred in a primary school in London where the headteacher and some of his staff introduced radical changes in teaching methods – for example, in one class children watched television or played table-tennis whenever they wished. In addition, 'they disrupted the school routine (not to mention the cleaners) by coming into class early, staying late, ignoring break rules and wandering all over the building at will (they took to using the staff toilets)' (Gretton and Jackson, 1976, p. 18). Parents became so anxious about the way their children were being taught that they claimed at a meeting that it was not a question of how their children were being taught but that they were not being taught at all. The conflict between the dominant teaching methods used in the school and parental values became so great that a public inquiry was held and the headteacher and some other members of his staff were removed from their positions. However, this was an exceptional case and it is probable that parental pressure was only effective because the teaching methods were changed so abruptly; and also because the school inspectors, as well as some members of the school staff, who had been at the school before the arrival of the new headteacher, agreed in broad terms with the parents' complaints.

(3) Parental and community attitudes towards discipline

The use of corporal punishment in schools is far less common in the West than it used to be. Its use is retained in very few Western countries and even in those where it is still permitted, such as Britain, some educational authorities are moving to outlaw its use. There are many reasons for this movement away from physical punishment. For example, Good and Brophy write (1977, p. 65):

> ❝ The main problem with physical punishment is that it is a direct attack upon the student, and as such it is virtually

impossible to pull off without creating anger and resentment. Furthermore, this anger and resentment usually is much stronger than any feelings of fear or contrition, so that the end result is that the physical assault does not function as punishment. That is, it does not reduce the tendency for the student to misbehave. It may give the teacher a feeling of satisfaction in seeing that students 'get what they deserve,' but this obviously is not the same as meeting the students' needs. It constitutes revenge or possibly sadism, but not punishment. '

In addition, Good and Brophy note that its use in the USA has been shown in general to be ineffective. They write that its failure is most marked in the case of 'assaultive, antisocial juvenile delinquents and criminals'. These young people typically come from homes where physical punishment has already been used a great deal to little effect and therefore its use in school is likely to be equally ineffective.

In a similar vein, we have already noted that in the study of secondary schools done in London by Rutter and his associates it was found that schools that employed high levels of corporal punishment tended to have more discipline problems.

It is certainly our own view that corporal punishment should not be used in schools, both on moral and on practical grounds. Nevertheless, we acknowledge that sometimes a young teacher is put under strong pressure to use this method of discipline, if the majority of other teachers in the school do so. In such cases, even the pupils may expect the new teacher to make use of the cane, and in fact, if its use is widespread in the school, the young teacher may even be regarded by pupils as being 'soft' if she does not use it herself as well. Thus there are often pressures within the school, usually arising from a general cultural acceptance of physical punishment, which may be so strong that they are difficult to ignore. Consequently teachers may sometimes use corporal punishment against their own wishes.

In addition, where parents and communities commonly use such punishments themselves, they often attempt to exert pressure on teachers to do the same. The popular press in Britain is full of letters arguing that the increase in vandalism and rowdiness that has occurred recently within inner city areas could be checked by 'a short, sharp shock' to the young people concerned. By the phrase 'a short, sharp shock', such writers refer to the use of corporal punishment within a very repressive setting.

Seaga, too, found that there was strong parental pressure in Rural Ridge for teachers to use corporal punishment. By corporal discipline parents specifically meant 'flogging' though other varieties of physical discipline were also used in the school like forcing the child to kneel or stand for a long time. Thus (p. 243):

M's father came to see the head teacher on one of his infrequent visits to Rural Ridge. He requested the teacher to 'give de boy more floggins for 'im too rude and don' interested enough in school work'.

Seaga continues that teachers in Rural Ridge felt that they were forced to use extensive discipline in school both because of parental pressure and because the pupils expected them to, having been prepared for this by their parents. For example, Seaga actually heard a parent tell his child: 'Wait till you get to school. Ah going mek teacher stretch you out and tear yu skin' (p. 243).

It can be seen that, potentially, parental attitudes to discipline and how it should be imposed may play an important part in school life both by direct pressure on the part of parents and also by creating expectations within pupils that such disciplinary measures are both common and effective.

(4) *Parental attitudes towards the characteristics of good schools and good teachers*
The reader may remember that parents at Rural Ridge saw education in strictly 'instrumental' terms. By instrumental we mean that they saw the school experience, not as valuable in itself – say, in the sense of broadening the child's horizons – but as valuable because schooling provided access to desirable occupations and social status. Not surprisingly, then, the school and the teacher were judged mainly by the results of the Jamaican Local Examination. 'If sufficient students are successful, it is to the glory of the teacher. If, on the other hand, too many fail, it reinforces the argument that "teacher not forcing de pickney [children] dem to learn enough, for so much of dem couldn't fail".'

In addition, parents judged teachers by the amount of time the teacher devoted to school activities outside school hours; for example, teachers were expected to conduct private classes for the Jamaican Local Examination students. Teachers were also expected to be intimately concerned in the running of the Sunday school and to take an active part in the conducting of the Sunday service at church. In other words, teachers were expected to play a certain sort of role outside the school as well as in the school. Clearly it would not do for a Rural Ridge teacher to be an unbeliever.

It is not only in small rural villages like Rural Ridge that such social expectations are brought to bear on the teacher. In many other societies teachers are expected to behave in certain fairly restricted ways outside school, as well as within the school situation. For example, recently in Britain the headmistress of a large secondary school was suspended because, although unmarried, she was expecting a baby. The father of the baby, who was also a teacher, was waiting for his divorce to come through and then the couple intended to marry. Interestingly, no action was taken against the man concerned. Thus, it can be seen that community values can extend not only to influencing what is taught in schools and how it is done, but also to helping to shape the kind of life a teacher leads.

We have used the Seaga study and other instances to illuminate the ways in which schools and teachers may have to respond to parental and community pressures. As we shall emphasise in the last section of this chapter, schools and what goes on in them must always be considered in the context of the larger community of which they can never be independent.

Different Approaches to Knowledge and the Formal Education system

(1)   *A reminder about disembedded thinking*
In different places in this book, when we have been looking at home background and cultural factors, we have argued that to succeed within a formal school system which is based on a Western model certain cognitive approaches are more helpful than others. For example, in Chapter 2 we suggested that both in the West and in other cultures children who come from homes where what Margaret Donaldson calls 'disembedded thinking' is encouraged are given a good preparation for the cognitive and learning tasks of school. By this term 'disembedded thinking' we referred to the capacity to isolate, within a tight logical system, the problems and tasks of the schoolroom. To remind the reader what

this entails, let us look at some research done by Cole and Scribner in Liberia. They were exploring the relation between culture and problem solving and set the following problem (1974, p. 163):

If Flumo or Yakpalo drinks cane juice, the Town Chief gets vexed [angry]. Flumo is not drinking cane juice. Yakpalo is drinking cane juice. Is the Town Chief vexed?

Now, within the Western tradition, a subject or pupil asked such a problem is expected to isolate the problem from any knowledge of any specific characters called either Flumo or Yakpalo, and is required to 'disembed' the problem by responding to the logical question in an abstract manner. In abstract, the subject then has to accept all the assumptions in the problem and come to the conclusion that the Town Chief would indeed be angry. But this is what the actual subject in the investigation replied: 'People do not get vexed with two persons.' The experimenter did not accept this reply as valid and repeated the question. The dialogue then proceeded as follows (p. 163):

Experimenter: (Repeats the problem).
Subject: The Town Chief was not vexed on that day.
Experimenter: The Town Chief was not vexed? What is the reason?
Subject: The reason is that he doesn't love Flumo.
Experimenter: He doesn't love Flumo? Go on with the reason.
Subject: The reason is that Flumo's drinking is a hard time. That is why when he drinks cane juice, the Town Chief gets vexed. But sometimes when Yakpalo drinks cane juice, he will not give a hard time to people. He goes to lie down to sleep. At that rate people do not get vexed with him. But people who drink and go about fighting – the Town Chief cannot love them in the town.

Now what had happened was the subject knew two characters with these particular names, and what is more, he knew how they reacted to drinking cane juice. Thus he discarded the first assumption of the problem – that people in authority get angry with everybody in the same way – and substituted for the first assumption his social knowledge that people interact in different ways with each other. (He replaced the experimenter's assumption with his own particular knowledge of how people in general react to the drinking habits of specific other individuals that they are acquainted with.) But once he had made this substitution of what he considered a valid reflection of social reality, the subject then proceeded to be absolutely logical. His reasoning ran thus:

Flumo's drinking gives people a hard time (Subject's actual knowledge of a person called Flumo)
Yakpalo's drinking does not give people a hard time (Subject's actual knowledge of a person called Yakpalo)
People do not get vexed when they are not given a hard time (Subject's knowledge of human relationships)
The Town Chief is a person (Logical inference)
Therefore the Town Chief is not vexed at Yakpalo (Second logical inference)

To us this example encapsulates and sums up a conflict in cultural assumptions. Within Western frames of cognition, when a problem is put, say, in a school situation, or by a researcher, the subject is assumed to be aware that in answering that problem he must confine himself *only* to what is given in the problem. He must not venture outside the problem set by reference to any specific knowledge he may have about what happens when that type of problem occurs in everyday life. Instead he must 'disembed' the problem.

As we noted in Chapter 2, this 'disembedded' thinking is the kind that is most applicable to subjects taught within formal education – like, for example, science, technology and mathematics. It is not, however, the kind of thinking that is typical of everyday life. Much of the time, both in the West, as Donaldson describes, and in other cultures, as noted by Cole and Scribner, a large majority of people do relate problems they encounter to their general knowledge of the social world around them rather than to a formal, logical, analytical system.

Thus conflict sometimes occurs within a formal school system, if there has not been a long-established tradition that encourages disembedded thinking within the society concerned or within a particular cultural sub-group. There are, however, other aspects of the interrelationship between the knowledge system used in formal schooling and cultural norms that can also be a potential source of conflict. In the following four sub-sections we shall look at four of these: what sort of knowledge is considered appropriate to the formal school system? what kind of explanations of natural phenomena are available within the formal school system? how fixed are cultural explanations of natural phenomena? and finally, whether certain 'cognitive' styles are more appropriate to the formal school system.

(2) *What sort of knowledge is important?*

In Western societies many older children have a great deal of knowledge covering a number of different areas that is not directly relevant to the *academic* content of their school work. Some of these areas are, for example:

(*a*) an extensive knowledge of television and radio shows
(*b*) an intensive knowledge of the personal history of celebrities like pop stars, film stars and sportsmen and women
(*c*) a detailed knowledge of pop music, often at a fairly complex level in that they can identify different movements within the pop music and disco music scene
(*d*) a sophisticated awareness of fashion in clothes, hair-styles and make-up and an astonishing ability to be aware of subtle changes in this area of life.

These are areas that form an intimate part of popular culture in societies like Britain, Western Europe and the USA. While some schools will now include reference to these areas in the more informal aspects of the curriculum, such areas seldom, if ever, form part of examinable material. Because such areas are not formally assessed for academic examinations, like those leading to university entrance, it can be argued that they are not regarded as centrally important to the academic life of formal schooling. Yet, in fact, each area we listed above has an academically acceptable analogue (see Figure 10.2).

Schools do regard as academically respectable:

(*a*) a knowledge of theatre, ballet and opera
(*b*) a knowledge of the lives of great historical figures
(*c*) a knowledge of classical music and more serious modern music
(*d*) a knowledge of fine art and fashions in graphics and design.

Theorists like Hebdige (1979) claim that this

Knowledge that can be, and often is, tested in academic assessment	Knowledge that is seldom, if ever, tested in academic assessment
 a knowledge of theatre, ballet, opera	a knowledge of television and radio shows 
 a knowledge of classical & serious modern music	a knowledge of pop music 
 a knowledge of fine art and graphics	a knowledge of fashion in clothes, hair and make-up 
 a knowledge of the lives of great historical figures	a knowledge of the lives of pop stars, film stars 

Figure 10.2 What kind of knowledge is important academically? (in this figure we are contrasting two kinds of knowledge that are characteristic of Western cultures. See pages.. 206-8)

second list is more typical of the *dominant ideology* in Western countries. By 'dominant ideology' such theorists refer to the attitudes to knowledge held by the most powerful groups of people in the society. The dominant ideology will thus be an important influence on what is taught in schools.

The concept that a dominant ideology determines, or at least influences, the type of knowledge that is taught within the formal school system has been put forward by social scientists working in Third World settings as well. They have argued that what is taught within the school systems of some non-Western countries is largely influenced by a dominant Western educational ideology, which is a remnant of the colonial experience. Thus in their book of essays entitled *The Indigenous for National Development*, a group of Nigerian social scientists contend that the education system of many Third World countries is dominated by a curriculum that is not appropriate because the Third World countries have lost

> ‘ the crucial initiative to determine freely what aspects of the new cultures being pressed on them they could meaningfully borrow and integrate into their own traditional corpus [body] of institutions, ideas and values. ’
>
> (Osoba, 1976, p. 75)

Such social scientists argue that in many Third World countries schools concentrate on knowledge that is not appropriate to the indigenous culture and emphasise instead the type of knowledge that is typical of the Western academic tradition. They point to the fact that in many developing countries that have been exposed to the Western tradition of education for some time there is often an overwhelming social problem because high schools produce thousands of graduates educated in a Western tradition but unable to find places in either higher education or employment that make use of their knowledge. For example, in Kenya, as Dore notes, 'By the early seventies the problem of secondary leaver employment was recognised to be acute' (1976, p. 68).

This leads to educationalists in countries where such problems exist arguing that the knowledge taught in their schools should be based on a realistic marriage of the indigenous knowledge system and *only* those aspects of Western knowledge that will lead to technological advances in fields like health, agriculture and communication.

Clearly not all aspects of Western education are necessarily in conflict with traditional knowledge. This was shown in a recent study done by Young in Papua New Guinea. Young (1977) conducted interviews with educated Papua New Guineans and also analysed the content of essays high school students wrote on the subject of the difference between 'village' knowledge and school knowledge.

In general, his subjects thought that traditional knowledge covered things like how to be a member of your family, and how to make things like bows and arrows. They thought that knowledge gained in the formal school situation was related to things like arithmetic, science and how people live in other countries. For example, the following was an example of a spontaneously provided distinction between what, Young claims (1977, p. 25), could be regarded as 'village' knowledge and 'school' knowledge:

Q. I want to talk about the different kinds of knowledge in Papua New Guinea ... what do you think are the different kinds of knowledge?

A. ... Well to my understanding, as for knowledge, I think ... the things that you learn from your environment where you were brought up ... things like you know ... learning to be one of the members of the family ... when you grow up you ... other members of the family ... teach you things like how to make a bow and arrow and build a house or a canoe ... some these things, but seeing that Papua New Guinea is in a sort of transitional ... let me say ... society ... as for myself, I left the village and when I came to school ... in a formal situation, I had to learn things like adding one and one makes two and somethings in sc. ... science and ... and learning about ... how other people live in other countries ... and sort of things like that ... I see these things as some kind of knowledge ...

Young found that when Western knowledge was explicitly compared with traditional knowledge many subjects mentioned the following characteristics that applied to Western rather than traditional knowledge: it allows communication with other groups; it helps understanding of members of other groups and other countries; and it enables people who gained it to be free of the constraints of locality, tradition and village life.

As a whole, Young's subjects were favourably disposed to the type of knowledge that they thought was typically taught in schools. It could be argued, however, that his subjects were part of the 'elite' of Papua New Guinea and therefore were not typical of their countrymen and women in that as comparatively highly educated people they stood to profit because such education is currently both highly regarded and well paid in Papua New Guinea.

It would seem that no matter which culture we are considering, we have to be aware that the knowledge that is taught in schools reflects the social structures of the country itself and may also reflect the influence of dominant foreign sources. There can be no unique body of knowledge that is suitable for all societies at all times. It is, however, most important that the body of knowledge that the schools in any country transmit is related to the functions that the particular society expects formal schooling to fulfil. We shall return to this subject in the final section of this chapter.

(3) What kind of explanations of natural phenomena are accepted in the school system?

As Nduka (1974) points out, despite the claims from some anthropologists that certain societies are more 'primitive' than others in their systems of thought, there are aspects of human rationality that are comparable across cultures. 'The logical categories of "true" and "false", "sense" and "nonsense" are obvious examples' (p. 154). Similarly, pre-industrial societies, just like industrial societies, have based their routines of living on principles of causation linking events.

However, the dominant type of explanations that are offered as underlying the causation of natural phenomena such as lightning, the seasons, sickness, and so on has differed from culture to culture. Over the past three or four centuries, in the *West*, the dominant explanations of such phenomena have been based on a scientific model, although within the Western world the degree to which science rather than religion provides the dominant model of causation has differed from country to country and cultural sub-group to cultural sub-group. Look, for example, at the Darwinian theory of evolution. In the nineteenth century, when it was first postulated, it was accepted by a very small minority and only within the academic setting. Even in this century, some schools in rural areas of the USA banned the teaching of a scientific approach to the creation of man and the universe,

and insisted that the biblical story of creation was taught in its stead.

Similarly, within countries where the most important religion is *Islamic* there has been an increasing tendency within the academic setting of colleges and universities to accept scientific models of the causation of natural phenomena (El-Gahr, 1971). But, as in the West, the degree to which science rather than religion provides the most commonly accepted explanation varies between countries and between types of educational institution. It also, of course, varies with respect to the subject area considered. For example, if we look at the question of sex differences in ability, in some Islamic countries this is still not considered an appropriate matter for research at all educational levels as Quiranic teaching is still very influential in areas pertaining to the place of women in society.

We notice the same general trend in *Hindu* societies as well. For example, in India science and mathematics have long been an integral part of the academic school and university curriculum, and scientific explanations of natural phenomena are widely accepted. However, a Hindu science teacher may present the scientific model of the origin of life in the academic setting, but retain a belief in reincarnation.

Looking at African societies, and at Melanesian societies, we find that acceptance of the scientific model of the causation of natural phenomena is, relatively speaking, more recent. However, there are exact parallels between religious thinking about the causation of natural phenomena in these societies and in Christian, Islamic or Hindu ones. Thus, according to Mbiti, in the case of Africans 'it is religion more than anything else, which colours their understanding of the universe and their empirical participation in that universe' (quoted by Nduka, 1974, p. 156). It is widely believed that there is an involvement of spirits in natural phenomena.

> Traditional African societies draw, with varying degrees of articulation, the ontological distinctions between man, nature and spirits or gods. Although the conception of a Supreme God or Spirit is also present in many cases, it must be remembered that traditional African religions have been polytheistic rather than monotheistic. Now in the cosmologies of the various African societies, it is widely believed that there is mutual involvement of nature and spirit. Thus a tree, a river, the sky, etc., may be

inhabited by a spirit or spirits. Similarly, a natural phenomenon, e.g. lightning, may be associated in one way or another with a god (in this case *Amadioha* among the Ibo, *Sango* among the Yoruba, etc.). It is also generally believed that gods and spirits, especially ancestral spirits, as well as other supernatural forces, directly influence everday occurrences and therefore the lives of people. Such cosmological beliefs as the foregoing provide the background for an understanding not only of traditional African religious and magical practices, including witchcraft and sorcery, but also of tra- ditional African systems of thought. '

Thus in societies with beliefs such as Nduka describes we would expect to find the same potential conflict between scientific models of causation of natural phenomena and religious explanations as we have shown exists in other cultures. We can see this illustrated, perhaps, in attitudes to sickness and ill-health. There are medical schools and hospitals in Africa of a very high standard and para-medical services are becoming more and more widespread, showing a general acceptance of the medical model of sickness. Nevertheless, there are still numbers of people, many educated within the Western tradition, who believe that ill-health may also be caused by bewitchment (Jahoda, 1970). This is because at the same time as accepting the medical model they retain a belief in the traditional religious explanation that personal misfortune may sometimes be caused by the 'anger of one's ancestral spirits consequent, for instance, upon one's failure to perform some filial duties' (Nduka, 1974, p. 157). Or they may believe that someone whom they have displeased is using witchcraft on them (Erinosho, 1978). However, we consider that such explanations should not be referred to as 'magico-mythical' (ibid.); it seems to us they are religious explanations of the same type as the Christian belief in the Creation of the World, or as the Islamic belief in the power of the prophet Mohammed, or as the Hindu belief in reincarnation.

In this sub-section we have tried to show that, in any society, there is bound to be some contradiction between scientific models of causation and the explanations offered by the indigenous religion. This contradiction becomes less marked as science and technology begin to play a larger part in national life. However, there is no ground for the commonly held stereotype that certain societies are handicapped in the development of science and technology because of their indigenous religion and beliefs. All societies have attempted to understand natural phenomena and in doing so all societies have displayed an awareness of the principles of causation. There is no difference in the basic process underlying religious thought in different societies. We have argued that it is only a very superficial assessment of differences in religious thought that has labelled the religious and traditional beliefs of some African and some Asian societies as 'pagan' or 'magical' or 'pre-logical' and regarded Christian and Islamic beliefs, in contrast, as conceptually superior.

(4) *Are explanations of natural phenomena regarded as fixed?*

Perhaps the most important distinguishing characteristic between the scientific approach to knowledge and the religious approach lies in the relatively 'open' nature of scientific models (Nduka, 1974).

The essence of the scientific approach is that it is empirical in nature; that is, it is based on experience, observation or experiment. This means that scientific models of knowledge are continually changing as a result of research. Scientific systems do not remain closed for long. Although scientists are sometimes reluctant to accept the implications of new findings that totally revolutionise the way they have been looking at certain natural phenomena, in the end they inevitably accept the findings and amend their theoretical systems accordingly.

As Nduka puts it, 'Science is knowledge which has been obtained largely through observation and experiment and has been subjected to sustained, critical scrutiny and passed through a many-layered ... filter' (1974, p. 159).

On the other hand, it is characteristic of some religions that, although they allow for analytical examination and scrutiny of written or oral statements pertaining to their beliefs, they do not encourage basic modifications of their fundamental explanatory models. Where such religions are very influential in a society, and in particular where religious leaders regard questioning of fundamental doctrines as unacceptable, there may be a clash between religious explanations of man and the universe and scientific models of knowledge. However, in modern times it is seldom that such conflict obstructs the teaching of science in schools.

In fact, in most societies, different models of knowledge coexist, often within the same individual. As we noted above it is quite possible to teach about the nature of evolutionary change and believe in personal reincarnation, and Jahoda (1970) had shown that in Ghana students were quite able to reconcile their traditional supernatural beliefs with Western-influenced education. Similarly, in Western societies science graduates may believe that their future may be affected by the movement of the stars and planets (astrology) even though there is no acceptable scientific explanation of why such heavenly movements should affect any individual's personal destiny.

Conflict between religious and supernatural beliefs and science is only likely to become significant in the educational context if the religious or spiritual leaders insist that they are the only authority in matters pertaining to the causation of natural phenomena. Furthermore, such conflict will be aggravated to the extent that the religion or belief system concerned is 'closed', that is, does not see its fundamental doctrines as open to change.

Thus, if a child comes from a home which is orthodox in the sense of the paragraph above, that is, where it is not regarded as permissible to question religious doctrine or to compare it with other knowledge systems, he may find the critical attitude that science demands very difficult to adopt. Similarly, to the extent that a society is influenced by an authoritarian and doctrinaire religious approach to the causation of natural phenomena, such a society may be relatively handicapped in its scientific progress.

(5) *Are some cognitive styles superior to others?*

In this section we have been considering cultural influences on the systems of knowledge that form the basis of formal schooling in Western societies and in many Third World societies that have been influenced by the Western model of formal schooling. In doing so we have made the following points.

In order to perform well at academic tasks in such school systems, pupils must learn to be *disembedded* in their thinking. That is, they must learn to abstract academic problems from their social knowledge of the world around them. They must learn to think generally and not to relate problems to any specific knowledge they may have of their personal world.

We have showed that schools tend to regard only *certain kinds of knowledge as appropriate* for academic treatment, and we noted that in making this selection they are influenced by the dominant ideology of the society. We also noted that in some Third World societies such a dominant ideology may be influenced by Western approaches to education.

We looked at the *different kinds of explanations* that exist in any culture *to explain natural phenomena*. We argued that in all societies these have been explained in the past with the aid of causational models that rested on religious beliefs and pointed out that nowadays such religious beliefs tend to coexist with scientific explanations of natural phenomena. On the whole, formal schools tend to offer scientific explanations. We also noted that all religious thinking is basically comparable and there is no ground for regarding the traditional or religious beliefs of some cultures as superior to those of others.

We pointed out that if religious beliefs are imposed in a very doctrinaire way, in any culture, then *children who come from very orthodox homes may find it difficult to accept the 'open' nature of scientific thinking*.

In this last sub-section on approaches to knowledge we should like to look critically at claims that have been made that some societies encourage 'cognitive styles' that are more helpful in the school situation than other cognitive styles.

A great deal of research has been generated all over the world by the ideas of an American psychologist, H. A. Witkin. In fact, in terms of impact on volume of psychological research in non-Western countries, Witkin comes second only to Piaget. Witkin based his original theory on work done in America, but as we noted above, this theory has sparked off work in numerous different cultures. Basically, his theory proposes that each individual has a particular 'cognitive style' which affects the whole range of his psychological activity from thinking to personal relationships.

You will, of course, be curious as to the dimensions of this wide-ranging personal characteristic. According to Witkin, individuals basically fall somewhere between two extremes of 'cognitive style'. These two extremes are 'field independence' and 'field dependence'. According to Witkin, *field independent* individuals are analytical in their approach to the world; they are highly 'differentiated', by which Witkin means they have a number of different, independent subsystems in their functioning which allow them to be discriminating and flexible both in their intellectual and their personal responses. *Field dependent* individuals, on the other hand, are more 'global' in their responses; they are not analytical and tend to respond in a less 'differentiated' way, that is, they do not have well-developed subsystems of functioning that allow them to be flexible and cognitively discriminating.

How do you find out whether a person is field dependent or field independent? Witkin has two major tests. In the first, the subject has to pick out a small design hidden in a larger more complex design. (This is called an Embedded Figure Test and you can see the type of item used if you look at Figure 4.7, page 52.) The quicker the subject can pick out the small shape, the more field independent he is. In the second test, called the Rod and Frame Test, the subject is taken into a completely dark room and seated on a chair. He is given a switch which is attached to a rod which, as we will describe, he is required to adjust. In front of him is a rectangular, luminous frame. Inside the frame is a luminous rod. The frame is tilted and the subject has to move the rod in such a way that the rod is vertical. He must not be influenced by the degree of tilt of the frame. The more nearly vertical he brings the rod, the more field independent he is (see Figure 10.3).

Thus, as you can see, whether or not a person is judged as field independent results from his performance at two tests which are concerned with visual perception. Witkin argues that if a person is analytical at this level of visual perception, he will tend to be analytical over the whole range of his psychological functioning.

What does Witkin think is the cause of these differences in psychological approach? What does he see as the determiner of whether or not a person is field independent? According to Witkin it all depends on child-rearing practices. If a mother encourages her child to be independent and urges him to explore his environment, he will tend to be field independent. If, on the other hand, she is overprotective and hampers the child's attempts to explore the environment, the child will tend to be field dependent. And, according to Witkin, some societies produce more field independent individuals than others because they encourage their young to be autonomous, independent and

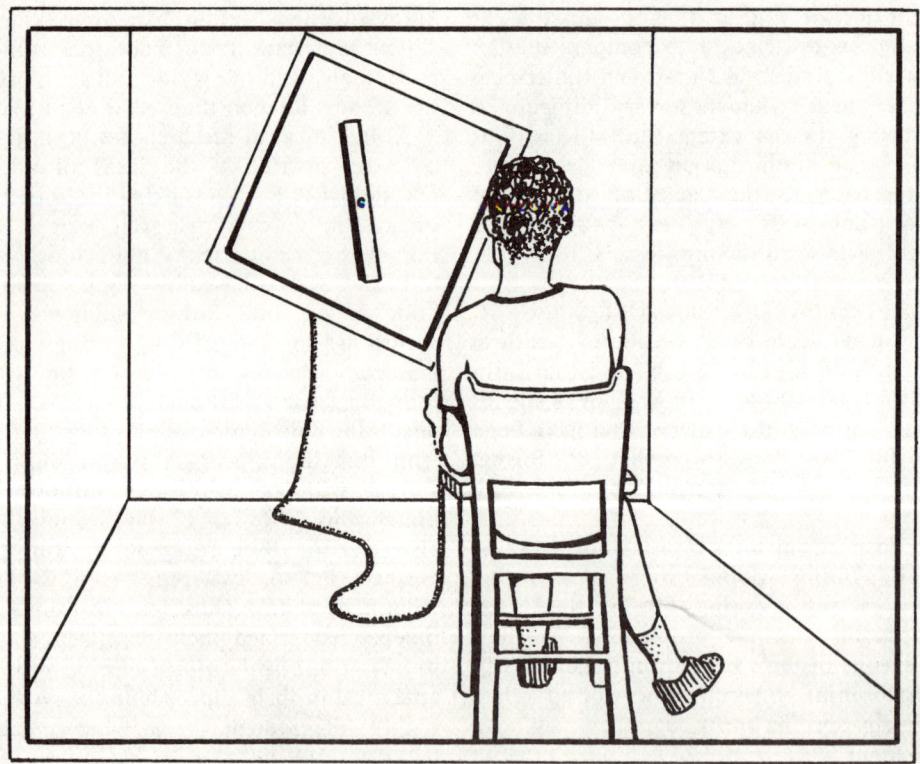

Figure 10.3 The Rod and Frame test

exploratory; while other societies tend to produce field dependent individuals because they do not allow children to be independent and autonomous in their behaviour (Witkin, 1967).

It seems to us that Witkin's work and theories can be criticised in a number of important ways.

(a) A number of studies, done in the West, have indicated that Witkin's tests of field independence measure largely spatial ability (Vernon, 1972) and little else.

(b) The studies in non-Western countries that Witkin and his associates have done have been reinterpreted by other psychologists who have disputed Witkin's interpretation of his results. In looking at their results, Witkin and psychologists who have been influenced by him have interpreted the fact that many non-Western subjects were low in field independence (i.e. did not score well at his tests) as being due to the child-rearing practices used in these cultures. Another interpretation that can very often be made instead is that the low scores resulted because such subjects were not at all familiar with the type of material and kind of tasks used in the tests. Indeed, a number of studies have shown that the more exposed to Western culture the subjects were, and consequently to the test tasks and test material, the higher their scores were (Okonji, 1969; Siann, 1972).

(c) People can be trained very easily to score better at Witkin's tests if they are coached. If these tests are really indicators of overall functioning as Witkin claims they are, we would not expect performance at these tests to be so subject to practice effects.

(d) The way that Witkin's tests have been administered in non-Western settings has often been very insensitive. It does seem that sometimes subjects just did not understand what they were being asked to do. Researchers very often seemed to have wrongly assumed that simply translating Witkin's instructions into the local language would ensure that subjects were quite clear about the demands of the task.

(e) Related to the point above, Witkin's approach has tended to be very affected by his own background. For example, it does seem that those societies whose child-rearing practices are closer to the American norm have tended to be regarded by psychologists associated with Witkin as providing a better cognitive approach than those societies whose practices were less similar to those common in the USA.

We have included some reference to Witkin's work because it has led to so many studies all over the world. We feel, however, its focus has been what Wober (1969) calls 'centri-cultural' rather than 'cross-cultural'. By this Wober means that Witkin's research carries over with it from the USA assumptions that are not justified in other settings. As Serpell says of the concept of field independence which he (Serpell) regards as 'centri-cultural' (1976, p. 54):

> The 'centri-cultural' approach acquires unattractively ethnocentric overtones when the dimension of behaviour investigated is value-laden, as appears to be the case for field-dependency. If theories originally formulated to explain the behaviour of Western populations are to be productive in cross-cultural research they will need to be prised free of particular standardized tests, and new instruments devised appropriate for measuring the same psychological constructs in different cultural settings.

In sum, then, we consider there is little evidence to support the contention that different 'cognitive styles', of the type postulated by Witkin, are characteristic of different cultures. Further, we do not regard the fact that members of certain cultures do not score highly on tests of field independence as having any relevance to the academic potential of members of those cultures.

In this section we have been looking at areas where conflict may arise from a clash between cultural approaches to knowledge and cognition and those approaches to knowledge that are characteristic of the formal school system. In the next section we consider how the language medium used in the school can affect school performance.

The Language Medium of the School and Learning

Some Third World countries conduct education primarily through an indigenous language while others rely primarily on a foreign tongue like English or French. In many countries where the latter course is followed, there is at present some dissatisfaction with the use of a non-indigenous medium as the primary language of instruction. Recently there has been an increasing tendency to switch to an indigenous language. In this short section we do not attempt to explore the social and political implication of such decisions. Instead we concentrate on the psychological implications of whether or not the child is taught primarily in the mother tongue. In doing this we contrast four possible broad approaches, and discuss, in turn, the effect each approach may have on cognitive and affective (social and emotional) development. In presenting our material in this way we do not draw directly on any particular project in any specific place to represent any of the contrasting approaches. Rather we discuss each approach to begin with 'in abstract' so as to highlight the theoretical issues involved and we follow this, where possible, with relevant research findings.

Before presenting these approaches we shall have to define some terminology. In the excellent survey of this area edited by Bamgboṣe, *Mother-Tongue Education*, the contributors tend to call the indigenous languages they write about the 'mother-tongue', indicating of course that in the countries they write about there are a number of different mother-tongues. As we are going to discuss in sub-section (5) below the particular difficulties experienced by the child whose mother-tongue is not the indigenous language used in the school, we shall have to define some terms.

By the 'mother-tongue' we mean the language used in the child's home.

By the 'foreign language' we mean the principal foreign language used in the country like English in Nigeria or Papua New Guinea or India and French in Benin, Zaire or Senegal.

By an 'indigenous' language we mean a language that is used as a medium of instruction in the school and that is indigenous to the country but is not the child's mother-tongue. We only refer to this term in sub-section (5).

In the following four sections we are going to look at four possible approaches to language in the primary schools, and while doing so we are going to assume that it is the child's mother-tongue that is the principal national language taught in the school. (In the fifth and last sub-section we shall discuss the child who is facing the task of dealing with three languages, that is, whose own mother-tongue is not the indigenous language primarily used in schools in his area.)

The four approaches we shall discuss are:

(1) Teaching in the primary school is only through the medium of the mother-tongue; the foreign language is only introduced at secondary school level.

(2) The mother-tongue is the main medium of instruction in the primary school; the foreign language is introduced at the primary school after the child can read in the mother-tongue.

(3) The mother-tongue is the major medium of instruction in the primary school; but the foreign language is introduced simultaneously with the mother-tongue.

(4) The foreign language is the major medium used in the primary school.

We shall now discuss the psychological implications of each of these approaches.

(1) *Teaching in the primary school is conducted only through the medium of the mother-tongue. The foreign language is not used at all in the primary school.*

In this situation the child is taught through the medium of his own home language throughout the primary school and only encounters a foreign language or languages in the secondary school. It is, of course, the system that is used in the majority of schools in many Western countries. For example, in Britain and America foreign languages are seldom presented before secondary school.

The major advantage of this system is that right from the beginning there is a close match between the learning medium of school and the home background. This serves two important psychological functions. To begin with, as Fafunwa (1975, p. 226) notes, there can be a close linkage between parents and the school: 'Parents [can] assist the classes through their children by supplying information on local mores [customs], folklores, festivities etc., whenever requested by the teachers – both parents and children now communicate in a common language in regard to school education.'

Secondly, as we pointed out when we discussed the teaching of reading, reading is a psycholinguistic skill, so that it is most important that the child has an intimate knowledge of the language he is being taught to read in. This condition is of course fulfilled if the mother-tongue is the medium of instruction in the primary school.

Thus socially, culturally and intellectually there is a great deal to be gained in psychological terms by using the mother-tongue as the medium of instruction in the primary school. There are, however, two areas of possible disadvantage. The first is a practical one; in the case of countries with many different languages, the problems of producing teaching materials in all the languages involved may be a very time-consuming and expensive task. Nevertheless, as the Rivers Readers Project in Nigeria shows, this particular difficulty can be overcome by a disciplined and constructive approach. In this project, in which an attempt is being made to teach all children, in the first instance, in their mother-tongue, readers in fifteen different languages were produced in the first year of the project (Williamson, 1976).

The second possible disadvantage lies in the fact that if this approach is used, and if there are insufficient textbooks in the mother-tongue, then those children who proceed to the secondary school may have difficulty in obtaining adequate reference books and textbooks, particularly in science subjects. For this reason, and also to aid communication with those who do not speak the same mother-tongue, it is often advisable to teach the principal foreign language (such as English or French) used in the country at some stage in the primary school. Broadly speaking we can differentiate two opposing ways that this can be done. First, the foreign language can be introduced simultaneously with the mother-tongue, or, secondly, the second language can be introduced in the primary school after the child has learned to read in his mother-tongue. It is to the second and, in our opinion, preferable alternative that we turn now.

(2) *The mother-tongue is the major medium of instruction in the primary school, and some time after reading in it has been established the foreign language is introduced.*

This approach retains the major advantages of the first approach in that the child is provided with a close match, culturally, socially and psycho-linguistically, between school and home. In addition to these advantages, by introducing a foreign language in the primary school he is provided with the basis, if he continues to secondary school, of reading textbooks in the major foreign language used in his country.

In this approach the child only starts to learn the second language (the foreign one) after basic literacy skills are established in his mother-tongue.

Research summarised by Downing (1974) seems to point to the psychological advantages of delaying second language teaching until literacy is established in the first language. This is because, as he notes (1974, p. 80) and as we described in Chapter 6:

' Literacy development is a problem-solving process. The child begins in an initial state of cognitive confusion regarding the nature and purpose of the tasks of reading and writing. He gropes his way out of this confusion mainly by solving a series of conceptual learning problems which yield increasing cognitive clarity. For example, he must develop concepts for such categories as work, phoneme, syllable, letter, character, etc. according to the language and its coding units in the writing system. He must understand the concept of a code in which one symbol can represent another, as well as the concepts of the units of language used in the particular code he is required to learn. '

Thus, as Downing claims and as we noted above, reading is best established when the child has an intimate knowledge of the language he is learning to read. This is because the child's knowledge of his own language enables him to predict what is likely to come next in the passages or texts he learns to read from, and thus he is provided with vital clues in solving the cognitive problems of reading. *But once he has learned the beginnings of reading skills in his mother-tongue, he is then well able to transfer his general understanding of what literacy and reading is about to a second language.*

In his analysis of the research findings which led him to conclude that literacy skills are best first established in the mother-tongue, Downing points out that if reading is taught in two languages simultaneously then cognitive confusion is likely to occur as the child struggles to solve the problems of reading using two entirely different sets of sounds, rules and sometimes even alphabets. On the other hand, once the child has solved the basic process of reading in the language he knows best, he is prepared for the *kind of tasks* learning to read in the second language will present.

' When one has learned to speak the mother-tongue, one does not have to learn how to speak all over again in learning a foreign language. One simply transfers the speaking skills to the second language. Similarly, once one is literate in the first language of literacy one does not have to acquire literacy over again when one learns to read a second language. One need only extend one's existing literacy. '

(Downing, 1974, p. 82)

Thus this particular approach to the problems of language teaching seems to offer the best psychological advantages in those countries where there is still a heavy reliance on a foreign language like English or French at the secondary school and university and college level. By initially introducing the home language, the child has the best possible match between home and school at all levels, social, cultural and cognitive. If the second language is then introduced in the primary school some time after literacy skills have been established, the child should experience little difficulty in transferring his reading and writing skills to the second language. In some areas, however, the second language is introduced simultaneously with the mother-tongue and we now discuss this approach.

(3) *Although the mother-tongue is the major medium of instruction in the primary school, the second language is introduced simultaneously.*

In the last sub-section we noted that research indicates that reading is always easier to learn in the mother-tongue than in any other because of the child's familiarity with the language. If, at the same time as the child is expected to acquire reading in his mother-tongue, he is also asked to acquire reading in a second and relatively unfamiliar language, then, as we noted before, he may become confused because of the differences that are bound to exist in the reading rules applicable in the two languages.

However, our claim that it is theoretically better to introduce reading in the mother-tongue before introducing it in a second language rests mainly on research reported from the West and our own analysis of the nature of reading – that it is a psycho-linguistic problem-solving task. As we noted in the beginning of this section, many Third World countries are now moving to replace the foreign languages as the major medium of instruction throughout the primary school. Very often when this is done the child is introduced to both the mother-tongue and a foreign language at the same time. Further, in many such cases, as in the careful experimental project being carried out in Ife, Nigeria (Fafunwa, 1975; Afọlayan, 1976), these changes are being meticulously monitored. The results of such projects, when they are reported in detail, should enable us to validate or reject our present hypothesis that it is better to first establish reading skills in the mother-tongue before introducing reading in a foreign language.

However, it does not seem to be in any doubt that whether or not a second language is introduced at the same time, one of the first languages a child learns to read should be his mother-tongue. It is for this reason that we find the last approach we describe to language-use in the primary school the least satisfactory of the four.

(4) *The primary teaching medium in the school is a foreign language rather than the mother-tongue.*

This approach to primary school education is the one that is still used in some Third World countries. For example, writing in 1976, Fyle reports that 'In Sierre Leone, English is used as the medium of instruction for all primary education' (p. 47).

As we have noted throughout this section, it seems to us that on both cognitive and affective grounds such a policy has psychological disadvantages. We acknowledge that, in a multilingual country, it can be very difficult to cater for all the mother-tongues that there may be. Nevertheless, we would echo Fafunwa's cry that 'It is universally accepted ... that a child learns best in its mother-tongue and that the mother-tongue is as natural to him as the mother's milk' (1975, p. 216).

It has sometimes been argued that it is necessary to use a foreign language in Third World countries as the major language of education because indigenous languages lack sufficiently sophisticated vocabulary and conceptual approaches to deal with the technological demands of present-day life. However, as the Ife primary education project has shown, there are little grounds for such a view. This project has 'proved an obvious fact that any dynamic language has a means of adapting to new situations and new challenges' (Fafunwa, 1975, p. 222). Similarly, Serpell concludes in discussing this issue that 'There is no good reason to suppose that, if it is used in the context of advanced education, *any* language cannot adapt ... to the requirements of technology' (1976. p. 68).

In sum, it seems to us that there are no clear psychological advantages in retaining the use of a foreign language as the major medium of instruction in the primary school.

(5) *Special difficulties encountered by children when the indigenous language used in the school is not their mother-tongue.*

Sometimes young children who start primary school come from homes where the mother-tongue differs from the language spoken by the rest of the community and used in school. In general this will not cause any special difficulty if such children are well integrated into the local community and understand and speak the locally used indigenous language. It is well known, in fact, that young children often find it far easier to learn the language of a new community into which their parents have moved than do the adults in the family.

If, as is the case with many immigrant children in Britain, young children do not speak or even understand the local language used in the school, some remedial help is usually needed; for such children do not have the very valuable linguistic knowledge that aids reading that their peers have. In addition, such children often feel inadequate because they cannot follow what is said to them, or even if they do understand, they may have difficulty in responding. In some cases they may be mocked at by the other children in the class. Clearly, in such circumstances teachers have to make a very special effort to help these children, both in the cognitive tasks of the classroom and at the level of social and emotional adjustment to their new environment.

Sometimes a rather different difficulty may arise, when a country decides to teach only one, two or a few of the indigenous languages. Such is the case, for example, in countries with so many indigenous languages that adopting each indigenous language in the area it is spoken is not a practicable solution to the problem of switching the teaching medium away from a foreign language to an indigenous language or languages. In such cases, however, the language adopted is usually one of which all the children will have some knowledge. This means that there will not necessarily be any particular cognitive strain in learning to read it, though, as we have pointed out, it is always easier to learn to read in your own mother-tongue. In addition, as all the children in the area will face the same difficulties, such a situation is not likely to lead to any of the social or emotional problems which arise when children are in the relatively unusual position of not speaking a language in a community where everyone else does.

In summary, then, learning a language at school that is not the mother-tongue only tends to give rise to psychological difficulties if children have no previous knowledge of the language or if they feel isolated because they alone do not know the language that is used as a teaching medium.

We have been looking in this section at the psychological implications of the language used as the major medium for teaching in the school. In the last section of this chapter which follows we look briefly at how the functions society ascribes to education can affect teacher–pupil and parent–teacher relationships.

A Broader Perspective

In his book, to which we have referred before – *The Diploma Disease* (1976) – Dore looks at the underlying beliefs that people may hold about why school learning is necessary. He distinguishes between two major orientations – first, people may regard learning as important because they see acquiring knowledge as an important *end in itself*. Secondly, they may see acquiring knowledge as important because the knowledge can then be used to achieve other purposes – that is, knowledge is *instrumental in helping to reach other objectives*.

Educationalists tend to hold both these orientations. They can obviously see the importance of promoting learning in order to equip individuals and society as a whole with useful knowledge and skills, that is, they can acknowledge the instrumental aspects of learning. At the same time they usually have invested so much personal time and effort in learning and teaching that they are bound to have experienced the intrinsic rewards of teaching and learning. As Dore says, any educationalist who did not attach some absolute value to learning as an end in itself 'would not ... be much of an educationalist' (p. 138).

Parents, on the other hand, tend to see learning more instrumentally. They want their children to leave schools equipped with knowledge and skills that will ensure that they are at least as well equipped as other young people to get employment or higher education.

Similarly, most pupils, even if they find learning intrinsically exciting and rewarding, expect their schooling to equip them to compete effectively for jobs and places in higher education. Thus, as we have stressed throughout this book, if pupils and their parents do not perceive school as fulfilling the functions they want it to, there will be repercussions in the schoolroom.

In a recent survey on drop-out in Ibadan primary schools, Yoloye (1975) concludes that many of the children who drop out of school do so because parents weigh up the advantages and disadvantages of children continuing to attend school and find that the disadvantages like cost, loss of child labour, severe discipline, outweigh the advantages. They think their children are not making enough progress in learning, and they are not convinced that keeping them at school will lead to better job opportunities. In such circumstances, parents are unlikely to be persuaded to keep their children in school for the intrinsic rewards of learning.

As we have mentioned before, such perceptions of whether or not education is useful to pupils may differ depending on the social class of the family and their economic position. Further, as we noted in discussing Wilson's study of school-leavers in Papua New Guinea, the perception of the usefulness of education may also depend on whether the family live in the rural or urban areas. For example, a country may decide to switch its educational emphasis primarily to ensuring that primary schools prepare children for participating in rural development. If this is done, parents who were themselves educated within a more formal academic system may become very dissatisfied, particularly if the family live in an urban area. And even within rural areas, as Wilson's study showed, the skills taught at school are not made use of in the same way throughout a society.

There are, however, far more fundamental questions relating to the function of school learning, that lie outside the scope of this book. These are concerned with the beliefs the society holds in general about the role of education in a society. In some countries there is an emphasis on what Dore calls 'society-regarding achievement learning'. By this he means that in some societies learning at school is viewed through the perspective of how each pupil can serve the overall needs of society. If this perspective is held, then decisions about who should go on to higher education may lie primarily outside the sphere of influence of the individual and his family. In other societies, on the other hand, the emphasis may be placed on what Dore calls 'self-regarding qualification-seeking learning'. By this he means that individuals and their parents regard school as a place where qualifications are gained which will primarily be of use to the individual as he makes his way through life. If this perspective is held, then parents may be able to use their resources to aid their children in doing well at school and going on to higher education; they may, for instance, be able to pay school fees, buy books and uniforms, or pay for extra coaching to achieve this aim.

Another very fundamental issue in education is concerned with the overall direction that a society regards itself as pursuing. If a society, in general, regards the acquisition of sophisticated technology as an important national aim, schools will, on the whole, have curricula that are significantly affected by the content of examinations. If a society regards its overall aims as lying more urgently in the direction of what President Nyerere has called 'self-reliance', there will probably be rather more emphasis on linking the content of the school curriculum to the kind of employment that most adults will follow.

Thus it cannot be stressed too emphatically that in considering the interactions between schools, communities, parents, teachers and pupils, these must be viewed in their societal setting.

Summary

(1) In the introduction we pointed out that all societies have had educational systems, but that these have varied with respect to how closely they were allied to formal institutions like schools, colleges and universities.

(2) We then looked at some areas where conflict may arise between the more and less formal aspects of education.

(3) In discussing the effect of parental and community values on schools, we considered, in turn, the effect of parental and community attitudes to education in general, to what the school should teach and how it should do so, to discipline and to the characteristics of good schools and good teachers. In each case, we showed that parental and community values in these areas are bound to affect pupil–teacher and pupil–school interactions.

(4) We also looked at the effect on education of indigenous approaches to knowledge. We pointed out that schools must be affected by such approaches but that there is no evidence to support a view that any such approaches impede academic progress.

(5) Following this we looked at the psychological implications of the major language used in schools. We concluded that the available

evidence supports the view that this should be the child's mother-tongue, particularly in the area of acquiring literacy skills.

(6) Finally, we argued that schools and their effect on teachers, pupils, parents and communities cannot be viewed in isolation from generally held social values and aspirations.

Chapter 10: Selected Bibliography

Parental and community values and the school
Figueroa, P. M. E., and Persaud, G., *Sociology of Education: A Caribbean Reader* (London: OUP, 1976).

Different approaches to knowledge
Serpell, R., *Culture's Influence on Behaviour* (London: Methuen, 1976).

Witkin's theory of cognitive style
Siann, G., 'Measuring field dependence in Zambia', *International Journal of Psychology*, vol. 7, no. 2 (1972).

The use of the vernacular in schools
Bamgboṣe, A., *Mother Tongue Education: The West African Experience* (London: Hodder & Stoughton, 1976).

A broader perspective
Dore, R., *The Diploma Disease: Education, Qualification and Experience* (London: Allen & Unwin, 1976).
Nyerere, J. K., *Education for Self-Reliance* (Dar es Salaam: Government Printer, 1967).

THE NATURE AND ASSESSMENT OF INTELLIGENCE AND THE ASSESSMENT OF ACADEMIC ACHIEVEMENT

11

> ' An individual's potential can only be measured in terms of the specific demands and background skills of his own culture. Should not his 'intelligence' be related in the same way, and not to an alien culture? (Serpell, 1973, p. 81). '

Introduction

As the reader might have observed, we have avoided any discussion of the term 'intelligence' until this stage in the book. We have done this for two reasons.

First, we consider that each culture rewards and promotes particular cognitive skills, and thus, in our opinion, 'intelligent' behaviour must be related to the values, culture and expectations of the society in which that behaviour takes place. Obviously, then, as the Serpell quotation at the beginning of this chapter points out, 'intelligence' should be viewed within a cultural context.

However, for many people who have been influenced by the educational values of the West, 'intelligence' means something far more restricted and narrow and has been equated with performance within the academic situation and with skill at psychological tests like intelligence tests. In this chapter we shall argue that this particular view of intelligence is too specific and limited to be of any great use within the cross-cultural perspective. Further, we shall show that such a view, while popular amongst psychologists

and educationalists in the first part of this century, has been increasingly criticised lately as more and more evidence points to the importance of factors other than cognitive ability in academic and intelligence test performance.

It is because we see the definition of 'intelligence' and discussions about its nature as intimately linked to culture that we have delayed our treatment of the subject to this part of the book which deals with the interaction of educational variables and culture. However, there is a second reason for delaying our discussion of intelligence to the end of the book.

This second reason is related to our view of the determinants of performance in the academic situation and within the psychological test situation. We regard such performances as having a great many determinants. Obviously the level of an individual's cognitive skills is very important in such situations. But, as we have tried to show throughout this book, such skills are related to many factors besides the inborn potential for cognitive growth.

For instance, we demonstrated in Chapter 2 that home background factors may affect such performances. So can both the area an individual comes from, whether rural or urban, and the individual's degree of exposure to particular educational practices (Chapters 3 and 4). In Chapters 5 and 8 we argued that an individual's level of self-esteem may also affect such performances. Finally, in Chapters 8 and 9, we showed that sometimes factors lying right outside the individual, like the social climate of the school and community and cultural attitudes to education, can affect levels of academic performance.

It is with this background in mind that we now turn our attention to the specific area of 'intelligence'. We shall present the view that 'intelligence' is best regarded as a dynamic cluster of skills. And we shall suggest that such skills are largely determined by the individual's environment and that they are always capable of being improved. While we would not deny that there may be individual differences in cognitive potential that are due to genetic factors, we shall argue that environmental factors are at least as important as these inborn factors in determining the individual's performance on the psychological tests that are labelled 'intelligence tests'.

In this chapter we discuss the nature and measurement of 'intelligence', bearing these perspectives in mind – that 'intelligence' is a concept that must be considered in relation to cultural values and social expectations, that the amount of 'intelligence' a person is regarded as showing cannot be thought of as fixed, and that behaviour in academic and test situations is determined by a number of factors of which 'intelligence' is only one.

After discussing the nature and measurement of 'intelligence' we shall turn our attention to the assessment of academic achievement. We shall look at the functions assessment serves, both within schools and in the broader social context. Following this we shall look at two different approaches to assessment – normative assessment and criterion assessment. Finally, we shall tie together many of the themes we have explored in this book by looking at the determinants of academic performance. (See Figure 11.1.)

The Nature of Intelligence

(1) *History of interest in the concept*

The rise of 'IQ tests'. As Butcher points out in his book, *Human Intelligence: Its Nature and Assessment* (1970), it is only comparatively recently that the terms 'intelligence' and 'intelligent' have come into general use in the English language. Indeed, until the early part of this century intelligence was not a term that was used to describe children and their school performance. But by the middle part of this century it had become a term that was constantly used in the West within

the discipline of education psychology. How did this situation arise?

Perhaps the earliest work in the area was done by Francis Galton in England towards the end of the nineteenth century. Galton observed that in certain English families there were a far higher proportion of eminent scholars than there were in others and he became firmly convinced that the reason for this lay in the fact that the determinant of such distinction, which he regarded as intelligence,* was inherited. He assumed that intelligence was a function of the individual's sensory faculties and devised a series of tests of reaction time and sensory acuity to measure intellectual ability. Thus, as Sprinthall and Sprinthall put it, he can be 'considered, therefore, to be the father of intelligence testing' (1974, p. 343).

If we look at Galton's work within a historical perspective, we can see that he was influenced by the rapid growth of knowledge and interest in both the natural and physical sciences that was taking place at that time in Britain. Scientists were beginning to be able to measure physical variables with great accuracy and it was not therefore surprising to find a movement within the study of human behaviour that was similarly concerned with testing and measuring. Thus one of the precursors of the interest in intelligence and its assessment derives from the scientific climate of the late nineteenth century. Britain, however, was not the only European country to produce workers in the field of cognitive ability. Starting from quite a different perspective, Binet in France produced the first usable test of intelligence in 1905. He had been commissioned by the French Minister of Public Instruction to develop a testing procedure that could help to identify students whose academic skills and ability were so low as to make it necessary to place them in special schools. He therefore produced a practical diagnostic instrument to distinguish such children.

It is important to remember that, unlike Galton and many later workers who used and modified his tests, Binet himself did not believe that he was testing an attribute that was largely inherited and unchangeable. On the contrary, Binet regarded intellectual skills as always being capable of being improved by appropriate teaching. He disapproved greatly of teachers who believed that such remediation was not possible. He wrote of such

* From now on we shall refer to this general area as intelligence, acknowledging that the different workers in this field that we shall discuss use the term in different ways.

INTRODUCTION

THE NATURE OF INTELLIGENCE
(i) History of interest in the concept
(ii) Some models of intelligence
(iii) Viewing intelligence in a cross-cultural context

THE ASSESSMENT OF INTELLIGENCE
(i) Defining intelligence for assessment purposes
(ii) Intelligence is not a fixed attribute
(iii) Bias in tests and the test situation
(iv) Why assess intelligence ?
(v) Questions to ask about any intelligence test

THE FUNCTIONS OF ASSESSMENT
(i) Assessing for pedagogic reasons
(ii) Assessing for selection purposes
(iii) Assessing for social reasons

THE DIFFERENT KINDS OF ASSESSMENT
(i) Norm-referenced assessment
(ii) Criterion-referenced assessment

THE DETERMINANTS OF ACADEMIC ACHIEVEMENT

SUMMARY

Figure 11. 1 Structure of Chapter 11

teachers that it was entirely unsuitable of them to say things of their pupils like 'This is a child who will never accomplish anything ... He is poorly gifted.' He noted of such remarks, 'Never! What a large word!' (Binet, quoted by Kamin, 1977, p. 22).

Binet, then, believed that intelligence was an evolving collection of skills that was always capable of being improved. As we have noted, this was a view that was completely opposed to the way Galton regarded intelligence. You will remember that Galton saw intelligence as almost entirely dependent on the individual's inborn characteristics and therefore, as far as Galton was concerned, intelligence was a relatively fixed quantity. This viewpoint of Galton's found a ready audience in the USA, where a number of psychologists, and Terman in particular, became very interested in intelligence testing. They believed that by using intelligence tests they could establish who were mentally defective and then they could act to prevent such people from having too adverse an effect on society in general. Terman modified the Binet tests and his version of these tests became known as the Stanford-Binet.

From some of his writing, we can see that Terman linked his interest in intelligence testing to fairly pronounced views about society.

> ❛ ... in the near future intelligence tests will bring tens of thousands of these high-grade defectives under the surveillance and protection of society. This will ultimately result in *curtailing the reproduction* of feeble-mindedness and in the elimination of an enormous amount of crime, pauperism, and industrial inefficiency. It is hardly necessary to emphasize that the high-grade cases, of the type now so frequently over-looked, are precisely the ones whose guardianship it is most important for the State to assume. ❜

> (our italics; Terman, quoted by Kamin, p. 20).

Kamin's book *The Science and Politics of IQ* documents this perspective held by Terman and other American psychologists like Yerkes and makes a convincing case for seeing part of the popularity of intelligence testing, in the earlier part of this century, as lying in the political convictions of such psychologists who were convinced that intelligence was largely inherited and that those of low intelligence were concentrated in certain sectors of the population – the poor, Spanish-Indian, Mexican and black. Further, these psychologists considered that people of low intelligence were not the equal of the majority of the citizens of the USA and therefore required different treatment. Thus the Binet test was used to classify numbers of unfortunate people as mentally defective and to assign them to state institutions (Kamin, 1977).

However, Terman and his colleagues were not the only psychologists who encouraged the use of intelligence tests for social or political reasons. Another group of educationalists, located primarily in Britain, were convinced that such tests could be used to identify children of high academic potential and, having identified them, place them in academic schools where their special gifts could be encouraged. In this way, psychologists like Godfrey Thomson saw intelligence tests as an important means of bringing about social equality. Thus Britain spearheaded the use of selection examinations which were largely based on intelligence tests in order to filter children into different types of schooling. It was hoped by many dedicated psychologists that gifted children from comparatively disadvantaged social backgrounds could in this way be given an education that was equivalent to that enjoyed by children who were more privileged socially.

Thus far, then, we have seen the increasing popularity of intelligence testing in the first half of this century as springing from:

(a) A scientific interest in the testing and measurement of human abilities (Galton).
(b) A practical desire to be able to diagnose those children who required special remedial education (Binet).
(c) A politically motivated desire to be able to identify mental defectives and then control their behaviour (Terman and Yerkes).
(d) A socially motivated desire to be able to identify gifted children and provide them with a more academic type of education than those who were identified as less able (Thomson).

Looking at these influences on intelligence testing, it seems to us quite clear that, perhaps more than any other area in psychology, perspectives on intelligence must be related to the social, political and cultural environment.

In any event, by the 1940s the following views derived from the growing emphasis on intelligence testing were widely held by most Western psychologists:

(a) Intelligence is a recognisable attribute which is responsible for differences among children and adults in their learning, reasoning and other cognitive capacities.

(b) This attribute is essentially stable and does not change throughout an individual's lifetime.

(c) Intelligence tests are adequate measures of this attribute.

The fall of IQ tests. By the late 1970s all three of the statements we have just listed would be disputed by most psychologists (Vernon, 1979). They would dispute that intelligence is easily defined or identified as a distinct attribute. They would not agree that intellectual skills do not change over time. And finally they would not, in general, accept that intelligence tests measure anything as clear-cut as 'intelligence'. How is it that such a reversal of attitudes to intelligence and intelligence testing has occurred? To begin with, there has been an accumulating amount of scientific evidence that indicates that the views held earlier about the nature of intelligence are incorrect and we shall return to this evidence in the next section of this chapter. But, in addition, there were once again cultural, social and political factors that also influenced views on the nature of intelligence and its assessment.

As in the nineteenth century the scientific climate had influenced Galton's views on intelligence, so in the second half of the twentieth century the scientific climate has influenced our views on intelligence. Scientists at present are rather more relativistic in their views than scientists were in the last century. They are aware that even in the physical sciences there has to be an acceptance that any scientific theory is shaped to some extent by the assumptions of the person who puts it forward. Also, they are aware that the very act of recording an observation must be taken into account when considering the observation. Similarly, psychologists have become aware that psychologists themselves sometimes draw conclusions which are not free of their individual biases. Further, they have also begun to acknowledge that in any experimenter–subject interaction the subject himself may be influenced by what he thinks the psychologist wants him to do. An increasing amount of data has been produced that indicates that subjects sometimes respond not only to the variables the experimenter is trying to manipulate but to others that spring from the interaction between the subject and the experimenter. Thus many psychologists have begun to be sceptical about psychological tests and measurements.

In America, too, political factors began to affect the testing movement. In general black American and other minority groups had tended to score at lower levels than white Americans on intelligence tests. With the advent of the Black Power movement and other organisations of black consciousness, it began to be pointed out that such group differences were due to the culturally biased nature of the tests. Further, it was pointed out that most members of minority groups lived in far less advantageous conditions than the majority of white Americans, and that these environmental factors undoubtedly affected test scores. Consequently, intelligence testing fell into disrepute in the USA.

In Britain political factors also contributed to a growing rejection of intelligence tests. It became clear that the intelligence measures used in selection tests favoured middle-class students in that they reflected middle-class, rather than working-class, culture and values. Further, middle-class children tended to do better than working-class children on these selection tests, largely because the schools they attended were better, because teachers expected such children to pass the selection tests and because, in many cases, specialised coaching was provided.

Thus, subtle and complex social factors were involved in the decline in popularity of the testing movement. It can be seen, then, that interest in intelligence and its assessment cannot be separated from social and cultural variables.

In this sub-section we have aimed to show the reader that the way intelligence and intelligence testing have been viewed is intimately related to the cultural context. Before we present our own views on moving towards a cross-cultural perspective on intelligence, we should like to present some models of the nature of intelligence that have been influential in educational psychology. We shall look at three of these models: (a) the general factor model of intelligence proposed by Burt and Vernon, (b) Thurstone's primary mental abilities and (c) Guilford's multi-factorial approach to intelligence.

(2) *Some models of intelligence*

The intelligence testing movement was started largely by Terman in America and his modification of the Binet test, the Stanford-Binet, became widely used in the assessment of intelligence. Terman did not develop any model of intelligence but modified the sub-tests used by Binet, which Binet himself had produced without any specific theoretical base except that, as we noted before, he (Binet) regarded intelligence as composed of a cluster of abilities which could be modified by teaching.

Terman defined intelligence as 'the ability to carry on abstract thought' but did not propose any detailed model of this ability although, as we have seen, he did regard it as largely innate. It was left to Spearman (1863–1945) to make the first attempts in the USA to formulate a detailed model of the structure of intelligence. Spearman became convinced that performances in 'all branches of intellectual activity have in common one fundamental function (or group of functions)' (Spearman, quoted by Butcher, 1970, p. 45). Thus he has been regarded as the first modern theorist to develop the idea that there is a general factor of intelligence which largely determines the level of intellectual functioning. His approach, though he was an American, was most influential in Britain.

(a) *The general factor model of intelligence – Burt and Vernon.* Sir Cyril Burt has, until very recently, been the most influential figure in the field of intelligence in Britain. He proposed that there was a hierarchy of mental abilities. By this he meant that the most important factor underlying performance at intellectual tasks was a general factor of mental ability, but that, in addition, there were other less important factors that characterised different groups of tasks. From our point of view the most interesting aspect of Burt's work has been his view that this general ability was largely innate; that is, he regarded intelligence as largely inherited, defining it as 'innate general cognitive ability' (Butcher, 1970).

How did he come to this conclusion? He reached it largely by looking at 'twin studies'. In such studies, identical twins, who share the same genotype (who are born with identical genes) are studied. In particular he looked at identical twins who had been separated at birth and reared in very different homes and he calculated how closely their intelligence quotients (scores on intelligence tests) resembled each other. Then he looked at identical twins who had been reared together and he calculated how closely their intelligence quotients resembled each other. He reported that there was almost as close a resemblance between the scores of separated identical twins as there was between the identical twins who had been reared together. He

reasoned that this proved that the genotype was more important than the environment in determining intelligence. There is nothing wrong with this conclusion from a logical point of view. Unfortunately for Burt's case, it has recently been demonstrated that his figures were inaccurate and in many cases misleadingly reported. Further, it seems that some of the people Burt claimed to have worked with were unknown to other psychologists working in the field and it has proved impossible to track down and show any independent evidence of the actual existence of these people. (Gillie, 1976; Kamin, 1977).

This has led Kamin and many others to the conclusion that 'The numbers left behind by Sir Cyril Burt are simply not worthy of our current scientific attention' (p. 71) and even Vernon (1979), who is more sympathetic to Burt's position, has recently reported: 'I'm afraid then that we will have to jettison [abandon] his [Burt's] individual test data' (p. 12). Leaving aside, for the moment, Burt's claim that this general factor of intelligence is largely inherited, let us turn our attention to the work of P. E. Vernon, who has been the most eminent of Burt's British followers.

Vernon has developed Burt's model in the following way. He, like Burt, argues that there is an underlying general factor which he considers to be largely inborn, though he has recently conceded that 'the total evidence of environmental effects on individual intellectual growth is very strong' (1979, p. 19). As well as this general factor, he claims there are two major group factors: the 'verbal educational factor' and the 'psychomotor factor'. Then there are minor group factors which will vary with the cultural and environmental variables. Finally, there are specific factors which are associated with the particular intellectual task in question.

Vernon has conducted a large-scale cross-cultural study of intelligence and the cultural environment (1969) and he has concluded that his general model in intelligence is applicable in all the cultures he studied, though the way that the factors group themselves may differ from culture to culture.

The chief disadvantage about Vernon's approach to the cross-cultural field has, however, been its centri-cultural nature. By this we mean that Vernon has both explicitly and implicitly identified intelligence as the ability to do well at the tasks he used in his survey. As we have argued throughout this book, such tasks, which are imported directly from Western cultures, and modified only to the extent of translation into the vernacular and removal or reinterpretation of unfamiliar terms, are most unlikely to be adequate tests of anything more general than familiarity with Western modes of education and Western ways of categorisation. As Serpell writes of the use of such tests in Zambia (1975, p. 2):

> ' The form of all currently available standardised intelligence tests in Zambia appears to be biased towards Western culture in using either the English language or Western conventions of pictorial and symbolic representation. Thus the possibility arises that their use for educational (and occupational) selection guides into positions of privilege and responsibility not those endowed with the greatest 'adaptability' ... and creativity, but those who by whatever means, have made the fullest adaptation to certain facets of Western culture. '

(b) *Thurstone's primary abilities model.* L. H. Thurstone (1887–1955) has been one of the most influential American workers in the field of cognitive abilities. He introduced a new principle into the field which he called 'simple structure'. This principle postulated that there are fundamental human abilities which enter into cognitive task performance. Each cognitive task calls on some, but not all, of these primary abilities. He isolated seven of these factors from a battery of fifty-six varied tests. The seven he isolated were:

S – spatial ability
P – perceptual speed
N– numerical ability
V – verbal meaning
M– memory
W– verbal fluency
I or R – inductive reasoning (reasoning from the particular to the general).

Later he dropped the M factor and added a 'motor' factor.

Thurstone's work has been criticised on a number of counts. To begin with, British workers in the field have argued that if he performed further statistical analyses he would find that there is a more general factor underlying his abilities. (Thurstone responded to this criticism by agreeing that there was some evidence for a general factor or factors if alternative statistical techniques were used.) Secondly, it has been argued that the abilities he lists as primary are primary only in a statistical sense – that is, they emerge as primary from the statistical analyses he performed – rather than primary in any neurological or psychological sense. Finally, as we mentioned in Chapter 6, this way of looking at intelligence came under fire in America because such models made no allowance for the kind of skills we discussed in our section on creativity-divergent skills.

It is certainly our view that these criticisms were justified. In particular, it seems that to extend the results obtained by giving groups of American students a battery of tests to making general statements about the primary structure of mental abilities is an unjustified leap. Nevertheless, we have made some reference to Thurstone's work because it demonstrates the very limited areas of human behaviour which some psychologists considered when they were producing their theories of human intelligence. You will notice, for example, there are no references at all to skills in interpersonal areas.

The final model of intelligence that we shall look at is the multifactorial model produced by J. P. Guilford and his associates (Guilford, 1967).

(c) *The multi-factorial model of Guilford.* Unlike Spearman, Burt, Vernon and Thurstone, in his later years the eminent American psychologist J. P. Guilford has completely rejected the concept of a general factor or factors underlying intellectual skills.

He examined the performance of numbers of different subjects on large batteries of tests and concluded that in 7,000 combinations of different tests there was little evidence to show that individuals who did well on one test did well on any other. He concluded that intellectual abilities are spread very unevenly within people, and pointed to the finding that 'individuals who test as mentally deficient frequently make surprisingly good social and economic adjustments' (1967, p. 27). He continued that such individuals may have abilities in the areas of social intelligence which intelligence tests do not measure.

Instead of regarding intelligence as being governed largely by a general factor, Guilford has proposed a model in which abilities vary according to basic and underlying psychological processes. He has proposed three basic dimensions in his model and these are:

Operations (5) This refers to the following processes – cognition, memory, evaluation, divergent production (we discussed this in Chapter 6 in the section on creativity) and convergent production.

Contents (4) The material on which operations are performed. These are – figures, symbols, semantic (meaningful material) and behavioural.

Products (6) The form the contents take after being operated on. These are – units, classes, relations, systems, transformations and implications.

In this three-dimensional model, then, there are five operations, four contents and six products and therefore as $5 \times 4 \times 6 = 120$, according to Guilford 120 tests would be needed to classify human abilities. In his massive book *The Nature of Human Intelligence* (1967), he describes how he and his co-workers set about producing such tests.

In considering the basis of intelligence, Guilford concludes that both heredity and environment contribute conditions which affect the intellectual abilities of individuals. Thus he would not regard it as appropriate to regard any individual as having a fixed amount of intelligence. Instead he claims that 'Development of the intellectual skills, as in acquiring any kind of skills, depends on practice' (1967, p. 476).

In evaluating Guilford's model we note that, unlike the other models we have presented, Guilford is concerned with the way the individual functions in everyday life, as well as in academic and test situations. For example, he has devised some tests of social sensitivity. Further, he takes into account interpersonal skills and it seems to us his perspective on intelligence is far removed from that of, say, Vernon, who regards it as best tested (in the West anyhow) by tests which examine how individuals 'grasp relations' and by what he calls 'symbolic thinking' (Vernon, 1969, p. 10).

It seems to us that Guilford's theoretical view of intelligence comes near our own which is that intelligence refers to a dynamic cluster of skills which are always capable of being improved. In addition his model seems preferable to others because he does not confine his attention as narrowly as other workers. However, the complex details of his model remain to be confirmed. With respect to Guilford's individual tests Butcher notes that research studies using them have not found that the individual tests produced by Guilford are of much predictive value. In our own experience,

the tests are more useful from a theoretical, rather than a practical, perspective and certainly require extensive revision if they are to be used outside the American culture for which they were designed.

(3) *Viewing intelligence in a cross-cultural context*

In a study done in eastern Zambia, Serpell (1975) studied forty-two children aged between 6 and 13 years. He asked adults who knew the children well about how competently they thought the children dealt with tasks in the village, how well they could carry messages and how well they could answer riddles. Thus, for example, the adults were asked which child they would choose to fetch help, carry messages, and so on. In addition Serpell tried to discover the basis on which the adults ranked the children's ability to do such tasks.

From a detailed analysis of the adults' responses Serpell concluded that 'in the Chewa community we have been studying, the disposition to use one's capacity in a socially productive way forms an integral part of what is valued as intelligence' (1975, p. 25). Thus Serpell pointed out that in a rural society where it is important for people to live in a co-operative manner intelligence is regarded as the ability to contribute to the general social welfare.

It seems to us that this conclusion pinpoints a fundamental proposition which we have been making; that is, intelligence must be related to cultural values. In the West intelligence has been related to the kinds of ability needed to excel in technological and scientific fields, so that, particularly in the case of workers like Burt and Vernon who have focused on a general ability, intelligence is seen as manifesting itself in the ability to reason using largely symbolic material.

Should this Western perspective on intelligence be extended beyond the societies in which it originated? To answer this question let us look at why it is necessary for a society to hold a particular perspective on intelligence. We have seen that before this century, in the West, interest in either defining or measuring intelligence was not very pronounced. Interest in defining and measuring intelligence rose when it was believed that each individual had a fixed amount of the attribute and that this fixed amount of intelligence was largely due to the individual's genotype or his inborn genetic equipment.

This perspective on intelligence led to the production of intelligence tests which were used predictively; that is, children were given such tests and depending on their performance on such tests decisions were made about the children's futures. In Britain, for example, selection for more advanced forms of education rested largely on performance on tests of this nature. When it was discovered that it was not easy to define the underlying basis of such tests and that the ability to do such tests was not fixed, the predictive nature of the tests was called into question, and as we noted, the last fifteen years have seen a dramatic decline in the use of such tests for selection purposes in the West. (Very recently there has been a resurgence of interest in such tests in Britain, but this interest is shown more at the political level than by psychologists or educationalists.)

If we are not very interested in *measuring intelligence* because, as we shall show in the next section, such measurements are of limited predictive value except when dealing with individual children in a diagnostic situation, it seems to us that the subject of the nature of intelligence is not one that should occupy educationalists and developmental psychologists too much.

It would seem sufficient to note the following points in viewing intelligence in a cross-cultural perspective.

(a) Different societies make different demands on cognitive and social functioning. In some societies abilities concerned with the rapid and systematic analysis of symbolic data are highly regarded. In others abilities relating to the sensitive interaction with other members of the community are highly regarded. In some the creative abilities of song, dance and art are seen as particularly valuable. In others the emphasis is on technological skills.

(b) In any society such skills are not evenly distributed within particular individuals. For example, in the West we find highly productive artists who can barely add a column of figures. And in many Third World countries we find very prosperous business men and women who dropped out of school at an early age and lack the basic skills of literacy. In all societies we can identify elderly people who would never have scored well on tests of abstract reasoning like intelligence tests, but who have lived happy and successful lives.

(c) Evidence shows that with training people can improve their ability in most areas of human endeavour. For example, McFie, working in Uganda, showed large increases on scores at a test that is regarded as a measure of 'general intelligence' when he coached some schoolboys at the task (McFie, 1961).

(d) It would seem, therefore, that intelligence is best regarded as a dynamic cluster of skills that are always capable of improvement. Further, the particular cluster of skills that are regarded as important in human functioning will change from culture to culture and time to time.

In this section we have been concerned to show that we cannot consider the nature of intelligence and its measurement in the abstract. Such issues must always be viewed within a social and cultural context.

In discussing the decline in interest in intelligence and intelligence testing, we noted on page 224 that the following three views that were once held about the area are now largely disputed. These were that intelligence is a recognisable attribute, that it is a stable attribute and that intelligence tests are an adequate measure of this attribute. In the next section we examine the grounds for the rejection of these three points about intelligence that were so firmly held when the popularity of intelligence testing was at its height.

The Assessment of Intelligence

(1) *Defining intelligence for assessment purposes*
In the last section we presented three models of intelligence, and the reader will have noted that they differed considerably – Vernon and Burt regarding intelligence as lying largely in the amount of the general factor possessed by any individual, Thurstone regarding intelligence as showing itself in the degree to which an individual possesses what he called the 'primary abilities' and Guilford regarding intelligence as being characterised by the three dimensions of operations, contents and products.

These three models, and we have selected only three of a number of different models that have been proposed, reflect the general lack of agreement shown by psychologists working in the field of intelligence. For example, even among psychologists who would agree that intelligence can be measured by intelligence tests (and many psychologists would not agree that this can be done) there is no generally accepted definition of intelligence.

Nevertheless, despite this lack of agreement in the definition of intelligence, a significant number of Western psychologists have been using intelligence tests for a great many years. They have argued in defence of this procedure, that these tests have a high predictive value – that is, they are able to select those children who will do well in the academic situation. Further, they have argued that these tests are able to differentiate well between children of varying ages, in that in general the older the child the better he will score on these tests. Such psychologists are often quite happy with an operational definition of intelligence. They would define intelligence as 'what intelligence tests test' (Butcher, 1970).

However, it is quite possible for tests to predict who will do well at school and to differentiate between children of varying ages without necessarily measuring this elusive attribute 'intelligence'. Precisely what it is that such tests measure remains an open question. We, for instance, would argue that intelligence tests measure, as much as anything else, the capacity to 'disembed' one's thought. And, as we have indicated, such a capacity is largely dependent on home background and the degree of exposure to academic tasks. Other psychologists, however, remain convinced that intelligence tests do measure, or at least tap, an inborn potential for cognitive growth.

Assuming, however, that intelligence tests *do* tap the inborn potential for cognitive growth, even those psychologists who hold this view would agree that they cannot measure this inborn capacity directly. Such psychologists recognise that the environment must play some part in the development of such a capacity. They also recognise that even the most refined intelligence tests cannot adequately test the whole scope of intelligent behaviour.

Thus Vernon (whom you will remember believes that intelligence is largely controlled by innate factors), following the work of Hebb, makes a distinction between three types of intelligence. He calls the inborn potential for cognitive growth 'Intelligence A'. He sees the interaction between this innate potential and the environment as producing another level of intelligence – 'Intelligence B'. Finally, he regards the intelligence measured by intelligence tests as 'Intelligence C'. In making this third distinction, he takes notice of the fact that any test can only sample the area it is produced to test.

In this short discussion we have tried to indicate that there is no general agreement on a standard definition of intelligence. The conviction that was held earlier in this century that intelligence is a distinct and recognisable attribute seems very questionable. Particularly in view of the differing models that have been suggested for the nature of intelligence, it does not seem appropriate to regard intelligence as a concept that is clear-cut enough to allow for a generally agreed definition to be formulated.

Another problematical area in attempting to define intelligence and to assess it has been the growing awareness that whatever it is that intelligence tests measure it is not a fixed attribute. It is to this aspect of testing intelligence that we turn now.

(2) *Intelligence is not a fixed attribute*

As we mentioned above, the chief use to which intelligence tests have been put is a predictive one; that is, intelligence tests scores have been used to make decisions about the way people would behave in the future. Typically, a group of children might have been given an intelligence test, their intelligence quotients (or IQs) computed, and on the strength of their individual IQs the children might have been assigned to different teaching programmes or different schools. This procedure makes the assumption that such IQs are fixed and do not change with changing circumstances. We shall now consider some evidence that challenges this assumption. But before doing so we might pause to look at intelligence tests in a little more detail and consider how such 'IQs' are computed.

As we mentioned before, the first test to be used widely was Terman's modification of Binet's test, the Stanford-Binet. This test is an individual test; that is, it is given to one subject at a time, in contrast to a group test, which is administered to a number of subjects simultaneously. The Stanford-Binet consists of a number of sub-tests like vocabulary, comprehension, spotting absurdities (or inappropriate features) in pictures and in verbal material, memory tests and verbal reasoning items.

When Terman first introduced the test he gave it to a large number of American children of different ages. From the results of this administration he produced average scores for each age level. This procedure is known as 'standardisation'.

In order to compute a particular child's IQ on the Stanford-Binet the psychologist used to proceed as follows. First, he would give the child the test, then he would add up his raw score. This raw score would then be referred to the standardisation tables and the psychologist would note at what age children, on average, achieved such a raw score. This age level would then be the subject's 'mental age', or MA. The psychologist would then find out the child's actual age – his 'chronological age', or CA – and would insert the CA and MA in the following formula:

$$\text{Intelligence Quotient} \quad \text{or IQ} = \frac{\text{CA}}{\text{MA}} \times 100$$

(For example, if the child's actual age was 8, and his mental age was 10, then his IQ would have been $\frac{10}{8} \times 100 = 125$.) Thus a child whose mental age exactly matched his chronological age would have an IQ of 100 and using this formula the average IQ of any group of American children was likely to be around 100.

When the Stanford-Binet was revised in 1960 this method of calculating IQ was abandoned and the following adopted. A child's raw score is related to the percentage of children of his age who, according to the standardisation tables, achieve his particular score. So, nowadays, a psychologist simply looks up the raw score in that section of the standardisation table that deals with the child's age level and reads off his IQ or, as it is sometimes called, deviation IQ. As with the earlier method, this revised method gives an average IQ of 100 for children from the same kind of population as the standardisation population.

The Stanford-Binet in its amended version is still used. But both in the USA and in Britain its popularity as an individual test has been rivalled by the Wechsler intelligence scale. Like the Stanford-Binet, this test consists of a number of sub-tests. Unlike the Stanford-Binet, however, the Wechsler test yields two raw scores: one relates to verbal skills, like vocabulary, information, comprehension, verbal reasoning, and so on; and the other relates to performance skills, like copying designs with blocks, arranging pictures to tell a story, assembling objects out of standard pieces, and so on. The advantage offered by this test, then, is that it can be used more analytically in diagnosis; for example to compare children's performance on verbal as compared to non-verbal skills.

Very often, however, intelligence tests are given as group tests. These are always of the pencil-and-paper variety, as it is not possible to use different bits of apparatus with a number of subjects at the same time. They also tend to be speeded. Typically they consist of items of verbal reasoning like 'Sun is to day as moon is to …?', or completion of number series like '1, 1, 3, 3, 5, ?'. In addition there are often arithmetical items, items concerned with spatial abilities like the ability to recognise different views of the same shape, comprehension items and vocabulary items. Many of these skills seem to us to be intimately related to the kind of skills that are used in the academic situation, and all can be coached.

Having given you a brief introduction to some IQ tests, their contents and the way IQs are calculated, we should now like to turn to the particular question we are considering in this sub-section. This is, do children score the same IQ if they are tested at different times?

Let us look at group tests first. IQ scores on these tests are not nearly as stable as scores on individual tests, and even as enthusiastic a supporter of psychological tests as P. E. Vernon has called results on these tests 'chancy' (Vernon, 1979, p. 7).

But how consistent are scores on individual tests? They do tend to be relatively consistent, if children remain in the same environment, but a growing number of studies show that if children are exposed to more stimulating environments large increases in IQ scores can be made. Lack of space prevents us documenting these studies but the reader is referred to the series of readings by Clarke and Clarke (1976) to which we referred in the first part of this book, and in particular to the articles by Bronfenbrenner and Gray and Klaus. These studies refer on the whole to large-scale interventions made in areas of social deprivation and the detailed findings indicate that when children from disadvantaged homes were exposed to more stimulating environments, 'Almost without exception, children showed substantial gains in IQ and other cognitive measures during the first year of the program, attaining or even exceeding the average for their age' (Bronfenbrenner in Clarke and Clarke, 1976, p. 247).

If such children complete such an intervention programme and are returned to their previous unsatisfactory environments, then typically after a while their IQs do drop a little, but the most recent long-term evaluations of such studies show that there are enduring cognitive gains. If they remain within a more stimulating environment the gains in IQ remain, and may increase with age. Such was the case in the study of twin boys studied by Koluchová, who made an IQ gain of twenty and twenty-nine points respectively over a period of six years between their eighth year and their fourteenth year (Clarke and Clarke, 1976, p. 58).

The claim that IQs remain stable and are fixed is clearly not supported by these studies. However, these studies all refer to changes in IQ that were associated with the intervention of professional workers who specifically aimed to change IQs. Have changes been observed in IQs when children remained within the same homes and were not subject to this kind of intervention? The answer to this question is that schooling, in itself, can lead to shifts in IQ. Not just whether or not children continue at school, but the type of school they continue to attend can affect IQ scores. Thus in a British study reported by Clarke and Clarke (1978) the IQ scores of boys of 14 years was compared with their IQ scores of three to four years earlier, and it was found that those who went to a more academic type of school showed an upward shift of IQ of up to twelve points. Clarke and Clarke conclude: 'In general the IQ is a fairly stable measure over time, but in individual cases the prediction of IQ in adult life from scores obtained in childhood is subject to considerable error' (1978, p. 127).

In summary, it seems that IQ scores are not at all stable if there are large-scale environmental interventions, but in general individual tests of IQ tend to give fairly stable results if there are no such environmental changes. However, IQs are likely to shift upwards with particular kinds of educational practices.

If IQs are not fixed, then it does seem that whatever intelligence tests measure it cannot be only innate ability. If you are interested in this area, you might like to follow up the references to it in the two books by Butcher and Kamin respectively to which we have been referring throughout this chapter. However, the general consensus held by most psychologists is that intelligence, no matter how it is defined, must be affected to some extent by the individual's genotype. And that this innate potential is always modified by environmental variables. It is our own view that environmental factors are, on balance, more important than innate factors in determining how well any individual adapts to the cognitive, emotional and social demands of life.

(3) *Bias in tests and the test situation*

In the last sub-section we indicated that IQ test scores were very likely to be affected by changes in environment. As we pointed out, this suggests that whatever they measure IQ tests do not measure only innate cognitive potential. They also clearly measure learning experiences as well.

This leads us to ask whether there is any bias in IQ tests that would make certain children more likely to have had relevant learning experiences than others when it comes to IQ test performance.

The answer to this question is surely positive. To the extent that children share the same culture or sub-culture as the psychologists who framed the tests, to that extent they will be at an advantage compared with children from a different background.

Thus, considerable literature exists in the West that would appear to indicate that middle-class children in Britain and members of the dominant racial groups in the USA are at an advantage when it comes to the performance of IQ tests. How does this extend to the cross-cultural perspective?

Right through this book we have argued that great care must be exercised in interpreting the results of tests originating in a culture other than the one for which they were designed. To illustrate this point yet again, let us look at some work done by Serpell (1973) in the area of visual copying which is often a component of intelligence tests.

In most Western tests such visual copying is usually done with either geometric blocks or pencil and paper. Serpell pointed out that young children in Third World countries have very limited experience with these materials compared with their Western counterparts. He devised two other copying tasks – one was mimicking hand positions and the other was wire-modelling which is a commonly found activity among the young Zambian children he worked with.

He then compared two sets of 8-year-olds on three visual copying tasks: copying designs with pencil and paper, copying hand positions and copying wire models. The first set were urban Zambian children and the second set were urban British children. He found that the British children, not surprisingly, did better on the pencil-and-paper task, scores on the hand mimicking tests were much the same for both groups, and scores on the wire-modelling task were higher for the Zambian children. This study would seem to show the importance of drawing on observation of the indigenous environment before constructing tests.

Another study which points to the importance of fitting test procedures to local conditions was that done by Harkness in Kenya (1975). In it she pointed out that many Western tests require children to talk to the experimenter or tester but that in the culture she studied in Kenya children are brought up in such a way that they are discouraged from talking freely to adults. Instead, there is a traditional emphasis on language comprehension rather than language production.

If this is the case, then in such societies tests should be produced which concentrate on the language skills that are highly developed – like understanding – rather than on the language skills like verbal expressiveness, which children undoubtedly have, but which they may be reluctant to use in the presence of an adult, particularly a strange adult.

We have suggested that tests may be biased. In addition to this, test situations may also be biased. We see this most clearly in the atmosphere that is generated in the group test situation. Here children are treated very formally, and required to handle material that may be very strange to them, like, for example, multiple-choice answer sheets. In addition such tests are very often highly speeded. Children who come from societies where there is an emphasis on slow, courteous interpersonal relationships may find such an atmosphere most disturbing.

If IQ tests do not produce very stable scores, if they are so subject to environmental effects and if tests have to be so carefully constructed in order to avoid bias, we may ask the question 'Why use IQ tests at all?'. And it is to this question that we turn now.

(4) Why assess intelligence?

In the West the two main uses of intelligence tests have been to predict future performance at school and to make clinical diagnoses. In addition they have been used extensively in psychological research.

Using such tests for prediction, particularly in order to make selections, is now far less prevalent in Western societies than it was. The reasons for this have been documented in the first part of this chapter.

However, many Third World countries currently use psychological tests, such as tests of verbal reasoning, as part of a battery of tests in order to select children for secondary education or higher education. The advantage of such tests is that they can be marked quickly and objectively, often by means of a computer. In addition, these tests are often favoured because it is thought they are less dependent on previous education than achievement tests are; that is, they are seen as testing actual

cognitive potential rather than learning.

As we have made plain throughout this section, we would not agree with this last view, because so much evidence points to the marked effect environment has on performance on such tests.

So far we have quoted Western studies that show how much environmental factors can affect performance on intelligence tests. But, as Obmeata (1973) shows, environmental factors can affect performance on intelligence tests in other settings as well. Thus, reporting on his own investigation of this area, he notes that in Nigeria children who come from homes where English is spoken are at an advantage when it comes to performance on intelligence tests compared with children who do not come from bilingual homes. Further, in many Third World countries certain parents are able to arrange for extra coaching in the skills that these tests measure.

Nevertheless, in the absence of enough secondary school places to satisfy public demand, such tests will undoubtedly continue to be used, and in the next sub-section we list some of the questions that educationalists should ask themselves about specific intelligence tests they may be faced with.

The use of intelligence tests for diagnostic purposes is far more justified. In the hands of a skilled and sensitive psychologist, an individual test like the Wechsler Intelligence Scale for Children (WISC) or the British Abilities Scale (BAS) or any other test that consists of a number of varied sub-tests can yield a great deal of very valuable information about a child who has learning or behavioural difficulties.

Finally, the use of intelligence tests in psychological research is a practice that is bound to continue. If this is done, however, psychologists should always bear in mind that 'intelligence' should only be considered within a cultural context.

(5) Some questions that should be asked if IQ tests are used

Before you use the results of an IQ test for a pupil or a group of pupils you might consider the following questions.

(a) Is the particular test reliable? By the question 'is the test reliable?' we mean 'does the test measure consistently?'. In order to answer this question, the test manual or test instructions should supply an estimate or estimates of reliability in the form of 'reliability coefficients'. These coefficients may refer to two kinds of reliability – 'test-retest' reliability and 'internal consistency'.

Test-retest reliability is concerned with the consistency with which the test can differentiate between people. For a test to be a good measuring instrument, we would expect it to make the same sort of judgements about a group of people on repeated administrations. Thus we estimate this property of reliability by administering the test twice to the same group of people. This can be done in two ways. Either the same test can be given to the same group of people at an interval of at least three or four weeks apart. Or, if there are two parallel versions of the test, both versions can be administered to the same group of people. In either case, this test-retest approach will yield two sets of scores which can be compared.

It is the comparison between these two sets of scores that gives an estimate of how consistently the test differentiates between people. Obviously, if the same person comes first on both administrations, and the same person comes second, and the same person comes third, and the same person comes last and so on, the test will be differentiating between them very well and very consistently. We would then say that the test had high test-retest reliability, because it ranks people in the same order each time it is given.

Test manuals should inform the user that such a test-retest exercise has been done. The manual should also report an index of the relationship that was found between the two sets of scores that were yielded by the test-retest exercise. This index is called a test-retest 'reliability coefficient'. For most purposes, this coefficient should be at least 0.80 and preferably above 0.90. (The highest value such a coefficient can in fact take is 1.00.)

In addition to reporting test-retest reliability, some test manuals report the *internal consistency* of the test. This refers to the homogeneity of the test and reflects the extent to which the parts of the test are similar. You would only be interested in this measure if all the sections of the test are meant to be testing one thing, and, as most intelligence tests are composed of a number of sub-tests, this statistic is probably not very important in the case of intelligence tests.

Thus, in general, the test-retest reliability is more important in the case of intelligence tests than the internal consistency reliability. Further, it should be acceptably high or the test will not be capable of making stable comparisons between individuals.

(b) *Is the particular test valid?* By the term validity we refer to the extent to which the test measures what you want it to measure. For example, if you wish to use the test to make selections for further education, it is essential to know that, in the past, this test has been accurate in making such predictions.

Thus, before using an intelligence test, it is important to check to see if this test has been used before to make decisions of the sort you are going to use it for. And if this is the case, you should satisfy yourself that it differentiated between individuals in such a way that those who did well at the test did well later in the field you are using it to select for.

(c) *Is the test only testing convergent kinds of skills?* If the test appears to be only looking for answers of a particular kind to stereotyped sorts of questions, that children may have been coached on over and over again, you may not be able to use the test to predict original thinking.

(d) *On whom was the test standardised?* If you are going to use the tables in the test manual to give you an estimate of children's IQs, you must ensure that the standardisation tables given in the manual were derived from testing a similar population to your own group of children. For example, if you are planning to use the test on a group of children who live in a very isolated rural area, you would not wish to relate their scores to standardisation tables obtained from testing children in a large city.

(e) *Where was the test constructed, by whom and for whom?* Ideally you would wish to use a test that was constructed by psychologists from within the local culture, and was designed with the kind of children you intend to use it on in mind.

(f) *Is the test speeded?* Some cultures do not place as much emphasis on working at speed as other cultures do. If your group of children are not used to working under great pressure of time, do not choose a test that is highly speeded. By 'highly speeded' we mean a test that barely allows enough time for the average candidate to finish.

(g) *Who is administering the test?* In some societies girls find it very threatening to be tested by a strange male tester. In such cases, perhaps it would be better to use a female tester.

(*h*) *Are the test conditions comfortable?* Anxious and uncomfortable candidates do not do well at intelligence tests. Make sure that the desks are comfortable and the room is large and airy. Also, do not test late in the afternoon or when the children are hungry.

(*i*) *Are the instructions clear enough?* Check that all pupils understand how to use the answer books. Enough practice should be given to ensure that all pupils are absolutely certain about the way they are to enter their answers.

In this section we have looked at the nature of intelligence and how it has been assessed by psychologists. We have also made some recommendations about extending the use of such tests from the West where they originated into other cultures. We now move away from the field of intelligence and look at the assessment of academic achievement.

The Functions of Assessment

For most pupils and most students, assessments, tests and examinations are very much a part of the educational process. If these assessments are made in an atmosphere of intense competition, then the very words 'assessments, tests or examinations' can produce very definite feelings of discomfort in those about to be assessed. This is because to most consumers of education, like pupils and students, assessment is associated with selection – into the next class, into a particular stream or into higher education. But, of course, selection should not be the only function of educational assessment. Indeed, if education is primarily concerned with the transmission of knowledge and skills, then selection should be one of the least important functions of assessment.

In this section we look at some of the functions of assessment. In doing so, we consider first of all those aspects of assessment that are part of the learning-teaching situation and we refer to these as the 'pedagogic' functions of assessment. Following this we look at those aspects of assessment that are concerned with its selection function and finally we consider some functions of assessment that are linked to social variables. These latter two functions of assessment are intimately related to the functions that any society ascribes to educational institutions and it is for this reason that we consider

assessment in this last part of the book which deals with school in its social setting.

(1) *Assessing for pedagogic reasons*
As Payne (1974) writes, 'The process and results of educational assessment constitute a very powerful force that can be used to improve the effectiveness of teaching-learning situations' (p. 3). In this sub-section we look at some of those aspects of assessment that are directly concerned with the refining of teaching method and the enhancement of learning.

(*a*) Let us look first at the ways in which a teacher can use assessment to give her feed-back about her teaching. To begin with, a teacher may give a test or an assignment to discover whether the class, as a whole, have any general gaps in understanding or whether the class, as a whole, are experiencing any specific difficulties. Assessment used in this manner can help her to identify particular deficiencies in her own presentation of the subject matter under consideration.

If a number of parallel classes in a school cover the same syllabuses but are taught by more than one teacher, a teacher can use the results of common examinations which are given to all the parallel classes to inform her how her teaching methods compare to those used by her colleagues. If she discovers that her particular class performs relatively badly in some areas, she can seek help for the future presentation of such areas. If, which is obviously more pleasing, she discovers that her class perform relatively better in some areas, she can share her clearly effective methods with other teachers. In each of these cases, such mutual co-operation is easier to achieve if teachers themselves do not see themselves in competition with each other, but see teaching as an activity that is always helped by discussion and the sharing of information.

(*b*) Assessment can also be a very effective diagnostic device when it comes to finding out about the progress of individual pupils. If this is one of the primary functions that a teacher is using assessment for, then total scores for each student are far less useful than a careful scrutiny of each individual script so that particular areas of difficulty can be identified for particular pupils.

(*c*) Once a teacher has identified such specific areas of difficulty for particular pupils, assessment can then serve the equally useful function of giving the pupil feed-back about his own strengths and weaknesses in the area that has been assessed.

(*d*) But for a pupil, this kind of individualised feed-back does not only serve the purpose of informing him about his particular strengths and weaknesses, it also performs the important function of satisfying the psychological need for recognition which we discussed in Chapter 1. Because, as we noted then, it can be extremely frustrating for students if their work is returned to them with only the barest indication that the teacher has looked at it. Individualised feed-back goes a long way to motivating students. It can serve as a very useful opportunity for a teacher to enhance a pupil's self-esteem by recognising, not only achievement, but also effort.

(*e*) Such individualised assessment can also provide an opportunity for the exchange of ideas between teacher and student which can be an extremely valuable aspect of education, not only for the student but also for the teacher.

(*f*) Some teachers use assessment to provide incentives to study. Thus a teacher may explicitly reward good marks gained on an assessment exercise. She may, for instance, wish to ensure that certain basic concepts in a particular subject area are learned to mastery. In order to achieve this objective, she may arrange that students who achieve full marks on exercises in that subject area gain a particular privilege. In doing this there is no reason why students should not be given a number of chances to achieve this reward. Her prime objective should be to encourage mastery of the area, and therefore the fact that certain students have to repeat the assignment exercise a number of times until such mastery is reached should not worry her.

(*g*) In fact, a careful attention to the way work is assessed can help to shape constructive study habits. By steady and consistent assessment of work right throughout the year, the teacher can ensure that new concepts are not introduced before the ones on which they rest have been thoroughly revised and understood by students.

In Chapter 6 we defined learning as a change in behaviour or in the predisposition to behave in a certain way. If a teacher wants to ascertain whether in fact learning has taken place, she has to measure this change. And it is this aspect of assessment that has concerned us in many of the points listed above. In addition, assessment can be used to reinforce the interpersonal relationships between teachers and pupils and this is another aspect of the assessment process that we have been concerned with in this discussion. If a teacher treats assessment in the light of these two goals – to evaluate learning and to improve her interactions with her pupils – she may be able to remove at least some of the traditional fear and dislike with which most of her pupils regard assessments and tests. Unfortunately, in most societies, assessment is, of necessity, concerned with selection. And it is to this function of assessment that we turn now.

(2) *Assessment for selection*

Whenever educational resources are short, assessment will be used for selection purposes. Thus, many Third World countries use achievement tests that are based on the material covered in the primary school as the chief mechanism for selection into secondary school. They may use intelligence tests as well as such achievement tests, but as we noted at the beginning of this chapter, intelligence tests often themselves reflect previous learning experiences.

The tension engendered by such selection procedures will be familiar to all readers. Very often the tension is accompanied by extremely high levels of anxiety. And, as we noted before, high levels of anxiety can interfere with cognitive functioning, particularly in the area of reasoning. But because the issues at stake are so important for the vast majority of candidates, there is little teachers can do to reduce such anxiety. In the very nature of selection, some must succeed, and others fail.

Trying to reduce such tension and anxiety lies outside the hands of most teachers. The issues concerned in such selection procedures are social and political in nature, and therefore fall outside the scope of this book. We might perhaps just mention that anxiety levels may not be so high if there are prospects within the particular society of what has been called 'continuing education'. By 'continuing education' we refer to opportunities for adult education, whether at night school or at special further education colleges for mature students.

As we have stressed before in this book, cognitive development occurs at different rates. Faced with the prospect of selection examinations, pupils may be able to prepare themselves for the possibility of failure if this difference in developmental rate is pointed out to them, and they can then therefore accept that some of them may be able to cope better with the cognitive demands of higher education later in life. But they will only be able to treat the prospect of failure in this comparatively philosophical manner if they know that opportunities for continuing education will be available to them later in life.

It is most important for a teacher who is preparing pupils for such entrance examinations to accept that it is unlikely that all her pupils will succeed. And she must strive to make the prospect of failure acceptable to her pupils by stressing that those who do not succeed in being selected, or are sent on to schools that they consider second best, are not failures as individuals. This is particularly important if parental pressure to succeed at such examinations is being very strongly exerted.

In this discussion we have, up to now, considered selection for movement from one institution to another. But of course, examinations are often used for selection procedures within particular institutions. For example, examinations may be used to choose which pupils are to move into the top streams in certain subjects and, in some schools, examinations may be used to stream pupils into slower or quicker classes. Once again, if such selection procedures are used, particular care must be exercised in order to prevent pupils who fail to be selected into the more academic sets or streams from labelling themselves as failures.

In general, if it is desired to separate pupils into ability groups, two points should be borne in mind. The first is that there should always by an opportunity for pupils who show a marked improvement in their performance to be reassessed and moved upwards. Mobility between sets and streams must exist or else the motivation to work may be considerably reduced in the lower sets or streams. The second is that, in general, it is better, psychologically speaking, to keep children in mixed ability classes, setting them in different groups only when the subject matter demands it, rather than streaming children into top or 'A' streams and bottom streams. The latter practice often leads to the creation of a cohesive group of pupils in the bottom streams who, perceiving themselves as failures, adopt a set of anti-school values. (You may remember that we discussed this in Chapter 8 when we referred to the study made by Hargreaves into the values, attitudes and self-perceptions of boys in the top and bottom streams of an English secondary school.)

In the last two sub-sections we have looked at assessment in the two areas for which it is most commonly used. In the next sub-section we look at a third function which may be served by assessment – assessment for social reasons.

(3)   *Assessing for social reasons*

Educational institutions do not exist in vacuums. In most instances they are funded by governmental sources and in many countries such institutions absorb a great deal of the national budget. Because of this, educational institutions are accountable to the public as a whole.

When one of the present authors (Siann, 1973) conducted a survey into attitudes to assessment in a large British university, she found that a small minority of students and staff argued that assessment of student progress was not necessary and, indeed, was counter-productive. Such critics of assessment claimed that there should be sufficient motivation on the part of students to study without the 'carrot and the stick' practice of passing or failing examinations. Consequently they argued that all assessment should be abolished.

Others, who were in the majority, argued that such a viewpoint (that the only motivation to study should be the intrinsic interest of the material) was totally unrealistic and that abolishing assessment would lead to a group of students who would spend their time in idle discussion rather than in serious academic work.

In evaluating these different attitudes to assessment, it seems that both possess a certain validity. It is true that too much emphasis on assessment can destroy vital aspects of the learning process because students may strive to learn what they think will be assessed rather than concentrate on learning material that really interests them. On the other hand, exerting no demands at all on students would certainly lead to some students, at any rate, paying less than full attention to their studies.

One principle, however, emerged very clearly from the surveys, and that was that educational institutions need to assess students or else they are not seen as properly fulfilling their social roles. It is unlikely that the public in any country would wish to support an institution such as a secondary school, college or university which was not seen to operate some kind of assessment system.

In addition, assessment within institutions is a necessary part of the procedure whereby certain individuals are licensed to perform certain tasks. Many educational institutions play a very valuable role in administering external examinations, which enable those who pass them to follow particular careers. For example, secondary schools may teach secretarial skills like typing, shorthand and book-keeping. They may also prepare pupils who study these subjects for external examinations in these areas. Then, if such pupils pass these examinations at school, when they leave school they will be equipped for obtaining office jobs.

These are two of the functions that assessment serves in schools which relate to society in general. There are, of course, others. But by briefly discussing these two aspects we have tried to show how intimately assessment in schools is related to the pressures of the world outside the school gates.

Different Kinds of Assessment

In the preceding section we showed that when we measure or assess educational achievement we do so in order to obtain information that will be useful to us in some way – to optimise learning, to make selections and to validate our educational institutions. But the results of these measurements can only be utilised within a frame of reference. Thus, if we are interested in learning, we have to have a standard of mastery of the subject matter to be learned against which we can check the achievements of those we are assessing. Similarly, when we are assessing for selection purposes, we have to refer individual scores to those of the group.

Basically, then, there are two frames of reference we can use. First, we can check assessment scores against a predetermined standard of mastery that we have set up; and we call this *criterion-referenced* assessment. Or we can check individual assessment scores against the range of scores exhibited by other candidates; and we call this *norm-referenced* assessment. In this section we look briefly at these two different approaches to assessment.

(1) *Norm-referenced assessment*
Until recently, and with the exception of certain skill areas, like passing a driving test, most assessment has been of the norm-referenced kind; that is, a student's performance has been rated with respect to the performance of his peers.

The basic principle on assessment of this kind has been to provide a kind of continuum of performance ranging from the highest in the group to the lowest. The measure or mark assigned to a student usually represented his place on the continuum. The group, as a whole, has a *normative* function – it sets the standards.

This procedure as a whole tells us nothing about the performance in absolute terms of any individual. As a whole, the reference group providing the standard may be 'bright' or 'dull', and this way of looking at scores simply allows us to rank pupils. But obviously such a procedure is useful if we want to make selections.

For example, we may have twenty places available in the top set of mathematics in the third year at secondary school. If we give all the prospective candidates a test, and we are satisfied that the test is a good measuring instrument, then we can simply take the twenty candidates with the highest scores and give them places in the top stream.

In drawing up a norm-referenced test, our major objective in choosing particular items to include will be the extent to which such items differentiate between superior candidates and those of lesser ability. Thus all norm-referenced tests tend to have a fair proportion of rather difficult items.

There are certain drawbacks on relying on this system of assessment. First, much research on the reliability of testing (you will remember from the last section that reliability refers to the consistency of measurement) indicates that it is extremely difficult to make accurate and reliable discriminations when only a few marks are concerned.

Secondly, research tends to show that by labelling and grading we depress the performance of those students who do not fall in the top, say, 40 per cent of the class list.

Research also shows that while a certain amount of stress may be desirable to prompt optimum motivation, greater levels of stress may seriously handicap some students, and indeed at advanced levels of testing may lead to fairly severe emotional disturbances.

The advantage often cited for norm-referenced testing is that competition 'brings the best out' in the top candidates. This leads one to consider whether we wish to encourage the 'extrinsic' motivation engendered by competition or would prefer that motivation to learn and study was more related to the 'intrinsic' qualities of the study area – that is, the student wants to learn for the sake of academic or vocational interest.

However, whatever the psychological disadvantages of norm-referenced testing, it is the only method of assessment when we are selecting candidates for a comparatively small number of places. In using such tests, however, we must always satisfy ourselves that they are both reliable and valid measures; that is (see the previous section on intelligence testing), the tests must be consistent in their measurement and we must ensure that they measure the particular attribute or attributes we are interested in testing.

(2) *Criterion-referenced assessment*

While norm-referenced testing centres primarily on distinctions between individuals, criterion-referenced testing centres on the effectiveness of learning. Criterion-referenced measures are concerned with the individual's status with respect to some criterion-referenced performance standard.

Thus a teacher may decide not to embark on teaching long division until the class or individual concerned gains at least 90 per cent on two tests — one on short division and one on long multiplication. Each student will have to fulfil this criterion, maybe by repeating the test a number of times, before he moves on to the new material.

Criterion-referenced measures, then, are those which are used to ascertain an individual's status with respect to some criterion, that is, performance standard. It is because the individual is compared with a specific criterion, rather than other individuals, that these measures are described as criterion-referenced. The meaningfulness of an individual score does not depend on comparison with other candidates.

In criterion-referenced testing we want to know what an individual can do, not how he stands in comparison to others. For example, when a candidate sits a driving test, the examiner wants to ensure that he can drive safely. He is not interested in how any candidate compares to those who came before him. Instead he will have a list of skills that he expects the candidate to possess. For example, he will expect him to know the highway code, to steer accurately, to change gears at the appropriate time, to brake smoothly and to be able to park properly.

Criterion-referenced testing, then, focuses primarily on the uses to which the knowledge or skill it is testing is to be put. In criterion-referenced testing each item should be chosen to represent a particular aspect of the skill or knowledge that you wish the candidates to master. In this respect, then, there is a major difference in construction compared to norm-referenced testing, where each item is normally chosen to discriminate between those who are superior and those who are comparatively poor in the subject area.

It would seem then, that criterion-referenced testing is most appropriate for the first and third functions of assessment that we distinguished in the last section. That is, it is helpful in refining teaching and learning because it gives information about specific areas of ability and disability. Further, it is also useful in licensing students for particular careers. To go back to our example of using assessment in the area of secretarial skills, we can see that if we set up a shorthand speed of 120 words per minute and a typing speed of 70 words per minute, then as soon as students reach these criteria we can give them their certificate. In essence, it will not matter how many times such assessments are conducted, all the examiner should be interested in is whether the candidate has reached the criteria skills or not.

Thus one of the advantages of such an approach lies in the reduction of anxiety such methods can bring. Other advantages lie in the extent to which there can be a very close interplay between teaching and learning. As each aspect of the subject is taught, it can be assessed. Those that have achieved mastery with respect to the criteria set up can move on to the next section of the subject area. Those who have failed to reach the criteria can revise the material, and be reassessed. This can be repeated until mastery of the criteria is reached.

The chief disadvantages of criterion-referenced testing lies in the construction of the assessment procedures. Before these can be constructed, the skill or knowledge area must be analysed into its component parts, aspects or sub-skills. Further, the items included in the test must be adequate and representative examples of these parts. This kind of analysis, is, of necessity, much easier in certain subject areas than in others. For example, it is easier to construct a criterion-referenced test for mathematics than it is for literature.

In summary, then, in psychological terms, assessment that is centred on the mastery of specific criteria is bound to be less anxiety-provoking than norm-referenced testing. In our opinion it should be the preferred method of testing for the first (pedagogic) and third (social) functions we identified assessment as serving. It cannot, of course, be used for selection purposes.

The Determinants of Academic Achievement

This book has been concerned with educational psychology within a developmental context. Right through the book we have attempted to stress the interaction between all the aspects of a child's life in determining how well he adjusts to schooling and to his emotional and social life.

We hope the reader will now regard academic achievement as multiply–determined. Whether a child does well or not at school is not just dependent on any attributes he happens to be born with. Instead, it is a complex response to his family and home environment, his community and its values, his peers and his other social contacts, his teachers, his school or schools and their assessment procedures, and the overall climate of his school or schools. Finally, and perhaps most important, it depends to a very large measure on his perceptions of himself, his education and how much value he places on academic achievement.

Summary

In this chapter we were concerned with the areas of assessment, both of intelligence and of academic achievement. In both areas we showed that how these attributes are assessed depends largely on social variables.

(1) We first considered the nature of intelligence.
  (a) We demonstrated that interest in the concept could be related to social and political factors.
  (b) We then presented three models of intelligence, indicating how diverse these were.
  (c) We noted that we regard intelligence as a dynamic cluster of skills that are always capable of being improved. Further, we noted that such skills differ from culture to culture, depending on the types of demands each culture exerts on social and individual behaviour. However, we pointed out that all individuals anywhere are capable of learning new and diverse skills.
(2) We then looked at the assessment of intelligence.
  (a) We discussed the difficulties of defining intelligence for the purposes of assessing it.
  (b) We indicated that however it is defined, it cannot be regarded as 'fixed' and that it is not appropriate to regard intelligence as depending only on inborn or innate capacities. *However intelligence is defined, it is always affected by environmental factors*.
  (c) We discussed the difficulties of eliminating bias both in the testing situation and in tests themselves.
  (d) We noted that intelligence tests would probably continue to be used both for selection and for diagnosis.
  (e) We listed some of the necessary properties an intelligence test should have before any decisions can be taken on the results of administering such a test.
(3) We then looked at academic assessment and differentiated three major groups of functions such assessment can serve.
  (a) Assessment for improving and refining teaching and learning (or 'pedagogic' purposes).
  (b) Assessment for selection.
  (c) Assessment for validating educational institutions and their teaching ('social' reasons).
(4) We distinguished two different approaches to assessment.
  (a) Norm-referenced assessment. In this approach an individual's scores are related to those of his peers. It is best used for selection purposes.
  (b) Criterion-referenced assessment. In this approach, an individual's scores are related to his mastery of a set of criteria that are covered in the assessment. It is best used for the pedagogic and social purposes of assessment.
(5) Finally, we argued that academic achievement is multiply–determined for any particular individual – depending on his home, family, community, peers, school and its assessment procedures and, most crucially, on his perception of himself and the importance of educational achievement.

Chapter 11: Selected Bibliography

The nature of intelligence
Kamin, L. J., *The Science and Politics of IQ* (Harmondsworth: Penguin, 1977).

The assessment of intelligence
Butcher, H. J., *Human Intelligence: Its Nature and Assessment* (London: Methuen, 1970).

The purpose of assessment
Ohuche, R. O., and Akeju, S. A., *Testing and Evaluation in Education* (Lagos: African Educational Resources, 1977).

Different kinds of assessment
Payne, D. A., *The Assessment of Learning: Cognitive and Affective* (Lexington, Mass.: D. C. Heath, 1974).

Bibliography

Abiola, E. T., 'Understanding the African school child', *West African Journal of Education*, vol. XV, no. 1 (1971).

Afọlayan, A., 'The six-year primary project in Nigeria', in *Mother-Tongue Education: The West African Experience*, ed. A. Bamgbọṣe (London: Hodder & Stoughton, 1976).

Aronson, E., *The Social Animal*, 2nd edn (San Francisco: Freeman, 1976).

Ashem, B., 'Cultural and social class differences in maternal communication and teaching strategies of the Nigerian mother', *African Journal of Educational Research*, vol. 1, no. 1 (1974).

Ashem, B., and Janes, M. D., 'Deleterious effects of chronic under-nutrition on cognitive abilities', *Journal of Child Psychology and Psychiatry*, vol. 19, no. 1 (1978).

Ault, R. L., *Children's Cognitive Development* (New York: OUP, 1977).

Ausubel, D. P., and Robinson, F. G., *School Learning: An Introduction to Educational Psychology* (London: Holt, Rinehart & Winston, 1971).

Ayonrinde, A., Ashem, B., and Ugwuegbu, D. E. C., 'Effects of educational film show on the attitudes of nursery school authorities', *Ilorin Journal of Education*, vol. 1, no. 1 (forthcoming).

Bakare, C. G. M., 'Some psychological correlates of academic success and failure', *African Journal of Educational Research*, vol. 2, no. 1 (1975).

Bamgbọṣe, A., *Mother-Tongue Education: The West African Experience* (London: Hodder & Stoughton, 1976).

Beard, R. M., 'An investigation into mathematical concepts among Ghanaian children', *Teacher Education*, May 1968 and November 1968.

Beard, R. M., *An Outline of Piaget's Developmental Psychology* (London: Routledge & Kegan Paul, 1969).

Bethlehem, D. W., 'The effect of westernization on cooperative behaviour in Central Africa', *International Journal of Psychology*, vol. 10, no. 3 (1975).

Bexton, W. H., Heron, W., and Scott, T. H., 'Effects of decreased variation in the sensory environment', *Canadian Journal of Psychology*, vol. 8 (1954).

Bidwell, C. E., 'The administrative role and satisfaction in teaching', *Journal of Educational Sociology*, vol. 29 (1955).

Blair, G., Jones, R. S., and Simpson, R. H., *Educational Psychology*, 4th edn (New York: Macmillan, 1975).

Bowlby, J., *Attachment and Loss: 1. Attachment* (London: Hogarth Press, 1969).

Bronfenbrenner, U., *Two Worlds of Childhood: US and USSR* (Harmondsworth: Penguin, 1974).

Bronfenbrenner, U., 'The origins of alienation', in *Influences on Human Development*, ed. U. Bronfenbrenner and M. A. Mahoney (Hinsdale, Ill.: Dryden, 1975).

Brookover, W., Paterson, A., and Thomas, S., 'Self-concept of ability and school achievement', final report of Cooperative Research Project No. 845, US Department of Health, Education and Welfare, Office of Education (East Lansing: Michigan State University, 1962).

Brown, C. W., Ni Bhrolcháin, M., and Harris, T., 'Social class and psychiatric disturbance among women in an urban population', *Sociology*, vol. 9 (1975).

Bruner, J. S., *Towards a Theory of Instruction* (Cambridge, Mass.: Harvard University Press, 1966).

Bruner, J. S., *Beyond the Information Given* (London: Allen & Unwin, 1973).

Bruner, J. S., 'Child's play', *New Scientist*, 18 April 1974.

Bruner, J. S., 'From communication to language – a psychological perspective', *Cognition*, vol. 3, no. 2 (1974–5).

Bruner, J. S., 'The beginnings of intellectual skill: 2', *New Behaviour*, 9 October 1975.

Bruner, J. S., and Goodman, C. C., 'Value and need as organizing factors in perception', *Journal of Abnormal and Social Psychology*, vol. 42, no. 1 (1947).

Bruner, J. S., Jolly, A., and Sylva, K., *Play – Its Role in Development and Evolution* (Harmondsworth: Penguin, 1976).

Bryant, P., *Perception and Understanding in Young Children* (London: Methuen, 1974).

Bullock, A., *A Language for Life: Report of the Committee of Inquiry appointed by the Secretary of State for Education and Science under the Chairmanship of Sir Alan Bullock, FBA* (London: HMSO, 1975).

Burns, R. B., *The Self Concept in Theory, Measurement, Development and Behaviour* (London: Longman, 1979).

Burridge, K. O. L., 'A Tangu game', in *Play – Its Role in Development and Evolution*, ed. J. S. Bruner, A. Jolly and K. Sylva (Harmondsworth: Penguin, 1976).

Burton, R. V., and Whiting, J. W. M., 'The absent father and cross-sex identity', *Merrill-Palmer Quarterly*, vol. 7 (1961).

Butcher, H. J., *Human Intelligence: Its Nature and Assessment* (London: Methuen, 1970).

Calder, J. R., *Understanding Number Bases* (Edinburgh: Moray House College of Education, 1971).

Callaway, A., 'The employment problem of secondary grammar school leavers', *NISER Monograph Series No. 4* (Ibadan: Nigerian Institute of Social and Economic Research, 1975).

Castle, E. B., *Growing up in East Africa* (London: OUP, 1966).

Chaikin, A. I., Sigler, E., and Derlega, V. J., 'Nonverbal mediators of teacher expectancy effects', *Journal of Personality and Social Psychology*, vol. 1, no. 30 (1974).

Chowo, H., 'Child-care in Tanzania', talk given August 1978 to The Three Rs Seminar, Moshi, Tanzania.

Clark, H. H., and Clark, E. V., *Psychology and Language: An Introduction to Psycholinguistics* (New York: Harcourt Brace Jovanovich, 1977).

Clark, M. M., *Young Fluent Readers* (London: Heinemann, 1976).

Clarke, A. M., and Clarke, A. D. B., *Early Experience: Myth and Evidence* (London: Open Books, 1976).

Clarke, A. M., and Clarke, A. D. B., *Readings from Mental Deficiency: The Changing Outlook* (London: Methuen, 1978).

Cockram, L., and Beloff, H., *Rehearsing to be Adult* (Leicester: National Youth Bureau, 1978).

Cole, M., and Gay, J., 'Culture and memory', *American Anthropologist*, vol. 74, no. 5 (1972).

Cole, M., and Scribner, S., *Culture and Thought* (New York: Wiley, 1974).

Coleman, J., 'Current contradictions in adolescent theory', *Journal of Youth and Adolescence*, vol. 7, no. 1 (1978).

Coleman, J., George, R., and Holt, G., 'Adolescents and their parents: a study of attitudes', *Journal of Genetic Psychology*, vol. 130 (1977).

Condon, W., 'Speech makes babies move', in *Child Alive*, ed. R. Lewin (London: Temple Smith, 1975).

Conger, J. J., *Adolescence and Youth: Psychological Development in a Changing World* (New York: Harper & Row, 1977).

Coopersmith, S., *The Antecedents of Self-esteem* (San Francisco: Freeman, 1967).

Cortis, G., *The Social Context of Teaching* (London: Open Books, 1977).

Dale, P. S., *Language Development: Structure and Function*, 2nd edn (New York: Holt, Rinehart & Winston, 1976).

Dasen, P. R., 'Are cognitive processes universal? A contribution to cross-cultural Piagetian psychology', in *Studies in Cross-Cultural Psychology*, Vol. 1, ed. N. Warren (London: Academic Press, 1977).

Dastoor, D. P., and Emovan, A. C., 'Performance of nine-year-old Nigerian children on Block Design Test', *West African Journal of Education*, vol. XVI, no. 3 (1972).

Davis, K., 'Final note on a case of extreme isolation', in *Early Experience: Myth and Evidence*, ed. A. M. Clarke and A. D. B. Clarke (London: Open Books, 1976).

Deregowski, J. B., 'Difficulties in pictorial depth perception in Africa', *British Journal of Psychology*, vol. 59 (1968).

Deregowski, J. B., Muldrow, E. S., and Muldrow, W. F., 'Pictorial recognition in a remote Ethiopian population', *Perception*, vol. 1 (1972).

Donaldson, M., *Children's Minds* (Glasgow: Fontana/Collins, 1978).

Dore, R., *The Diploma Disease: Education, Qualification and Experience* (London: Allen & Unwin, 1976).

Douvan, E., and Gold, M., 'Modal patterns in American adolescence', in *Review of child development research*, Vol. 2, ed. L. W. Hoffman and M. L. Hoffman (New York: Russell Sage Foundation, 1966).

Downing, J., 'Bilingualism and learning to read', *The Irish Journal of Education*, vol. VIII, no. 2 (1974).

Downing, J., 'The psychological foundations for effective communication in reading', in *Reading: Problems and Practices*, 2nd edn, ed. J. F. Reid and H. Donaldson (London: Ward Lock, 1977).

Downing, J., 'Making literacy equally accessible to females and males', paper presented in July 1979 to World Federation for Mental Health Congress, Saltzburg, Austria.

Dunphy, D. C., 'The social structure of urban adolescent peer groups', *Sociometry*, vol. 26 (1963).

Durojaiye, M. O. A., 'A study of socio-metric choice in a Nigerian international secondary school', *West African Journal of Education*, vol. XVI, no. 3 (1972).

Durojaiye, M. O. A., *A New Introduction to Educational Psychology* (London: Evans, 1976).

El-Garh, M. S., 'The philosophical basis of Islamic education in Africa', *West African Journal of Education*, vol. XV, no. 1 (1971).

Elkind, D., *Children and Adolescents: Interpretative Essays on Jean Piaget*, 2nd edn (New York: OUP, 1974).

Elkind, D., and Weiner, I. B., *Development of the Child* (New York: Wiley, 1978).

Epelboin, S., and Epelboin, A., 'Female circumcision', *People*, vol. 6, no. 1 (1979).

Erikson, E. H., *Identity, Youth and Crisis* (New York: Norton, 1968).

Erinosho, O. A., 'Sociocultural antecedents of magical thinking in a modernizing African society', *Journal of Cross-Cultural Psychology*, vol. 9, no. 2 (1978).

Fafunwa, A. B., 'Education in the mother-tongue: a Nigerian experiment. The Six-Year (Yoruba Medium) Primary Education Project at the University of Ife, Nigeria', *West African Journal of Education*, vol. XIX, no. 2 (1975).

Fagbongbe, E. O., 'Reappraising the relationship between discipline, school authority and the Nigerian secondary school student', *West African Journal of Education*, vol. XVII, no. 3 (1973).

Fantz, R. L., 'Visual perception and experience in infancy', in *Early Behavior*, ed. A. W. Stevenson (New York: Wiley, 1967).

Fargo, G. A., Behrns, C., and Nolen, P., *Behavior Modification in the Classroom* (Belmont, Calif.: Wadsworth, 1970).

Ferguson, C. A., 'Baby talk as a simplified register', in *Talking to Children: Language Input and Acquisition*, ed. C. E. Snow and C. A. Ferguson (Cambridge: CUP, 1977).

Fiedler, F. E., *Leadership* (New York: General Learning Press, 1971).

Figueroa, P. M. E., and Persaud, G., *Sociology of Education: A Caribbean Reader* (London: OUP, 1976).

Flavell, J. H., Beach, D. R., and Chinsky, J. M., 'Spontaneous verbal rehearsal in a memory task as a function of age', *Child Development*, vol. 37 (1966).

Flavell, J. H., Friedrichs, A. G., and Hoyt, J. D., 'Developmental changes in memorization processes', *Cognitive Psychology*, vol. 1 (1970).

Floyd, A. (ed.), *Cognitive Development in the School Years* (London: Croom Helm, 1979).

Fogelman, K., *Britain's Sixteen-Year-Olds* (London: National Children's Bureau, 1976).

Fortes, M., 'Social and psychological aspects of education in Taleland', in *Play – Its Role in Development and Evolution*, ed. J. S. Bruner, A. Jolly and K. Sylva (Harmondsworth: Penguin, 1976).

Frandsen, A. N., *Educational Psychology* (New York: McGraw-Hill, 1967).

Furth, H. G., *Piaget for Teachers* (Englewood Cliffs, NJ: Prentice-Hall, 1970).

Furth, H. G., and Wachs, H., *Thinking Goes to School* (New York: OUP, 1974).

Fyle, C., 'The use of the mother-tongue in education in Sierre Leone', in *Mother-Tongue Education: The West African Experience*, ed. A. Bamgbose (London: Hodder & Stoughton, 1976).

Gagné, R. M., *The Conditions of Learning*, 3rd edn (New York: Holt, Rinehart & Winston, 1977).

Garvey, C., *Play* (London: Methuen, 1977).

Gay, J., personal communication (1979).

Geber, M., and Dean, R. F. A., 'The state of development of newborn African children', *Lancet*, no. 272 (1957).

Getzels, J. W., and Guba, E. G., 'The structure of role and role conflict in the teaching situation', *Journal of Educational Sociology*, vol. 29 (1955).

Getzels, J. W., and Jackson, P. W., *Creativity and Intelligence* (New York: Wiley, 1962).

Ghuman, P. A. S., *The Cultural Context of Thinking* (Windsor: NFER, 1975).

Gillie, O., *Who Do You Think You Are? Man or Superman: The Genetic Controversy* (London: Hart Davis MacGibbon, 1976).

Good, T. L., and Brophy, J. E., *Educational Psychology: A Realistic Approach* (New York: Holt, Rinehart & Winston, 1977).

Gordon, C. W., *The social system of the high school* (Glencoe, Ill.: The Free Press, 1957).

Goslin, D. A., *The School in Contemporary Society* (Glenview, Ill.: Scott Foresman, 1965).

Graves, P. L.,'Infant behavior and maternal attitudes', *Journal of Cross-Cultural Psychology*, vol. 9, no. 1 (1978).

Greenfield, P. M., 'On culture and conservation', in *Studies in Cognitive Growth*, ed. J. S. Bruner, R. R. Oliver and P. M. Greenfield (New York: Wiley, 1966).

Gretton, J., and Jackson, M., *William Tyndale: Collapse of a School – or a System* (London: Allen & Unwin, 1976).

Gruneberg, M. M., and Morris, P., *Aspects of Memory* (London: Methuen, 1978).

Guilford, J. P., *The Nature of Human Intelligence* (New York: McGraw-Hill, 1967).

Hagen, J. W., Jongeward, R. H., and Kail, R. V., 'Cognitive perspectives on the development of memory', in *Cognitive Development in the School Years*, ed. A. Floyd (London: Croom Helm, 1979).

Hake, J. M., *Child Rearing Practices in Northern Nigeria* (Ibadan: Ibadan University Press, 1972).

Hamachek, D. E., *Encounters with the Self*, 2nd edn (New York: Holt, Rinehart & Winston, 1978).

Hargreaves, D. H., *Interpersonal Relations and Education*, revised student edition (London: Routledge & Kegan Paul, 1975).

Harkness, S., 'Child language socialization in a Kipsigis community of Kenya', unpublished PhD thesis, Harvard University (1975).

Harkness, S., 'Aspects of social environment and first language acquisition in rural Africa', in *Talking to Children: Language Input and Acquisition*, ed. C. E. Snow and C. A. Ferguson (Cambridge: CUP, 1977).

Hasan, P., and Butcher, H. J., 'Creativity and intelligence. A partial replication with Scottish children of Getzels' and Jackson's study', *British Journal of Psychology*, vol. 57 (1966).

Hebb, D. O., *Textbook of Psychology*, 3rd edn (Philadelphia, Pa.: Saunders, 1972).

Hebidge, D., *Subculture: The Meaning of Style* (London: Methuen, 1979).

Henry, J., and Henry, Z., *The Doll Play of Pilaga Indian Children* (New York: Vintage Books, 1974).

Heron, A., and Simonsson, M., 'Weight conservation in Zambian children; a non-verbal approach', *International Journal of Psychology*, vol. 4 (1969).

Hertzog, J. D., 'Initiation and high school in the development of Kikuyu youths' self-concept', *Ethos*, Winter 1973.

Hudson, L., *Contrary Imaginations* (London: Methuen, 1966).

Hudson, W., 'Pictorial depth perception in sub-cultural groups in Africa', *Journal of Social Psychology*, vol. 52 (1960).

Hulse, S. H., Deese, J., and Egeth, H., *The Psychology of Learning* (Tokyo: McGraw-Hill Kogakusha, 1975).

Hutt, S. J., Hutt, C., Lenerd, H. C., Bernuth, H. V., and Muntjewcuff, W. J., 'Auditory responsivity in the human neonate', *Nature*, no. 218 (1968).

Imoagene, O., 'Predicting success in a developing society', university inaugural lectures, University of Ibadan, (1979).

Ioannou, A. A., personal communication, 1979.

Isaacs, I., 'Environmental and other factors affecting the performance in mathematics of third-year students in Jamaican post-primary schools', *Caribbean*, vol. 3, no. 1 (1976).

Jahoda, G., 'Supernatural beliefs and changing cognitive structures among Ghanaian university students', *Journal of Cross-Cultural Psychology*, vol. 1, no. 2 (1970).

Jencks, C., Smith, M., Acland, H., Bane, M. J., Cohen, D., Gintis, H., and Michelson, S., *Inequality: A Reassessment of the Effect of Family and Schooling in America* (New York: Basic Books, 1972).

Jersild, A. T., *In Search of Self* (New York: Teachers College Press, 1952).

Jordan, D. R., *Dyslexia in the Classroom*, 2nd edn (Columbus, Ohio: Merrill, 1977).

Jordan, R. R., 'A survey of reading interests and reading abilities in some secondary schools in Sierre Leone', *West African Journal of Education*, vol. XVIII, no. 2 (1974).

Kadushin, A., 'Adopting older children: summary and implications', in *Early Experience: Myth and Evidence*, ed. A. M. Clarke and A. D. B. Clarke (London: Open Books, 1976).

Kagan, J., 'Resilience and continuity in psychological development', in *Early Experience: Myth and Evidence*, ed. A. M. Clarke and A. D. B. Clarke (London: Open Books, 1976).

Kagan, J., *The Growth of the Child* (London: Methuen, 1979).

Kagan, J., and Klein, R. E., 'Cross-cultural perspectives on early development', *American Psychologist*, November 1973.

Kagan, J., Klein, R. E., Finley, G. E., Rogoff, B., and Nolan, E., 'A cross-cultural study of cognitive development', *Monographs of the Society for Research in Child Development No. 180*, vol. 44, no. 5 (1979).

Kamin, L. J., *The Science and Politics of IQ* (Harmondsworth: Penguin, 1977).

Kandel, D. B., and Lesser, G. S., 'Youth in two worlds: a summary of research results', in *Influences on Human Development*, 2nd edn, ed. U. Bronfenbrenner and M. A. Mahoney (Hinsdale, Ill.: Dryden, 1975).

Kaye, B., *Bringing Up Children in Ghana: An Impressionistic Survey* (London: Allen & Unwin, 1962).

Keay, F. E., and Karve, D. D., *A History of Education in India and Pakistan*, 4th edn (London: OUP, 1964).

Kenyatta, J., *Facing Mount Kenya* (London: Secker & Warburg, 1961).

Kobayashi, T., *Society, School and Progress in Japan* (Oxford: Pergamon, 1976).

Kohlberg, L., 'The child as a moral philosopher', *Psychology Today*, September 1968.

Kounin, J. S., and Gump, P. V., 'The comparative influence of punitive and non-punitive teachers upon children's concepts of school misconduct', *Journal of Educational Psychology*, vol. 52 (1961).

Krech, D., Crutchfield, R., and Ballachey, E., *Individual in Society: A Textbook of Social Psychology* (New York: McGraw-Hill, 1962).

Kuppuswamy, B., *A Text Book of Child Behavior and Development* (Delhi: Vikas, 1974).

Lake, U., 'Research in the early learning centre, April 1978–March 1979', no. 1 (a Bernard van Leer Foundation project, Salisbury, 1979), cyclostyled.

Leach, M. L., 'Pictorial depth and space: procedural, instrumental, cultural and experimental factors contributing to their perception by Shona children', *Journal of Cross-Cultural Psychology*, vol. 9, no. 4 (1978).

Leacock, E., 'At play in African villages', in *Play – Its Role in Development and Evolution*, ed. J. S. Bruner, A. Jolly and K. Sylva (Harmondsworth: Penguin, 1976).

Leacock, E. B., 'Abstract versus concrete speech: a false dichotomy', in *Functions of Language in the Classroom*, ed. C. B. Cazden, V. P. John and D. Hyams (New York: Teachers College Press, 1972).

LeVine, B. B., 'Yoruba students' memories of childhood rewards and punishments', *Occasional Publication No. 2* (Ibadan: Institute of Education, University College, 1962).

Lewin, K., Lippitt, R., and White, R., 'Patterns of aggressive behaviour in experimentally created "social climates"', *Journal of Psychology*, vol. 10 (1939).

Lloyd, B. B., 'Education and family life in the development of class identification among the Yoruba', in *The New Elites of Tropical Africa*, ed. P. C. Lloyd (London: OUP, 1966).

Lloyd, B. B., 'Studies of conservation with Yoruba children of differing ages and experience', *Child Development*, vol. 42 (1971).

Lloyd, B. B., *Perception and Cognition* (Harmondsworth: Penguin, 1972).

Lloyd, B. B., and Easton, B., 'The intellectual development of Yoruba children: additional evidence and a serendipitous finding', *Journal of Cross-Cultural Psychology*, vol. 8, no. 1 (1977).

Maccoby, M., and Modiano, N., 'Cognitive style in rural and urban Mexico', *Human Development*, vol. 12 (1969).

McDonald, F. J., *Educational Psychology*, (Belmont, Calif.: Wadsworth, 1965).

McFie, J., 'The effect of education on African performance on a group of intellectual tests', *British Journal of Educational Psychology*, vol. 31 (1961).

Mackinnon, D. W., 'The personality correlates of creativity. A study of American architects', *Proceedings of the Fourteenth Congress of Applied Psychology*, vol. 2, Munkgaard (1962).

McMichael, P., 'Self-esteem, behaviour and early reading skills in infant school children', in *Reading: Problems and Practice*, 2nd edn, ed. J. F. Reid and H. Donaldson (London: Ward Lock, 1977).

Maddy, Y. A., *No Past, No Present, No Future* (London: Heinemann, 1977).

Madsen, M. C., and Shapira, A., 'Cooperative and competitive behaviour of kibbutz and urban children in Israel', in *Influences on Human Development*, ed. U. Bronfenbrenner and M. A. Mahoney (Hinsdale, Ill.: Dryden, 1975).

Madsen, M. C., and Yi, S., 'Cooperation and competition of urban and rural children in the Republic of South Korea', *International Journal of Psychology*, vol. 10, no. 4 (1975).

Majasan, J. A., 'Indigenous education for development', in *The Indigenous for National Development*, ed. G. O. Onibonoje, K. Omotoso and O. A. Lawal (Ibadan: Onibonoje, 1976).

Maqsud, M., 'Social interaction and moral judgement in northern Nigerian adolescents', *Journal of Social Psychology*, vol. 105 (1978).

Mays, J. B., *The Social Treatment of Young Offenders* (London: Longman, 1975).

Mbilinyi, M. J., *Traditional Attitudes towards Women: A Major Constraint on Rural Development* (Dar es Salaam: Universities of East Africa Social Sciences Conference, 1970).

Mead, G. H., *Mind, Self and Society* (Chicago: Chicago University Press, 1934).

Mead, M., *Male and Female* (Harmondsworth: Penguin, 1962).

Meeker, B. F., 'An experimental study of cooperation and competition in West Africa', *International Journal of Psychology*, vol. 5, no. 1 (1970).

Millar, S., *The Psychology of Play* (Harmondsworth: Penguin, 1968).

Millham, S., Bullock, R., and Hosie, K., 'On violence in community homes', in *Violence*, ed. N. Tutt (London: HMSO, 1976).

Mitchell, J. C., and Epstein, A. L., 'Occupational prestige and social status among urban Africans in northern Rhodesia', *Africa*, vol. 29 (1959).

Moely, B. E., Olson, F. A., Halwes, T. G., and Flavell, J. H., 'Production deficiency in young children's clustered recall', *Developmental Psychology*, vol. 1 (1969).

Moore, D. F., 'A review of education of the deaf', in *The Third Review of Special Education*, ed. L. Mann and D. A. Sabatino (New York: Grune & Stratton, 1976).

Munroe, R. L., and Munroe, R. H., 'Obedience among children in an East African society', *Journal of Cross-Cultural Psychology*, vol. 3, no. 4 (1972).

Mussen, P. H., Conger, J. J., and Kagan, J., *Child Development and Personality*, 4th edn (New York: Harper & Row, 1974).

Nash, R., *Teacher Expectations and Pupil Learning* (London: Routledge & Kegan Paul, 1976).

Nduka, O. A., 'African traditional systems of thought and their implications for Nigerian education', *West African Journal of Education*, vol. XVIII, no. 2 (1974).

Neisser, U., *Cognition and Reality* (San Francisco: Freeman, 1976).

Nyerere, J. K., *Education for Self-Reliance* (Dar es Salaam: Government Printer, 1967).

Obmeata, J., 'Cultural and linguistic variables in intelligence test scores', *West African Journal of Education*, vol. XVII, no. 3 (1973).

Ogionwo, W., 'Social psychological mechanisms affecting high school drop-out', *West African Journal of Education*, vol. XVI, no. 3 (1972).

Ogunlade, J. O., 'Family environment and educational attainment of some school children in western Nigeria', *West African Journal of Education*, vol. XVII, no. 3 (1973).

Ogunmodede, E., 'End this mutilation', *People*, vol. 6, no. 1 (1979).

Ohikhena, T. O., and Anam, A., 'Leadership types among secondary school principals in the South-Eastern State of Nigeria', *African Journal of Education Research*, vol. 1, 1974.

Ohuche, R. O., and Akeju, S. A., *Testing and Evaluation in Education* (Lagos: African Educational Resources, 1977).

Okonji, M. O., 'The differential effects of rural and urban upbringing on the development of cognitive style', *International Journal of Psychology*, vol. 2, no. 4 (1969).

Okonji, M. O., 'Culture and children's understanding of geometry', *International Journal of Psychology*, vol. 6 (1971).

Oloruntimehin, O., 'Some factors contributing to juvenile delinquency in Nigerian children', *West African Journal of Education*, vol. XVIII, no. 2, (1974).

Olson, D. R., 'On conceptual strategies', in *Studies in Cognitive Growth*, ed. J. S. Bruner, R. R. Oliver, P. M. Greenfield *et al.* (New York: Wiley, 1966).

Omari, I. M., and Cook, H., 'Differential cognitive cues in pictorial depth perception', *Journal of Cross-Cultural Psychology*, vol. 3 (1972).

Onibonoje, G. O., Omotoso, K., and Lawal, O. A., *The Indigenous for National Development* (Ibadan: Onibonoje, 1976).

Opie, I., and Opie, P., 'Street games: counting out and chasing', in *Play – Its Role in Development and Evolution*, ed. J. S. Bruner, A. Jolly and K. Sylva (Harmondsworth: Penguin, 1976).

Osoba, S. O., 'Factors militating against creative and socially relevant intellectual activity in colonial and post-colonial Nigeria', in *The Indigenous for National Development*, ed. G. O. Onibonoje, K. Omotoso and O. A. Lawal (Ibadan: Onibonoje, 1976).

Otaala, B., 'Performance of Ugandan African children on some Piagetian conservation tasks: an exploratory investigation', in *Readings in Educational Psychology* in East Africa. Book Two, ed. H. A. El-Abd (Makerere: Department of Educational Psychology, Makerere University, 1971).

Owoc, P. J., 'On culture and conservation once again', International Journal of Psychology, vol. 8 (1973).

Oyemade, A., 'Institutional care, foster home care or family care?', Pediatrics, vol. 53, no. 2 (1974).

Page, R., and Clark, G. A., Who Cares? Young People in Care Speak Out (London: National Children's Bureau, 1977).

Palardy, J. M., 'What teachers believe – what children achieve', Elementary School Journal, no. 69 (1969).

Payne, D. A., The Assessment of Learning: Cognitive and Affective (Lexington, Mass.: D. C. Heath, 1974).

Pelto, G. H., and Pelto, P. J., The Human Adventure: An Introduction to Anthropology (New York: Macmillan, 1976).

Peluffo, N., 'Culture and cognitive problems', International Journal of Psychology, vol. 2 (1967).

Philips, S. U., 'Participant structure and communicative competence: Warm Springs children in community and classroom', in Functions of Language in the Classroom ed. C. B. Cazden, V. P. John and D. Hymes (New York: Teachers College Press, 1972).

Philp, H., and Kelly, M., 'Product and process in cognitive development: some comparative data on the performance of school age children in different cultures', British Journal of Educational Psychology, vol. 44, no. 3 (1974).

Piaget, J., The Origins of Intelligence in Children (New York: International University Press, 1952).

Piaget, J., The Child's Construction of Reality (London: Routledge & Kegan Paul, 1958).

Pilliner, A. E. G., 'Norm referenced and criterion referenced tests – an evaluation', in Issues in Educational Assessment, Scottish Education Department (Edinburgh: HMSO, 1979).

Poole, H. E., 'The effect of urbanization upon scientific concept attainment among Hausa children of northern Nigeria', British Journal of Educational Psychology, vol. 38, no. 1 (1968).

Prabhu, P. H., 'India: Chapter 14', in Psychology Around the World, ed. V. S. Sexton and H. Misiak (Monterey: Brooks Cole, 1976).

Prewitt, K., 'Education and social equality in Kenya', in Education, Society and Development, ed. D. Court and D. P. Ghai (Nairobi: OUP, 1974).

Price-Williams, D. R., Gordon, W., and Ramirez, M., 'Skill and conservation: a study of pottery-making children', Developmental Psychology, vol. 1 (1969).

Pringle, M. K., The Needs of Children (London: Hutchinson, 1974).

Pugh, G., Children of Working Mothers: Highlight No. 22 (London: National Children's Bureau, 1976).

Rappaport, M. M., and Rappaport, H., 'The other half of the expectancy equation: Pygmalion', Journal of Educational Psychology, vol. 67, no. 4 (1975).

Reid, J. F., and Donaldson, H. (eds), Reading: Problems and Practices, 2nd edn (London: Ward Lock, 1977).

Reid, L. H. E., 'School and environmental factors in Jamaica', in Sociology of Education: A Caribbean Reader, ed. P. M. E. Figueroa and G. Persaud (London: OUP, 1976).

Richards, M. P. M., 'First steps in becoming social', in The Integration of a Child into a Social World, ed. M. P. M. Richards (Cambridge: CUP, 1974).

Ricks, D. M., 'Vocal communication in preverbal normal and autistic children', in Language, Cognitive Deficits, and Retardation, ed. N. O'Connor (London: Butterworth, 1975).

Robertson, K., personal communication (1979).

Rogers, C. R., On Becoming a Person (Boston, Mass.: Houghton Mifflin, 1961).

Rogers, C. R., Freedom To Learn (Columbus, Ohio: Merrill, 1969).

Rosch, E., 'Human categorization' in Studies in Cross-Cultural Psychology, Vol. 1, ed. N. Warren (London: Academic Press, 1977).

Rosch, E., 'Principles of categorization', in Cognition and Categorization, ed. E. Rosch and B. B. Lloyd (New Jersey: Erlbaum, 1978).

Rosenshine, B., Teaching Behaviours and Student Achievement (Slough: NFER, 1971).

Rosenthal, R., and Jacobson, L., Pygmalion in the Classroom (New York: Holt, Rinehart & Winston, 1968).

Rutter, M., Maternal Deprivation Reassessed (Harmondsworth: Penguin, 1972).

Rutter, M., and Madge, N., Cycles of Disadvantage (London: Heinemann, 1976).

Rutter, M., Maughan, B., Mortimore, P., and Ouston, J., Fifteen Thousand Hours (London: Open Books, 1979).

Samuels, S. C., Enhancing Self-Concept in Early Childhood (New York: Human Sciences Press, 1977).

Santrock, J. W., and Ross, M., 'Effects of social comparison on facilitative self-control in young children', Journal of Educational Psychology, vol. 67, no. 2 (1975).

Schaffer, H. R., Mothering (London: Fontana/Open Books, 1977).

Schaffer, H. R., and Emerson, P. E., 'The development of social attachments in infancy', Monographs of Social Research in Child Development, 29, serial no. 94 (1964).

Schmuck, R., 'Some relationships of peer liking patterns in the classroom to pupils' attitudes and achievement', The School Review, vol. LXXI, no. 3 (1963).

Schofield, M., The Sexual Behaviour of Young People (London: Longman, Green, 1965).

Seaga, E. P. G., 'Parent Teacher Relationships in a Jamaican Village', in Sociology of Education: A Caribbean Reader ed. P. M. E. Figueroa and G. Persaud (London: OUP, 1976).

Seaver, W. B., 'Effects of naturally induced teacher expectancies', Journal of Personality and Social Psychology, vol. 28 (1973).

Serpell, R., 'Intelligence tests in the Third World', *New Guinea Psychologist*, vol. 5, no. 3 (1973).

Serpell, R., 'Estimates of intelligence in a rural community of eastern Zambia', HDRU Report, No. 25 (Lusaka: University of Zambia, 1974), cyclostyled.

Serpell, R., *Culture's Influence on Behaviour* (London: Methuen, 1976).

Shaikh, M. S., 'A study of the Nigerian problem pupil and his milieu', *West African Journal of Education*, vol. XVIII, no. 2 (1974).

Siann, G., 'Measuring field dependence in Zambia', *International Journal of Psychology*, vol. 7, no. 2 (1972).

Siann, G., and Pilliner, A. E. G., 'A survey of undergraduate assessment at the University of Edinburgh', *Scottish Educational Studies*, vol. 1 (1973).

Siegel, I. E., Roeper, A., and Hooper, F. H., 'A training procedure for acquisition of Piaget's conservation of quantity', *British Journal of Educational Psychology*, vol. 36 (1966).

Silvey, J., 'The occupational attitudes of secondary school leavers in Uganda', in *Education in Africa*, ed. R. Jolly (Nairobi: East African Publishing House, 1969).

Skinner, B. F., *Contingencies of Reinforcement* (New York: Appleton, 1966).

Slobin, D. I., *Psycholinguistics*, second edition (Glenview, Ill.: Scott, Foresman, 1979).

Smith, F., *Understanding Reading: A Psycholinguistic Analysis of Reading and Learning to Read* (New York: Holt, Rinehart & Winston, 1971).

Sprinthall, R. C., and Sprinthall, N. A., *Educational Psychology: A Developmental Approach* (Reading, Mass.: Addison-Wesley, 1974).

Sprott, W. J. H., *Human Groups* (Harmondsworth: Penguin, 1958).

Stoch, M. B., and Smythe, P. M., 'The effect of undernutrition during infancy on subsequent brain growth and intellectual development', *South African Medical Journal*, vol. 41 (1967).

Stones, E., *An Introduction to Educational Psychology* (London: Methuen, 1969).

Stott, D. O., 'Children in the womb: the effects of stress', *New Society*, 19 May 1977.

Super, C. M., 'Environmental effects on motor development: the case of "African infant precocity"', *Developmental Medicine and Child Neurology*, vol. 18 (1976).

Suran, B. G., and Rizzo, J. V., *Special Children: An Integrative Approach* (Glenview, Ill.: Scott Foresman, 1979).

Thomas, A., Chess, S., and Birch, H. G., 'The origin of personality', *Scientific American*, no. 223 (1970).

Thomas, J., 'Tutoring strategies and effectiveness: a comparison of elementary age tutors and college tutors', unpublished doctoral dissertation, University of Texas at Austin (1970).

Tizard, B., *Adoption: A Second Chance* (London: Open Books, 1977).

Toch, H., *Violent Men: An Enquiry into the Psychology of Violence* (Harmondsworth: Penguin, 1969).

Torrance, E. P., *Education and the Creative Potential* (Minneapolis: University of Minnesota Press, 1963).

Trevarthen, C., personal communication (1979).

Trower, P., Bryant, B., and Argyle, M., *Social Skills and Mental Health* (London: Methuen, 1978).

Turner, J., *Psychology for the Classroom* (London: Methuen, 1977).

Ugwuegbu, D. C. E., 'High school students' attitude towards unethical behaviour in West African School Certificate examinations', *African Journal of Educational Research*, vol. 2 (1975a).

Ugwuegbu, D. C. E., 'Attitude of Igbu high school students towards cheating in examinations', *West African Journal of Education*, vol. XIX, no. 3 (1975b).

Ugwuegbu, D. C. E., 'Ethnic preferences and behavioural intentions of primary school pupils', an invited paper presented at Department of Guidance and Counselling Seminar, (1979a).

Ugwuegbu, D. C. E., 'Effectiveness of self-persuasion in producing healthy attitudes toward polygyny', paper presented at the World Federation For Mental Health Workshop, Salzburg, Austria (1979b).

Uka, N., *Growing up in Nigerian Culture* (Ibadan: Institute of Education, University of Ibadan, 1966).

Uka, N., 'Peer group versus adults as a source of advice during late adolescence', *African Journal of Educational Research*, vol. 1, no. 1 (1974).

Vernon, P. E., *Intelligence and Cultural Environment* (London: Methuen, 1969).

Vernon, P. E., 'The distinctiveness of field independence', *Journal of Personality*, vol. 40 (1972).

Vernon, P. E., *Intelligence Testing 1928–1978: What Next?* (Edinburgh: Scottish Council for Research in Education, 1979).

Wallach, M. A., and Kogan, N., *Modes of Thinking in Young Children* (New York: Holt, Rinehart & Winston, 1965).

Ware, H. R. E., 'The Changing African Family in West Africa', talk given on 3 March 1975 to the Commonwealth Students' Children's Society Seminar on the African Child in Great Britain.

Warren, N., 'African infant precocity', *Psychological Bulletin*, no. 78 (1972).

Warren, N. (ed.), *Studies in Cross-cultural Psychology*, Vol. 1 (London: Academic Press, 1977).

Washburne, C., and Heil, L. M., 'What characteristics of teachers affect children's growth', *School Review*, no. 68 (1960).

Waterlow, J. C., 'Adaptation to low-protein intakes', in *Protein-Calorie Malnutrition*, ed. R. E. Olson (New York: Academic Press, 1975).

Watkins, M. J., 'Theoretical issues', in *Aspects of Memory*, ed. M. M. Gruneberg and P. Morris (London: Methuen, 1978).

Weis, L., 'Education and reproduction of inequality: the case of Ghana', *Comparative Education Review*, vol. 23, no. 1 (1979).

Whiting, B. B., and Whiting, J. W. M., *Children of Six Cultures: A Psycho-Cultural Analysis* (Cambridge, Mass.: Harvard University Press, 1975).

Williamson, K., 'The Rivers Readers project in Nigeria', in *Mother-Tongue Education: The West African Experience*, ed. A. Bamgboṣe (London: Hodder & Stoughton, 1976).

Willmott, P., *Adolescent Boys of East London* (London: Routledge & Kegan Paul, 1966).

Wilson, M., 'School leavers in a coastal area', *Papua New Guinea Journal of Education*, vol. 12, no. 1 (1976).

Winick, M., Meyer, K. K., and Harris, R. C., 'Malnutrition and environmental enrichment by early adoption', *Science*, no. 190 (1975).

Winnicott, D. W., *The Child, the Family and the Outside World* (Harmondsworth: Penguin, 1964).

Witkin, H. A., 'Cognitive styles across cultures', *International Journal of Psychology*, vol. 2, no. 4 (1967).

Wober, M., 'Distinguishing centri-cultural from cross-cultural tests and research', *Perceptual and Motor Skills*, vol. 28 (1969).

Wober, M., 'Explorations on the concept of self esteem', *International Journal of Psychology*, vol. 6, no. 2 (1971).

Wober, M., *Psychology in Africa* (London: International African Institute, 1975).

Worchel, S., and Cooper, J., *Understanding Social Psychology* (Homewood, Ill.: Dorsey Press, 1976).

Wright, D., *The Psychology of Moral Behaviour* (Harmondsworth: Penguin, 1971).

Yoloye, E. A., 'The pattern of dropout in Ibadan primary schools', *African Journal of Educational Research*, vol. 2, no. 1 (1975).

Young, R. E., 'Education and the image of Western knowledge in Papua New Guinea (Part I)', *Papua New Guinea Journal of Education*, vol. 13, no. 1 (1977).

INDEX OF AUTHORS CITED IN THE TEXT

Joint works are indexed under the name of the author mentioned first in bibliographical information, with cross-references from the names of collaborators.

Abiola, E. T. 14, 15, 162, 241
Acland, H., see Jencks, C.
Akeju, S. A., see Ohuche, R. O.
Anam, A. 196; see also Ohikhena, T. O.
Argyle, M., see Trower, P.
Aronson, E. 82, 241
Ashem, B. 15, 21, 23, 38, 241; see also
    Ayonrinde, A.
Ault, R. L. 49, 59, 67, 241
Ausubel, D. P. 113–14, 123, 241
Ayonrinde, A. 17, 38, 241

Bakare, C. G. M. 75, 241
Ballachey, E., see Krech, D.
Bamgbose, A. 214, 219, 241; see also
    Fyle, C.
Bandura, A. 111
Bane, M. J., see Jencks, C.
Beach, D. R., see Flavell, J. H.
Beard, R. M. 61, 67, 241
Beeby, C. E. 199–200
Behrns, C., see Fargo, G. A.
Beloff, H., see Cockram, L.
Bernuth, H. V., see Hutt, S. J.
Bethlehem, D. W. 166, 241
Bexton, W. H. 8, 241
Bidwell, C. E. 197, 241
Binet, A. 221–3, 225, 229–30
Birch, H. G., see Thomas, A.
Blair, G. 186, 190, 194, 241
Bloom, B. S. 12
Bowlby, J. 6, 241
Bronfenbrenner, U. 6, 85, 163, 230, 241
Brookover, W. 77, 241
Brophy, J. E., see Good, T. L.
Brown, C. W. 17, 241
Bruner, J. S. 22, 28, 34, 40, 49–52, 81,
    111–13, 114–15, 123, 241
Bryant, B., see Trower, P.
Bryant, P. 45, 67, 241
Bullock, A. 96, 97, 98–9, 123, 241
Bullock, R., see Millham, S.
Burns, R. B. 150, 241
Burridge, K. O. L. 35–6, 241
Burt, C. 224, 225, 227
Burton, R. V. 152, 241
Butcher, H. J. 221, 225, 229, 239, 242; see
    also Hasan, P.

Calder, J. R. 109, 242
Callaway, A. 177, 242
Carlson, A. J. 135
Castle, E. B. 35, 36, 105, 106, 200, 242
Chaikin, A. I. 78, 242
Chess, S., see Thomas, A.
Chinsky, J. M., see Flavell, J. H.
Chowo, H. 11, 19, 65, 242
Clark, E. V., see Clark, H. H.
Clark, G. A., see Page, R.
Clark, H. H. 30, 33, 40, 242

Clark, M. M. 96, 97, 123, 242
Clarke, A. D. B., see Clarke, A. M.
Clarke, A. M. 4, 7, 9, 10, 14, 27, 230–1,
    242
Cockram, L. 135, 142, 144, 156, 160, 165,
    242
Cohen, D., see Jencks, C.
Cole, M. 10, 21, 27, 59, 60, 63–4, 67,
    105–6, 242
Coleman, J. 156, 160, 242
Condon, W. 5, 242
Conger, J. J. 127, 130, 132, 133, 136–7,
    143, 150, 151, 156, 160, 164, 165, 173,
    179, 242; see also Mussen, P. H.
Cook, H., see Omari, I. M.
Cooper, J., see Worchel, S.
Coopersmith, S. 82, 242
Cortis, G. 188, 189, 242
Court, D., see Prewitt, K.
Crutchfield, R., see Krech, D.

Dale, D. S. 33, 34, 242
Dasen, P. R. 60, 242
Dastoor, C. P. 23, 242
Davidson, A. 145
Davis, K. 9, 242
Dean, R. F. A., see Geber, M.
Deese, J., see Hulse, S. H.
Dennis, W. 7
Deregowski, J. B. 61, 62, 242
Derlega, V. J., see Chaikin, A. I.
Donaldson, H., see Reid, J. F.
Donaldson, M. 41, 46, 59, 60, 65, 205,
    206, 242
Dore, R. 176–7, 208, 217, 219, 242
Douvan, E. 164, 242
Downing, J. 24, 97, 215–16, 242
Dunphy, D. C. 162, 242
Durojaiye, M. O. A. 6, 14, 27, 119, 129,
    130, 132, 133, 150, 155, 159, 162, 164,
    167, 242

Egeth, H., see Hulse, S.H.
El-Gahr, M. S. 209, 242
Elkind, D. 136, 145–6, 163, 178–9, 242
Emerson, P. E., see Schaffer, H. R.
Emovan, A. C., see Dastoor, C. P.
Engel, B. 135
Epelboin, A., see Epelboin, S.
Epelboin, S. 133, 242
Epstein, A. L., see Mitchell, J. C.
Erikson, E. H. 134–5, 150, 242
Erinosho, O. A. 210, 242

Fafunwa, A. B. 216, 242
Fagbongbe, E. O. 172, 242
Fantz, R. L. 5, 243
Fargo, G. A. 123, 243
Fay, J., see Davidson, A.
Ferguson, C. A. 33, 243

Figueroa, P. M. E. 219, 243
Flavell, J. H. 54–5, 243; see also
    Moely, B. E.
Floyd, A. 67, 243
Fogelman, K. 160, 176, 243
Fortes, M. 35, 37, 243
Frandsen, A. N. 193, 243
Freud, A. 155–6
Friedrichs, A. G., see Flavell, J. H.
Furth, H. G. 46–7, 61, 67, 90–1, 243
Fyle, C. 216, 243

Gagné, R. M. 88, 93, 94–5, 123, 243
Galton, F. 221, 223
Garvey, C. 34–5, 36, 37, 40, 243
Gay, J. 154, 155, 243; see also Cole, M.
Geber, M. 19, 243
Ghai, D. P., see Prewitt, K.
Ghuman, P. A. S. 10, 65–6, 105, 136, 243
Gillie, O. 225, 243
Gintis, H., see Jencks, C.
Gold, M., see Douvan, E.
Goldfarb, W. W. 6
Good, T. L. 24, 78, 81, 123, 186, 203–4,
    243
Goodman, C. C. 51
Gordon, C. W. 197, 243
Gordon, W., see Price-Williams, D. R.
Goslin, D. A. 185, 186, 187, 243
Graves, P. L. 25, 243
Gray, J. L. 230
Greenfield, P. M. 60, 243
Gretton, J. 203, 243
Gruneberg, M. M. 67
Guilford, J. P. 102, 103, 224, 226, 227, 243
Gump, P. V., see Kounin, J. S.

Hagen, J. W. 55, 243
Hake, J. M. 9, 10, 19, 34, 243
Halwes, T. G., see Moely, B. E.
Hamachek, D. E. 71, 72–3, 74, 76–7, 87,
    131, 141, 142, 150, 156, 243
Hargreaves, D. H. 138, 169–70, 175, 179,
    236, 243
Harkness, S. 33, 231, 243
Harris, R. C., see Winick, M.
Harris, T., see Brown, C. W.
Hasan, P. 102, 243
Hebb, D. O. 8, 18, 229, 243
Hebidge, D. 206–8, 243
Heil, L. M., see Washburne, C.
Henry, J. 38, 243
Henry, Z., see Henry, J.
Heron, A. 61, 243
Heron, W., see Bexton, W. H.
Hertzog, J. D. 138, 154–5, 172, 243
Hooper, F. H., see Siegel, I. E.
Hosie, K., see Millham, S.
Hoyt, J. D., see Flavell, J. H.
Hudson, L. 102, 105, 243

Hudson, W. 61, 62, 243
Hull, C. L. 108
Hulse, S. H. 123, 243
Hutt, C., see Hutt, S. J.
Hutt, S. J. 5, 34, 244

Imoagene, O. 196, 244
Ioannou, A. A. 12, 244
Isaacs, I. 172, 244

Jackson, M., see Gretton, J.
Jacobson, L., see Rosenthal, R.
Jahoda, G. 211, 244
Janes, M. D., see Ashem, B.
Jencks, C. 23, 171, 244
Jersild, A. T. 73, 244
Jones, R. S., see Blair, G.
Jongeward, R. H., see Hagen, J. W.
Jordan, D. R. 123, 244
Jordan, R. R. 96, 244

Kadushin, A. 7, 18, 244
Kagan, J. 10, 24, 26, 65, 244; see also
    Mussen, P. H.
Kail, R. V., see Hagen, J. W.
Kamin, L. J. 223, 239, 244
Kandel, D. B. 160–1, 162, 163–4, 244
Karve, D. D., see Keay, F. E.
Kaye, B. 190, 193, 244
Keay, F. E. 199, 244
Kelly, M., see Philp, H.
Kelman, H. C. 82
Kenyatta, J. 35, 36–7, 179, 200, 244
Klaus, M. H., see Gray, J. L.
Klein, R. E., see Kagan, J.
Kobayashi, T. 199, 244
Kogan, N., see Wallach, M. A.
Kohlberg, L. 147–9, 244
Kounin, J. S. 190, 244
Krech, D. 188, 244
Kuppuswamy, B. 6, 105, 130, 136, 166–7,
    244

Lake, U. 24, 244
Leach, M. L. 62–3, 244
Leacock, E. 35, 36, 60, 105, 106, 244
Lenerd, H. C., see Hutt, S. J.
Lesser, G. S., see Kandel, D. B.
LeVine, B. B. 14, 244
Lewin, K. 165, 189, 244
Lippitt, R., see Lewin, K.
Lloyd, B. B. 22, 23, 61, 67, 244
Lloyd, P. C., see Lloyd, B. B.

Maccoby, M. 64–6, 244
McDonald, F. J. 186, 189, 244
McFie, J. 228, 244
Mcgarrigle, J. 46., see also Donaldson, M.
MacKinnon, D. W. 104, 244
McMichael, P. 18, 75–7, 245
Maddy, Y. A. 142–3, 245
Madge, N., see Rutter, M.
Madsen, M. C. 165–6, 245
Majasan, J. A. 137, 138, 199–200, 245

Mann, L. 123, 245
Maqsud, M. 149, 245
Maughan, B., see Rutter, M.
Mays, J. B. 12, 245
Mbilinyi, M. J. 22, 25, 245
Mbiti, J. S. 209
Mead, G. H. 72, 74, 245
Mead, M. 127, 131, 152, 154, 156, 179,
    245
Meeker, B. F. 166, 245
Meyer, K. K., see Winick, M.
Meyerson, L. 156
Michelson, S., see Jencks, C.
Millar, S. 40, 245
Millham, S. 144, 245
Mitchell, J. C. 176, 245
Modiano, N., see Maccoby, M.
Moely, B. E. 55, 245
Moore, D. F. 123, 245
Morris, P., see Gruneberg, M. M.
Mortimore, P., see Rutter, M.
Muldrow, E. S., see Deregowski, J. B.
Muldrow, W. F., see Deregowski, J. B.
Munroe, R. H., see Munroe, R. L.
Munroe, R. L. 10, 245
Munjewcuff, W. J., see Hutt, S. J.
Mussen, P. H. 45, 51–2, 54, 56–7, 245
Myers, R. E. 197–8

Nash, R. 78, 87, 245
Nduka, O. A. 209, 210, 245
Ní Bhrolcháin, M., see Brown, C. W.
Njau, E. 106
Nolen, P., see Fargo, G. A.
Nyerere, J. K. 218, 219, 245

Obmeata, J. 232, 245
Ogionwo, W. 169, 170, 173, 245
Ogunlade, J. O. 20, 245
Ogunmodede, E. 133, 245
Ohikhena, T. O. 196, 245
Ohuche, R. O. 240, 245
Okonji, M. O. 21, 61, 213, 245
Oloruntimehin, O. 179, 245
Olson, D. R. 57, 59, 245
Olson, F. A., see Moely, B. E.
Omari, I. M. 62, 245
Opie, I. 37, 245
Opie, P., see Opie, I.
Osoba, S. O. 208, 245
Otaala, B. 21, 245
Ouston, J., see Rutter, M.
Owoc, P. J. 61, 246
Oyemade, A. 7, 246

Page, R. 13, 246
Palardy, J. M. 77, 246
Paterson, A., see Brookover, W.
Pavlov, I. 107–8, 110
Payne, D. A. 234, 240, 246
Pelto, G. H. 127, 155, 246
Pelto, P. J., see Pelto, G. H.
Peluffo, N. 61, 246
Persaud, G., see Figueroa, P. M. E.

Philips, S. U. 6, 246
Philp, H. 61, 246
Piaget, J. 41–7, 56, 60–1, 66, 67, 135, 145,
    149, 246
Prabhu, P. H. 159, 246
Prewitt, K. 23, 246
Price-Williams, D. R. 60, 246
Pringle, M. K. 5, 7, 8, 9, 12, 13, 14, 25, 28,
    112, 246
Pugh, G. 17, 246

Ramirez, M., see Price-Williams, D. R.
Rappaport, H., see Rappaport, M. M.
Rappaport, M. M. 78–80, 104n, 246
Reid, J. F. 123, 246
Reid, L. H. E. 200, 246
Richards, M. P. M. 30, 246
Ricks, D. M. 30, 246
Rizzo, J. V., see Suran, B. C.
Robertson, K. 97, 246
Robinson, F. G., see Ausubel, D. P.
Roeper, A., see Siegel, I. E.
Rogers, C. R. 71–2, 187, 246
Rosch, E. 57, 246
Rosenshine, B. 8, 246
Rosenthal, R. 77, 246
Ross, M., see Santrock, J. W.
Rubin, T. 51
Rutter, M. 6, 8, 11, 12, 17, 24, 142, 170–1,
    172, 174, 179, 246

Sabatino, D. A., see Mann, L.
Samuels, S. C. 76, 246
Santrock, J. W. 77, 246
Schaffer, H. R. 6, 14, 17, 246
Schmuck, R. 193, 246
Scott, T. H., see Bexton, W. H.
Scribner, S., see Cole, M.
Seaga, E. P. G. 202, 203, 204–5, 246
Sears, R. R. 19
Seaver, W. B. 77–8, 246
Serpell, R. 62–3, 67, 216, 219, 226, 227,
    247
Shaikh, M. S. 143, 247
Shapira, A., see Madsen, M. C.
Siann, G. 52–3, 146–7, 213, 219, 236, 247
Siegel, I. E. 46, 247
Sigler, E., see Chaikin, A. I.
Silvey, J. 176, 247
Simonsson, M., see Heron, A.
Simpson, R. H., see Blair, G.
Skinner, B. F. 108, 110, 123, 247
Slobin, D. I. 31–3, 247
Smith, F. 96, 123, 247
Smith, M., see Jencks, C.
Smythe, P. M., see Stoch, M. B.
Spearman, C. 225, 226
Sprinthall, A. N., see Sprinthall, R. C.
Sprinthall, R. C. 50, 221, 247
Sprott, W. J. H. 185, 247
Stoch, M. B. 21, 247
Stones, E. 185, 247
Stott, D. O. 16, 247
Super, C. M. 18, 247

Suran, B. C. 105, 117, 118, 123, 247

Terman, L. M. 229
Thomas, A. 26, 81, 247
Thomas, S., *see* Brookover, W.
Thomson, G. 223
Thorndike, E. 107
Thurstone, L. L. 224, 226
Tizard, B. 7, 18, 247
Toch, H. 144, 247
Torrance, E. P. 105, 106, 123, 247
Trevarthen, C. 6, 247
Trower, P. 179, 247
Turner, J. 67, 104, 123, 247

Ugwuegbu, D. C. E. 38, 178, 185, 186, 193, 247
Uka, N. 9, 11, 14, 19, 36, 163, 247

Vernon, P. E. 9, 20, 60, 105, 136, 213, 224, 226, 227, 229, 230, 247

Wachs, H., *see* Furth, H. G.
Wallach, M. A. 102, 247
Ware, H. R. E. 6, 247
Warren, N. 18, 67, 247
Washburne, C. 8, 247
Waterlow, J. C. 21, 247
Watson, J. B. 110–11
Weiner, I. B., *see* Elkind, D.
Weiss, L. 23, 248

White, R., *see* Lewin, K.
Whiting, B. B. 85–6, 87, 248
Whiting, J. W. M., *see* Whiting, B. B.
Williamson, K. 215, 248
Willmott, P. 162, 164–5, 248
Wilson, M. 202, 218, 248
Winick, M. 21, 248
Witkin, H. A. 211–13, 248
Wober, M. 10, 18, 27, 67, 75, 248
Worchel, S. 188, 248
Wright, D. 149, 150, 248

Yerkes, R. M. 223
Yi, S., *see* Madsen, M. C.
Yoloye, E. A. 218, 248
Young, R. E. 208–9, 248

GENERAL INDEX

ability, level of 12, 15
abstraction 22, 56, 57, 60, 64–5, 104, 145
adjustment 71–87, 168–9
adolescent: acquisition of identity 134–5;
    alienation 74, 156–7; emotional
    problems 142–4, 150, 179;
    psychological problems 130, 134–47;
    radicalism 156–7; rebellion 146;
    rejection of parents' values 157; self-
    concept 130–1; sexual behaviour 132–3,
    166–8; sub-culture 169, 178
adoption 7, 18
affection, need for 6–8, 17, 18, 73, 82, 136,
    159
'ages and stages' 135
aggression 26, 82–3, 111, 141, 144, 190
analytic thinking 20, 47, 65, 66, 146
Anancy stories 203
Arapesh (New Guinea) 131–2
areas, play 38–9
arithmetic 49, 80, 81, 90
arousal 8–9
assessment 115, 121, 220–39, see also tests
association learning 88–91, 95, 107–8, 121
astrology 211
attention 28, 52, 53, 59, 88, 119
attitude: of child 4, 158, 170, 175; of
    parent 9, 10, 13, 19, 21–2, 23, 25, 82,
    139, 158, 200, 202; of school-manager
    197; of society 11, 13, 138, 200, 202; of
    teacher 11, 12, 73–4, 77–8, 111
Australia 60
'authoritarian-aggressive' 85
authority 82, 106, 147
autonomy 82, 135, 136, 137, 138, 143

babbling 30
Baoule (West Africa) 60
Baroda 130
BAS, see tests
behaviour 11, 80, 82–4, 108, 147, 172,
    177–9
behaviourism 11–12, 107–11, 122
Bengal, West 25
Benin 214
bias: cultural 10, 103, 159, 193, 226, 231;
    social 118, 161, 193, 224
Birmingham 65
blindness 16, 117–18
'bloomers' 77
Bobo doll 111
boredom 8, 83, 138
braille alphabet 117, 118
bricks, building 39
bullying 83, 144, 168; ceremonial 152

Canada 8
caretakers (of children) 6, 17, 26, 28, 82
cartoons 63
case-studies: Isabelle (deaf-mute's child) 9,
    20; Isak (dyslectic) 119–21; Jacqueline
    (Piaget's daughter) 43; Jane and Peter
    (adolescents) 156; Paul (fantasist) 145

categorisation 55, 56–7, 59, 64
centration 44
ceremonies: bar-mitzvah 155;
    confirmation 155; initiation 12, 127,
    131, 133, 152–5
characteristics, sexual 129–33
cheating 149, 185
Chewa 227
child-care 5–7, 16–19, 22, 24, 161
Children's Bureau, National 13
China 185
choice, vocational 175–7, 179
circumcision: female 133; male 154–5
class, socio-economic 21, 23, 24, 170, 173,
    176, 193, 224
class-management 171
clay, modelling 39
climate, school 170–5
coaching 23, 103, 224, 233
colour-discrimination 19
communication: non-verbal 28, 30; pre-
    linguistic 28–30, 40
competition and co-operation 75, 165–6,
    185, 227
compliance 82, 147, 150
computer analogy of cognitive system 7, 8
concepts: abstract 49, 56, 93; complex 56;
    concrete 91–3; formation of 64;
    scientific 61; valid 56
concrete-operations period 43–5
conditioning 109–11, 185
conflict: family 158, 159, 161; school 195
conformity 13, 106, 169
Confusianism 199
conservation 41, 44–6, 60–1
consistency 7–8, 71
control group 78, 79, 104
convergence 102, 105
co-ordination 18, 20, 46
cortex, visual 51
councils, pupil 12
counselling 130, 134, 143, 149, 155, 195
creation-stories, traditional 209–10
creativity 36–9, 101–6, 113, 122
crèches 7, 17
cues 53, 55, 61, 90, 91
culture: and cognitive development 24, 41,
    59–66, 205, 211; and creativity 105–6;
    and intelligence 225; and language
    development 36–7, 60; and self-concept
    74–5, 86; and social relationships 85–7
curiosity 22, 105, 111
curriculum 77, 170, 173, 176–7, 179, 199,
    206
Cyprus 12

Dakar 60
dancing 36–7
Darwinian theory 209
'dating' 167
deafness: associated with rubella 16; and
    language development 116–17

defence mechanisms 139–42, 150
deformity 11
delinquents, social 178–9
'dependent-dominant' 85
depression 17, 144
deprivation 4, 6, 24, 121, 137, 230
determinism 4
development: character 26, 82; cognitive 7,
    9, 20, 40–65, 144; emotional 5–6, 8,
    80–6, 134, 135, 142–4; intellectual 36,
    145, 221–39; language 9, 28, 36; moral
    82, 147–50; perceptual 19, 20, 21;
    physical 16, 19, 21, 117, 129–34, 149,
    155; skills 34, 37, 97, 145; social 6, 10,
    111, 137, 160–1; temperament 25–7
development, rate of 26–7
deviance 12, 137, 149, 169, 177–9
diagrams 63
disadvantage 21, 24, 118, 119, 172
discipline: home 7, 159; school 7–8, 12,
    82–5, 111, 147, 149, 190, 203–4
discovery learning 111, 113, 122
disembedded thought 22–3, 56–7, 205,
    206, 211
displacement (defence mechanism) 141–2
disruptiveness 26, 82–3, 106, 144, 168, 171
disturbance, emotional 17, 143, 144, 150,
    157
divergence 102, 103, 105
dog, Pavlov's 107–8, 110
dolls 38, 43
dolls' house 39
drawing 46, 101
dress, adolescent style of 157, 169
dressing-up 39
drink, alcoholic 16, 144, 149
drop-outs 169, 170, 173, 218
drugs, addictive 16, 141, 144, 149
dyslexia 119–21

Ebrie 60
EEG (electroencephalograph) 21
egocentrism 43–5, 46, 116
Einstein, A., school performance of 15
elite 23, 61, 173, 209
empathy 146
enactive representation 49, 50, 81, 112
England 199
English language 30–2, 213, 214
environment ix, 4, 9, 10, 17, 19, 21, 22, 25,
    34, 35, 43, 47, 61, 64, 93, 129
Eskimos 61
esprit de corps 195
examinations 23, 204, 206–7, 272, 277–8,
    285
expectation 51, 77–80, 81, 131, 137, 143,
    169
experiences, need for new 5, 9, 14, 34, 35,
    37, 80, 136–8, 159
experiments, psychological 44–6, 54, 57,
    59, 66, 75, 107, 165–6

exploration, natural 9, 15–16, 18, 21, 28, 34–5, 43, 65, 80, 81, 106

family: extended ix, 6, 13, 17, 23, 85, 86, 158–60, 166–7; matrifocal 161; nuclear 13, 86, 158, 159–61; one-parent 161
fantasy 37, 139–40, 145, 175
feedback 18, 23, 80, 91, 112, 234
field-dependence 211–13
figure: embedded 52; reversible 51
Finnish language 32, 97
firmness 190
folk-tales 49, 203, 214
France 135–6, 199, 221
French language 213, 214
friendship 74, 137, 164–5

games: Ayo, Dara, or Okwe (Nigeria) 10; co-operative 81–2; 'counting-out' (Great Britain) 37; Ekak (Nigeria) 36; improvised 34; make-believe 39; Monopoly (Great Britain) 36; reasoning 46–7; Taketak (New Guinea) 35; traditional 37
'gender development' 23
generation gap 85, 138, 157
genetic factors 25–7, 42
genotype 26, 174, 225, 227, 231
German Democratic Republic 6
German language 31, 32
Ghana 23
grapheme 97
graphic thinking 46–7
Great Britain 17, 23, 24, 36, 37, 195, 203, 221
Greece 33
Greenland 60
grouping 56–7
growth-spurt 128–9, 149
Guatemala 10, 24, 65
guilt 11, 135, 158
gypsy children 202–3

hair-style, adolescent 157, 169
handicaps 11, 21, 115–23
Hausa 18
headteacher 195–8
Hinduism 159, 199, 210
homework 195, 200
Hopi 37
hormones, sex 129, 132–3
hypotheses 57–9, 144

Ibadan 7
iconic representation 49–50, 81, 112
identification 82, 96, 147, 150
identity crisis 134, 135
illness 15–16
illusions, visual ix, 51
inadequacy, feelings of 27, 129, 139, 142–4
incest taboo 133
India 6, 65
Indians, North American 6, 155
inference 21, 45, 59, 62, 65, 101

initiation 121, 127, 131, 133, 152–5
institutions: basic social 149; child-care 6–7, 12, 13; educational 175, 236; for mentally defective 223
instruction, language of 33, 60, 200, 213–17, 218–19
insulation, emotional 142
intelligence 220–34
interaction: adult-child 3–4, 5–6, 17, 22, 23, 28, 30, 78, 137; peer 85, 137; social 10, 148, 149, 193, 194
interest 90, 91, 114
internalisation 82, 144, 147, 150
IQ 102, 119, 221–4
Islam ix, 147, 209, 210
Israel 17, 165–6

Jamaica 200, 202, 204
Japan 199
Japanese language 97
jokes 36

Kampala 167
Kenya 10, 18, 23, 33, 35, 36, 231
kibbutzim 17, 165–6
Kikuyu (Gikuyu) 35, 36, 138, 154–5, 200
Kpelle 63–4

labelling 54–5
Lagos 143
language: and communication 20, 33, 115; and conceptualisation 33; children's 30–3, 40; foreign 213–17; learning 9, 20, 28, 31–2, 40, 48; mediating function of 20; playful use of 36–7
laws 148
leadership: autocratic 190, 197; 'consideration' 188, 195; democratic 189; 'initiating structure' 188, 195; laissez-faire 189; transactional 196
learning: abstract concept 93–4, 121–2; association 88–91, 121; discrimination 91–3, 121
Lebanon 7
left-handedness 13–14
Lesotho 154, 155
level, (pre-, post-) conventional 148
Liberia 21, 27, 63, 155, 166
lies 37
lip-reading 116–17
logical thinking 22, 45, 46–7, 59, 64–5
London 8, 11, 17, 170, 203
'look and say' 98
Luo language 32

McCarthy scales 24
Malawi 24
'mainstreaming' 118
malnutrition: in adolescence 129; in infancy 21, 119; in pregnancy 15
maltreatment of children 13, 17
marksmanship 35
marriage: arranged 85, 167; early 166–7
mass media ix, 11

mathematics 22, 49, 93, 99–101, 145, 172
'meaningful learning' 90–1, 95, 113–14, 122
medical services 115
memory 49, 53–4, 55, 57, 59, 60, 63–4, 88, 119, 145
menarche (onset of menstruation) 131–2, 154–5
method, instructional 186–7
Mexico 60, 148, 165–6
misbehaviour 11, 82–3, 85, 110
missionaries 106, 200
mnemonics 90, 91, 114
model-making 38–9, 62, 80, 101
monotropy 6
morale 12
morality 82, 85
Morocco 33
morphemes 98–9
motivation 90, 101, 108, 141, 237
mother 5, 6, 13, 15, 17, 19, 25, 26, 33, 153, 160–1
motor skills 18, 26
Muslims, see Islam

Nairobi 155
'nature and nurture' 26, 27
'Naughty Teddy' 46
needs 3–14, 80–4, 86, 111, 136–9
New Guinea, see Papua New Guinea
Nigeria: adolescent problems 130; bias against women's education 147; board game 10; counselling programme 143; employment of school-leavers 177; family strictness 9–10; infant-care 6, 9; infants' motor skills 18; language project 215; left-handedness, attitude to 14; malnutrition, study of 21; moral development 149; parent–child interaction 26; self-concept 75; social class and education 23
norms of good behaviour 20
novelty, principle of moderate 48, 90
number 91, 93
'nurturant responsible' 85

obedience 10, 136
occupations 175
operation (Piagetian theory) 43, 45, 145, 227
orientation (of shapes) 97–8, 120
orphanages 13
outings 171
'overlearning' 108
over-regularisation (child language) 31–2, 33, 94

paper as play material 39
Pakistan 199
Papua New Guinea 75, 173, 202, 208–9, 214
parents: conversations with children 9, 23, 29, 173; deaf-mute 9; effect on child's temperament 26; illiterate 19;

relationships with adolescents 136–7,
    139, 143, 158–61, 179; teacher's contact
    with 18
partially-sighted children 117–18
participation, pupil 185, 186
peer-group 161–8
perception 19, 49, 51–3, 57, 60, 61–3, 88,
    108, 111
periods, developmental: concrete
    operations 43–5; formal operations 45;
    sensory motor 43
Philippines 85, 86
phonemes 99, 215
phonic system 98–9
pictures 47, 50, 61–3, 75, 103
Pilaga 38
play 9, 12, 18, 33–9
play therapy 38
polygamy 159
polytheism 209–10
popularity 163, 164, 193
posture development 18, 19
poverty 18, 21, 24, 51, 137, 161, 178, 187
practice 107
praise 10–12, 23, 80, 82, 138
'precocity' (motor development) 18–19
pregnancy: drugs and smoking in 15;
    malnutrition in 15; mother's attitude to
    16–17, 19
primer, reading 96
problem-solving ix, 34, 57, 99–101, 177,
    205, 215
problems, emotional 178
processes: cognitive 48–59, 88;
    instructional 106–115; memory 54–5
programmed learning 108–10
projection (defence mechanism) 139, 141
pronunciation 97
psychologists, clinical 71–2
puberty 25, 127, 129, 135, 155, 157
punishment 3, 7, 25, 108, 148, 190, 203;
    corporal 203–4
Punjab 10, 65
puns 36
pupil-centred education 12, 111, 113

questions, child's 9, 19, 20–1

reading 20, 24, 25, 27, 76, 77, 95–9, 119,
    122, 215
reality, denial of 139, 150
reasoning: intellectual 49, 57–9, 60, 88,
    101; moral 147–9
rebellion in adolescence 146, 152, 157
recall 54–5, 63–4
reciprocity 6
recognition: in memorising 54; need for
    10–12, 82–3, 138
reference group 193
reflex 43
regard, unconditional positive 11
regression 142
rehearsal (memorising) 54, 119
reinforcement 11–12, 91, 107–10, 121, 185

rejection 11, 76
relationships: boy–girl 159–60; family 6,
    17, 18, 158–61; headteacher–teacher
    196–8; parent–teacher 202;
    teacher–pupil 81, 82–4, 86, 174, 183–7,
    198, 202, 218; teacher–teacher 194–6
relativity of concepts 56
remediation of low ability 15, 221
repetition 91, 114, 119
research, empirical 71, 86
respect for elders 9–10
response: sensory 5, 52; sexual 132, 133–4,
    141, 159–60
responsibility, need for 12, 81, 136, 138
retardation, mental 15, 118–19, 145
retina 51
retrieval 55
revision 108–9
reward 25, 82, 108, 148, 171
riddles 36, 65
rite de passage 127, 155
rituals 7, 35
rivalry, sibling 38, 74
role confusion 135, 156
roles, sexual 24–5, 159; differentiation of
    152; 'traditional' 159
rote learning 91, 94, 95, 106, 114
rubella (German measles) 16
rule learning 31, 49, 94–5, 97, 99, 122
rural areas 10, 60–1, 64–5, 166, 173
'Rural Ridge' 202, 204–5
Russian language 32

Samoa 105–6; language 32
sand and water play 39
Scandinavia 17, 18, 23
scarification 152–4
schemata 49, 50, 53, 59, 66
schools: co-educational 60, 167, 171;
    community 18; infant 22, 27; nursery
    27, 38–9; organisation of 194–8;
    primary 26, 69–87, 91, 125, 134, 135,
    159, 170, 203; secondary 10, 23, 125,
    159, 170, 215
science 35, 63, 99, 105, 221
Scotland 18, 60, 146
SEC, see class, socio-economic
security, need for 6–7, 73, 80, 82–3, 84,
    113, 136, 137
self-: concept 10, 27, 71–87, 131, 134–5,
    136, 138–9; deception 141; esteem
    72–4, 75–6, 77, 80, 86, 116, 129, 131,
    138, 143, 158, 172; image 10, 145–6;
    perception 4, 131
semantics 31, 55
Senegal 18, 60, 214
sensory-motor period 43
sequence of learning material 112
sewing 39
sex: differences 24, 25, 144, 146–7, 173–4;
    education 133
shape: discrimination 19; orientation 97–8,
    120
Sierra Leone 96, 142–3

sign language 116
singing 19
'sociable-intimate' 85
socialisation 3, 5, 6, 12, 20, 34
sociologists 72
sociometry 191–3
South Africa, Union of 21
spatial ability 24, 60
special needs, children with 115–121
speech 9, 20, 30–3, 40
spelling 113, 114, 119
spiral approach 112–13
stages of development: cognitive 41–7;
    emotional 134–5; language 28–33;
    physical 135
'stars' 193
status: aggregation 164, 193; inequality
    187; of concepts 56
stereotypes 24–5, 129, 146–7, 155–6, 193
strategies: cognitive 21, 59; memorising
    55, 90; staff-relationship 197–8; task-
    appropriate 54; teaching 80, 81
structure: games 35–6; language 31–3, 40;
    learning material 112, 113–15
suicide 144
superordinate mode 57, 64
surrogate mother 6
Swahili language 97
symbolic representation 50–1, 81, 112
symbols 20, 43, 49
system, educational 199–200, 203–8, 218

Taiwan 148
Tale (West Africa) 35
Tangu (New Guinea) 75
Tanzania 6, 11, 18
taxonomic mode 56–7, 64
teachers: attitudes to pupils 11, 12, 73–4,
    77–8, 111; characteristics of 174;
    feedback from 18, 91; style of 17,
    187–90; values 146, 169, 187
techniques, instructional 106–15, 117,
    118–19, 121, 122
technology 21, 66, 105
tests and testing: aptitude 20; batteries 226;
    bias 231–2; British Abilities Scale (BAS)
    232; coaching 224, 233; creativity
    102–3; criterion-referenced 238, 239;
    diagnostic 234; field-dependence 212;
    group 230–1; Guilford's 226–7; in
    learning process 90, 234–5, 238, 239;
    intelligence 21, 102, 119, 200, 220–34;
    239; motivation of 221–4; norm-
    referenced 237–8; reliability 232–3, 237;
    selection 235–7; standardisation 233;
    Stanford-Binet 229–30; validity 233;
    Wechsler Intelligence Scale for Children
    (WISC) 230, 232
text-books, 199, 215
three-dimensional perception 46, 61–3
thumb-sucking 7
timidity 83–4, 139
toys, educational 19, 23, 35, 36
'transitional objects' 7

truancy 168, 169
Turkey 148–9
twins 225, 230

Uganda 21, 105, 167
urbanisation 21, 60–1, 63, 64, 66, 166
USA 7, 19, 23, 24, 104, 144, 223–7
USSR 6

validity of concepts 56
values: cultural 35, 85, 111; parents' 146,
157, 203; secondary pupils' 169;
teachers' 146, 169, 187
vandalism 137, 204
verification 100–1
vocabulary 90, 108, 113, 121, 145
vocational choice 175
Vygotsky blocks 65

warmth 187
West Indies 203; immigrants from 161
Wight, Isle of 170

Wisconsin 18
witchcraft 210
work 175–7, 179
working mothers 6, 17
worth, areas of personal 75–6
writing 46

Zaire 214
Zambia ix–x, 18, 24, 34, 195, 227, 231
Zimbabwe 24